BRITISH SPORTING ART IN THE TWENTIETH CENTURY

BY THE SAME AUTHOR

Horses of Renown

The Controversial Horse
(with R.S. Summerhays)

Enamoured of an Ass

Sporting Art: England 1700–1900

BRITISH SPORTING ART IN THE TWENTIETH CENTURY

STELLA A. WALKER

Foreword by Paul Mellon, KBE

THE SPORTSMAN'S PRESS
LONDON

Published by
The Sportsman's Press 1989

NOTE

The black and white illustrations are referred to in the text thus (*1*), (*2*), and the colour plates as *Plate 1*, *Plate 2* and so on. A complete list of illustrations can be found starting on page 211. Measurements are given as height by width.

British Library Cataloguing in Publication Data

Walker, Stella A. (Stella Archer), *1907–*
British sporting art in the twentieth century.
1. British visual arts. Special subjects:
Sports
I. Title
704.9′49796

ISBN 0-948253-36-3

Photoset and printed in Great Britain by
BAS Printers Limited, Over Wallop, Hampshire

Contents

Author's Acknowledgements

Owing to various circumstances the completion of this book has been long delayed; and its ultimate publication has been made possible only by the generous co-operation of many people. I am deeply indebted to artists, sculptors, private owners and to art galleries for permitting me to use reproductions of pictures and sculpture. A detailed list of acknowledgements is made on page 214.

In particular I would mention the kindness and help given to me in this respect by Arthur Ackermann & Son, the Court Gallery, Frost & Reed Ltd, Richard Green Gallery, Oscar & Peter Johnson Gallery, the Sladmore Gallery, Spink Ltd, the Tryon Gallery; and especially to the Trustees of the Sir Alfred Munnings Art Museum who also allowed me to quote from the Munnings' Autobiographies and to include the Royal Academy Dinner Speech.

My sincere appreciation is extended to Christie's and Sotheby's for the privilege of being able to browse through their photographic files, and to William Marler who kindly permitted me the use of material from his research into the life and work of Gilbert Holiday; also to William Heinemann Ltd, and Reginald Pound to quote from *The English Gentleman*. I must also thank the Editors of *Horse and Hound*, and *The Field* for permission to include extracts from certain articles that first appeared in these periodicals.

On countless occasions experts in various spheres shared their time and knowledge with me to solve many problems. Amongst these I am especially grateful to David Fuller of Arthur Ackermann & Son Ltd, Mark Flower of the Court Gallery, Stephen Ling of Fores, Claude Berry of the Tryon Gallery, Lionel Lambourne of the Victoria & Albert Museum, Miss Molly Garwood of the Sir Alfred Munnings Art Museum, Miss Mollie Luther of the Tate Gallery, and Miss Norah Titley of the British Sporting Art Trust.

Valuable help was given me in verifying details and tracing reproductions by Mrs D. Biegel, Miss Beverly Carter, Rupert Collens, Major J. Crawford, Sir Stephen Furness, W.S. Gadsby, Roy Heron, Mrs J.J. Phipps, Mrs M. Kenney, Mrs J. Kennedy, Malcolm Innes and Sir Nicholas Lyell, MP, Peter Johnson, Michael Lyne, Major A.G. Mann, David Messum, Sir John Miller, KCVO, DSO, MC, Sally Mitchell, Peter P. Nicholls, D.H. Piper; The Rev. Donald O. Prichard the Rector of St. Albans Church, Mells, and the Earl of Oxford & Asquith; Sidney T. Sabin, John Southern, MBE, Brian Stewart, Anne, Duchess of Westminster; and not forgetting E.G.H. Davey and Sir Stephen Lycett Green who at great inconvenience arranged photography of the Brian Hatton and Charles Furse paintings.

I also wish to thank the officers of the British Sporting Art Trust, the All-England Jumping Course, the Goldsmiths' College of the University of London, Kent County Cricket Club, the Royal Worcester Porcelain Company, Masters of Foxhounds Association, National Greyhound Racing Club Ltd, the National Horseracing Museum, the Royal & Ancient Golf Club of St. Andrew's and the Wimbledon Lawn Tennis Museum for supplying relevant information.

It is impossible to express adequately my appreciation to Mr Paul Mellon for the splendid Foreword; as on so many occasions, British sporting art is in his debt; and to Dr Robert Fountain, Chairman of the Executive Committee of the British Sporting Art Trust, for his unflagging encouragement and co-operation which certainly resulted in the book achieving completion.

Finally, my sincere thanks to my secretaries Barbara Kinsey and Patricia Seton, and to my indexer Jean Morris, for so patiently and efficiently coping with an author who, in this electronic age, tiresomely clings to the quill pen era. To all of these and many other kind, clever people unmentioned who have so generously given me their help, I am deeply grateful.

Stella A. Walker
February 1989

Foreword
by Paul Mellon KBE

As a complete amateur of the hunting field and Thoroughbred racing as well as other sports and the history of sporting art, I have found this book a treasury of information about sporting art and artists of this century. I have been struck by the fact that not only the outstanding masters of the trade such as Munnings, Edwards, Skeaping and Aldin but also the majority of later and younger aspirants, have themselves been eager practitioners of their chosen sports and have fused their first-hand athletic skills inextricably with their skills in brush, pencil and clay.

Stella Walker, while paying homage to the great names of the late nineteenth and early twentieth centuries, has clearly illustrated their pervasive influence on later and younger artists. She has also made clear the dividing lines between the forces of these older influences and the innate, highly personal and creative talents of their younger followers. Equally interesting and pertinent, she produces striking evidence of the influence of earlier eighteenth and nineteenth century artists such as Stubbs, Marshall, Alken and Herring on the great masters of this century. She traces not only the influence of British artists, but also the impact of the Impressionists and Post-Impressionists across the Channel, such as Manet, Degas and Toulouse-Lautrec.

It is not often realised how great was the sudden awakening caused by Eadweard Muybridge's photography of the horse in motion in the late nineteenth century. It must have made great demands upon the skills of even the most adept painters and draughtsmen, to capture on paper and canvas the newly visible, intricate movements of the four legs of the horse. Also, one is struck by the sharper images that careers in advertising and journalism have demanded of the works of many of these artists. The importunity of deadlines (and poverty) and the necessity of making lightning sketches from instantaneous observation have honed their art to a special brilliance.

For my own part, I shall use this book as an invaluable biographical reference work long after I have reread, absorbed and enjoyed the narrative. As a longtime (and some might say, greedy!) collector, I admit to considerable envy that I have missed so many opportunities to acquire not only works of the early masters but also those of the younger stars of the postwar decades. As a corollary, I would hope that we may see more comprehensive and lively exhibitions of contemporary British sporting art both in London and in the United States. Beyond reading about works of art, seeing them is the best education and the greatest pleasure.

If my comments have dwelt largely on the delineators of racing, hunting and other equestrian sports, it is only because I myself have been a lifelong addict of foxhunting, racing and of the horse himself, in sport and in art. However, although equine artists receive somewhat greater attention in her book, the author has in no way neglected those whose specialities have encompassed other field sports and country pursuits.

Stella Walker has deftly illuminated a firmament of glowing planets in describing the talents of those earlier twentieth century masters. By subtle magnification she has also defined the brightness of their satellites as well as the sparkle of younger stars more recently observed. In so doing she has given us a Stellar performance!

Paul Mellon
Rokeby Farms
Upperville
Virginia

1 Paul Mellon, KBE (*right*) with the sculptor, John Skeaping, RA, and the bronze of *Mill Reef*, 1973.

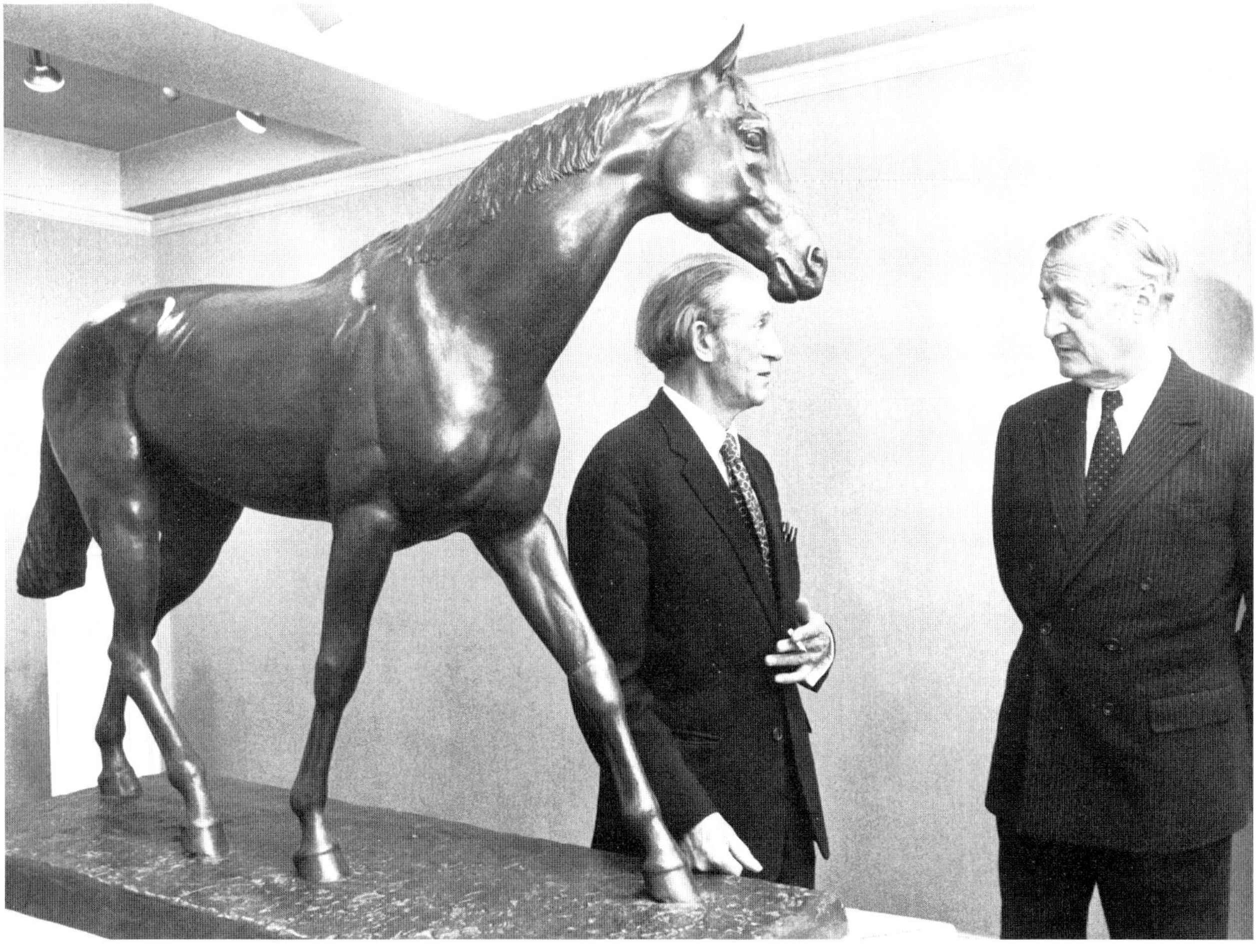

INTRODUCTION

The Changing World

For over 300 years the British school of sporting art has recorded the leisure diversions of our nation allied to the contemporary way of life. The pictures of the eighteenth and nineteenth centuries reflect not only the native addiction to the sports of hunting, fishing, shooting and racing but must be valued, also, as lively observations of our agriculture, bloodstock breeding, of our transport, customs and costume as enjoyed, in general, by the leisured classes.

In the twentieth century this social bias was to change and by the 1980s more than half the population was taking part in some sporting activity. In a contemporary Sports Council Report nearly seventy pastimes are listed, ranging from ballooning to water skiing, with angling, swimming and walking rated as the most popular pursuits. Nevertheless in the context of British sporting art it is evident, even towards the end of the twentieth century, field sports and the equestrian scene still provide the major pictorial inspiration, though unrelated subjects with bat and ball and other diversions share a growing representation.

The present generation has survived a cataclysm of catastrophe and change which, during the past century, has included two World Wars, social revolution, the take-over of life by the internal combustion engine and the chilling arrival of nuclear fission. However, our national inherent addiction to sport and love of rural life has remained constant, though conservation organisations have been compelled to protect our threatened country landscapes as motorways and airports have brought ever increasing deserts of concrete. With the abolition of blood sports beginning to appear an actual possibility, British sporting art as a documentary record assumes a relevance stronger, perhaps, than ever before in spite of the challenge and expertise of colour photography.

The devastating poverty of the agricultural depressions of the 1890s and 1930s has passed away; but for how long? Over-production now threatens the diligent husbandman and, with the total mechanisation of farming, much natural beauty and many country customs are disappearing for ever. Gone are the country fairs and harvest suppers; the tractor and combine harvester, allied to the functional buildings of factory farming and uprooting of hedgerows have engulfed the scene and completely metamorphasised rural existence. In the sporting sphere the horse box has supplanted the covert hack, game carts have become Land Rovers and estate shoots are profitably syndicated. Racing has assumed international status, oceans are no barriers to bloodstock breeding projects or to participation in competitive events in any part of the world.

But as this century nears its end, contrary to prophecy and even with increasing pressure from the anti-blood sports faction rarely have hunting and hunt supporters clubs been more popular. In 1987, 337 packs of hounds were registered compared with 305 in 1905.[1] Never have point-to-point meetings been better supported, angling and shooting clubs more numerous, and polo and harness driving events are enjoying a spectacular renewal. Today transport presents no problems and town dwellers share in rural activities to an extent never remotely possible in the days of Surtees. Every game fair and agricultural show attracts thousands of provincial visitors, and here art dealers' stands with sporting prints are thronged, which makes one think that the Englishman is still a countryman at heart, possessing an inbred love of sport and sporting art.

Perhaps the greatest revolution in the twentieth century sporting scene has been in the role of women. Intrepid Dianas had always existed as a minority; there was also that famous women's cricket match depicted by Rowlandson and modest Victorian maidens drew a pretty bow in archery tournaments. The equestrienne transition from side-saddle to astride has been almost total (though the recent revival of ladies in elegant habits has been a feature of the last decade but for decorative show events rather than practical purposes). Today, in virtually no field of activity is a woman debarred from taking part, holding her own in international competition with men, whether it is riding in the Grand National, sailing the Atlantic single-handed or competing equally in the equine career market. Inevitably sporting art in the second half of the twentieth century strongly reflects this feminine influence which has been complemented by the significant arrival of many gifted women artists to portray the contemporary sporting scene.

With the transformed conditions of the twentieth century the school of British sporting art has also faced a controversial challenge which in many ways it has been reluctant to accept. Artists, with only a few exceptions, have clung with almost pathological intensity to the traditional approach and techniques, and only recently has an original conception of this new world begun to appear. This book, therefore, aims to interpret something of the success and failure of sporting art during this century and to illustrate how the familiar has learnt to co-exist with some interesting innovation. It is realised omissions abound, that some inclusions may be considered irrelevant, but the subject has many facets and, for full appraisal, should not be surveyed for another couple of decades. But time does not stand still and writers are not immortal.

It is a curious fact that only recently have a few artists ventured away from field sports and emerged into the wider (and, some consider, inapplicable) aspects of the sporting scene, into the show arena, the football stadium, the athletics track and the tennis court. It must be admitted, however, that sporting art today, as yesterday, still reflects with skill and perception our country pursuits, and the horse, even in a modern mechanised environment, remains, as in the past, its major inspiration with hunting and racing its predominant subjects.

Talent has certainly not been lacking; Munnings, Edwards and Skeaping the sculptor must rank as the twentieth century masters for future generations, but we have been singularly blessed in this epoch with a rich diversity of artists, which also includes such names as G.D. Armour, Lynwood Palmer, Snaffles, Gilbert Holiday, Michael Lyne and Susan Crawford amongst a myriad of others; names to carry the school of British sporting art, a unique heritage of the past, triumphantly into the twenty-first century.

NOTES

1 *Baily's Hunting Directory, 1986–7*, J.A. Allen, London

1

A Watershed in British Sporting Art

In the first half of the nineteenth century the sporting pursuits of hunting, racing and coaching reached a zenith of popularity and, happily for posterity such artists as Marshall, Herring, Pollard, the Alkens, and Wolstenholmes and a wealth of others had been on hand to leave memorable pictures.

These masters passed away and the golden age of the road was also quickly superseded by a network of railways. Nevertheless the late Victorians of leisure and wealth continued an unbroken enthusiasm for foxhunting; huge shooting parties became a prestige seasonal pursuit and coursing and racing received popular support from all levels of society. Rochefoucauld's statement of over 250 years earlier that 'one of the Englishman's greatest joys is in field sports – they are all quite mad about them' [1] was still a basic truth.

But towards the end of the century British sporting art appeared to lose much of that robust quality and gusto which had formerly emphasised the enjoyment and excitement of these sporting activities and which had been the hallmark of its artists. Landseer and Ansdell had left a legacy of grandiose realism but, too often, simplicity and truth were overshadowed by sentiment and sentimentality and there was an overall lack of distinction and definition in the works of the next generation of painters who bridged the centuries.

In all fairness, however, direct comparison with the more lively, dynamic approach characteristic at the beginning of the nineteenth century must be considered against the impact on the late Victorian scene of the arrival of instantaneous animal photography based on the researches in Palo Alto in Southern California of English-born Eadweard Muybridge and others between 1872–1885. Of course the camera obscura and projected images in painting had been in use as long ago as the sixteenth century but with the eventual perfection of Muybridge's 'Zoopraxiscope', camera exposures of 1/6000th in regular sequence became possible. This exact reproduction of motion aroused widespread interest in this country and on the continent but few realised that it heralded a transformation in animal art and was the precursor of the 'movies'. He published in the 1880s *The Attitudes of Animals in Motion*, followed by the *The Horse in Motion* and in 1887 *Animal Locomotion*.

In the *Gentleman's Magazine* of December 1881 the full ingenuity of the idea became apparent in an article '*Photographs of a Galloping Horse*' by Richard A. Proctor, the astronomer, which included sixteen photographic positions of just one stride of the galloping horse. Three months later Muybridge himself gave an illustrated lecture at the Royal Institution before a distinguished audience which included the Prince and Princess of Wales and other members of the royal family, Sir Alfred Tennyson the Poet Laureate and Sir Robert Leighton the President of the Royal Academy. Reported in the *Illustrated London News* of 18 March 1882 as 'a Magic

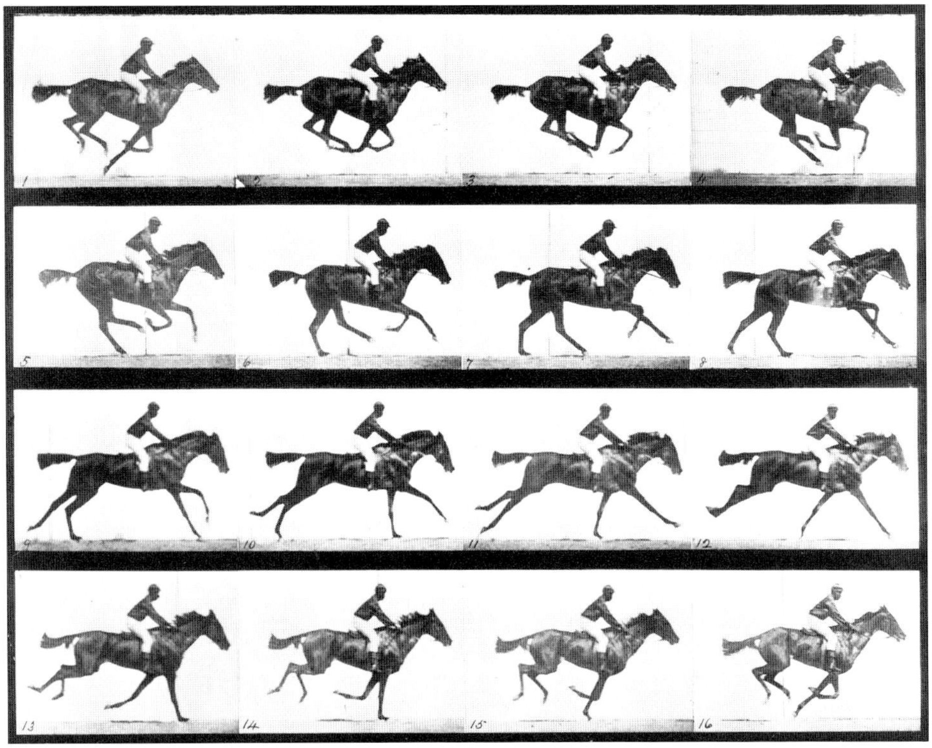

2 Eadweard Muybridge, Photograph of a Thoroughbred 'Annie G' with jockey, 1887.

Lantern Run Mad' it was admitted that 'animals suddenly become mobile and beautiful, and walked, trotted, cantered, ambled, galloped and leapt in a perfectly natural manner'. In Muybridge's series of sixteen photographs of a Thoroughbred, 'Annie G' with Jockey in 1887 this was clearly elucidated (*2*). Thus the fallacy of the invariable rocking horse gallop of equestrian art became apparent and immense problems simultaneously faced the sporting artist of the day.

Since 500BC in scenes of Greek chariot racing and in the Roman Quadriga teams of a thousand years ago, this pose of the fore and hind legs laterally outstretched had been accepted as the absolute symbol of the horse at speed. Admittedly, some naive attempts at more realistic representation can be traced even in paleolithic cave drawings, and the Greeks had recognised the importance of an alternative locomotion of limbs in the animal kingdom but left no information as to the actual manner of movement. The Duke of Newcastle in his seventeenth century classic work on horsemanship devoted a chapter on 'The Movement of the Horse in all his Natural Paces' and had come to the conclusion that 'his [the horse's] four legs may then plainly appear to be in the air at the same time'.[2]

George Stubbs had made one or two unsuccessful attempts at rationalising the position of the galloping horse as in his racing study of *Baronet*. James Ward, in his small painting of *The Finishing Post*, *c.* 1820, has the leading brown horse with all four feet off the ground, which caused some surprise to King George III but the artist produced sketches to support this advanced perception of animal movement. A picture by Ward's son-in-law, George Garrard, shows the Duke of Hamilton riding a trotting horse at speed with its legs in what Muybridge terms 'a period of unsupported transport'. This portrayal was unacceptable both to other artists and to the public.

Sometimes the sporting painter had succeeded, perhaps fortuitously, in a truthful portrayal of the moving horse but even as late as 1871, on the other side of the Channel, Meissonnier's examples of equine action outside the traditional position had been ridiculed by the French Academicians.

These isolated endeavours to elucidate the intricacies of equine movement failed to modify the general acceptance of the rocking horse syndrome. Even when British sporting artists such as J.F. Herring Snr, in the nineteenth century, exaggerated the pose in racing scenes into a bizarre *ventre à terre* gallop, the conventional association of outstretched front and hind legs was so longstanding that its viability went unquestioned (*3*).

Muybridge himself explained this lack of perception by the fact that over the ages there had been a complete absence of careful observation, of unprejudiced impression and also of serious reasoning on the actual locomotion of the horse; therefore acceptance of an alternative representation of the gallop presented formidable problems for the artist. There was a natural reaction. The mind refused to accept the idea of great pace founded on correct principles and the eye rebelled; and understandably, for, in the transition to increased speed, the eye fleetingly receives the impression of a lateral extension. Realism, therefore, was not entirely absent in these pictures of past racing scenes.

The camera's dénouement also had to be equated with some artistic licence. Proctor in his first lecture had considered that a picture should represent 'what we see and also be true to what the eye seems to see'. Lowes Luard in *The Horse: its Action and Anatomy* suggested that instantaneous photography should be considered as the anatomy of movement. For many artists Muybridge was to prove a false prophet. They assumed that to paint an animal in an attitude revealed by photography, but unperceived by the human eye, would spontaneously create an impression of movement and reality. Representational efficiency, however, can negate artistry.

But inevitably, in the light of Muybridge's instantaneous photography the sporting artist had reached the end of an era. The publication of his book in 1892, *The Horse in Action: an Electric Photographic Investigation of Consecutive Phases of Animal Progressive Movements* meant that the rocking horse pose had finally become unacceptable. This work is, in its way, as instructive and illuminating for any animal artist as Stubbs' *The Anatomy of the Horse*.

Few of the contemporary artists such as Thomas Blinks, John Charlton, Heywood Hardy, Godfrey Giles or even Lynwood Palmer could immediately adjust their talents to this new conception of the horse at speed. Compromise was the accepted solution with a static pose – a verdict that stultified spontaneity. It was a precedent much encouraged by the contemporary

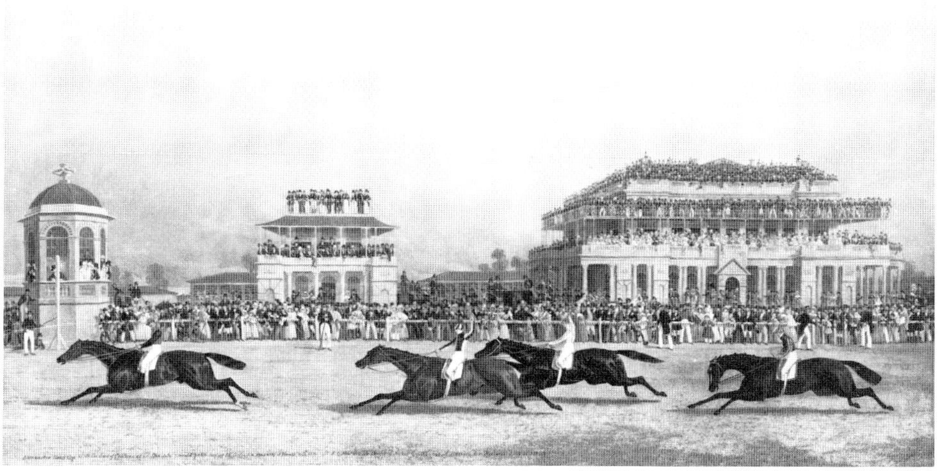

3 John Frederick Herring, Snr and James Pollard, *The Doncaster Gold Cup, 1838*. Oil on canvas, 40 × 81 in (101.6 × 205.7 cm).

prestige in England of the work of the Bavarian artist, Emil Adams, who was acclaimed in the English magazine *The World* as 'the finest horse painter in Europe' and was considered unequivocally by the Duke of Westminster as 'the only artist I know who can really conceive and paint on canvas a Thoroughbred as it really is'. Seven of his repetitive portraits hang in the Jockey Club Rooms at Newmarket to illustrate the artist's undoubted ability to suggest the elegance and quality of the contemporary racehorse, but he rarely chanced his reputation by painting his Classic winners in motion.

British artists even in their hunting scenes at this period seldom present the field following hounds in full cry. The riders are more often seen gathered at the meet, moving off or pulling up. It was a safe but somewhat ineffective compromise. The stirring hunt scurries of John Ferneley Snr, and Henry Alken's scenes of disasters in the galloping Shires of fifty years earlier certainly distorted the facts of animal action, nevertheless they brought a remarkable sense of zest and excitement into the sporting occasion lamentably lacking in the pictures at the beginning of the twentieth century.

Portrayals of hounds also (and indeed of all animals) had to be adjusted to this new conception. Though the mechanics of equine and canine action were not exactly similar, the contemporary artistic approach appeared less inhibited where hounds were concerned and John Emms, John Charlton and others presented packs in action with some reality.

Thus time to adjust to Muybridge's new definition of animal movement was required by the artist and a discriminating presentation and execution had to be balanced by intelligence and the critical faculty. The demise of the perennial rocking horse symbol was gradually, but surely, established and its passing must be considered a watershed in British sporting art.

In addition it must also be remembered that the late Victorian artists had been exposed for some years to the influence of the French Impressionists and Post Impressionists. This artistic revolt against the academic conventions of beauty, shocking and stimulating in its impact, was ignored by the British animal painters of the period with few exceptions. Only Robert Bevan, Joseph Crawhall and William Huggins (in his idiosyncratic studies of lions and tigers) reflected in their work this new approach to light and colour, as illustrated across the Channel in the equestrian pictures of Manet, Degas and Toulouse-Lautrec. It was Degas also who modelled a unique series of thirteen wax statuettes based on Muybridge's photographs of the horse in *Animal Locomotion*.

Though the school of British sporting art in its observation and structure for over 200 years had remained fundamentally representational, in modified form in the twentieth century Impressionism was eventually to bring a new vitality to the sporting scene illustrated by the liberated works of Munnings, Holiday and Skeaping – influences that imbued many young artists of the new era with a fresh vision even though their talent often lacked the magic of these earlier masters. But in general the late Victorian sporting artists were impervious to the new exciting phenomenon of Impressionism and old traditions died slowly in the shadow of the ageing Queen.

NOTES

1 François de la Rochefoucauld: *A Frenchman in England 1784*. [Being the Melanges sur l'Angleterre of François de la Rochefoucauld] translated with notes by S.C. Roberts, Cambridge University Press, 1933, p. 52.

2 William Cavendish, Duke of Newcastle: *A General System of Horsemanship*, trans. 1743, Book II, Chap II.

2

Bridging the Centuries: Edwardian Days

With the accession of Edward VII to the throne in 1901 English sporting activities were to enjoy a period of unprecedented popularity and prosperity. The new king, though in his sixtieth year, had always been identified with the national love of sport. Victorian decorum so strictly enforced in court circles had never dimmed his enjoyment of hunting and racing. As Prince of Wales he had hunted in the Shires and the Provinces with enthusiasm and G.D. Giles also portrays him with the Queen's Staghounds on an undistinguished grey taking a stile with great aplomb and, in a poor painting by John Sturgess, when out with the Quorn his horse is seen wisely refusing a stiff timber jump to avoid inevitable disaster over a fallen rider. But increasing weight proved a decisive handicap and hunting had to be abandoned – the royal soubriquet of 'Tum-Tum' was no idle allusion. Polo also had to be enjoyed from the sidelines but there are many engravings in the sporting periodicals, several after Cuthbert Bradley's drawings, of the King and Queen Alexandra watching play at fashionable Hurlingham, (a venue originally opened for pigeon shooting fifty years earlier) and the sport reached a zenith of popularity with sixteen clubs sited around London before the First World War.

It was King Edward's keen participation in racing, however, that brought him popular prestige with the sporting fraternity of all classes. In 1875 he had registered his colours, purple, gold braid, scarlet sleeves, black velvet cap and gold fringe; but success was long delayed until Persimmon, sired by the renowned St Simon, won the first royal Derby in 1896, a triumph greeted with great public enthusiasm. Four years later, in the sixtieth year of the old Queen's reign, the aptly named Diamond Jubilee (Persimmon's full brother) won for him not only the Blue Riband of the turf but the Triple Crown, and then, when at last King, in 1909, and to the delight of all England, Minoru gave him the hat trick – a success that triggered off Minoru racing board games and printed scarves. What a spate of commissions this trio of horses was to provide for the contemporary artist – Lynwood Palmer, Alfred Havell, Alfred Haigh, C.H.A. Lutyens, G.D. Giles and many others. And there were pictures of His Majesty himself holding social court on the Newmarket July Course by that rather uninspired exponent, Isaac Cullin.

In 1900 his 'chaser, Ambush II had won the Grand National. The King impulsively commissioned Mr N. Arthur Loraine, Clerk of the Course at Sandown and an amateur artist of small note, to paint a portrait of the horse with A. Anthony up and the royal owner alongside. Posed stiffly the result is hardly a masterpiece but does illustrate the animal's fine front and limbs. These qualities are emphasized in Alfred Haigh's more formal portrayal of the big bay at the start of the race but noticeably the brushing boots on the hind legs are omitted (*4*).

Edward VII's successes on the turf were always received with euphoric cries of 'Good old Teddy' and achieved more for the King's popularity with his people than all his skill in diplomatic circles as 'Edward the Peacemaker'. But his ready friendships with commoners whose

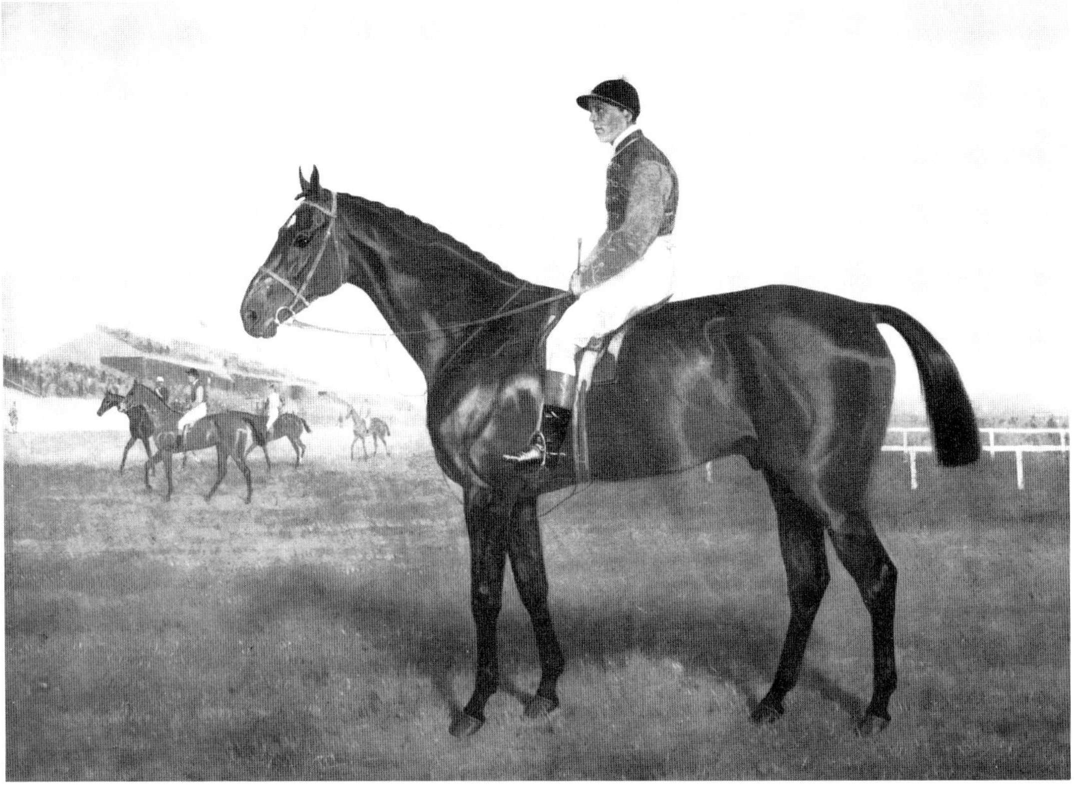

4 Alfred Grenfell Haigh, *Ambush II at the Start of the Grand National*, 1900. Oil on canvas, 20 × 25 in (50.8 × 63.5 cm).

wealth had been recently acquired from interests in grocery, brewing or banking were not approved by the Establishment; nevertheless under royal patronage these *nouveaux riches* enjoyed the entrée to Cowes and the most exclusive circles of the racing world. The King, like most Englishmen, demanded that his friends should be good sportsmen – their wealth was an added bonus.

At the turn of the century there was an invasion of foreigners into the racing hierachy and a welcome influx of cash and influence by such men as the Hungarian Prince Batthany, breeder of the notable sire, St Simon, the Russian Prince Soltykoff, the Jewish financier Baron Meyer de Rothschild, Baron de Hirsch and others – the first three were elected to the Jockey Club and all were accepted into the royal circle. After the King's third Derby triumph however, the Sandringham stud fell into decline and it was Colonel W. Hall-Walker, a highly successful breeder, who leased colts, including Minoru to bring new blood into the royal stock. He was to become Lord Wavertree after he had sold his training stables in 1915 to the nation, at Government valuation, and given four stallions and forty-three brood mares as the foundation of the National Stud. In 1904 he was instrumental in persuading perhaps the most important foreigner of all, the Aga Khan, to race in Europe. This influential sportsman was to commission portraits of his classic winners from most of the leading artists of the day.

There had also been a great renewal of interest in racing by the important English sporting families. The Stanleys revived their former traditions with the turf and built Stanley House at Newmarket and, with George Lambton as trainer, the 17th Earl of Derby was to win over 1000 races. Lord Rosebery of Mentmore and the Duke of Westminster were also amongst

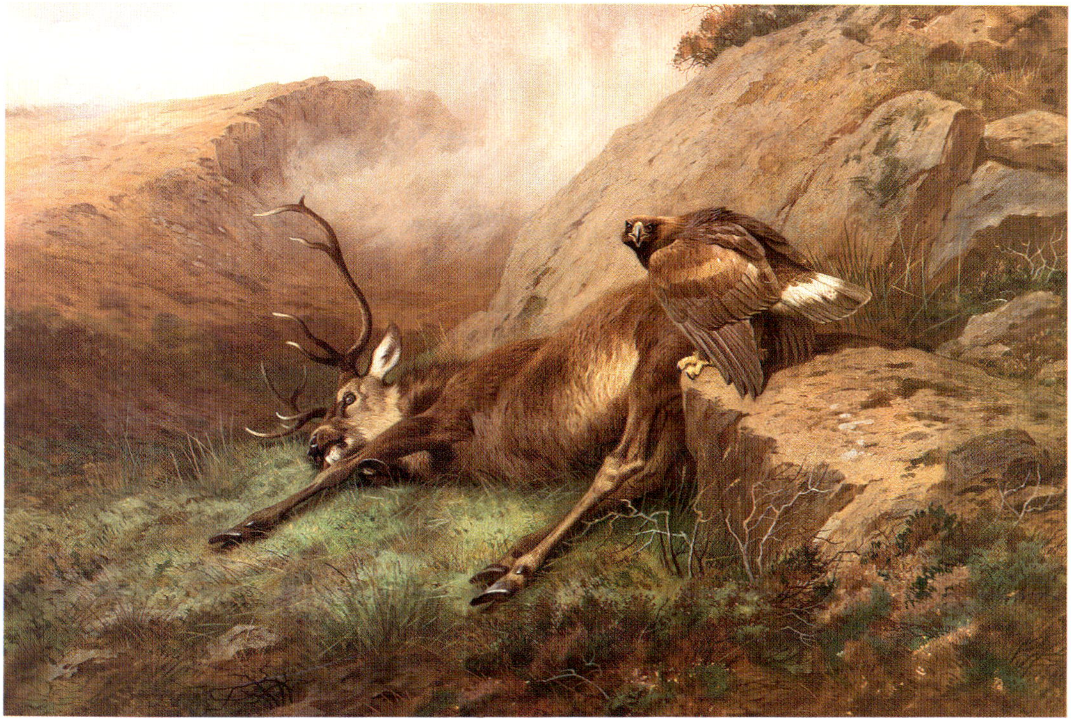

PLATE I (*above*) Archibald Thorburn, *The Lost Stag*, 1899. Watercolour, 30 × 46 in (76.2 × 116.8 cm). (*below*) John Emms, *After the Hunt*, 1907. Oil on canvas, 40 × 61 in (101.6 × 154.9 cm).

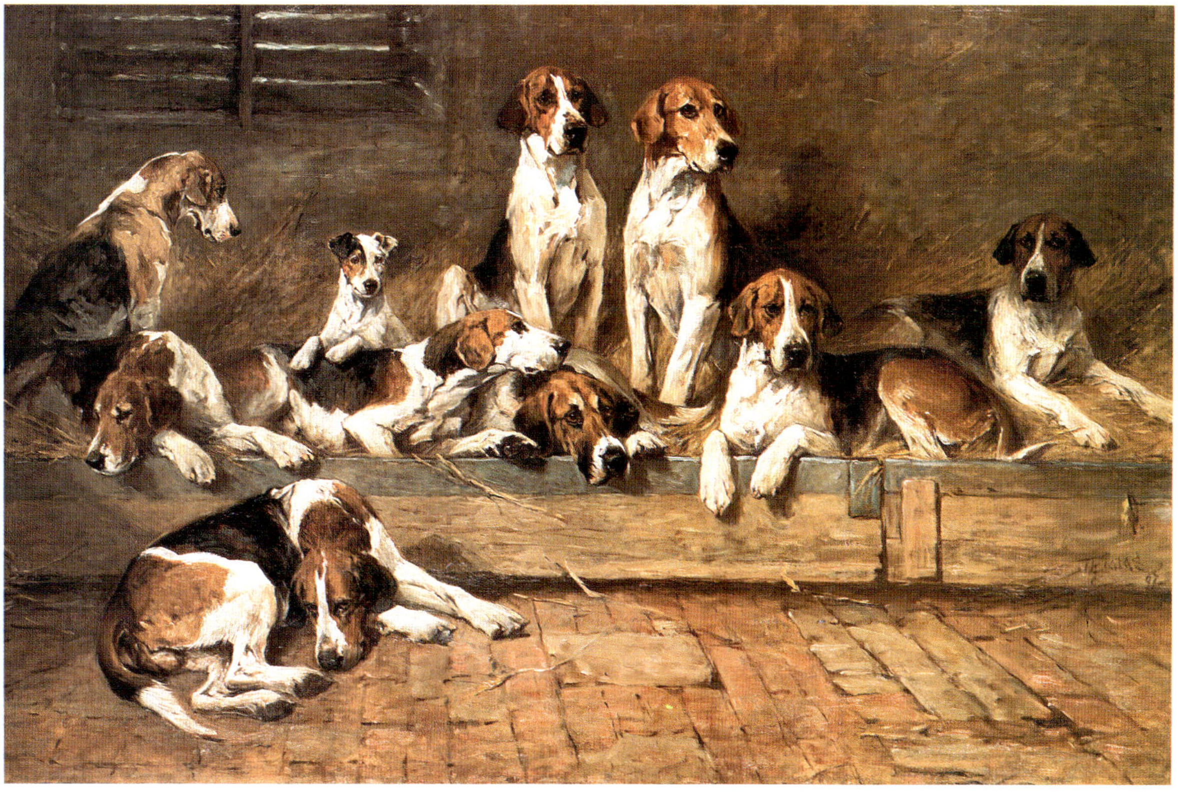

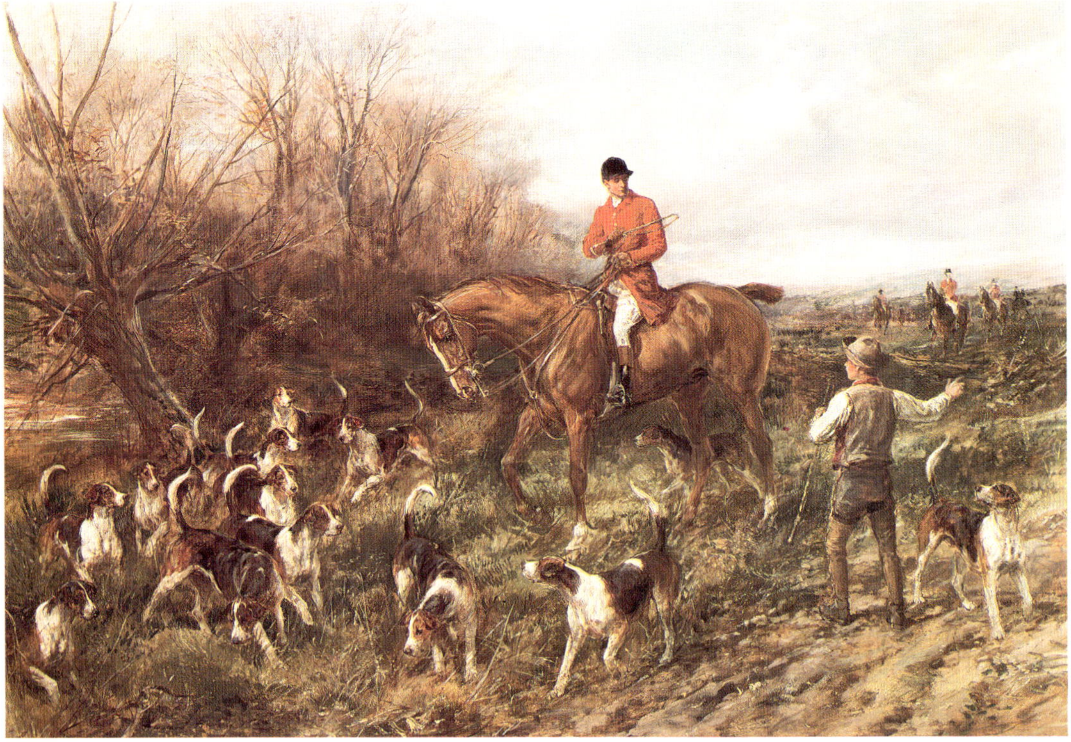

PLATE 2 (*above*) Heywood Hardy, *The Lost Scent*, 1906. Oil on canvas, $31\frac{3}{4} \times 46$ in (80.6 × 116.8 cm). (*below*) James Lynwood Palmer, *Stallions belonging to the Duke of Portland*, 1900. Oil on canvas, 66 × 108 in (167.6 × 274.3 cm).

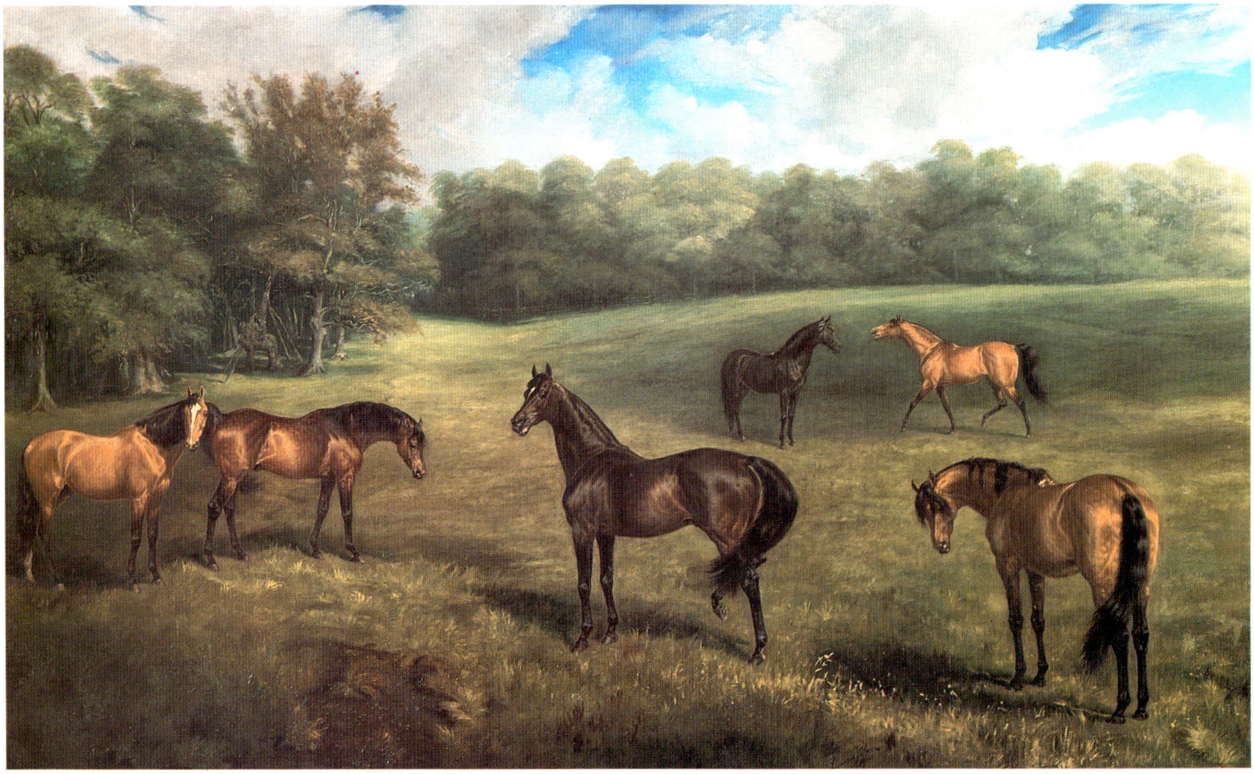

the wealthy aristocrats breeding horses of outstanding merit and dominating the racing scene. In addition American-born Viscount Astor bought Cliveden and started an important stud and bred twelve Classic winners; all gave important patronage to sporting art.

There was a big influx from the United States into English racing which had, indirectly, a spectacular effect on the pictorial scenes of the sport with the arrival in 1895 of the jockey Tod Sloan, who introduced the exaggerated short-legged forward racing seat with amazing success, immediately winning twenty races on mediocre horses. Though denigrated scornfully as the 'Monkey on a Stick' style, within a brief period virtually every English jockey was copying Sloan's method of riding.[1] The balancing act was demonstrated in a poster style gouache impression of Tod Sloan by Joseph Crawhall. The Americans also brought simpler and more natural methods of training; they fed their horses more scientifically and shod them with light racing plates. A flood of American horses arrived in the country and over a 100 of their yearlings were sold at Tattersalls in 1899. In 1908 American-bred horses won both the Grand National and the 2000 Guineas – Rubio and Norman III.

New ideas, new money and new owners stimulated every facet of the racing scene and this prosperity produced a lucrative market for the sporting artist. Though photography had made dramatic improvements, horse portraits in oils were not superseded and the competent (and often less than competent) animal painter was assured of commissions. But for the contemporary artist this break with familiar sights and customs produced problems. Not only had the rocking horse gallop to be abandoned but the portrayal of jockeys riding with long leathers, sitting down in the saddle was also outmoded. Nevertheless, as late as 1899, Lynwood Palmer in the formal portrait of *The Flying Fox* shows jockey Mornington Cannon comfortably posed in the former long-legged seat for the occasion, but in actual fact he was one of the few race-riders never really to adapt to the Sloan crouch.

Under Royal protocol considerable social impetus was also given to the shooting scene. Until late in the nineteenth century landowners had walked their estates with a few friends to shoot birds as they were put up but, encouraged by innovations introduced by these new monied sportsmen in which enormous bags were an essential climax of the day, game was now driven in concentrated forays by beaters towards the guns. No expense was spared and the scale of the sport became staggering. In 1900 at Sandringham 12,000 pheasants were reared in addition to the partridges and hares already found on the estate. This royal example was followed by other aristocratic landowners such as those at Holkham, Althorp and Welbeck.

The King's love of shooting was insatiable; though not himself in the top class of shots, Lord Warwick acclaimed him as a good one and a first class sportsman. As he grew older his love of shooting mellowed but never died. His son, George V inherited this royal addiction to the sport and he became one of the best six shots in the country; but his grandson, the Prince of Wales (later Edward VIII) after the slaughter of 4,400 pheasants at one party felt some ethical doubts and remarked 'Perhaps we overdid things today.'

A fashionable shoot was organised down to the last detail with the expertise of a military manoeuvre. It must be regretted that these sporting occasions taking place in pleasing surroundings have resulted in few pictorial records from the leading sporting artists of the day; nothing showing the keepers wearing the decorative royal livery of green and gold (as seen in the John Frederick Lewis picture *Buck Shooting in Windsor Park*, *c* 1827), and beaters conspicuous in white smocks and red hatbands. The ladies joined the party for a four course luncheon and in trailing tweeds and feathered hats afterwards would watch the men show off their markmanship.

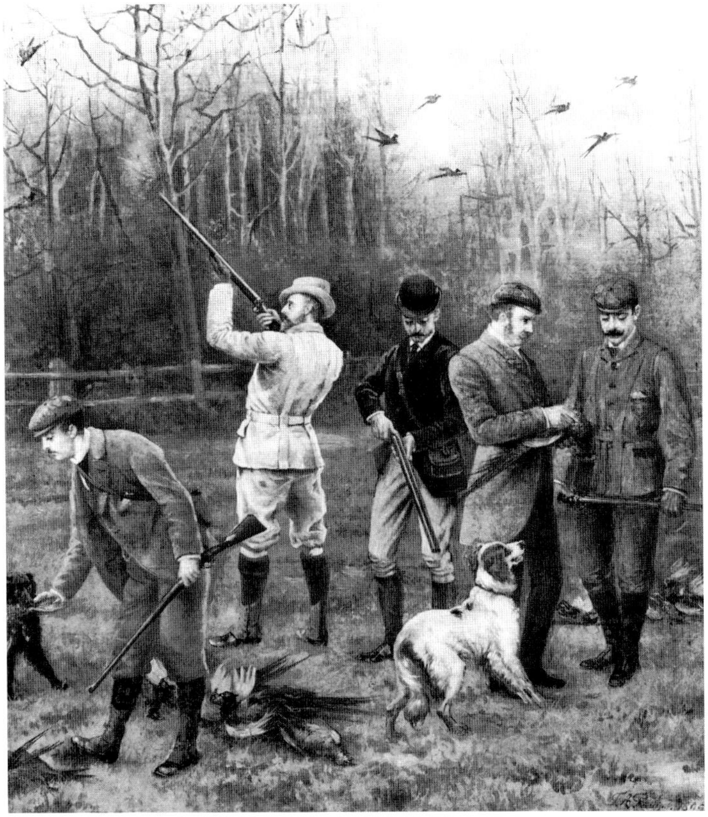

5 F.A. Phillips, *The Prince of Wales out Shooting*, 1899. Oil on canvas, $17\frac{1}{2} \times 15\frac{3}{4}$ in (44.4 × 40 cm).

There is a stiff portrayal by the illustrator F.A. Phillips of Edward VII in 1899 (when still Prince of Wales) attended by three busy loaders and a dog handler and more acceptable, perhaps, as an indication of contemporary fashion than a sporting occasion (5). With the advent of the patent ejector gun, clothes had become less encumbered by extraneous pockets and the King wears a well cut tweed Norfolk jacket and knickerbockers and the red tie he sported on these occasions, plus a trim Homburg hat and shooting spats, the latter a royal innovation quickly copied by others.

Queen Victoria's happy family holidays in Scotland had set the seal of approval on sport in the Highlands. By the twentieth century the glamour of the Glorious Twelfth had been established and several pictures were to emerge in these lovely surroundings in which deer stalking also provided an important activity.

Heywood Hardy and Thomas Blinks both painted scenes in which gun dogs played the major roles. With driven birds now the order of the day pointers had been largely superceded by setters with Gordons the favourite type. Heywood Hardy depicted convincing Highland scenes as in *The Twelfth* with the guns in action (6). Equally the Scottish artist, George Straton Ferrier in his *Twelfth of August* also pleasantly suggests the pleasures of grouse shooting with vistas of heather covered hills and banks of mist.

In a different category Archibald Thorburn, born in 1860, the son of Robert Thorburn, ARA, miniaturist to Queen Victoria, must be considered primarily as a great ornithological artist and with his fine draughtsmanship as one of the founders of modern bird painting. He was perhaps the first artist to work directly from life and not from the faded models of the taxidermist. In his early career he carried and used a gun but the piteous cries of a shot hare finished his enthusiasm as an active sportsman – an irretrievable loss for the documentary annals of sporting art as comparatively few pictures exist by Thorburn of the actual shooting occasion. He had, however, a considerable following amongst the shooting fraternity and early in the twentieth century he was also exhibiting stalking scenes in the Royal Academy.

Though somewhat predictable in composition he produced pleasing and evocative pictures of picturesque Highland venues in such works as *The First Right and Left* with a Gordon setter on point. More immediate in approach is *Not to be Turned*, a beater with a flag on a pole attempting with no success to deflect grouse towards the guns. These Scottish settings are depicted with care and sensitivity and Thorburn is one of the few colourists able to graduate with delicate variation the long stretches of purple heather. A dramatic, large watercolour *The Lost Stag*, exhibited in the Royal Academy in 1899, illustrates his bold use of colour and sense of tragedy, with a golden eagle about to pounce on its wounded prey (*Plate 1*).

A few studies by Thorburn of royal shooting scenes at Windsor emphasize his keen appreciation and understanding of the sport, though experts criticise technical details, but he must be primarily assessed for his renown as a bird illustrator outside the scope of the sporting scene. His ornithological studies remain unequalled and in his rendering of the colour, texture and form, allied to his appreciation of detail and expert field knowledge, lies his greatness. But, for a sporting artist these can become a limitation, for Charles Simpson in his work *Animal and Bird Painting* maintained, with some credence, that wild birds should be painted with an impressionism that uses space and light. Nevertheless fifty years after Thorburn's death in 1935 his works steadily augment in value and popularity.

The infusion of new wealth into the countryside compensated in some way for the acute agricultural depression at the end of the nineteenth century. Landowners had been faced by depleted rents and income tax, which had been 2d in the £ in 1875, rose with exigencies of the Boer War to over one shilling. Desperate days indeed! Nevertheless with free trade and industrial expansion the nation prospered as agriculture atrophied and hundreds of farm labourers left the land.

Rural society at this time was rapidly losing its social boundaries. Anyone rich with sporting pretensions, however plebeian were the origins of his wealth, could become a country gentleman especially if he indulged in the sport of foxhunting. This was not a new element; hunting in the nineteenth century had never been reserved solely for the landed gentry and had been

6 Heywood Hardy, *The Twelfth*. Oil on canvas, 28 × 40 in (71.1 × 101.6 cm).

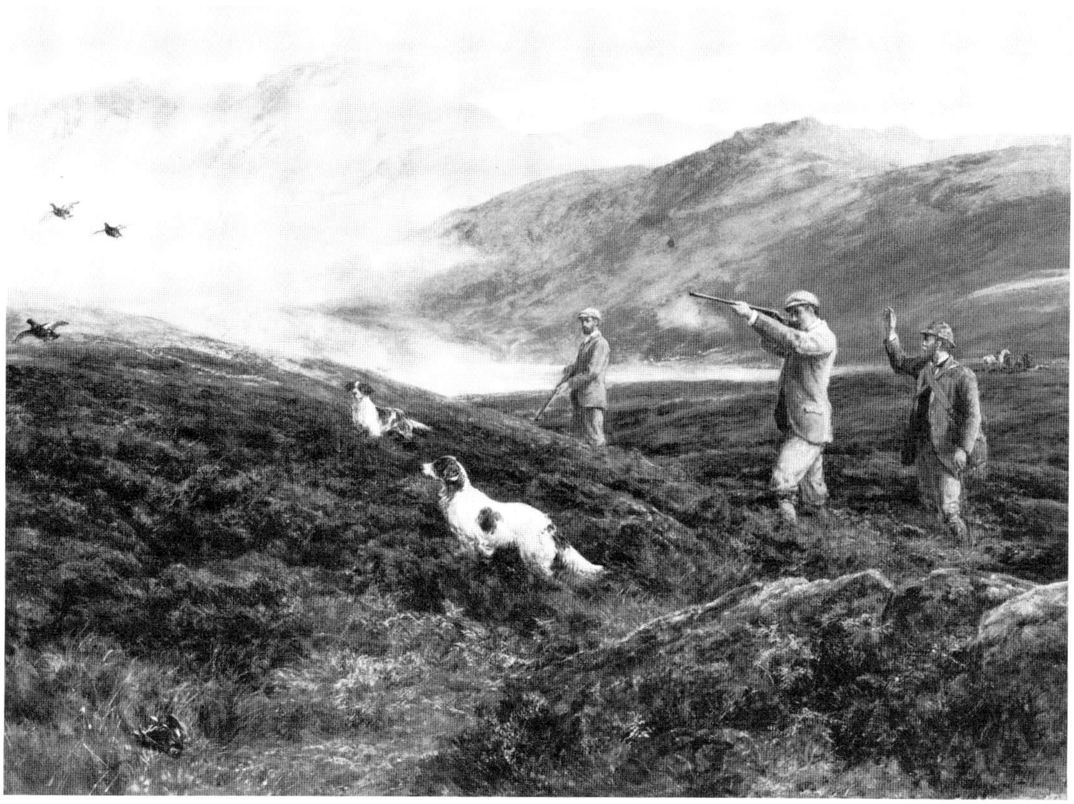

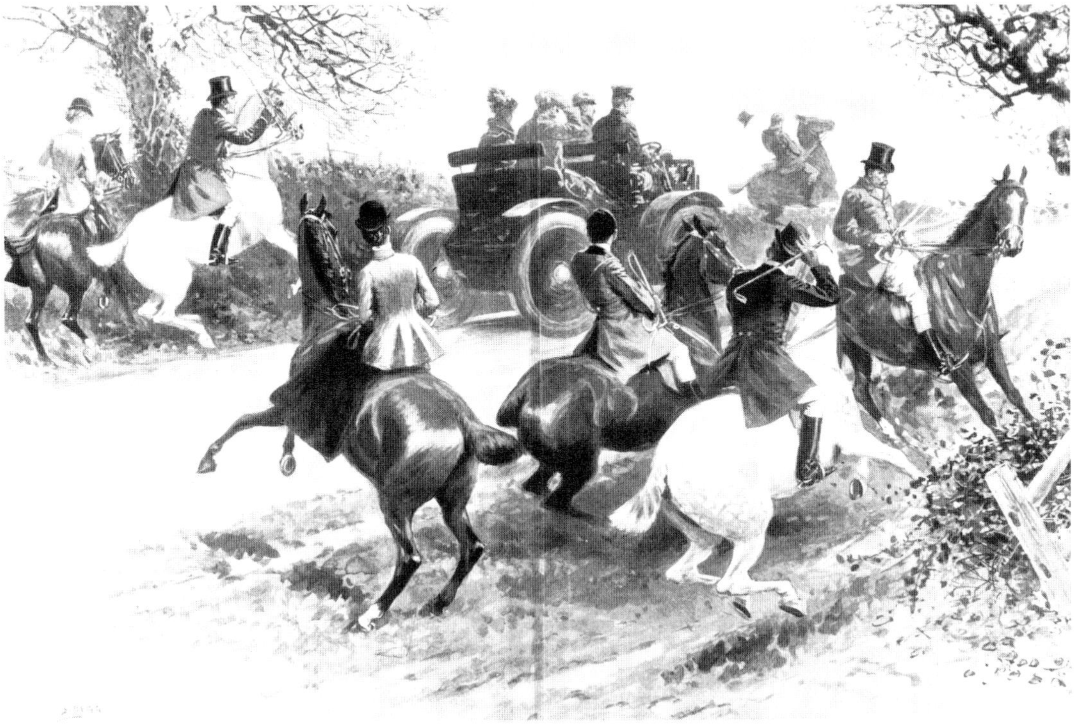

7 Samuel Begg, *Worse than Wire – a Motor in the Hunting Field*. Engraving reproduced from a printed copy of the *Illustrated London News* of 21 December 1901.

8 Cuthbert Bradley, *The Quorn Opening Meet at Kirby Gate, 1901*. Lithograph, image size 13 × 18 in (33 × 40 cm).

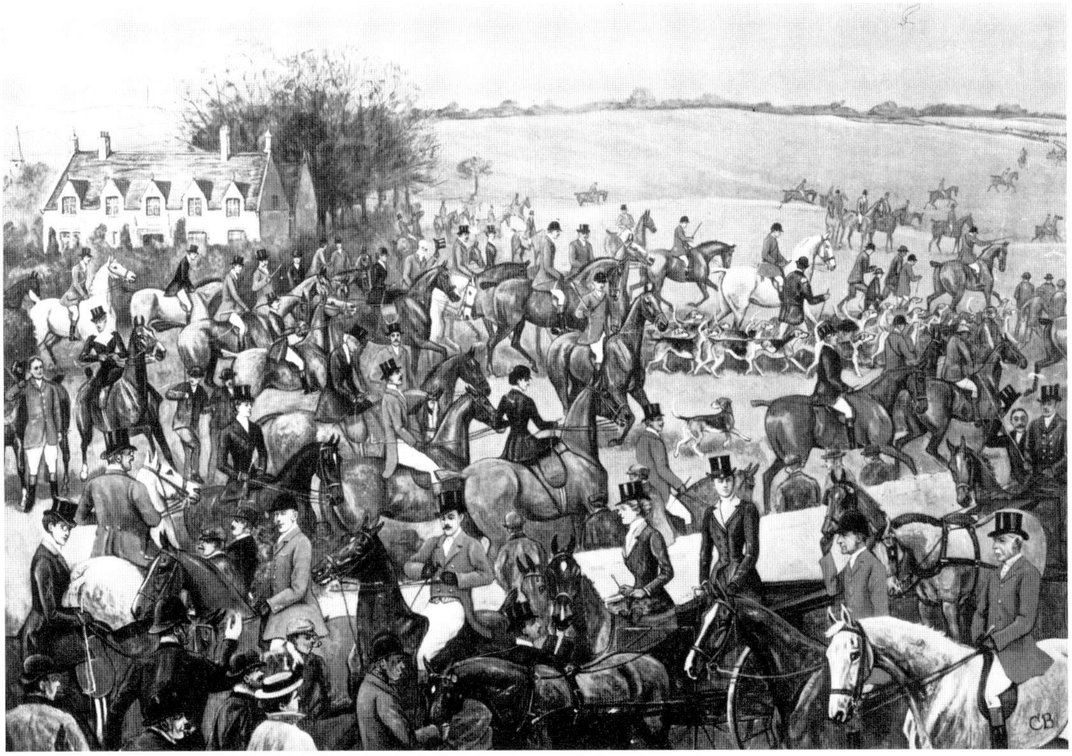

regularly enjoyed by local clerics, doctors, farmers and horse dealers. One of John Ferneley's striking hunting portraits in 1844 shows Mr George Marriot, *Old Marriot*, the Melton Mowbray haberdasher jumping a very big place in fine style with the Quorn, and equally Surtees' inimitable Mr Jorrocks, though a Cockney grocer, assumed greatness as a Master of Hounds. Subscription packs became the order of the day with long members' lists and guarantors; and as agriculture declined the prosperity and popularity of foxhunting soared. Fields were enormous and contrary to prophesy the network of railways across the country had not proved the death of both foxes and hounds. Instead more people from further afield were able to enjoy sport in pastures new and the years immediately preceding the first World War brought a second golden age before the final decline of landed society and the onslaught of the motor car. But in these contemporary pictures the decline in horsemanship became noticeable. In past centuries equitation with fencing, dancing and the classics had been considered a necessary part of a young gentleman's education but now the teaching of riding was left, more often than not, to the children's groom.

A foretaste of future problems is depicted in the *Illustrated London News* of 21 December 1901 with an engraving after Samuel Begg, a prolific contemporary illustrator of somewhat mundane talent, which bears the title *Worse than Wire – a Motor in the Hunting Field.* It shows a chauffeur-driven car with a man and two ladies and mayhem everywhere (7)! Hats flying, horses shying – two equestriennes in disorder. Below is printed in serious vein 'The Hon. Greville Verney, Master of the Warwickshire, had begged that motor cars would not be used for travelling to the meet or for any purpose connected with Foxhunting within the limits of the Hunt . . . a spectacle quite out of harmony with the spirit of foxhunting!'

Predictably the regular appearance of ladies in the hunting field now going across country in great style, riding side-saddle of course, provided artists with a new aspect of the sport. In a crowded composition of *The Quorn Opening Meet at Kirby Gate, 1901*, (with all persons identified on the original) Cuthbert Bradley, an adept journalist and caricaturist and also a sporting artist of minor talent, depicts half a dozen smart top-hatted ladies (and a glimpse of famous Tom Firr, retired huntsman in the right foreground), (*8*). Decorum seems to have dictated that these feminine riders were never portrayed upside down in a ditch as so often appeared the situation of husbands and brothers. Until the First World War, with few exceptions, girl teenagers and even their little sisters all rode side-saddle, pictorially with decorative results.

Few animal artists of any consequence were short of commissions at this time for, as in the days of Marshall, Ferneley and Alken, sporting pictures were the inevitable decoration for the walls of country houses. Every participating sportsman still required some record of victorious racehorses, favourite hunters and record runs but few mementoes of days with the guns were demanded.

NOTES

1 James Forman Todhunter Sloan introduced this style into England in 1898 but the forward seat had actually been used here without success three years earlier by a Negro, named Sims. A picture of *Tommy and Toddy – Loates and Sloan at Newmarket* in 1898 by an unknown artist shows the finish of a race contrasting the two styles. Tommy Loates was one of three jockey brothers. (Roger Longrigg, *The History of Horse Racing*.)

3

The Transitional Scene

There was no dearth of established artists to carry on the sporting pictorial tradition in the Edwardian age. Never had the dictum that demand produces supply proved more factual and, at a modest count, over fifty talented names could be listed. But it was such exponents as John Charlton, Heywood Hardy, Thomas Blinks, Godfrey Giles and others of their contemporaries who were to provide the transitional links, though much of their best work had been accomplished in Queen Victoria's reign. Many were, however, still exhibiting at the Royal Academy early in the twentieth century, but in general, they brought a stereotyped approach to the sporting scene with only modified action involved.

Though commercial photography was becoming ever more efficient and some detailed photographs of racehorses and British hunts began to appear in periodicals such as the *Illustrated London News*, *The Graphic* and *The Field* a steady market still existed for work by artists of even minor calibre, such as Ivester Lloyd, Finch Mason, John Beer and Ralph Cleaver, who could produce on the spot sketches which, from visual memory, were quickly embellished to illustrate the sporting events of the day for the topical magazines.

Ralph Cleaver possessed a versatile eye and could swiftly fulfil deadline dates on such diverse subjects as a lively version of the 1901 Oxford and Cambridge Boat Race as well as an impression of the sale of the King's heavy horses at Sandringham; and as early as 1900 produced *A Promising Run* – a huntsman with two couple of hounds and the horse galloping in convincing style.

But the facile skill of many of these artists providing regularly topical journalism for the popular weekly illustrated papers merits more appreciation than it has received. It may have been hack work but important social occasions were swiftly brought before the public.

Born in 1849, John Charlton (who did not die until 1917) must be considered in the context of the transitional painters of the Victorian/Edwardian eras. Somewhat unfairly the art historian Walter Shaw Sparrow regretted the influence on Charlton (and also other artists of the period) of innovating ideas from the Continent, though his training had been at the Newcastle School of Art and at South Kensington under the illustrator, J.D. Watson. The fact remains that John Charlton painted competently not only large ceremonial pictures of the Diamond Jubilee Procession arriving at St Paul's and such hunting groups as *Lord and Lady Spencer with the Pytchley Hounds in Althorp Park* with equal convincing confidence, but also his portrayal of foxhounds, when hunting and individually, are realised with exceptional perception, and with that keen, wistful look so peculiar to the breed. He had obviously been influenced by the fine kennel studies of his contemporary Victorian, John Emms, a master of foxhound character on large canvases (*Plate 1*). Such sporting portraits as Charlton's colourful painting of *The Lady Huntsman* (a curious title) in her scarlet coat on a grey horse, exhibited at the Royal Academy in 1907, hints possibly at the gallic ambience deplored by Shaw Sparrow (*9*). Incidentally a very similar

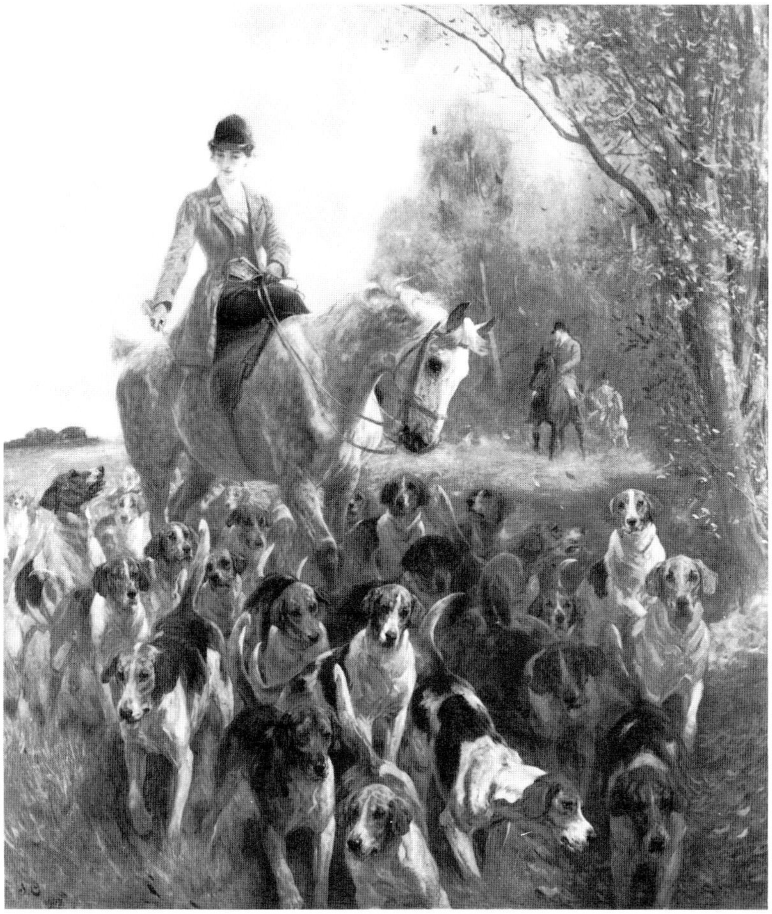

9 John Charlton, *The Lady Huntsman*, 1907. Oil on canvas, $82\frac{1}{2} \times 72$ in (209.5×182.8 cm).

picture by the artist of *Miss Cotton-Brown and Her Harriers* was exhibited in the Royal Academy in 1911.

Long-lived Heywood Hardy, a prolific contemporary of Charlton's, born in 1842, was nevertheless still exhibiting a Quorn hunting scene in the Royal Academy of 1918. Son of James Hardy, a portrait and landscape painter of difficult temperament, he spent his childhood in Bath before eventually escaping from family problems with his brother. In 1864 he went to Paris, entered the Ecole des Beaux-Arts and then studied under Pielse, painter of battle scenes, and later in Antwerp, copying pictures at the galleries and working in a small *atelier* run by the artist Coreine.

On returning to England in 1868 commissions for portraits of sporting pictures and animal studies were received from such influential patrons as the Marquis of Zetland, Colonel Wymndham Murray and the Sitwells of Renishaw. Heywood Hardy was a keen sportsman himself, possessing a good eye for a horse as in his portrayal of Mr F. Bibby's big raking steeplechaser, Glenside, winner of the 1911 Grand National, with Jack Anthony up.

His coaching scenes on the high road or with a spanking tandem never lacked action but his numerous hunting pictures, though competently composed and skilfully painted, appear devoid of real animation and seldom depict hounds in full cry, concentrating on such titles as *The Lost Scent* (*Plate 2*) or *Returning from the Hunt*. Nevertheless his gift for presenting the big hunting occasion is splendidly demonstrated in his fine composition *Captain Frank Forester and his Family at Kirby Gate*, *c* 1912. Forester was master of the Quorn for thirteen seasons and noted for never taking a fence slowly.

Unfortunately Heywood Hardy failed to escape the pervading Victorian sentimentality and often expended his undoubted talents in pseudo period hunting and coaching scenes. From 1873 he worked in London, exhibited forty-six pictures at the Royal Academy, and in most of the major galleries, and many of his works were published in the *Illustrated London News*, *The Graphic* and also appeared as popular prints. He was elected a member of several societies including the Royal Institute of Oil Painters, the Royal Society of Portrait Painters, the Royal Society of Painters and Etchers and an Associate of the Royal Watercolours Society.

In 1909 he moved to West Sussex and at the age of eighty-three painted a series of panels in Clymping church to commemorate its seven hundredth anniversary, as a gift for his old friend Canon E.F. Leach, the incumbent. The subjects, apathy, poverty, innocence and gaiety, brought some controversy as Christ is depicted walking on the Sussex Downs and in the nearby fields with (allegedly) local residents.

Heywood Hardy must be considered one of the most prolific Victorian painters typical of the period whose quality of brushwork and application was often obscured by a conventional approach to the subject, and unacceptably dated when confronted by the trends of the new century. But by the 1980s a revival in the appreciation of sporting Victoriana became apparent when a colourful hunting scene by this artist, *Drawn Blank*, dated 1899, was sold at Christie's in February 1986 for a record £62,640, more than double its estimate. This trend for appreciation of the early sporting art of this century will surely continue for these pictures have already become part of a fast disappearing heritage.

Another Victorian artist of ability to work on into the Edwardian era was Thomas Blinks, born in 1853 in Maidstone. Originally destined for a tailoring apprenticeship he received no

10 Thomas Blinks, *Over the Ditch*. Oil on canvas, 35 × 49 in (88.9 × 124.4 cm).

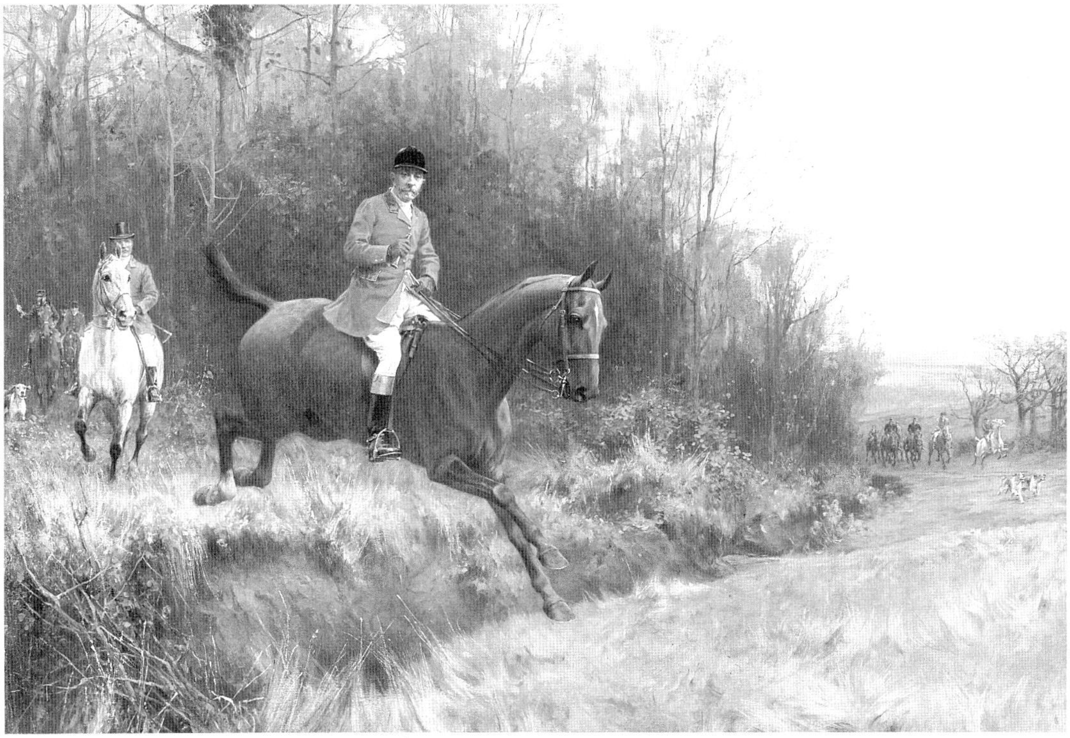

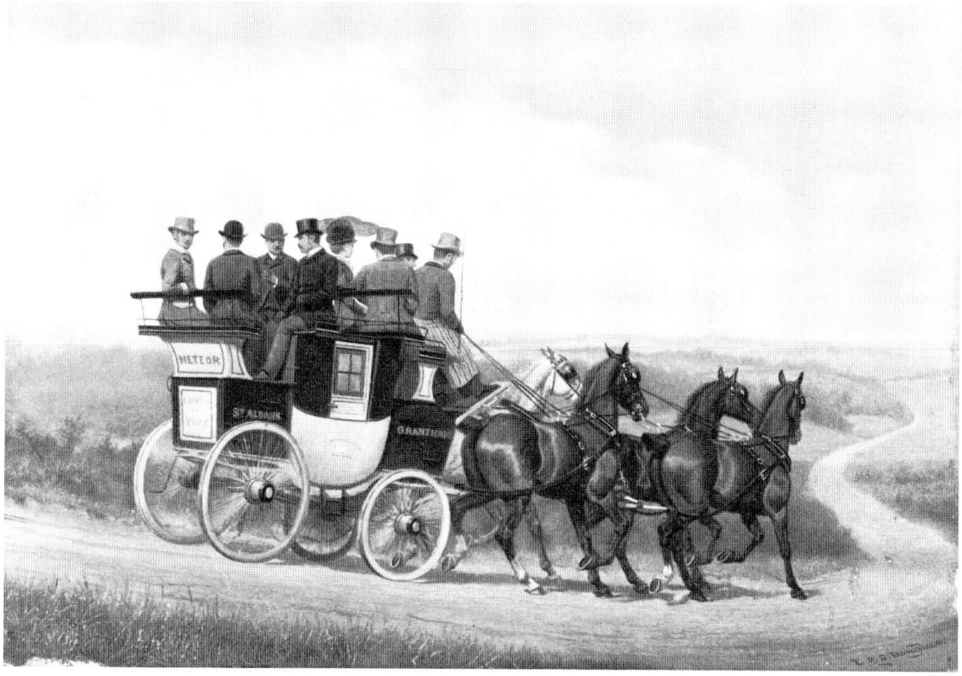

11 Edward Algernon Stuart Douglas, *Coaching in Summer* (from a set of four). Oil on canvas, $4\frac{1}{4} \times 5\frac{3}{4}$ in (10.7 × 14.6 cm).

formal artistic training but acquired a first class appreciation of horse anatomy and movement by watching horses at Tattersall's auction marts. Using both oils and watercolours he exhibited frequently in the Royal Academy, the first time in 1883 and he was one of the few artists who portrayed George V in the hunting field.

In his pictures there is an attempt to record accurate equine action but with varying success (*10*). He had a good appreciation of conformation and breeding in a hunter and there is a realism in his sporting scenes which at times could be almost photographic, as in the well known picture of *The York & Ainsty Hounds – on the Ferry at Newby* dated 1898, an occasion surprisingly free from any sense of apprehension at the situation. Understandably this and many other of his other popular works were reproduced as prints, several being engraved by J.B. Pratt. The talent of Thomas Blinks was also much in demand by the shooting fraternity for his accurate and pleasing portrayal of gun dogs on the moors. J.C. Wood coined the phrase for him as 'Master of the Immaculate Setter'.[1]

Among the many animal artists working at this time and finding successful careers in the prevailing enthusiasm for field sports must be mentioned Edward Algernon Stuart Douglas. Born in 1860, he exhibited ten hunting pictures in the Royal Academy and is one of the few late Victorians to have used coursing and coaching as a subject. An interesting set of four pictures of the road abound in knowledgeable detail sometimes found lacking in his hunting scenes (*11*). Though his death did not occur until 1915 most of his best work was completed before the end of the nineteenth century and this included some attractive sets of foxhunting on canvases as small as 8 × 10 inches.

Born in the same year was George Wright who was painting sporting pictures into nearly the middle of the twentieth century, sometimes collaborating with his brother, Gilbert, also a sporting artist which makes for some confusion. George Wright, small, dapper and a prolific worker could paint very competent horse portraits and also produce lively hunting and racing scenes. Regularly every fortnight he would turn up at Ackermann's with a couple of pictures

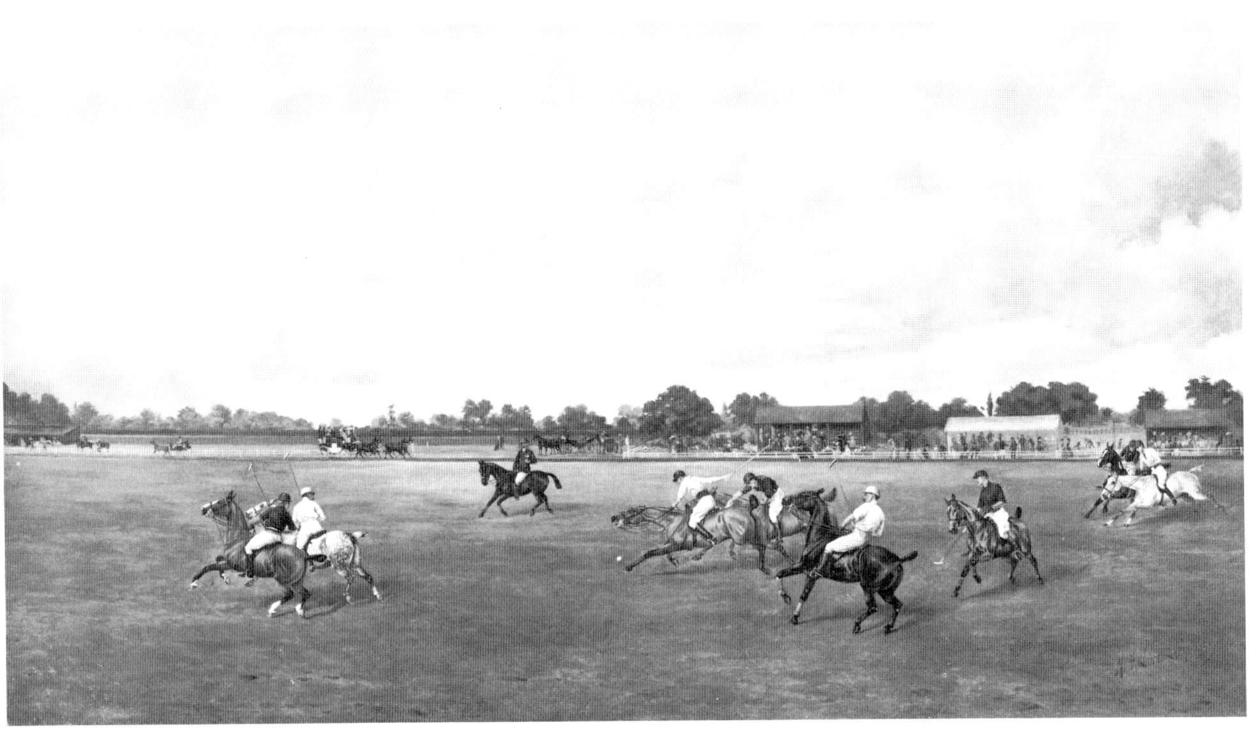

12 Henry Frederick Lucas-Lucas, *A Game of Polo at Rugby*, 1900. Oil on canvas, $33\frac{1}{4} \times 60$ in (84.4×152.4 cm).

13 George Wright, *Washing Down Polo Ponies in the Lines*. Oil on canvas, 14×21 in (35.5×53.3 cm).

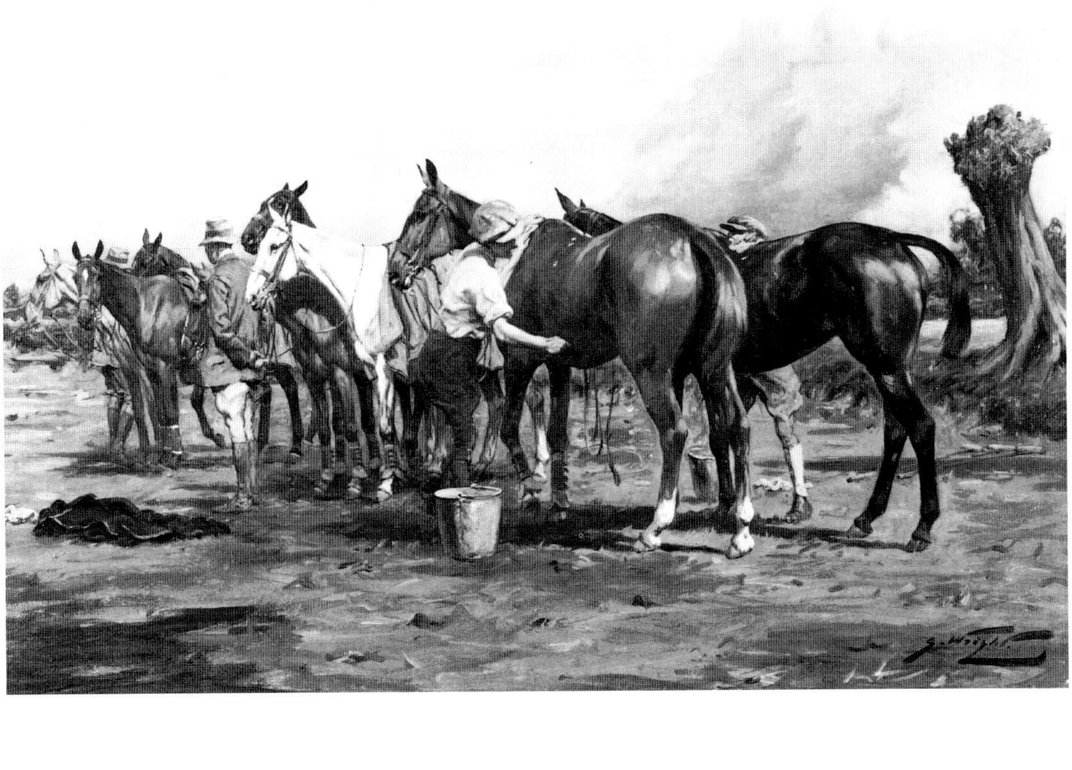

under his arm for which he received twenty guineas. In 1932, his seventy-third year, he held a very successful exhibition in their Gallery of twenty-four oil paintings of various sporting subjects. In the early part of his career he lived for a spell in Rugby which probably inspired some of his fine studies of polo for the popular club there. These dashing horsemen, invariably moustachioed, riding with long stirrup leathers on the 14.2 hh ponies, (the maximum height limit demanded by the rules of the day) provide a valuable documentary of the Edwardian game, especially in such studies as *Washing Down Polo Ponies in the Lines* (*13*).

His contemporary Henry Frederick Lucas-Lucas also painted action scenes as in *A Game of Polo at Rugby*, dated 1900 (*12*). Also of interest is a somewhat static scene *Getting into Line for Persimmon's Derby*, dated 1896. One of his most pleasing works is his portrait of the North Warwickshire's *Rally*, Champion Bitch Hound at Peterborough for three successive years in the early 1920s – a hat trick that afterwards resulted in the ruling that no hound would be permitted to win more than once.

Perhaps underestimated amongst these industrious early Edwardians was John Alexander Harington Bird, who studied at the Royal Academy Schools. Working in both oils and water-colours and with versatile talent he brought life and action into his hunting scenes, but more outstanding were his fine fluent studies of Arabian horses and native riders in desert settings. The elegant conformation of the oriental horses is sensitively allied to excitement and action.

Also of undoubted ability and patronised by influential sportsmen of the day was Thomas Percy Earl, whose portraits of top class racing winners included *The Mighty Sceptre* in 1901 and later popular, but somewhat ineffective, scenes of the 1927 and 1928 Grand Nationals. Four sporting artists with the surname Earl worked between 1836 and 1930, all believed to be family connections.[2]

The Aintree specialist, however, was John Beer, who from 1901–1913 was annually producing rather slick evocations of the great steeplechase in which the artist seems somewhat unaware of Muybridge's elucidation of true equine action. Though his work was uneven, (his horses often appear elongated) occasionally he veered from a style careless and predictable to emphasise with real flair the excitement and tension of the racing occasion. This is effective in his scenes at the post for the Grand National of 1901 when the race was run in a blizzard. Amongst other works of merit is his set of eight pictures of the Derby.

To make a considerable mark in this sporting world was Alfred Grenfell Haigh, born in 1870. Educated at Rossal where he won prizes for drawing, he later studied in Paris and with his own fine eye for accurate conformation, allied to being a first class horseman himself, he became one of the most popular equestrian artists of his day. Commissions were received from such renowned racehorse owners as the Duke of Portland, the Aga Khan and Lord Rosebery and he painted portraits of such classic winners as The Tetrarch, Bahram and Manna with striking success, but like many of his contemporaries he rarely portrayed the horse in motion, for he maintained that it was impossible to produce a horse at full gallop without making it appear unnatural. But a compensating gift for putting over equine character is illustrated by splendid head studies of Lieut Colonel T.R. Bodger's polo ponies, Dainty and Girton Girl, dated 1924 (*Plate 3*). We would recognise these stars of the international polo field anywhere. His pleasing paintings of greyhounds, winners of the Waterloo Cup, also exhibit the same perception and quality.

In the next decade, especially in hunting scenes, horses, hounds and the field were to be shown free moving and some animation and excitement gradually again began to prevail. But balanced and detailed appraisal of these early Edwardian artists is difficult as the 'Blitz' of the Second World War destroyed much relevant material. Ackermann's possessed a goldmine of records and catalogues but like many other London galleries received a direct hit. Nevertheless the popularity of sporting art on the London scene of the day, especially with hunting and racing as the subjects, is hard to exaggerate. Many works were exhibited in the Summer Exhibition of the Royal Academy and lithographic reproductions were much in demand.

Today many of these pictures appear to modern eyes inhibited in style and somewhat prosaic in their approach to 'a fast thing' across country or the rigours of competitive race riding. The majority, with their neat repetitive observation, lack the zest and impact of paintings of the eighteenth and early nineteenth centuries and few possess any landscape effects to stir the imagination. But, as the years pass, appreciation grows for here again, as in the past, artists have left a vivid documentary of national sporting ways and rural life that have already disappeared and these works are similarly destined to join the unique heritage of British sporting art.

It was an Indian officer, Major Godfrey Douglas Giles, born in Karachi in 1857, who became one of the most consistent of his generation in attempts to introduce some semblance of vigour and action into the sporting scene. On retirement, after service in India, Afghanistan and Egypt, he took up a career in art with only his experience as an intermittent animal painter of military subjects as background. He studied, however, in Paris with the distinguished painter and sculptor Carolus-Duran, founder and eventual President in 1898 of La Societé des Beaux Arts. Eventually Giles was to initiate a new and original conception of the hunting scene with the field spread out and events depicted as seen by followers in the rear (a familiar viewpoint for many foxhunters), (*14*). But Whyte-Melville wrote fifty years earlier, 'Every man that goes out hunting thinks he only wants an opportunity to show his back to the rest of the field.'[3]

Various identified hunting countries were Giles' frequent subjects, often to be reproduced as prints, though as in his set of three paintings of the Cheshire Hunt in 1904, problems of action are still apparent with the galloping field[4]; this was also visible in tense racing scenes

14 Godfrey Douglas Giles, *The Duke of Beaufort's – Brinkworth Brook*, *c* 1911. Print.

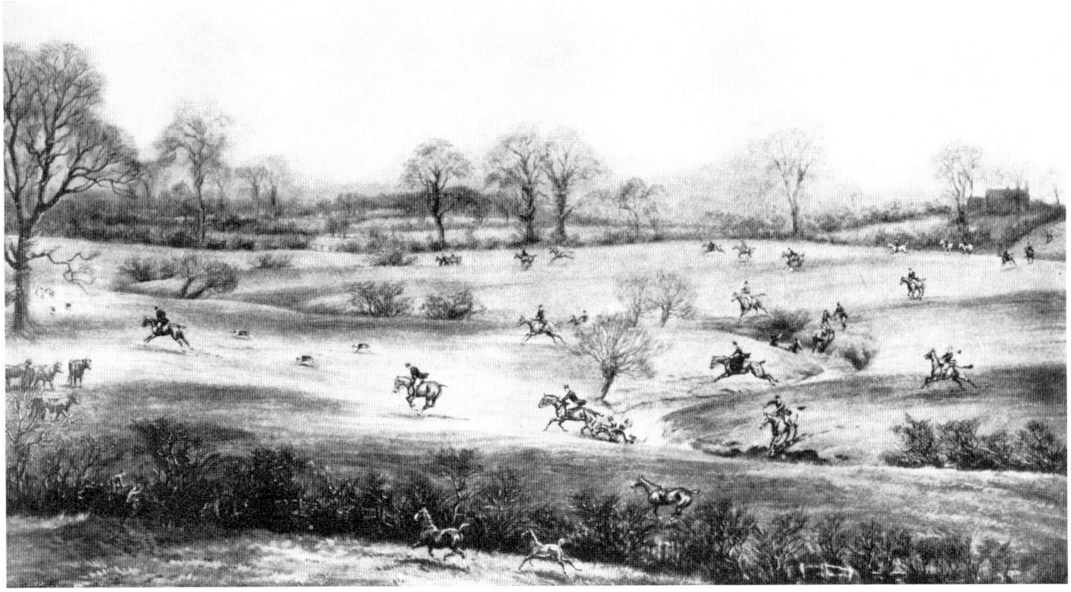

at the winning post. Nevertheless he could paint with great verve both hunting activities, people in crowded racecourse paddocks and most convincingly the speed and intricacies of polo matches at Hurlingham and elsewhere (*15*). Though his colour tones tended to be monotonous Godfrey Giles took a decisive step forward in bringing Victorian sporting art into the twentieth century.

It was, however, James Lynwood Palmer who was acclaimed by the public as the best equestrian artist of the day and amongst the leading racehorse owners he was eventually to supersede his exact contemporary, the popular German-born artist, Emil Adam, as their favourite portrayer of their classic winners. Born in 1868, third son of a Lincolnshire parson and possessed with an inherent artistic talent plus a passion for horses, Palmer ran away to Canada to avoid a destined legal career. After eleven years ranching, horse breaking, painting and sketching he finally finished up as horsemaster of one of the biggest cab proprietors in New York, where his salary depended on the fitness of his horses. His considerable artistic gifts were fortunately recognised by General Field of the US Army and his career as a painter was established.

Returning to England in the mid-1890s again fortune smiled, and under the immediate patronage of the Countess of Warwick, influential hostess, avid foxhunter and close friend of Edward VII, he quickly became established as the leading equestrian artist of the day and, in addition, one of the finest four-in-hand whips in the country. Palmer received many prestige commissions, including in 1900 one from the Duke of Portland for a group study (followed by individual portraits) of all the stallions at the Welbeck Stud with, of course, the legendary St Simon dominating the scene (*Plate 2*). Other celebrated patrons were to include such illustrious owners as Lord Rosebery, Lord Willoughby de Broke, Lord Woolavington, the Aga Khan and also Lord Lonsdale, MFH, whom he portrayed on a fine chestnut hunter, together with Lady Londsdale and the Cottesmore Hounds against a lovely panorama of High Leicestershire. Catalogue frontispieces for the International Horse Show at Olympia, of which Lord Lonsdale was the extrovert patron, followed this commission.

For King Edward in 1909 he painted the royal Derby winner, Minoru, and years later

15 Godfrey Douglas Giles, *Polo at Hurlingham*, 1918. Oil on canvas, 20 × 30½ in (50.8 × 77.8 cm).

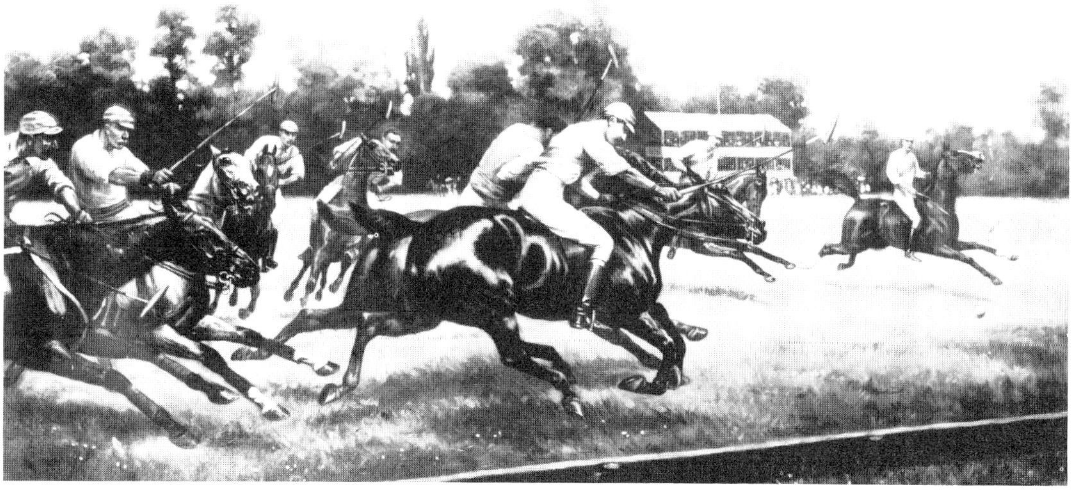

repeated the work in miniature for the Queen Mary's Dolls' House. Later Lord Woolavington was to commission a portrait of the massive chestnut Captain Cuttle, winner of the 1922 Derby and for Sir Abe Bailey, two fine portraits of the dark bay *Son-in-Law* who was to become leading sire in 1924 (*16*). But Lynwood Palmer's countless studies of Classic winners, like those by J.F. Herring Snr a century earlier, form a vital record of the early twentieth century Thoroughbred and many of his pictures today are to be found in various stately homes, in the Jockey Club rooms at Newmarket, and six hang in Boodles Club in London.

His practical knowledge of horsemastership was unique and in addition to painting many commissions for Lord Derby, including a vibrant portrait of that great little personality Hyperion, he was also retained as equine adviser to the stud. The trainer, the Honourable George Lambton (of whom he painted a brilliant portrait riding a dock-tailed cob on Newmarket Heath) wrote, after he had cured the famous Swynford's brushing problems, 'He is the cleverest man with a horse's foot I have ever come across!'[5] Some of his veterinary remedies were certainly unconventional – wounds were cleansed and dressed with pure linseed oil and his panacea for intestinal troubles was hard hay and turnips.

Apart from some excellent animated harness studies, Lynwood Palmer, as so many of his

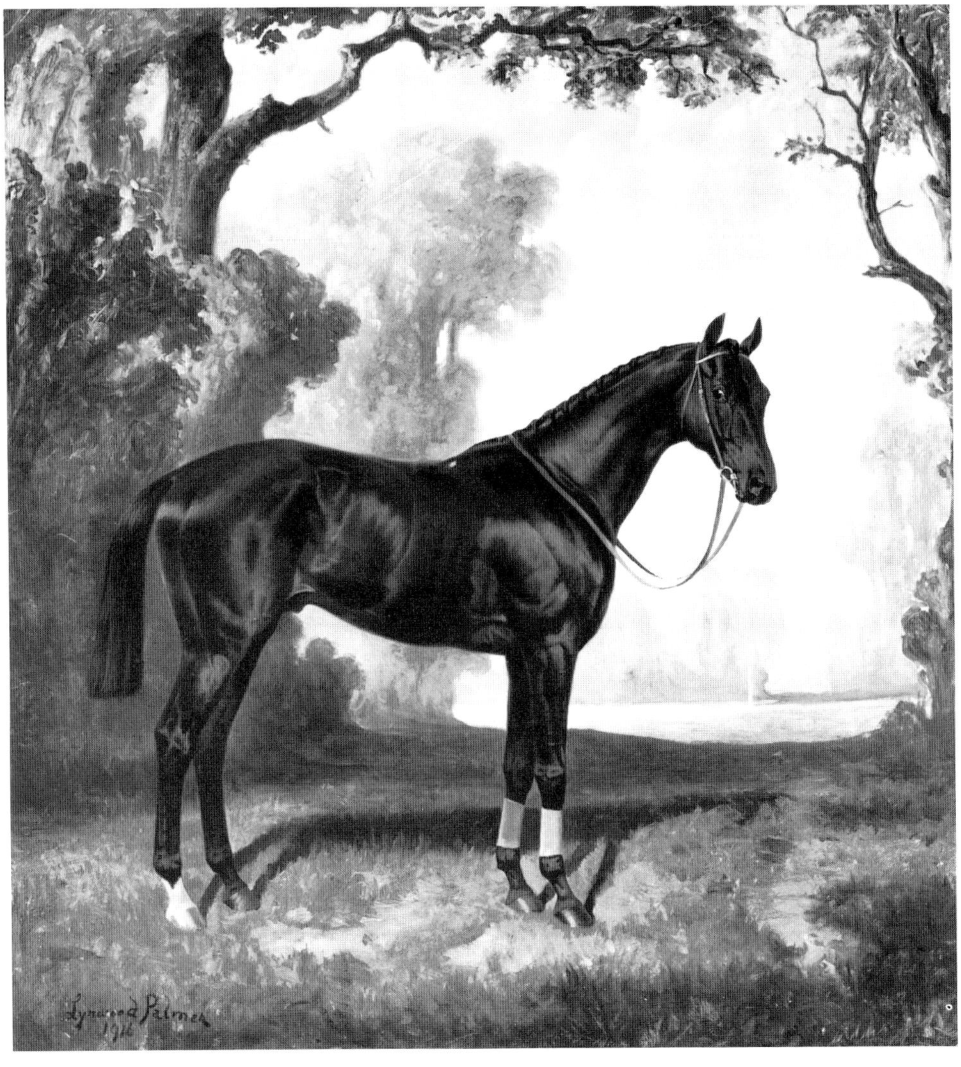

16 James Lynwood Palmer, *Sir Abe Bailey's Son-in-Law*. Oil on canvas, $31\frac{1}{2} \times 29\frac{1}{2}$ in (80 × 74.9 cm).

contemporaries, rarely portrayed the horse in action and today appreciation is almost exclusively based on his posed, but never lifeless, portraits of famous racehorses. Perceptive likenesses were often achieved by riding out alongside his subjects and afterwards briefly standing the horse for a small detailed watercolour embellished by neat written notes. He maintained that quickness was vital in capturing the alert nervous energy of the Thoroughbred. Later this information was developed into the finished picture when he would suggest with subtle touches the horse's individuality and temperament. In different vein, but pleasing in the Stubbs' tradition, are such compositions as *Mares and Foals at Lavington* and the study of Lord Wavertree's brood mares, *Cherry Lass, Black Cherry and Jean's Folly* with leafy trees to enhance the setting.

Lynwood Palmer's fluent ability to depict equine form is remarkable when it is realised he received no professional artistic training at any time in his career. Particularly indicative is his practical and strictly representational painting of Ambrose Clark's favourite grey carriage horse 'the best wheeler I ever drove', with its sporting American owner alongside and also a lively pair of greys in tandem. Munnings himself had small admiration for Palmer's talent because he felt the artist 'made the necessary portraits of horses as patrons wanted them to be'[6] – not an entirely just assessment. Like Munnings he could convey the stability of a horse to stand with weight on the ground and it was his own experienced technical knowledge of the horse, allied to his unerring eye, which gave both conviction and beauty to his studies of the Thoroughbred. He continued painting with undiminished skill until shortly before his death in 1941.

A thesis might be written on the ramifications of the Wheeler family in the Victorian era and their descendants into the twentieth century. John Alfred Wheeler, who died in 1903, was responsible for some enormous paintings of the Beaufort Hunt which incorporated nearly 130 figures. Nearer our own time it was his son and pupil Alfred Wheeler who lived until 1932 and fulfilled, in a somewhat stereotyped way, portraits of Classic winners for such distinguished patrons as Edward VII and the Baron Rothschild; he was responsible for helping his father on commissions. Alfred's eldest son, John Frederick, painted hunting scenes and his third son, Walter Herbert, was noted for his miniatures of horses and dogs but his portrait of HM The Queen's Aureole with Scobie Breasley was exhibited at the Paris Salon in 1955. He did not die until 1960 so some confusion arises when correct attributions are involved.

Another member of a distinguished and prolific family of artists was Alfred Charles Havell who worked for many years in a room always filled with his own tobacco smoke above the premises of the famous art dealers Fores in Piccadilly. His portraits of contemporary racehorses such as the famous St Simon and the Derby winner Minoru with King Edward VII, provided informative likenesses but with his first class hunting scenes, which were published as prints, sporting art still reflected the Victorian approach, often very competent but rarely innovative.

NOTES

1 Lieut Colonel J.C. Wood, *A Dictionary of Animal Painters*, p. 16.

2 George, the earliest (op. 1856–1883) was the father of Maud Earl (op. 1884–1919), painter of domestic animals especially dogs. (See Chapter 9, p. 89).

3 G.J. Whyte-Melville, *Market Harborough*, Chapman & Hall, 1861, p. 14.

4 Apparent in the dust jacket reproduction, typical of the Victorian tradition.

5 The Hon. George Lambton, *Men and Horses I have Known*, p. 290.

6 Reginald Pound, *The Englishman: A Biography of Sir Alfred Munnings*, p. 98.

4

Formative Influences and Innovations

Of all the late Victorian painters starting their careers at the end of the nineteenth century William Frank Calderon must be considered of major importance as an influence on the new generation of animal artists. Born in 1860, the third son of a Royal Academician, Philip Hermogenes Calderon, at fourteen years old he was awarded the Trevelyan Goodall Scholarship and studied at the Slade School for the next six years, aided by the addition of the Slade's own two years scholarship. He was not only himself an animal artist of versatile, though traditional, talent but also possessed a fundamental gift for imparting his knowledge to others. In 1894 he founded his School of Animal Painting in Baker Street, London, ran a summer school in the country and, until the outbreak of the First World War and afterwards, many sporting artists owed their growing reputations to skilled teaching under Calderon and his anatomy lecturer Dr Armstrong. These numbered such young men of ability as Cecil Aldin, Frank Stewart, Lionel Edwards, Frederick Whiting and Alfred Munnings.

Calderon's own equestrian works included horse fairs, hunting and rural scenes painted with keen observation. He was, unlike many of his generation, effective in the portrayal of animal character as in his arcadian composition *Shelter* exhibited in the Royal Academy in 1912 (*Plate 5*). Also he understood basic action and one of his finest pictures *The Crest of the Hill* with its straining team of heavy horses was bought for the National Gallery of Queensland.

Most valuable for the artists of this century was the publication in 1936 of his book *Animal Painting and Anatomy*, a work finely illustrated by the author himself (*17*). It covers not only the anatomical study of horses, cattle, dogs and cats but should rank as compulsory study for any ambitious animal artist, with its clear instruction on such complex and diverse subjects as muscle development and perspective, and also for its emphasis on such intangible facets as balance in composition and tonal colour values. One sentence, however, remains paramount; 'A beautiful picture may be done in spite of all laws, but it can never be beautiful if it is ill-drawn.'[1] Calderon's evaluation of important principles in animal form, both subjective and objective, certainly played their part in the shape of things to come.

It was, however, to the liberating influence of Joseph Crawhall and Robert Bevan that the more observant and creative animal artists of the new century owed their fresh approach to the sporting scene. Both Crawhall and Bevan worked into the second decade of the twentieth century but it is difficult to equate their original interpretation to sporting and equestrian subjects with the transitional compositions of their contemporaries. Though their influence made little immediate impact it was to grow with subtle effect over the years; only in retrospect is it possible to realise the value and potency of their innovations. For this reason their work and lives merit consideration in some detail.

It is curious that the 1860s saw the birth of both these men, who, whilst making their names

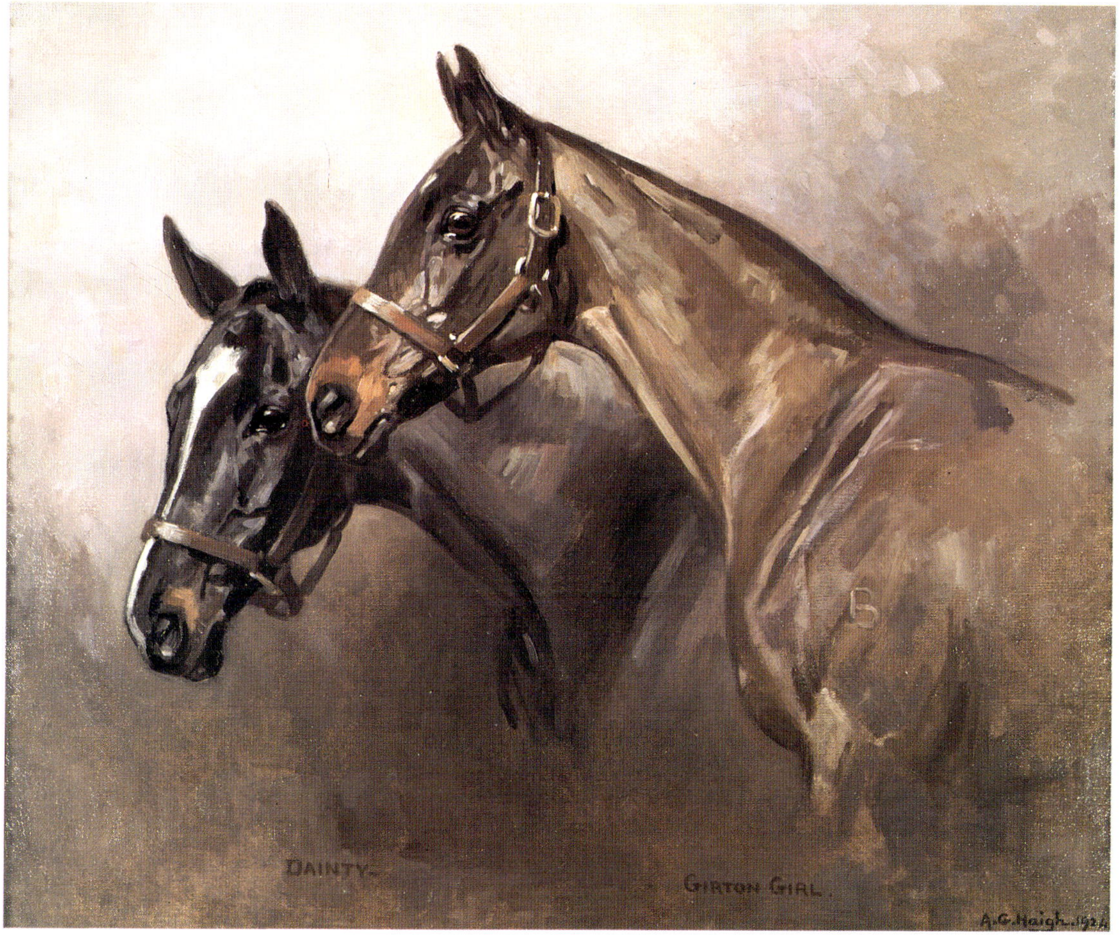

PLATE 3 (*above*) Alfred Grenfell Haigh, *Lt Col T. R. Bodger's Polo Ponies, Dainty and Girton Girl*, 1924. Oil on canvas, 19 × 23½ in (48.2 × 59.6 cm). (*below*) Lowes Dalbiac Luard, *Steeplechase*, *c* 1934. Pastel, 25 × 57 in (63.5 × 144.7 cm).

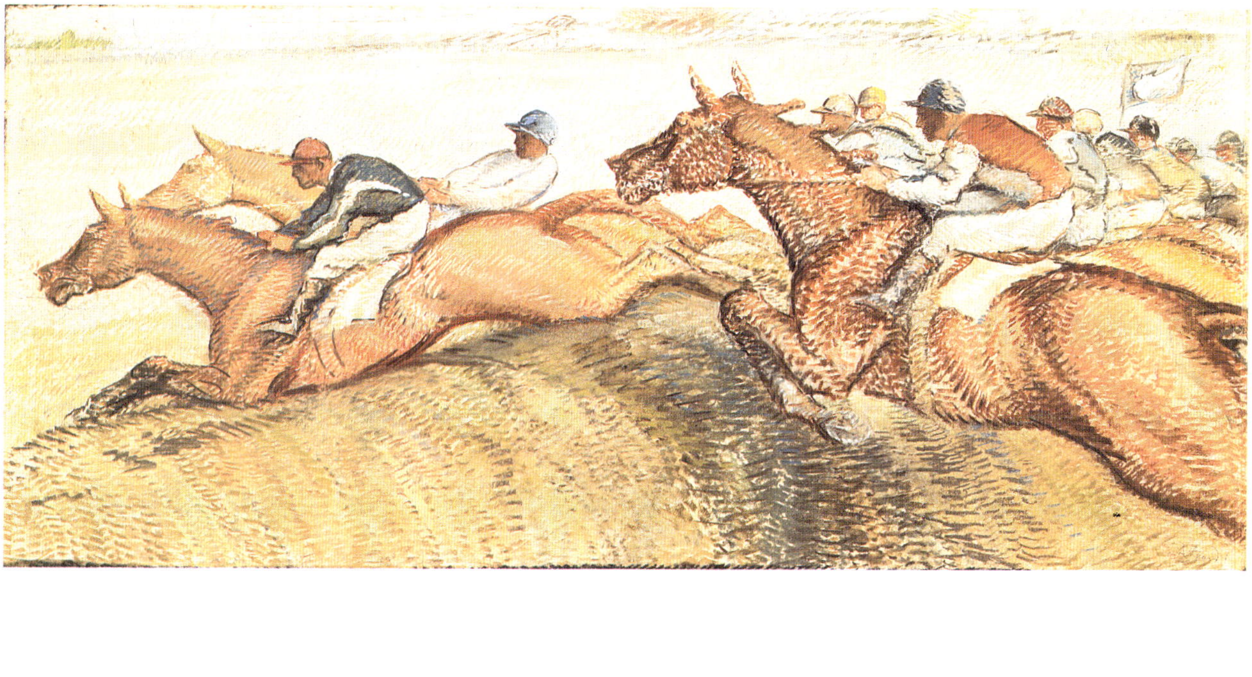

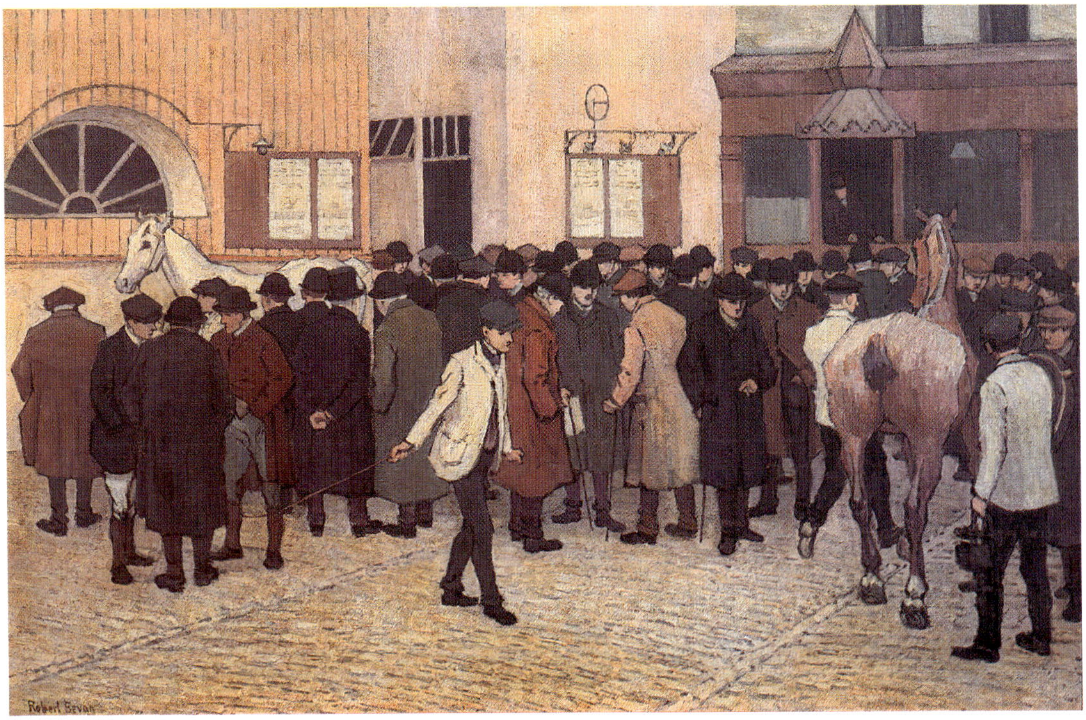

PLATE 4 (*above*) Robert Polhill Bevan, *Horse Sale at The Barbican*, *c* 1913. Oil on canvas, 31 × 48 in (78.7 × 121.9 cm).

(*right*) Joseph Crawhall, *The Meet*. Gouache on linen, 26 × 25 in (66 × 63.8 cm).

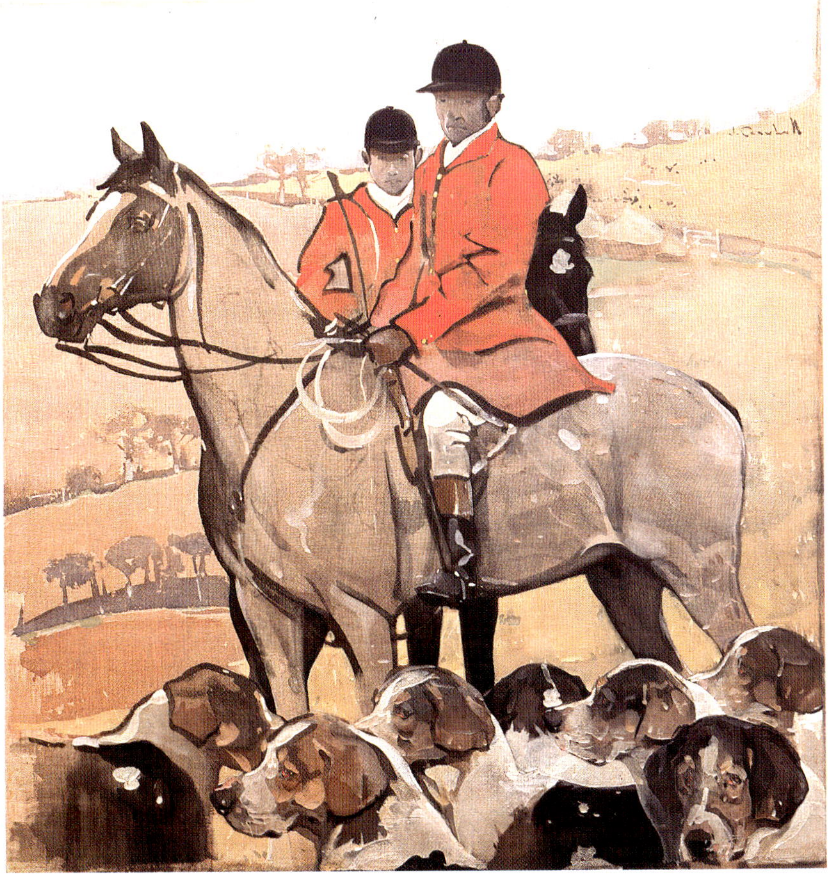

17 William Frank Calderon, *Drawing to show the pelvis of a horse resting*, from *Animal Painting and Anatomy*.

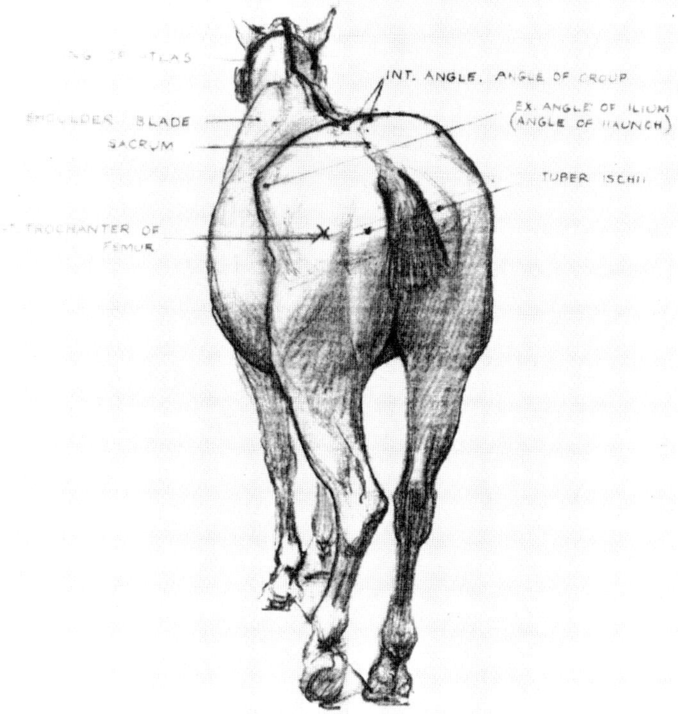

as artists in the Post-Impressionist genre in the sphere of landscape, were both also to use their considerable talents in sporting art, breaking away completely from the accepted conventions and bringing a new conception to the world of animal painting.

Most of our painters of field sports have been themselves active sportsmen and Crawhall and Bevan were no exceptions. Both had taken to hunting in their youth and were further indoctrinated by unconventional sport experienced in the unexpected terrain of North Africa.

In Crawhall's case, both as artist and sportsman, hereditary factors prevailed. He was born in Morpeth, Northumberland in 1861; his father, a successful rope manufacturer, was also a country squire of means and, like his grandfather, a talented amateur artist. Crawhall's close friend was Charles Keene, a constant contributor to *Punch* and a master of draughtsmanship. Crawhall studied with Edward Arthur Walton, the landscape painter and James Joseph Guthrie, the wood engraver.

A brief spell in 1882 at the Paris studio of Aimé Morot, the painter of animal subjects and battle pieces, decided Crawhall that there was little benefit in adapting to oils his own individualistic style of working in line and watercolours – his true affinity lay with the Chinese and Japanese schools. Nevertheless, his artistic life in France inevitably brought him in contact with the impressionist racehorse paintings of Degas and Manet and the vivid equestrian studies of his exact contemporary, Toulouse-Lautrec, which permanently stimulated his own sporting scenes.

Joseph Crawhall possessed his own expert understanding of animal anatomy and also a unique ability, working from memory and never from nature, to catch a likeness with sparkling precision in a few strokes of his brush, whether of horse, dog or bird. Like Robert Bevan, his friendship with Old Etonian, Bernardino de Velasco, the Duke of Frias and Hereditary Grand

Constable of Castile, who had established a pack of mongrel hounds to hunt fox and pig in Tangier, found him in North Africa acting as whipper-in with a polyglot field, mounted on anything from local Barbs to mules and donkeys. George D. Armour, the sporting artist, well known to readers of *Punch*, and John Lavery were also amongst this happy band, where sport consisted mainly of a good gallop in congenial company. The Hunt provided plenty of material for humorous sketches and Crawhall, always a first-class horseman, also achieved lasting fame by winning from 1893 the Tangier Hunt Cup for four years in succession.

A spell painting bull fights in Spain terminated this sowing of wild oats, after which the artist, first sharing a studio with Armour in London, then settled down to a somewhat dull existence with his devoted mother in Yorkshire. He took with him from Morocco an Arab stallion, Masmoud, renamed Beak, which sired several good ponies in the North and on which he hunted with great success with the Middleton, the Sinnington and the York and Ainsty. Reserved and reticent and nicknamed by Cunninghame Graham and Lavery as 'The Great Silence' but known by other contemporaries as 'Creeps', Crawhall was something of an eccentric. On one occasion he rode all the way from Yorkshire to the doors of the Chelsea Arts Club and he was never seen wearing anything but riding kit, except on Sundays. In spite of receiving awards for his work in Paris and Munich he hated publicity and, apart from a special rapport with children, he was only interested in people if they had animals.

Unfortunately, pressed by no financial stringencies, Crawhall painted only when in the mood, generally in watercolours, often on brown holland; being his own sternest critic he would then destroy much of his work. He held his first one man show in 1894 at Alex Reid's Gallery in Glasgow and his only other in 1912 at W.B. Paterson's in London. Most of his pictures were bought by the Scottish connoisseur Sir William Burrell and members of the Coats family and the present Burrell Gallery at Glasgow owns a fine collection of Crawhall's best work. Esteemed today are his exquisite studies of animals and birds, executed with stark economy of line or in fluent use of body colour or gouache, as in *The Black Cock* with the head of a white hen coming effectively into the picture.

His unforgettable watercolours of dour northern hunting types and other sporting scenes illustrate his flair for presenting the curious relationship that lies between horse and rider as in *The Meet* with its mounted hunt servants, a keen alert bay, and hounds filling the foreground (*Plate 4*). This quality is repeated in the back view of horse and rider in *The Huntsman* with the green harrier's coat a lovely contrast against the clear blue sky. These brought a new dimension to sporting art and a breakaway from the repetitive scenes of foxhunters streaming neatly across the pastures of the Shires. The spontaneous poster type drawing in gouache on paper of *Tod Sloan: the American Jockey* with its prancing racehorse, was to be echoed in the 1950s by John Skeaping's gouache studies of Thoroughbreds in action.

Robert Polhill Bevan, born in 1865, son of a Brighton banker, spent much of his childhood in the Sussex countryside. He studied later at the Westminster School of Art and at the Julian *atelier* in Paris, and then painted in Brittany, where one of his earliest studies was *The Old White Horse*. It was in 1891 he joined Crawhall and the sporting fraternity in North Africa and the following season became Master of the Tangier Hunt. He always deplored the fact that he came to hunting too late in life – he was all of sixteen years old when he first enjoyed the sport! When money ran out he returned to Brittany and came under the influence of Gauguin at Pont Aven – and here his Breton farm scenes, with their heavy horses, were painted in rich unconventional tones.

At the end of 1894 he lived alone on Exmoor for three years, painting and drawing and

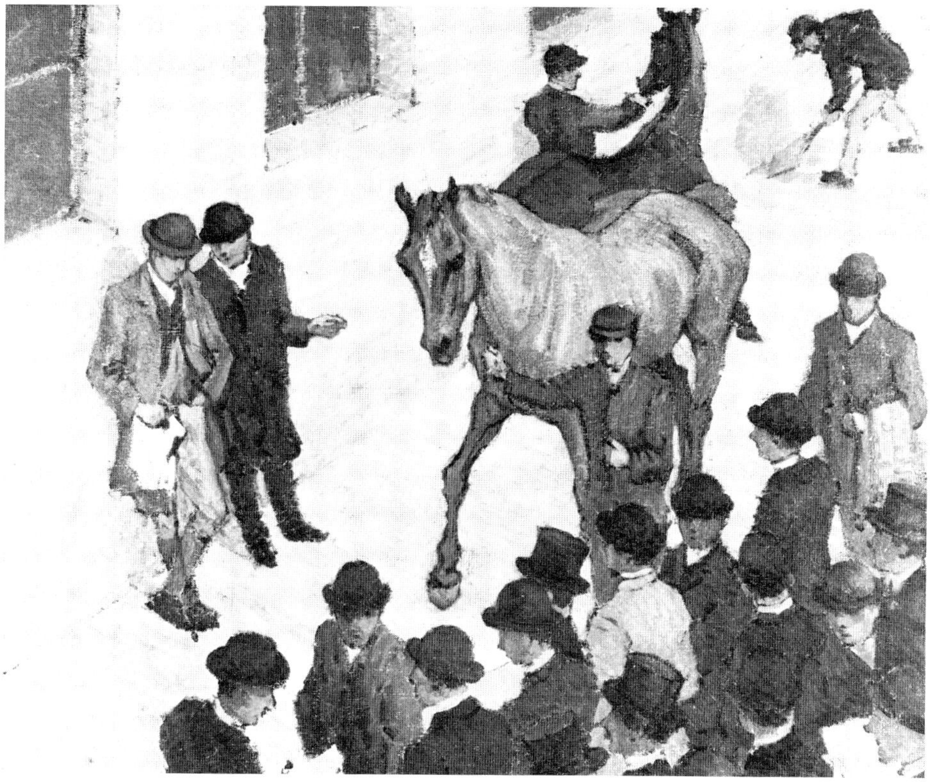

18 Robert Polhill Bevan, *A Horse Sale at Tattersall's*, 1911. Oil on canvas, 20 × 24 in (50.8 × 60.9 cm).

also hunting with two packs of hounds, for which the subscription to each was five guineas a year. Some lively sporting studies resulted from this period, including a set of hunting lithographs and a crayon *Hounds Feeding*, now belonging to the Ashmolean Museum.

In 1897 Bevan married a Polish girl of considerable beauty, and for the rest of his life there were long summer visits to Poland where he painted pictures in rich colour of peasant life and landscapes, with horses often supplying the central characters. Paternal responsibilites ended his aspirations as a foxhunting man but he remained a countryman at heart and, like Crawhall, always dressed the part. Horses never ceased to play a vital role in his life. Even when riding on a London bus he would occupy the top front seat to exchange horse lore with the driver.

But his favourite haunts became the horse auction marts of London – Tattersall's, Aldridge's, Ward's Repository and the Barbican, and here he found his most important subjects. In these paintings there are many variations on this one theme, but each picture is acutely observed, stamped with an unmistakeable spontaneity and each horse exudes personality – immediately recognisable with capped hock, hint of a dished action or wary, nappy eye – for Bevan was at his best, not with glossy Thoroughbreds, but with horses of plebeian antecedents.

Not less perceptively portrayed in *Horse Sale at The Barbican* are the bowler-hatted dealers, inscrutably scanning catalogues – a world of guile and plausibility (*Plate 4*). In *A Sale at Tattersall's*, dated 1911, the big free-striding roan with suspicious eye surveys the scene – a horse personality identifiable anywhere (*18*). These pictures by Bevan are painted with a direct urgency and possess subtle nuances which knowlegeable horsemen will appreciate.

The artist frequented the cabyards of Ormonde Place, St John's Wood, where seedy drivers and their gaunt broken-kneed horses are depicted in dim evening light with looming outlines of ancient hansoms making dramatic compositions. Here were facets of the equestrian world little exploited by previous artists of the horse and Bevan used them with originality and brilliant technique, but in spite of three one-man exhibitions he received little appreciation in his life-time. His contemporaries found him totally incomprehensible. Devoid of any sense of salesmanship on his own behalf it is doubtful if he earned £4000 as an artist during his whole career, but today four of his pictures are in the Tate Gallery and many others in important national collections.

After the Bevan exhibition at Colnaghi's in 1964 Sir Philip Hendy, the director of the National Gallery, stated, 'He is surely the best, if not the only painter of good horses that we have had in the twentieth century.' Enthusiasm is here carried to excess but Bevan's exciting post-impressionist colours and fresh, personal view of the *genus equus* certainly opened new vistas. In addition Bevan's paintings provide a pictorial documentary of a London still dominated by horse power, for it was not until the 1920s that the metropolis was taken over by the motor car. A scene in Cumberland Market shows loads of trussed hay. Horse-drawn buses, cabs, vans, carts, drays and private carriages still provided transport, and carriage ownership also included the middle classes of which every 200 families in 1000 owned a vehicle. It is estimated that in London alone, 300,000 horses required stabling and fodder so Bevan's pictures of cab yards, gloomy mews, auction sales and hay markets possess a contemporary relevance for posterity (*19*). That these scenes should be recorded with a spark of genius is our good fortune.

Robert Bevan was also a founder member of the influential Camden Town Group of artists and it was possibly his equestrian predilection that inspired such members as Lavery and Orpen later to make their occasional forays into the sporting arena, with Sir John Lavery's effective

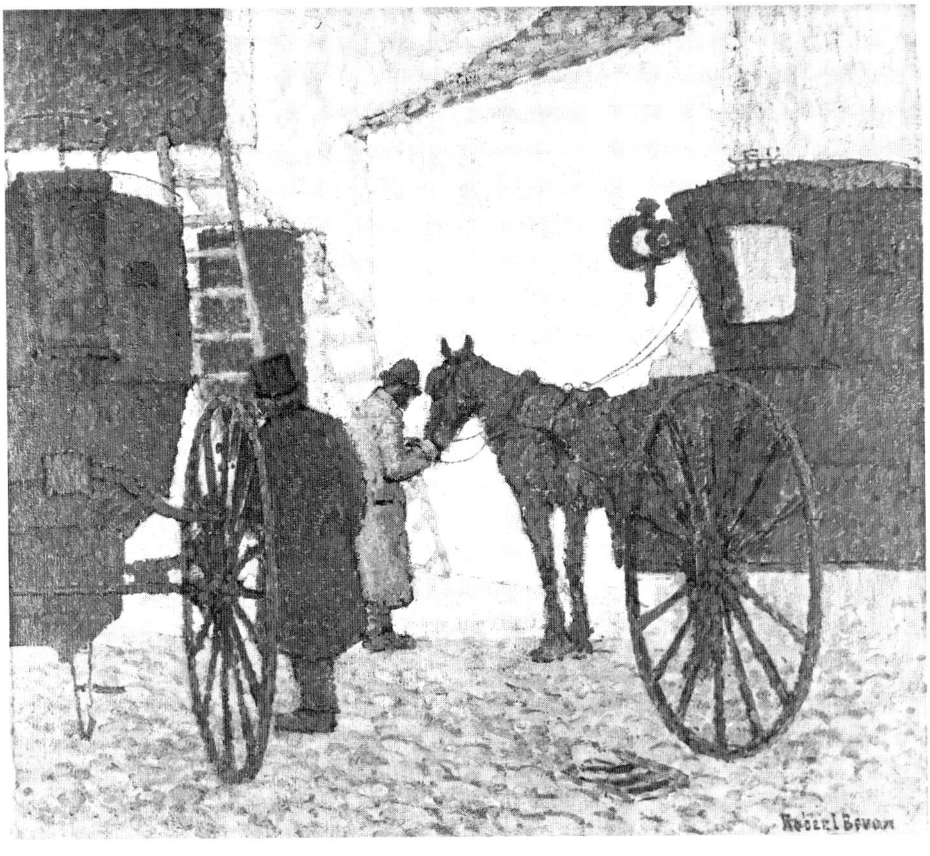

19 Robert Polhill Bevan, *Cab Yard at Night*, *c* 1910. Oil on canvas, 25 × 27½ in (63.5 × 69.8 cm).

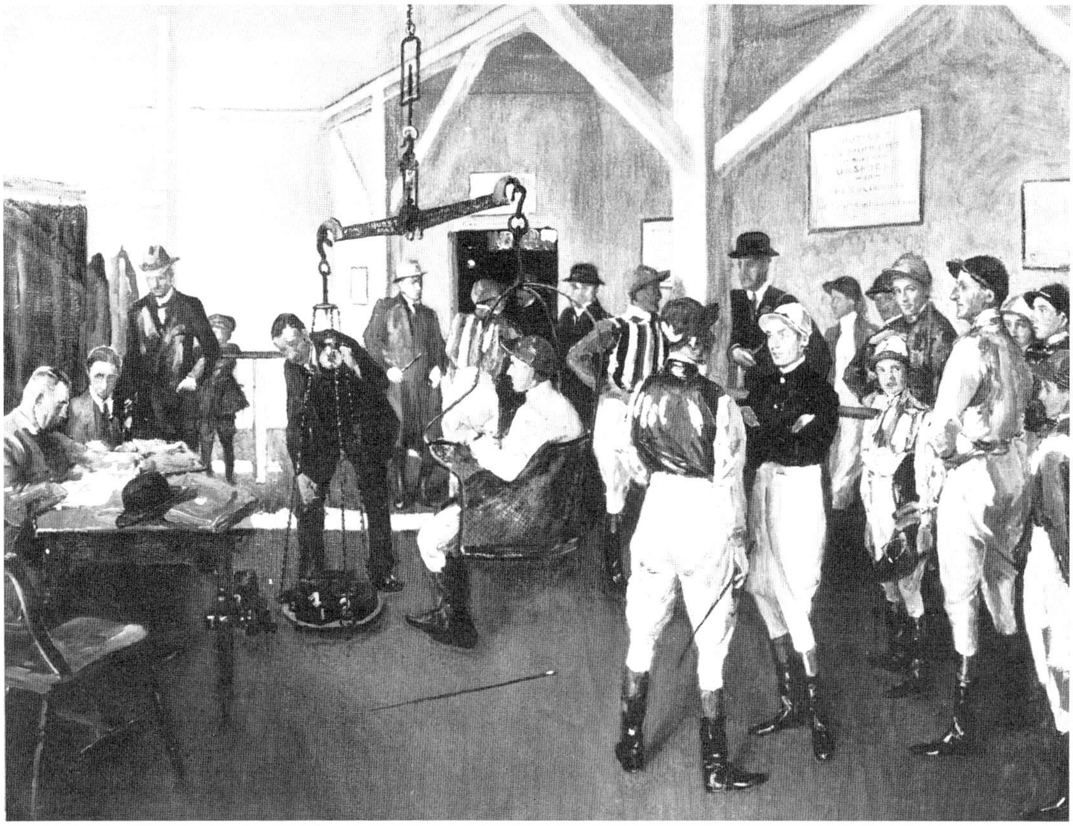

20 Sir John Lavery, RA, *Weighing Room at Hurst Park*, 1920. Oil on canvas, 30 × 40 in (76.2 × 101.6 cm).

behind-the-scenes paintings at important race meetings such as *The Jockeys' Dressing Room at Ascot*, now in the Tate Gallery, and *Weighing Room at Hurst Park* with clever portrayals of Donoghue (on the scales), Carslake, Wragg, Smyth and other leading jockeys of the day (*20*), and also *Weighing-in After the Epsom Derby 1924* with Tommy Weston, rider of Lord Derby's winner, Sansovino being checked in. His scenic *Derby Day in the Rain* suggests that this artist possessed his own innate appreciation for a day at the races whatever the weather. On the other hand Sir William Orpen's fine portrait of *Sergeant Murphy*, winner of the 1925 Grand National with his amateur rider Captain G.H. 'Tuppy' Bennett in the saddle, had, the artist admitted, only been put into the Royal Academy exhibition to prove he could paint horses as well as Munnings. But horse and landscape were successfully visualised as a pictorial entity.

An artist of outstanding talent appearing in the first decades of the century, who had been liberated not only by French Impressionism but had also derived exciting stimulus from the paintings of Crawhall and Bevan, was Charles Wellington Furse. Born in 1868, a brother of the sculptor John Henry Monsell Furse, at the age of sixteen he went to the Slade School and also worked in the evenings at Heatherley's before going to Paris to Julian's *atelier* for several months. His career was unfortunately hampered by tuberculosis, necessitating winters in Davos, Switzerland or, without doubt the fulfilment of his brilliant potential would have played a major role in the development of British sporting art, vying with the skill and mastery of Munnings.

He brought a new approach to the equestrian scene, abandoning the stereotyped for a free

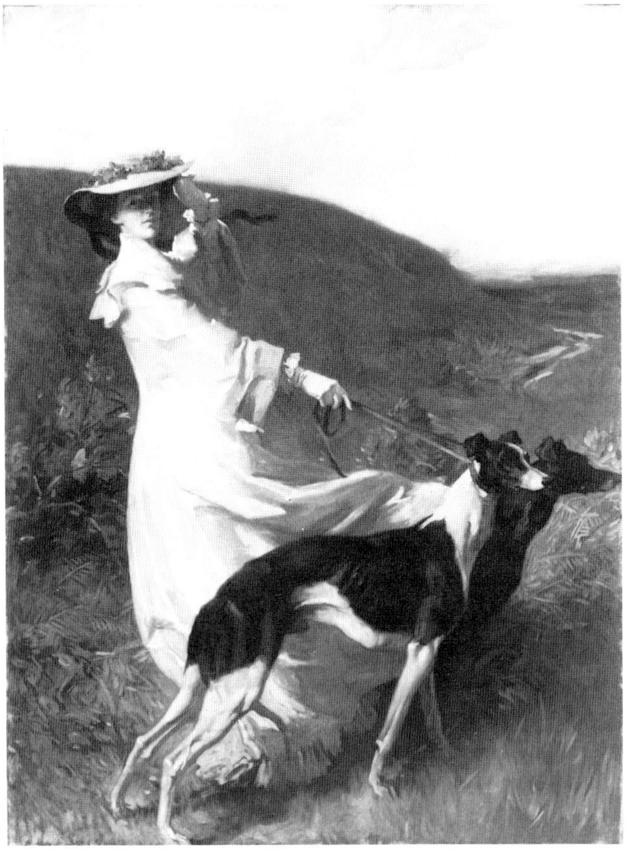

21 Charles Wellington Furse, *Diana of the Uplands*, *c* 1903–1904. Oil on canvas, $93\frac{1}{4} \times 70\frac{1}{2}$ in (236.8 × 179 cm).

powerful style on a big scale which made even his conventional hunting commissions such as the portrayal of *Mr John Lawrence, MFH of Llangbiddy Foxhounds, Monmouthshire* a lively and exciting occasion; hunter, rider and hounds exude personality. But all his life the artist, himself an all-round sportsman, took an intense interest in horses and in racing and possessed an encyclopaedic knowledge of bloodlines.

His last years, though swamped by numerous commissions for society portraits, at which Furse excelled, saw the full realisation of his talent in the much reproduced *Diana of the Uplands* – his beautiful wife leading the pair of greyhounds on a windswept common (now in the Tate Gallery), (*21*), and the sparkling colours and romantic beauty of the angling painting of his friends on holiday *Mr & Mrs Oliver Angling in Norway*, which created an unforgettable impression in the Royal Academy in 1903 when he was elected an ARA. Tragically the following year, when he was only thirty-six years old and with fame and fortune within his grasp, he died from a chill contracted after a wet day's shooting. In 1905 the striking composition *The Children of the Master of the York & Ainsty, Lycett Green Esq., out Cub-hunting* was exhibited posthumously in the Royal Academy and the huge canvas (nearly 7 ft × 9 ft 6 in) with its dramatic fluency, observation and technique brought full realisation of the loss to British sporting art sustained by the early death of Charles Furse (*Plate 5*).

Equally the outstanding artistic talent of Brian Hatton was also destined to unfulfillment. At the age of ten he had been awarded the Gold Star of the Royal Drawing Society, earned the approbation of the octogenarian artist G.S. Watts, and after his death on active service in Egypt in 1916 when only twenty-eight years old, Walter Shaw Sparrow referred to his possession of 'the rarest of all things – true genius'.

Born in Hereford, a countryside he never ceased to love, Hatton studied at George Harcourt's Art School in Arbroath and, very briefly, at Julian's in Paris. His first professional work for financial reasons was dedicated to portraiture, though horses, hunting and country life were interests always nearest his heart. With increasing maturity his equestrian pictures were considered comparable to Munnings and these major works included three paintings of the sporting Morris family of Higham Hall, Nuneaton where the dramatic picture of Mr C.J. Morris on his grey hunter, Meteor, strongly reflected the free fluent style of Charles Furse. Equally striking was his study of Lt Col Reginald Rankin with his grey Arabian, unconventionally posed with the rider sitting beside the unsaddled horse. But perhaps the true unrealised potential of the artist can be envisaged in his keenly observed drawings of countrymen (*Plate 22*) and in complete contrast such studies as *Sunday Morning in the Park* and the Crawhall-inspired *Butcher Boy*, alive with equine action. Almost all Hatton's pictures are in private collections and, apart from an exhibition in 1951 in the Hereford Art Gallery and another the following year in the Walker Galleries in London, little of his work had been seen in public until a small loan collection of his paintings, drawings and watercolours in 1978 at the Clarges Gallery in London. Today Brian Hatton is still a name virtually unknown in the sphere of sporting art.

Much of the technique and feeling for air and movement of Charles Furse was also to appear later in the equestrian portraits of Frederick (Fred) Whiting as illustrated in *The Children of Sir John Duthie* with its decorative girls astride on sensible hunters and, much later, in his oil painting of Miss Anne Elizabeth Holland, an attractive likeness of the Joint Master of the Old Surrey and Burstow Foxhounds riding an Irish mare, Tudor Gal, a successful competitor at Badminton Horse Trials and a reserve for the 1952 Olympic Games (*22*). Fred Whiting was born in 1874 and lived until 1962, studied at the Royal Academy schools and Julian's and exhibited at the Paris Salon. In 1945, in his seventies, he painted a pleasing picture of the Royal Princesses Elizabeth and Margaret riding in Windsor Park.

The fluency and vitality of Bevan's and Crawhall's individual approach to the equestrian scene is also recalled by the work of Lowes Dalbiac Luard, born in 1872. Of Norman Huguenot stock the greater part of his working life was spent in France, after studying at the Slade under Professors Tonks and Brown. In 1904 a visit of a few months to Paris to work under Lucien Simon and René Menard became extended to nearly thirty years, for Luard had become fascinated by the huge grey Percheron horses performing the heavy draught work on the city streets and quays. In these animals his love of muscular energy and movement was epitomised and from the French world of agriculture also he used teams harrowing and ploughing as subjects for his pictures, for he maintained that 'horses were the only nude models with movement really visible . . .'

Mentioned five times in despatches and winning the Croix de Guerre in the First World War, afterwards racing at Newmarket became a favourite subject for Luard. Here his explicit love of action is exploited in a style evocative of scenes by Manet and Degas. The nervous graceful form of the Thoroughbreds in his study *Race-*

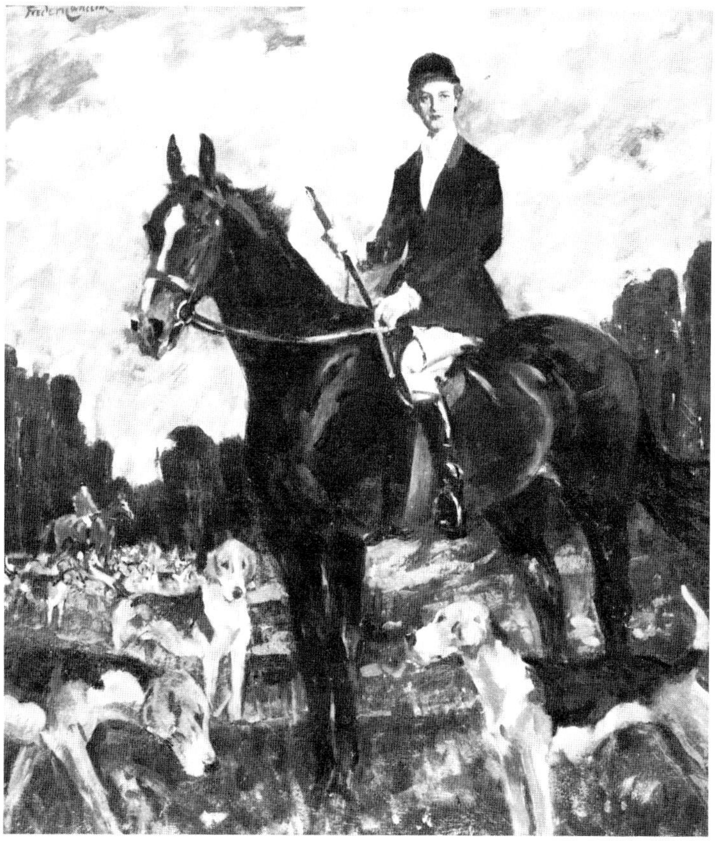

22 Frederick Whiting, *Miss Anne Elizabeth Holland at a Meet of the Old Surrey & Burstow Foxhounds*, *c* 1953. Oil on canvas, 40 × 36 in (101.5 × 91.4 cm).

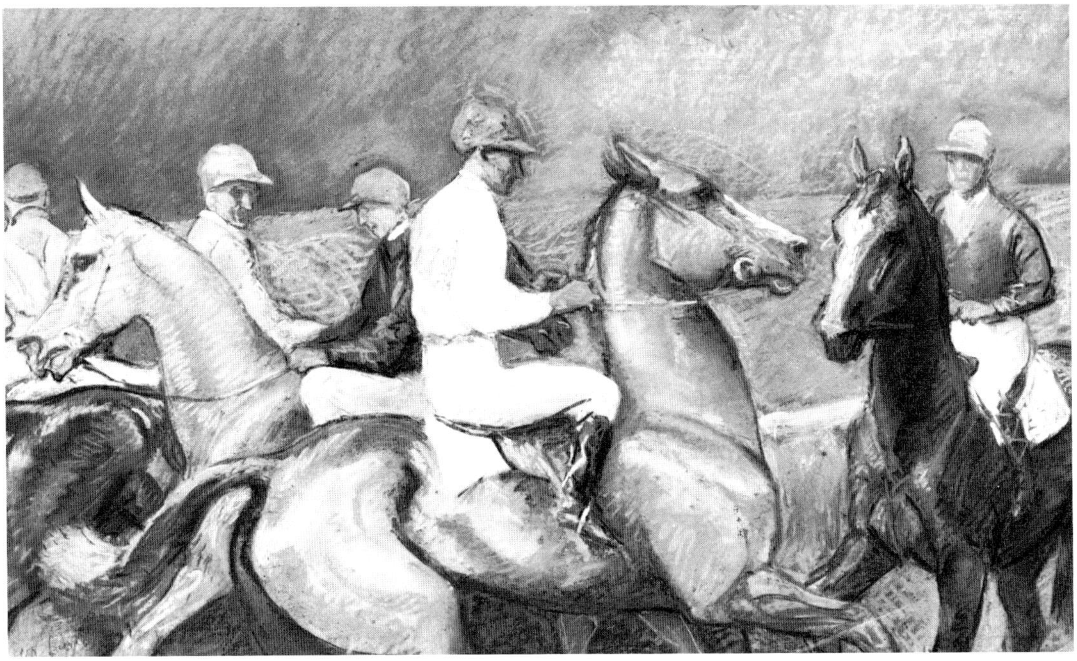

23 Lowes Dalbiac Luard, *Racehorses*, *c* 1934. Pencil and brush, 8 × 18 in (20.4 × 45.7 cm).

24 Jack Butler Yeats, *The Liffey Swim*, 1923. Oil on canvas, 24 × 36 in (61 × 91 cm).

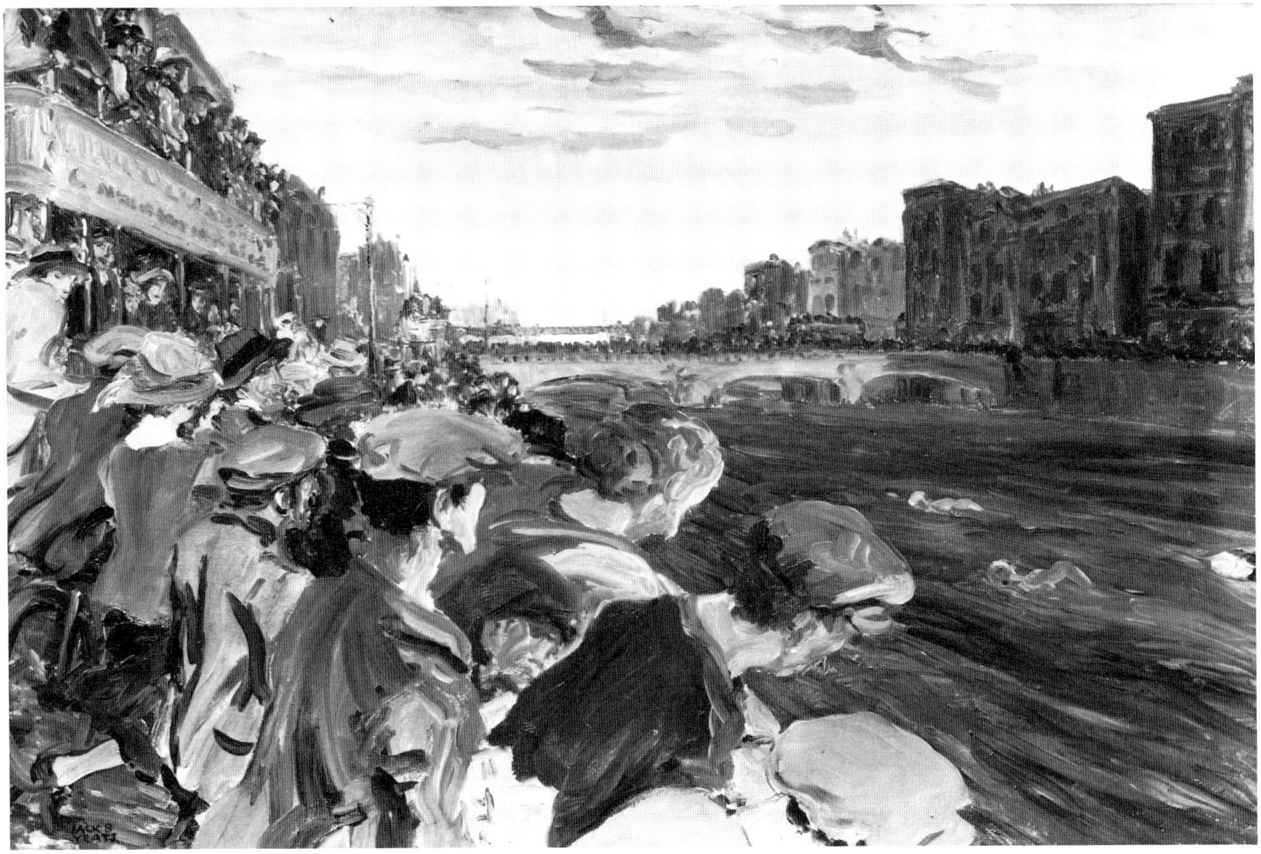

horses and the effective fluency of the painting *Steeplechase* stimulate the imagination by their vigour allied to an economy of line that relates not only to the Post-Impressionists but also to the influence of Bevan and Crawhall (*23*; *Plate 3*).

Lowes Dalbiac Luard died in 1945 and has never received the appreciation merited by his original talent, for he was working at a time when the sporting public still demanded a neat realism in its pictures. Happily a resurgence of interest in his work has been encouraged by two exhibitions in London put on in 1978 and 1980 in the Parkin Gallery. Of contemporary importance will be the republication of his two books, for during this century equestrian art has veered between traditional realism and slick Impressionism thus presenting conflicting guide lines in appreciation and understanding of animal movement. Lowes Luard's thoughts on the subject provide a valuable balance.

The first book, published in 1921, *Horses and Movement* is illustrated by finely coloured plates of his own works and deals briefly and succinctly with the drawing of movement. The second, *The Horse: its Actions and Anatomy*, published in 1935, illustrated again by the author's own plates in colour but, in addition, with diagrams, opens with the controversial statement, 'As the only purpose of an artistic anatomy is to help the artist in the observation of form, it can neglect the intricacies of nerves, veins, arteries and many other organs' – a sentence he later modifies by saying that 'this can only be achieved if it helps to a greater aesthetic enjoyment of form.'[2] But the book provides both practical and stimulating instruction in presenting the horse in action and allying beauty of form with landscape composition.

Another artist outside the conventional confines of British sporting art to bring a new facet to the scene was Jack Butler Yeats, an Anglo-Irishman by origin, born in London in 1891 and living and working for twenty-two years in southern England. However, boyhood holidays spent in Sligo ensured that the emotions of his pictures and political ideals were quintessentially Irish to contrast with some early scenes of boxing contests in London's East End.

There is a joy and glory in his work which Kenneth Clark described as 'so jauntily defiant of all the artistic fashions,'[3] nowhere more strongly illustrated than in the rich colours and thick paint texture of his racing scenes on the Kerry beaches and in his picture *The Liffey Swim*, with contestants in the annual event looking towards O'Connell Bridge (*24*). Jack Yeats, the most important Irish artist of his day, brought a creative element to sporting art outside the accepted context.

Liberation from Victorian confines was at last fully achieved by the innovative talent of such artists as Luard and Yeats but it was not until the mid-century that such long term influences were to become more strongly apparent in the works of John Skeaping, Peter Howell and others and finally to be used with vivid effect by newcomers in the 1980s.

NOTES

1 W. Frank Calderon, *Animal Painting and Anatomy*, Seeley Service & Co. Ltd., p. 41

2 Lowes Dalbiac Luard, *The Horse – its Action and Anatomy*, p. 1

3 Kenneth Clark, Introduction to Yeats Exhibition, Toronto, 1921.

5

New Artists in a New Century

During the splendid epoch of sporting art between 1700–1850 which had received the stimulus of such masters as Wootton, Stubbs, Marshall and Alken an interregnum was to follow with few successors of comparable calibre. Sporting activities were enjoyed with no less enthusiasm by the late Victorians; in fact hunting and racing reached a height of popularity, though most contemporary artists lacked a comparable zest in their style. However, towards the end of the nineteenth century the birth, all within twenty years, of a new generation of artists was to bring a renaissance of spontaneity and vigour to the sporting scene with, in addition, a welcome infiltration of humour. In some curious way this seemed to be endorsed by the appearance of the horses which, in accordance with current fashion, nearly all appear with docked tails and hogged manes.

Cecil Aldin, George Denholm Armour, Charlie Johnson Payne (Snaffles) were amongst the stars in this galaxy and in more serious vein Charles Simpson, Frank Algernon Stewart and Gilbert Holiday. The *anno mirabilis*, however, was 1878 which saw the birth of both Lionel Edwards and Alfred Munnings who, each in his own surperb style, became masters of the new century. Suddenly, therefore, a stimulating future for British sporting art was assured with a wealth of young talent.

Most of these artists shared a similar background, most inherited family sporting interests, nearly all enjoyed some professional training at an art school to be followed by a stint of hard bread and butter work for such periodicals as *The Graphic, Country Life, Punch,* the *Illustrated Sporting and Dramatic News*. All without exception possessed a love of horse and hound, and in addition an obsessive addiction to fox hunting which was, in some cases, to inhibit the fulfilment of artistic potential. It must be remembered also that each artistic career was sundered by the First World War; nevertheless their personal participation in sport brought to their work an ebullience and understanding not seen since the days of Henry Alken and John Ferneley Snr.

The trio, Aldin, Armour and Snaffles, were remarkable in their similarity of approach to sporting art and life. Each possessed energy, charm and a capacity for being able to identify humans and animals in a comical situation and also produce a work with an unerring eye correct in every essential sporting detail. These artists must be considered historians of field sports though their facts were spiced with laughter.

Their careers followed parallel paths, with illustrations galore profitably appearing in periodicals and books (by these lucrative activities they were enabled to hunt themselves) and all receiving popular acclaim for their hunting, racing and polo studies with, occasionally, an excursion into the picturesque deer stalking and angling world. Admittedly, quality varied depending on the vagaries of the hunting season and its temptations.

Cecil Charles Windsor Aldin was born in 1870 and during his long life his dedication to hunting always impeded his profession as an artist. Humour and *joie de vivre* might be considered the salient motifs of his work and, as a result, a happy spontaneity pervades his pictures of the sporting scene in that halcyon era at the beginning of the century.

He was an exception in having no family background of country or sporting heritage, his father being a Kensington builder. Nevertheless at an early age Cecil Aldin was obsessed by horses and began drawing tradesmen's vanners seen from his nursery window. His career started at the age of sixteen with a few weeks at the studio in Kensington of Albert Moore, an artist of classic pretensions; but he quickly went on to learn basic animal anatomy at the South Kensington School of Art, going thence to Frank Calderon's summer school at Midhurst in Sussex. Here he became involved in hunting with the local butcher's bobbery pack. It was a fatal infection never to leave him.

Like Mr Jorrocks whose first real hunting was based on St Botolph's Lane, Aldin also found himself hacking from the metropolis to meets in Surrey, graduating later, on an old polo pony stabled in the bicycle shed in his Chiswick studio, to hunt with the Surrey Staghounds. Equally he enjoyed something of the Bohemian artist's life, became an active member of the London Sketch Club and formed friendships with the incomparable caricaturist Phil May and above all, John Hassall, the king of poster artists in which sphere Aldin worked for Cadbury's Cocoa, Bovril and Rudge Whitworth bicycles. He rubbed shoulders with William Nicholson, who, with John Pryde, formed the Beggarstaff Brothers and enjoyed a *succès d'estime* for full-blooded posters. These were eclipsed in 1897 by Nicholson's brilliant woodcuts for *An Almanac of Twelve Sports* with words by Rudyard Kipling. First in the field is a galloping foxhunter epitomising January and this was to be followed more than thirty years later by the illustrations for a much valued edition of Siegfried Sassoon's *Memoirs of a Fox-hunting Man*. Little known is Nicholson's sparkling portryal of a boy *Hawking*, which raises regrets that this artist developed into the distinguished and innovative painter of portraits, landscapes and still life, forsaking

25 Cecil Charles Windsor Aldin, *The Garth Hunt*, *c* 1913. Print.

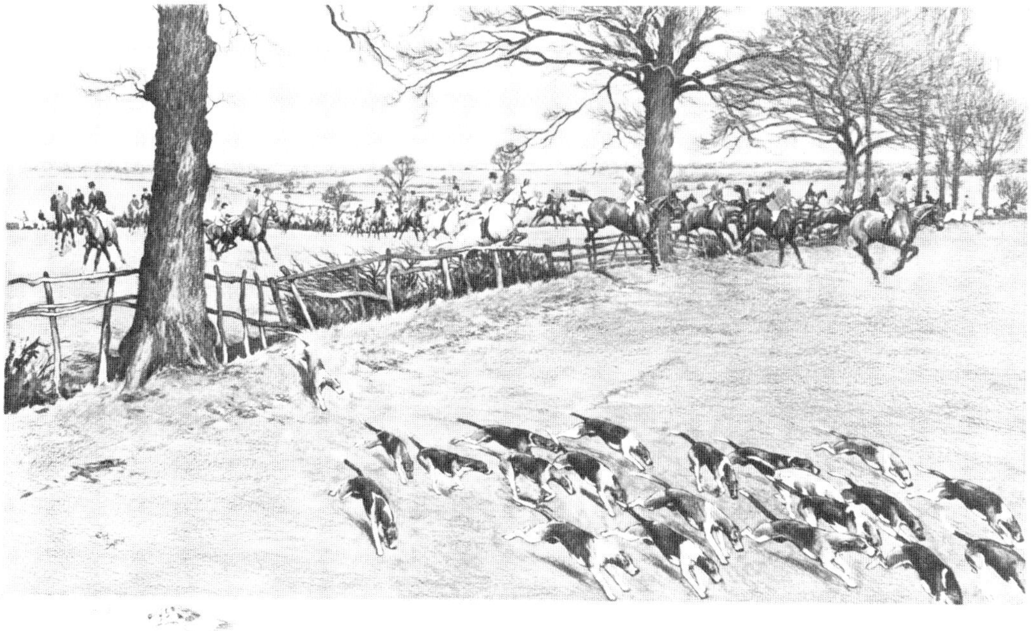

the sporting idiom, though he was a frequent visitor to Munnings' Chelsea studio.

Aldin himself was anything but parochial; he hunted in France with the Fôret d'Halette staghounds, held an exhibition in Paris and swapped canine sketches with Toulouse-Lautrec. For years, like many of his contemporaries, he was a regular contributor to such topical periodicals as *The Graphic, Black and White, Punch,* and *Pearson's Magazine* and even *The Lady's Pictorial.* His appointment as hunting correspondent for the *Land and Water Illustrated* (later incorporated into *The Field*) meant he was assured of a steady income of three guineas a week and could enjoy hunting in both Shires and Provinces. Modern foxhunters will be interested to know he was responsible for the 'banner' that for nearly a hundred years headed the front cover of *Horse & Hound* to illustrate the classic Whyte Melville quotation, 'I freely confess the best of my fun I owe it to horse and hound.'[1]

Moving house to near Henley, he hunted regularly with the Garth and the Berks and Bucks Staghounds, became Master of a pack of basset hounds, of the Peppard Farmers Harriers, hunting them two days a week for five seasons, and finally, in 1914, Joint Master (and subsequently sole Master) of the South Berks, a four day a week pack. Every year, until well in his fifties, he had a ride in the local point-to-point.

To fit in an artistic career among these sporting activities took some application, and after a long day's hunting Aldin would work late in his studio, a practice not conducive to the production of masterpieces. He seldom used oils, but his perceptive pen and ink sketches of dogs quickly became popular in the weekly papers.

With topical press photography in its infancy his drawings of racing and coursing events were much in demand. His work as a book illustrator was prodigious after his first important commission for Rudyard Kipling's series of *Jungle Stories* in the *Pall Mall Budget.* Imbued by Frank Calderon's golden rule that the only true pictures of animals are those drawn from life Aldin commuted between home and London's Zoological Gardens for his more exotic models. With the outbreak of the First World War, like several of his contemporary sporting artists, he became a Remount Purchasing Officer, but that is a story to be told later.

He illustrated scores of books but particularly pleasing are the colour plates and vivid line drawings to be found in his own autobiographical works *Ratcatcher to Scarlet* (1926), followed by *Scarlet to MFH* (1933), both containing advice as relevant today as when they were written. These were followed by the final volume, *Time I Was Dead* (1934).

His profitable series *Old Inns* (1920), in which he recorded twenty-eight of Britain's more picturesque hostelries and then *Old Manor Houses* (1923) were also produced as prints and became collectors' pieces here and in the United States where they were shamefully pirated. But it was his hunting and dog pictures that paid the forage bills.

Very early in his career a set of prints with the mythical *Fallowfield Hunt* for subject had sparked off public acclaim, but most highly prized is Aldin's series of *Hunting Countries* in the idiom of G.D. Giles which appeared in 1912–13, covering hunts as far afield as the Cheshire and the Devon and Somerset. His hunting scenes possess the evocative and simple realism of first hand experience allied to the nursery precision of Randolph Caldecott. They lacked the vitality of his quick line drawings which is explained by the fact that he would often attempt to make every horse and rider a recognisable personality (*25*).

Considerably gifted as an artist, with a perceptive eye for animal form and character, it is in his portrayal of dogs in which Aldin remains unique. He was a master at suggesting canine character and a relationship with man totally devoid of sentimentality. All his life he never ceased illustrating numberless dog stories written by himself and other authors. These drawings

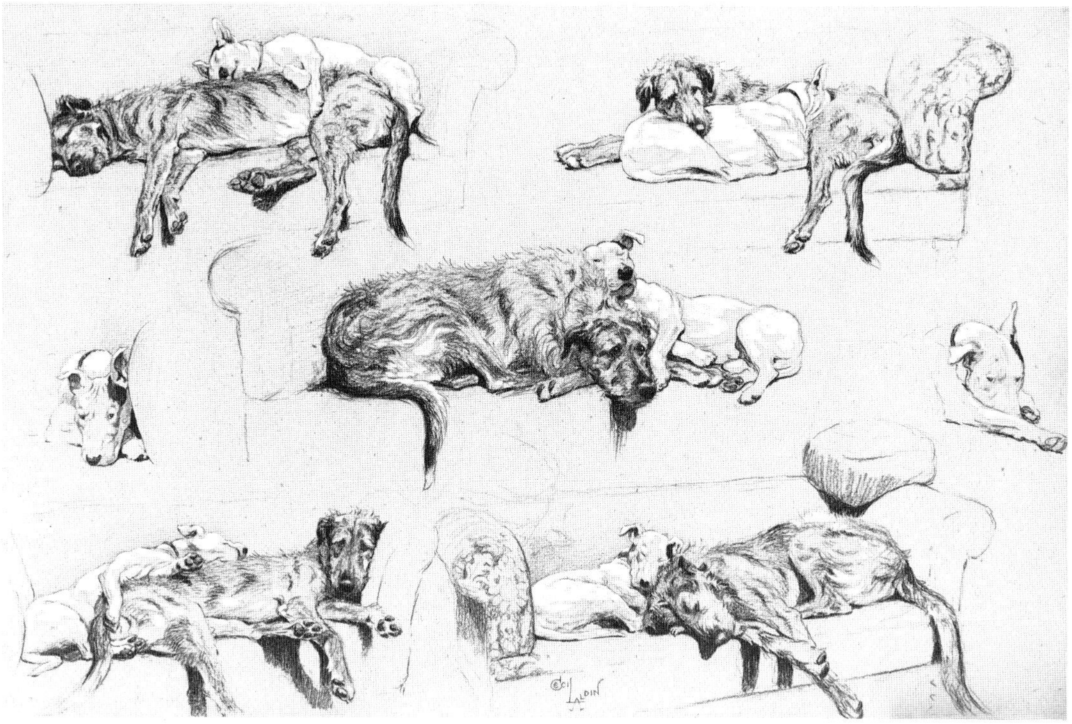

26 Cecil Charles Windsor Aldin, *Dog Studies. Micky and Cracker in a variety of poses*, *c* 1927–1929. Crayon drawing, 19 × 30 in (48.3 × 76.2 cm).

were rarely out of the public eye and brought him immense popularity. At one time he owned thirteen different breeds of dogs but his favourite models were his Irish wolfhound, Micky, and his bull terrier, Cracker, (*26*) reported in the *News Chronicle* as 'the most famous animal model in the world' and ultimately honoured with an obituary in *The Times*.

Cecil Aldin died in Mallorca in 1935 where he spent his last years to ease crippling arthritis and heart disease. Unpractical by nature, a born procrastinator and though some of his pictures were exhibited in the Royal Academy, never fulfilling his real potential; nevertheless, with gusto and humour, he made his own special mark in the world of twentieth century sporting art though the impact would have certainly been more impressive if hunting had not been his first love. But in a lengthy obituary in *The Times* it stated, 'there never has been a painter of dogs to hold a candle to him'.[2]

Equally popular with the public and fundamentally a more subtle and stylish artist than Aldin was George Denholm Armour who was referred to in his *Times* obituary as the first worthy successor to John Leech and certainly, with his brilliant draughtsmanship and scintillating wit, it was no exaggeration.

Born in 1864 in Lanarkshire, his father was a cotton broker but also a keen shooting man, and his mother followed hounds with enthusiasm, an inheritance passed on undiluted to her son. His early life was spent in Liverpool when, at six years old the local cab horses became his first models, followed by school at Madras College, St Andrews, Fife. The early death of his father necessitated earning a living and as drawing was his outstanding talent, apart from a fine tenor voice, he studied when sixteen years old at the Edinburgh School of Art before entering the Royal Scottish Academy of Art life school. As a student he won several prizes and was greatly helped and influenced by Robert Alexander, RSA, the animal painter and one of the finest horse artists of his time.

They travelled together to Tangier with painting in view but Armour had also heard that a horse could be kept for under one shilling a day: actually he hired one for fifteen shillings a month. It was the first of several visits and here he struck up a warm friendship with Joseph Crawhall and, like him, hunted avidly with the Tangier Hounds, each sportsman individually assuming the duties of first and second whippers-in. Horses were cheap, mostly Barb stallions and also pigsticking was another sport offering attractions. It was a period of carefree enjoyment but also immensely valuable to Armour's development as an artist. His strong, free pencil drawings and richly coloured watercolours as in *The Jockey* show Crawhall's impressionist influence (*27*).

Armour for two years had a studio in Primrose Hill in London and then until his marriage shared a Hertfordshire farmhouse with Crawhall where the latter did some of his best work. After a friendly introduction from Phil May, Armour contributed pen drawings to *Punch* for the next fifty years, not a job he really enjoyed, as pencil was his favourite medium. He also worked for *The Graphic* (a great favourite with impecunious young artists as payment was made weekly) and in 1911 he was invited to contribute to *Country Life*, eventually being sent to the United States to cover the international polo matches for the Westchester Cup. Here he noted with expert eye that 'the Americans were not pretty horsemen . . [but] they turned to good account their forward seat,' a position that shortly was to become universal for the next generation of riders and provide a new silhouette for the equestrian artist to master.

He visited Austria and produced some effective drawings of the Spanish High School horses and later was in France hunting and also visiting the Cadre Noir at Saumur. His addiction

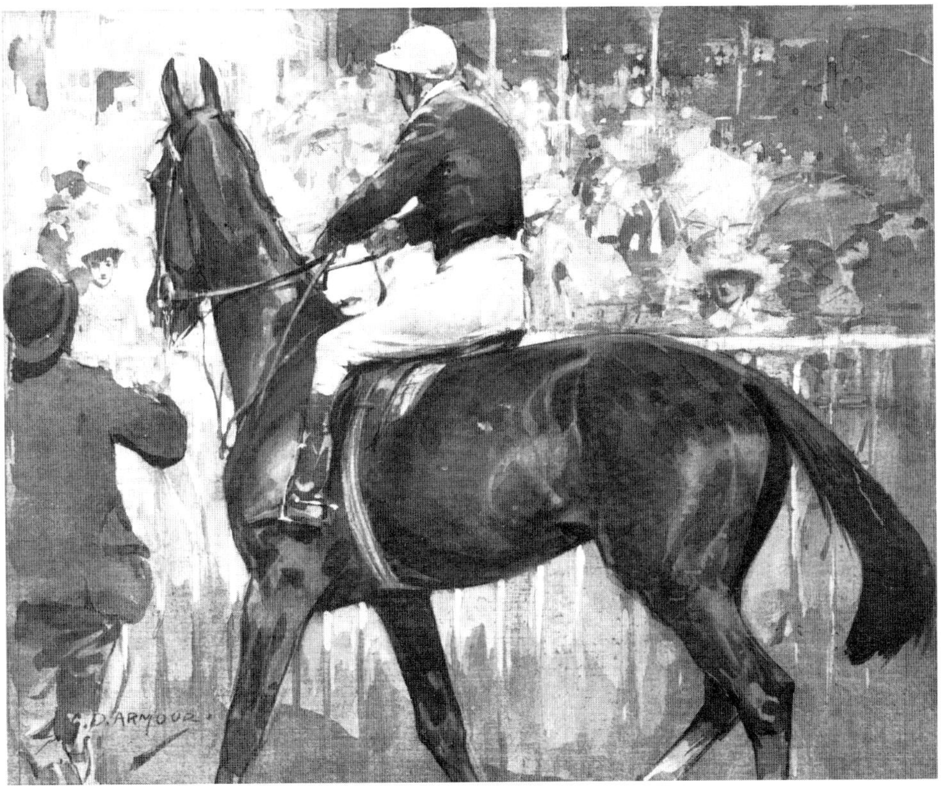

27 George Denholm Armour, *The Jockey*. Watercolour on holland, 10 × 12¾ in (25.4 × 32.3 cm).

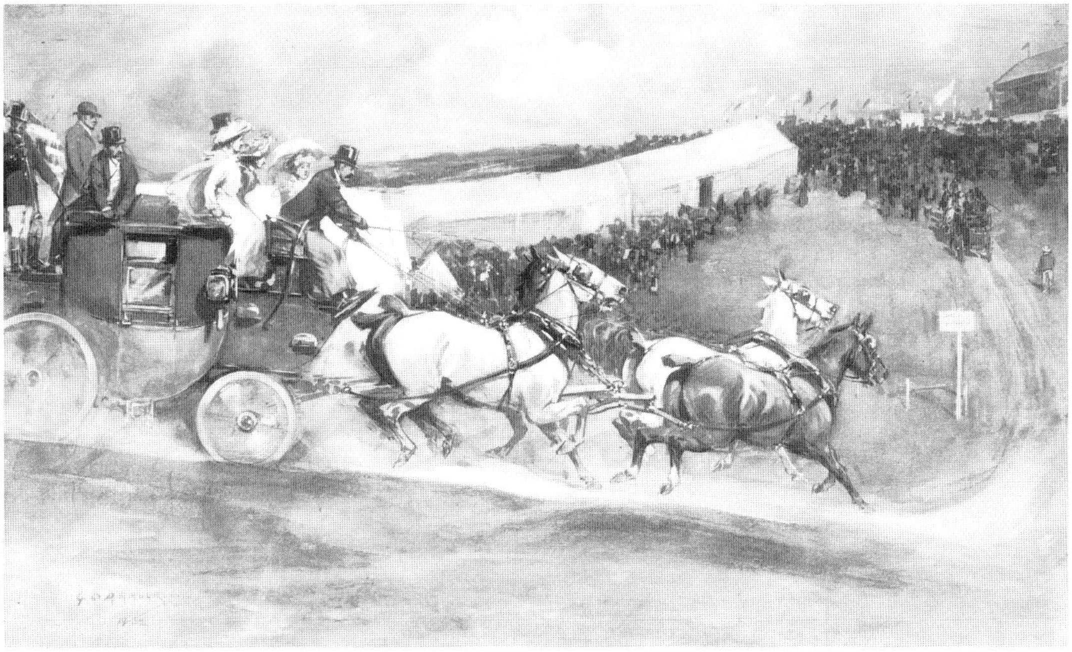

28 George Denholm Armour, *Derby Day*, *c* 1902. Sepia wash, $16\frac{1}{2} \times 27$ in (41.9×68.5 cm).

to fishing, grouse shooting and deer stalking year after year in Scotland also provided stimulating 'copy'. As a result he was much in demand as an illustrator and his work for such books as John W. Fortescue's *Story of a Red Deer* and John Masefield's *Reynard the Fox* made these volumes highly prized and, today, valuable possessions. Particularly successful were his rollicking illustrations in 1908 for *Hunts with Jorrocks* and *Jorrocks Lectures*, when he was careful never to duplicate any of the situations, except in one instance, previously depicted by John Leech. His supersize coffee table volume *Humour in the Hunting Field*, with comments by Crascredo, published by *Country Life* in 1928 with twenty engaging coloured plates and a wealth of acutely observed pencil sketches stamp him as a master of the subject.

In hunting of all subjects Armour emphasised action, humour and the unexpected with a lively expertise. He possessed a deft skill in putting over the naive ignorance of the tyro, in capturing the complaisance of the conceited as in '*When They Fancy Themselves*' and *In Tattersall's Auction* in fluent ink and watercolours (though blatantly inspired by Robert Bevan) he turned to good account a topical situation, as well as in the sparkling coach scene *Derby Day* with its galloping team and the tension of late arrival brilliantly portrayed (*28*). He had a wonderful eye for horse and hound but most important of all was his appreciation of the effects of British weather conditions on the countryside. Lionel Edwards wrote, 'He [Armour], I think, is the only contemporary artist who really gets the correct atmosphere in his winter hunting scenes,'[3] and Edwards was himself incomparable in this aspect of British sporting art, a facet virtually ignored by many artists.

Armour's equestrian portraits merit serious appraisal; several of his large works were exhibited in the Royal Academy. He was certainly more successful than either Aldin or Edwards in his ability to suggest a human likeness or catch a quirk of character as in his splendid picture of Mr and Mrs George Fenwick out hunting. Occasionally he would produce work of striking quality in gouache on holland (in the Crawhall tradition) as in his authoritative study *The*

Jockey or in his own telling portrait of Joseph Crawhall himself on some racing occasion in yellow silks, cap and white breeches.

Armour wrote, 'Anyone who has an eye for a horse or a little facility with paint can produce a recognisable presentation of a particular animal, even exaggerating good points and minimising faults and thus come to be ranked as a horse painter . . . But Robert Alexander, RSA, and, further back, Ben Marshall and Stubbs show what can be done with that great animal.'[4] He also stated with surprising naivety that both the latter were 'something very nearly, if not quite great artists.'[5] It was certainly Armour's long contact with Joseph Crawhall that brought definition and strength to his own considerable gifts as a draughtsman, even in his more humorous drawings for *Punch* and especially in some fine studies of bull fighting in Spain.

Service in the First World War absorbed some of his most active years; he was already fifty-five years old when the armistice was declared. He then moved to Wiltshire and later, to Somerset hunting with the Blackmore Vale and the V.W.H. (Vale of White Horse), never without a sketch book in his pocket, whether hunting, fishing or shooting for he was himself dedicated to all field sports. His studio was designed to open on to a stable so that quick reference to an actual horse was directly available. Amidst a galaxy of talent his work possesses an immediacy and conviction that never loses its appeal.

In the twentieth century world of sporting art nothing has been more remarkable in its final decades than the rocketing popularity of the works of Snaffles. For years his dusty prints, decorating the walls of village inns changed hands for the price of a double Scotch and a fiver, suddenly they became collectors' pieces and commanded hundreds of pounds and today are in demand all over the world.

Few people remember that the familiar pseudonym 'Snaffles' was the inspired alias of Charlie Johnson Payne. It had been assumed during his brief military career when he portrayed fellow soldiers in vivid sketches. In fact two linked snaffle bits ultimately became the stamp of authenticity on his later prints. Born in 1884 in Leamington Spa, son of a bootmaker, Snaffles, unlike many of his contemporaries, seemed to lack any direct family sporting background and any formal art training, though his father was interested in painting. But predictably with other artists of the period Snaffles developed an insatiable love of rural life and hunting.

In the euphoria of the Boer War he attempted, without success, at the age of fifteen to enlist in the Army but less than three years later he was accepted for the Royal Garrison Artillery, serving most of the time at Fort Widgley in Portsmouth. In 1906 after injury he found himself once more a civilian and, in a modest way, with watercolours and drawings mostly of officers, in semi-caricature style, began his career as an artist.

By nature reticent and retiring he was, however, to make friends in Aldershot with that great soldier and sportsman, 'Taffy' Walwyn (whose son Peter Walwyn was to become the successful trainer and his daughter Jean the equestrian sculptor), who lent him a horse and swiftly indoctrinated him into the joys of hunting. Impecunious, and with some diffidence, Snaffles offered five drawings of these sporting scenes for half a guinea[6] each to Fores, the well known print specialists then in Piccadilly, London, W1. To his dismay they were turned down at this price to be accepted by Mr Fores himself at fifteen shillings each. No wonder this firm acted as agent and mentor to Snaffles for all his long life, establishing a relationship of mutual esteem.

His hunting was first limited to such provincial packs as the Garth, the Chiddingfold and the Ripley Harriers in Hampshire and Surrey. In 1910 the leading publishers Lawrence & Jellicoe produced four prints of hunting types, the popular *The Gent With 'Osses to Sell, Blood & Quality,*

Plate 5 (*left*) William Frank Calderon, *Shelter*, 1912. Oil on canvas, 40 × 50 in (101.6 × 127 cm).

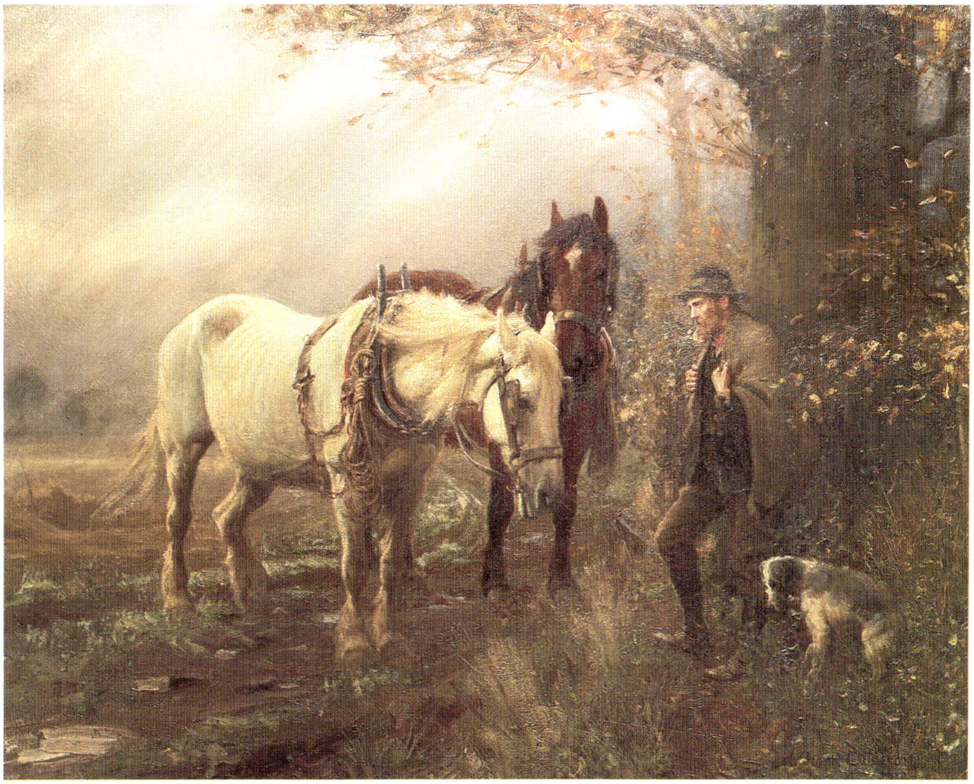

(*below*) Charles Wellington Furse, *The Children of the Master of the York and Ainsty, Lycett Green, Esq., out Cub-Hunting*, 1904. Oil on canvas, $82\frac{1}{4} \times 113\frac{1}{4}$ in (208.9 × 287.6 cm).

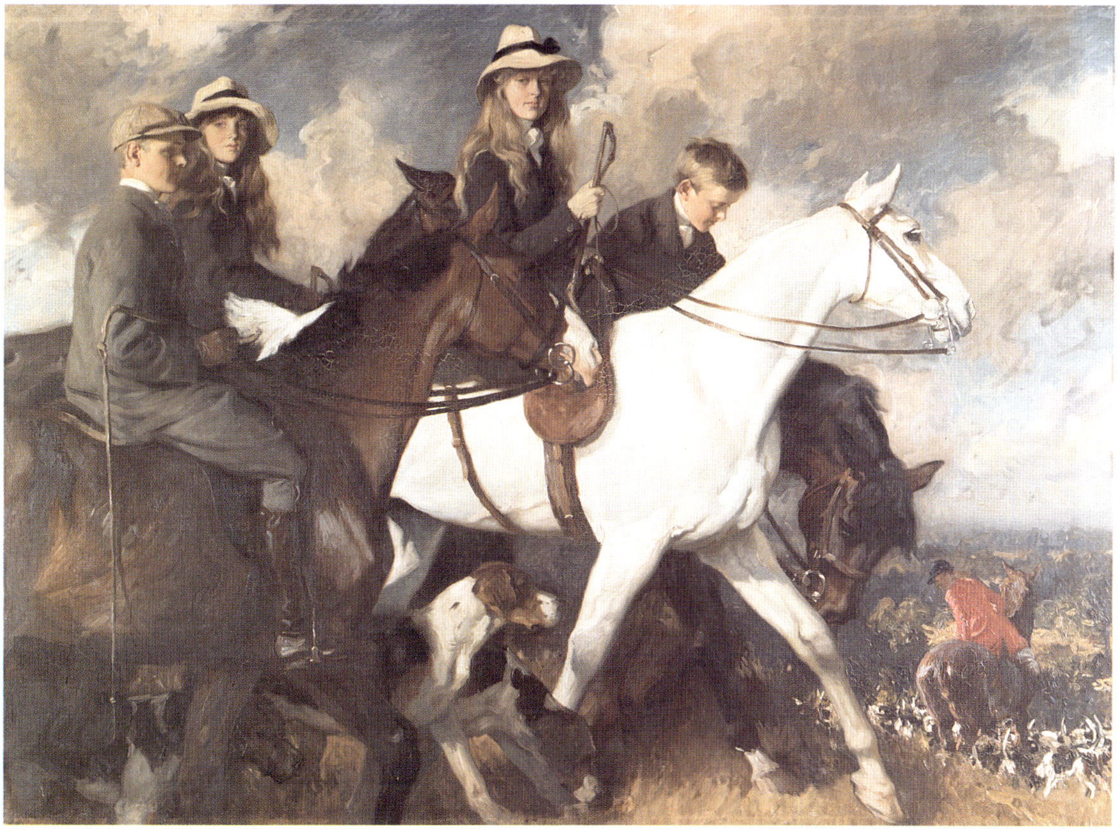

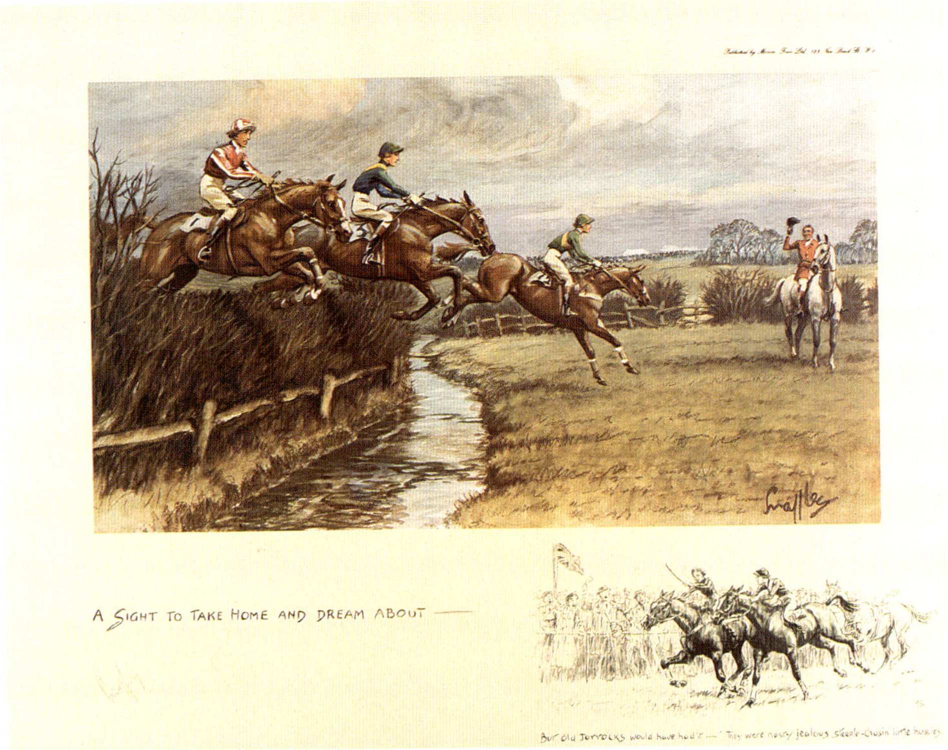

PLATE 6 (*above*) Snaffles (Charlie Johnson Payne), *A Sight to Take Home and Dream About*, 1950. Print, 20 × 24 in (50.8 × 61 cm). (*below*) Snaffles (Charlie Johnson Payne), *Carpet Beaters v Bobbery Wallahs*, 1930. Print, $19\frac{1}{4} \times 29\frac{1}{4}$ in (48.9 × 74.3 cm).

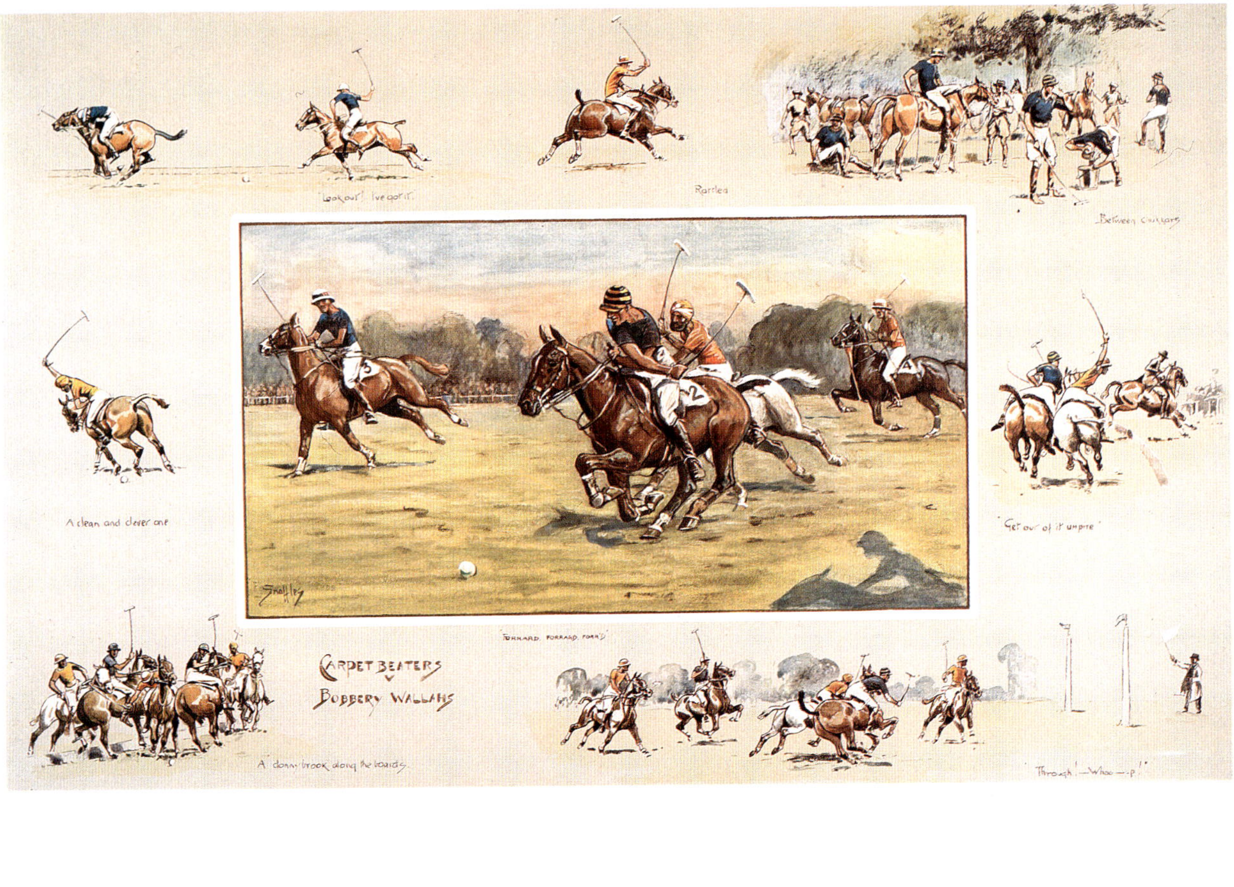

Old Tawny and *'Hogany Tops*. Hand coloured, (as usual, in his early days by Snaffles himself and his two sisters) they proved the turning point in his career with instant success. In the following year the *Illustrated Sporting and Dramatic News* republished these prints with additional numbers, including character studies from such fashionable hunts as the Pytchley and the Warwickshire all providing limitless subjects with humour and atmosphere. In 1912 he moved to Oakham and briefly enjoyed the style and panache of red letter days with the Cottesmore.

But in 1914 he was appointed one of the war artists of *The Graphic* and was sent to northern France. Later he served in the RNVR 'Dazzle' section, an interesting period to be explored later.

After the war a greater freedom of style materialised in his work with drawings more confident and fluid; he had come to terms with equine action and had escaped from what he termed his 'rocking horse' period.

By the late 1920s some of his prints in the *Illustrated Sporting and Dramatic News* were reproduced in colour and these featured a central picture encircled by ten small studies. In his later work this idiom in miniature became a personal hallmark with pencil vignettes illustrating different aspects of a situation with a masterly vitality. He was also a regular contributor to *Punch, The Tatler, The Field, Blackwoods* and other magazines, many of the illustrations being similar but often not identical to the prints that followed. Particularly effective are his Grand National pictures of this period.

In 1927–28 Snaffles made the first of his visits to India and Somaliland where he spent happy days with 'Taffy' Walwyn and contributed many paintings and drawings to the first volume of *The Hoghunter's Manual*, a magazine dedicated to the perilous and exciting activity of pig-

29 Snaffles – Charlie Johnson Payne, *''andsome is'*. Print, $18\frac{1}{2} \times 17$ in (46.9×43.1 cm).

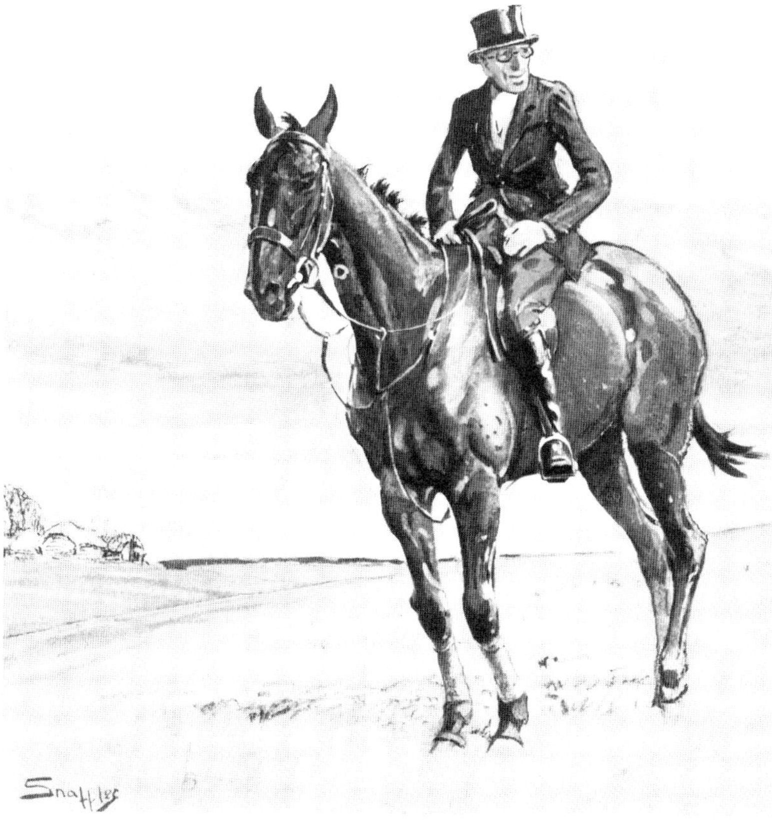

sticking. These exhibit the artist's own keen enjoyment of the sport and his appreciation of animal form whether boar, tiger, polo ponies or the Camel Corps in East Africa. Many examples of this work are to be found in his *Sketch Book of the Shiny*.

A prolific illustrator, it is in his own books that the diversity of his talent can be enjoyed, as in *'Osses and Obstacles* with its background of both Limerick and Leicestershire, *I Heard the Revelly* with contrasting simplistic sketches of army recruits and clever watercolours of the RHA gun teams, and not forgetting his 'rough idea' sketches, *Transmission & Power Units*, of Frederick Cody's Pioneer box kite aeroplane seen in 1908 on Farnborough Common! In *Half a Century of Memories* there are incisive pencil drawings of Meltonian thrusters and of country activities in wartime Devonshire all to give the wide scope of his works full range.

During his long life Snaffles produced nearly 300 prints in addition to his numerous watercolours, pencil and pen and ink drawings. Tragically many original plates of the prints, and the drawings and paintings themselves were destroyed in the Blitz and ironically the remainder accidentally by a firework on VE Day celebrations setting ablaze a Taunton storehouse, so all records were lost. *A Catalogue Raisonné of the Prints of Charlie Johnson Payne*, compiled in 1981 by the British Sporting Art Trust has done much to redress the absence of information and was included that year in the catalogue of their very popular Snaffles Exhibition in London, opened by HRH The Princess Anne.

In his own inimitable way Snaffles himself put on record half a century of field sports with all the changing customs and fashions. In his works can be traced the transition to the 'forward seat'; the nostalgia of those point-to-points when hunt members rode in scarlet and the runners looked like hunters and not racehorses; when the elegant hard-riding ladies side-saddle were metamorphasised into equally hard-riding competent girls astride. As late as 1952 in an exciting watercolour of a ladies point-to-point race '*A Sight to Take Home and Dream About*' he still paid homage to these dashing Dianas (*Plate 6*) but in the lively remarque drawing of the tight finish added the Jorrocks' suggestion that 'they were nasty jealous steeple-chasin' little hussies!'

Though commissioned portraiture was rarely the artist's occupation, nevertheless he possessed an uncanny knack of putting over with insight and humour, just short of caricature, the personality of both horses and riders. Immediately recognisable is the sardonic, spectacled foxhunter on the gaunt fiddle-headed bay, shockingly over at the knee, of *''Andsome Is' (29)* and embellished characteristically by a vivid margin sketch of the same tough pair clearing water in fine style with the caption '*Wot 'Ansome Does*'.

The studies of *The Best View in Europe* with hounds running across Leicestershire pastures and *The Worst View in Europe* with the sub-title 'Oh Murther! The dhrink died out of me the wrong side of Bechers' with a riderless grey ahead, the huge fence looming in all its unmitigated immensity and the big bay galloping on relentless in the rain . . . these have become classics.

Never a master of landscapes Snaffles' eye is, however, lively and perceptive for a country, whether it is the stone walls of Ireland, the stake and bound hedges of the Shires and the daunting width of the dread Whissendine or the dark hairiness of *The Bullfinch*, 'black as your hat on this side and glorious uncertainty on the other.'

As a result of his own conscious development of a photographic memory for the graphic incident, Snaffles provokes with more immediacy than any of his contemporaries nostalgic memories of the past. Pungency, vigour and wit, as in his polo impressions such as *Carpet Beaters v Bobbery Wallahs* always highlight his work but his pictures possess integrity and characterisation which capture indelibly for posterity sport as it was enjoyed in the first half of the twentieth century (*Plate 6*). Henry Alken Snr provided the same topical record a hundred years earlier.

In 1983 a sumptuous volume of eighty-two of Snaffles prints, with text by Donald Crawford and a foreword by HRH The Princess Anne, was published by the print specialist and dealer Mark Flower to commemorate the centenary of the artist's birth. The interest and acclaim received by this impressive work (it cost £350) would have amazed no one more than quiet retiring Snaffles himself.

Another artist of the period sharing the humorous approach to the sporting scene was Tomas Ivester Lloyd, born in 1873 in Liverpool. Self taught and never exhibiting his work, his abilities have perhaps been underestimated for, painting in both oils and watercolour, he possessed a sound eye for a horse, and many of his hound drawings were exceptional. He illustrated the British section of Sir John Buchanan Jardine's *Hounds of the World* and also exploited his gifts for the comical in scenes from Surtees.

It is difficult today to understand the importance enjoyed by the sporting book illustrator in the first half of the century. Direct black and white photography had swiftly acquired expertise but cameras still lacked the ability to record differing tones and quality of colour, and the results, in addition to being very expensive, could rarely be considered acceptable for prestige art books. Lithographic reproductions, with an improving mechanical technique, of artists' original paintings provided the solution.

It was a period when the sporting fraternity appreciated handsome volumes dedicated to their country activities. High in appeal as subjects were hunting countries and scenes, and in fact any pursuit connected with horse or hound. Authors and artists certainly cashed in on this situation. Publishers began to pride themselves on the design, style and, above all, the quality of their colour reproductions. Black and white drawings galore would be included but more important was a generous selection of colour plates.

Many artists supplied their own text, producing some of their best sketches and paintings as illustrations for their own books, as did Cecil Aldin in his many works on dogs, and G.D. Armour who was also particularly effective in his evocations of classic characters for reprints of Surtees and for books by E.W.D. Cuming. The illustrations by Snaffles for his autobiographies include much of his best and most popular work.

Charles Simpson, F.A. Stewart and Gilbert Holiday were also to join this band of skilled illustrators and, of course, most important of all Lionel Edwards. Over the years lithographic processes were to improve immeasurably, colour values approximated to the tones of the original paintings and he who possesses such a treasure as a copy of Will H. Ogilvie's *Collected Verses* with twenty-two colour plates of Lionel Edwards paintings, will realise the truth of this statement.

But in the future the sporting artist was to be in direct competition with the straight colour photographer for commissions by impatient and indiscriminating patrons for portrayal of their champion racehorses, favourite hunters and personal sporting occasions.

NOTES

1 J. Whyte Melville, 'The Good Grey Mare', *Baily's Magazine*, November 1871.

2 *The Times*, Obituary, 5 January 1935.

3 Lionel Edwards, R.I., *Reminiscences of a Sporting Artist*, p. 24.

4 G.D. Armour, *Bridle and Brush*, p. 378

5 ibid, p. 370.

6 One guinea equalled twenty-one pre-decimalisation shillings.

6

A More Serious Approach

In the trio Frank Algernon Stewart, Charles Simpson and Gilbert Holiday, all working before and after the First World War, sportsmen of the day possessed illustrators *par excellence*. Though recording the same field sports as Cecil Aldin, G.D. Armour and Snaffles they abandoned the humorous approach and individually their talents differed, with the sporting occasion playing a more serious role in its manner of composition and use of colour.

Frank Algernon Stewart, born in 1877, possessed the more traditional appeal and was another of that band of animal artists who had studied at the Calderon School and he also had enjoyed a spell with Fred Brown at the Slade. After working for the *Illustrated London News* in South Africa, making sketches in action in the thick of the Boer War, he was invalided home in 1901 and went to Julian's studio in Paris. Little evidence of this cosmopolitan experience is noticeable in his work which is almost entirely devoted to the hunting scene; and needless to say, like his contemporaries, he also was an inveterate foxhunter and, even when disability made riding impossible, he continued following hounds enthusiastically on foot from Cheltenham where he lived.

Watercolours were his most favoured medium and his hunting compositions were frequently of narrow rectangular dimensions. How John Ferneley's hunt scurries have influenced his successors! It is an idiom that many artists were to find ideal for the panoramic spread of field, huntsmen and hounds in full cry and F.A. Stewart made constant use of it.

As a sporting artist he has always been under-estimated, being overshadowed by the brilliance and sensitivity of the work of Lionel Edwards. His style is certainly less free with a slight inhibiting precision. But his horses and riders are drawn with observation as cleverly evoked in *Optimists at The Meet* – obviously a wet day ahead but foxhunters undeterred (*Plate 7*). The colour possesses an attractive clarity and he suggests for once the grey vagaries of English winter weather. He exhibited annually at Vicars Galleries in London.

Perhaps the best of Stewart's work can be enjoyed in the volumes with superb illustrations published between the wars, *Hunting Countries*, *Hark to Hounds* and *Cross Country with Hounds*, each incorporating different hunts, the first and second with the text by the artist and in the latter each section by a local foxhunter, e.g. Lt Col F.D.G. Colman, OBE, MFH for the Belvoir, Cecil Leveson Gower for the Old Surrey and Burstow; each is reproduced with a colour plate to include leading members of the hunt, and with considerable talent the artist proves this not such a restraining factor as might be expected. *The Atherstone from the Meet at Market Bosworth* though incorporating five greys in the forefront and the ladies showing the way (inevitably three of them members of the intrepid Inge family, mother and two daughters), clever composition and action dispels any monotony in the fine record of this famous hunt.

In *A Cubhunting Morning with the Cattistock* the scene is pleasingly detailed, with the leafy trees and the enthusiastic American H.A. Higginson, MFH, leading the field on a bay, with a glimpse in the distance of Cattistock Church from which at that time its carillon would play 'Do Ye Ken John Peel'. Does it still?[1] Clever black and white sketches abound of such characters as Mr Wilson, oldest member of the West Norfolk, and renowned Mr Sam Marsh,[2] 'He makes it look easy', sailing over a big fence at Puttenden Farm in Kent, all to demonstrate the immense pleasure to be obtained from finely illustrated books of a favourite sport.

Stewart's life seems to have been spent in some obscurity though he had a reputation for lavish entertaining which may explain why his effects at his death were valued at less than £300. One fact elicited by the British Sporting Art Trust that he always slept in a pink nightcap bears little relevance, however, to his undoubted talent as a sporting painter!

A contemporary of lesser renown was Basil Nightingale, born in 1864 at Malden in Essex, son of Robert Nightingale, a versatile artist whose subjects included equestrian works. Basil, early in his career, was painting hunting scenes and racehorses for Edward VII and, like his father, by his skilful use of pigment glamourised with a satin lustre the appearance of his horse subjects. His humorous sketches followed the Snaffles tradition but his most memorable work was the well known painting in 1899 of Tom Firr, the renowned huntsman of the Quorn, on the chestnut, 'Whitelegs', jumping timber in supremely nonchalant style, which became a popular print. Tom Firr in addition to becoming a legend in his own lifetime in the Shires was also praised by Brooksby the leading hunting correspondent of the day for being able 'to tie on an evening white tie better than any man I ever knew!'[3]

Hunting more than any other sport, provided the major inspiration for early twentieth century sporting artists but Charles Walter Simpson, born in 1885 and living until his eighty-seventh year, proved something of an exception. However, foxhunters will remain ever in his debt for three splendid volumes published in 1927, *The Harboro' Country*, *Leicestershire and Its Hunts* and, finally, dealing with the Yorkshire packs, *Trencher and Kennel*, each with a couple of dozen splendid colour plates and fifty or more black and white drawings. Though sometimes denigrated by the purists for occasional lapses in the finer points of foxhunting, nevertheless these studies of the finest hunting territories in the British Isles provide the artist with some

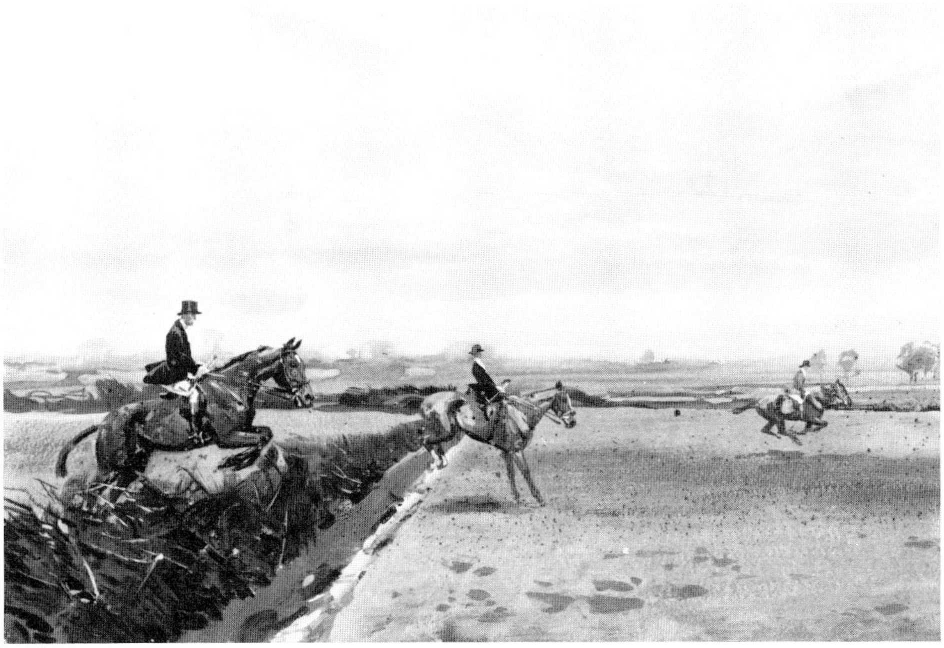

30 Charles Walter Simpson, *Over Plough and Fallow, Vale of York* (detail), *c* 1927. Watercolour, 15 × 21 in (38.1 × 53.3 cm).

wonderful landscape opportunities. His view of the Fernie country near Billesdon Coplow and bringing in stragglers at Ranksborough Gorse with the Quorn, capture rich memories for those fortunate enough to have hunted in the Shires; and his study of a run in the Vale of York suggests the joys of this galloping country (*30*). Certainly his ability to depict horse and rider is often less than masterly, though his portrait of that enthusiastic foxhunter, HRH The Prince of Wales (later the Duke of Windsor) out with the Quorn, effectively recalls the golden age of the late 1920s (*31*). For the Bramham Moor he painted a very effective picture of their dog pack relaxed on the benches in deep straw after a hard day. He was also the illustrator of more than a dozen other sporting books for various authors.

Born in 1885, son of Major General C.G. Simpson, CB, of the Lincolnshire Regiment, Charles Simpson was destined for a military career but a riding accident at the age of sixteen ended this ambition. Not surprisingly art became the substitute for, as he explained himself, that as a child 'as soon as my hands were big enough to hold a pencil I became an artist and started to draw animals.'[4]

He studied briefly under Lucy Kemp-Welch at her studio in Bushey, 'She was a great painter of horses and on that particular subject I learnt a lot from her',[5] and then with Stanhope Forbes, RA, in Newlyn and in 1910 he also went to Paris to Julian's *atelier* for a spell.

Few of the forty-eight pictures he exhibited at the Royal Academy during his long life had hunting as their subject and the first acceptance in 1907 was for one of his typical quiet agricultural scenes *Autumn Ploughing*. It was a visit to the rodeo staged at the British Empire Exhibition at Wembley in 1925 that generated his efforts to portray the horse in action and he produced a book *El Rodeo* from sketches made in the arena. For years he had been a regular visitor to the Grand National, siting himself at Becher's, and in 1927 he painted an effective scene of Sprig's triumph against a foreground frieze of spectators. In 1931 there was a spirited finish of the St Leger with Lord Rosebery's bay colt, Sandwich, beating Orpen.

Equestrian portraits brought commissions with such attractive paintings as Michael and John, the children of Mrs Carlos Clark, on their ponies. But later such notabilities as Colonel Harry Llewellyn on Foxhunter and Pat Smythe show-jumping on Tosca tended to an unpleasant stiff portrayal of both riders and horses.

Charles Simpson's talent came to fulfilment in his outstanding bird studies. He would take a large canvas out of doors and paint pictures in Cornwall of the sea and sea birds in all weather conditions. Here he brought a broad treatment to flight and to changing light and colour; themes which were brilliantly effective and clearly emanating from the influence of Joseph Crawhall. In his bird pictures such as duck in the estuary the vigorous brushwork and shadow variations produced works in exciting contrast to those quiet, and sometimes dull, compositions of High Leicestershire.

Amongst his most valuable contribution to sporting art is his notable book published in 1939, *Animal and Bird Painting: The Outlook and Technique of the Artist* with his own illustrations plus reproductions of famous paintings. Valuable advice for the aspiring sporting artist at the beginning of his career includes such guidance as 'No better training than to work . . . with a good landscape painter. Look at Constable, Cuyp and Crome'. But then follows a word of warning: 'English rural landscape has its own beauty but in unskilful hands it can be monotonous and without character in a picture'.[6] And perhaps most relevant of all for the mid-twentieth century artist he points out that the fault with inferior hunting paintings is that their execution is too laboured, too meticulously accurate in small things while missing the breadth and freedom that should be their outstanding qualities. As an artist the work of

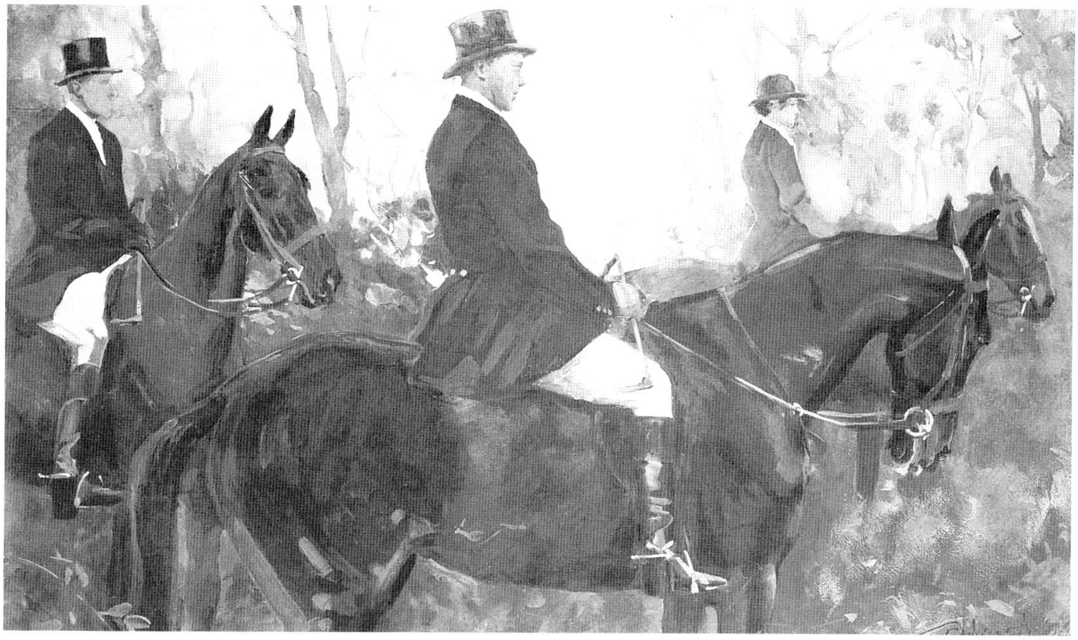

31 Charles Walter Simpson, *HRH The Prince of Wales out with the Quorn*, *c* 1927. Watercolour, 24 × 29 in (60.9 × 99 cm).

Charles Simpson is uneven, but this book provides inspiring guidelines for those at the beginning of a career in animal art. In addition, though somewhat outside the actual sporting context, his study of *Photography: The Figure in Colour and Monochrome*, published in 1939, makes a valuable appraisal of the relationship of the camera and the creative artist, using striking examples of his own skill as a photographer. He foretells the future takeover of acceptable colour from monochrome reproduction, an achievement which was to become a positive competitor for the animal painter.

Future generations surveying the sporting artists working in the first half of the twentieth century will be puzzled that Gilbert Holiday in his own day, and for many decades after, received appreciation from only a very small band of admirers. Overshadowed early in his career by the popularity of such humourists as Aldin, Armour and Snaffles, and then later outshone by the brilliance and productive longevity of two such masters as Lionel Edwards and Alfred Munnings, the rich sparkling gifts of Gilbert Holiday until recently have remained unacknowledged.

This relative obscurity is also explained by his early death in 1937 and by the fact that most of his best work was commissioned and remained in private hands and is only to be seen in country houses, many in Scotland and Ireland, and also in regimental messes. Many fine pictures remain in the Channel Isles where summer holidays were spent with his wife's family; several crossed the Atlantic to astute Americans. It was not until 1983 when William Marler, a noted art dealer based in Ludlow, put on a remarkable exhibition of 'The Art of Gilbert Holiday' at the Tryon and Moorland Gallery in London that prices in the sale rooms began a spectacular rise, indicating that collectors had at last discovered one of the most important talents of the century. It had taken William Marler over eight years to assemble the 103 items displayed, many of which had come to light when, after forty years, the contents of the artist's studio were dispersed.

Gilbert Holiday certainly shared his contemporaries' deep love of sport and of the English countryside and also their ability to capture both the vision and feeling, but in addition he excelled them all in his capacity for portraying the horse in action. In 1947 Lionel Edwards in his autobiography wrote, 'To my mind Holiday was almost the first artist to master the photographic action . . . By this I mean animals in motion as seen by the camera and not the artist's entirely conventional rendering . . . Holiday by clever manipulation of dust and mud and the consequent blurring of outlines was able to give a tremendous sense of speed. When handling a mass of horsemen he was even better and he would use even the most grotesque positions with success.'[7] Praise indeed from this master sporting artist and at last the facts of Muybridge's action photographs had been absorbed.

Born in Maida Vale, London, in 1879, a year after Edwards and Munnings, the second son of Sir Frederick Holiday, a distinguished civil servant, Charles Gilbert Joseph Holiday was always known simply as 'GH' and often signed his pictures solely with these initials. To his mother, a competent watercolourist and his uncle Henry Holiday, friend of such Pre-Raphaelites as Holman Hunt and Burne-Jones, and himself a noted exponent of that school, Gilbert Holiday owes his artistic leanings. From early boyhood drawing was his constant occupation and at Westminster School his gifts for the equestrian subject were fortunately recognised by his housemater, drawings of horses' heads being substituted officially for punitive 'lines'.

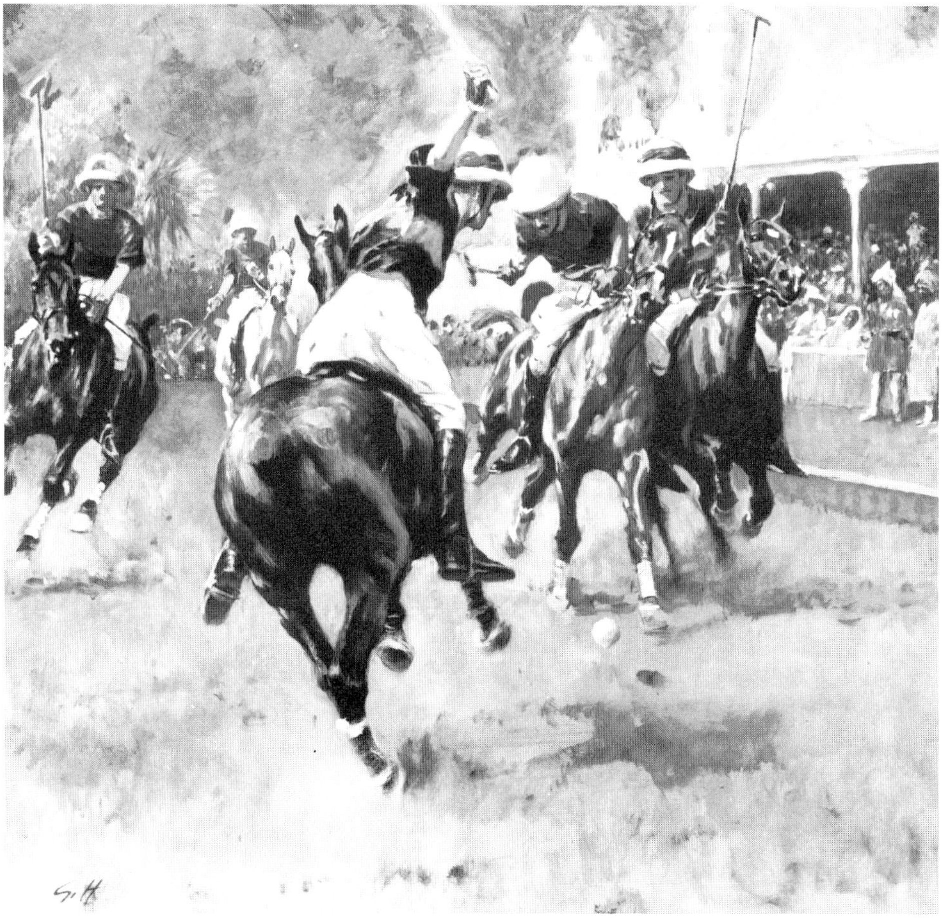

32 Gilbert Joseph Holiday, *A Polo Match*. Proof copy of an unsigned print, image size $8\frac{1}{4} \times 15\frac{1}{4}$ in (20.9 × 38.7 cm).

Trained later at the Royal Academy Schools, Holiday failed to accept the conventional approach to his subject but skilled draughtsmanship and a sense of form were never entirely sacrificed to his impressionist use of colour. Excitement, movement and truth were the hallmark of his pictures but always allied to expert accuracy of detail, for here was the work of a knowledgeable sportsman.

Like most of his contemporaries he first made his name in black and white work for the illustrated periodicals of the day but by 1904 he had exhibited an oil painting, *The Brewer's Dray*, the first of six works, at the Royal Academy. *The Graphic*, as so often, provided a financial lifeline and with ten pounds in the bank and the magazine's weekly contract for a page drawing he was in 1908 enabled to marry beautiful Marguerite Spencer from Guernsey who died, aged ninety-eight, only a year before the William Marler Exhibition. In later life Lionel Edwards maintained that he himself had regularly bought *The Graphic* just to enjoy the contributions of GH.

In spite of press commitments the artist painted brilliant studies of the equestrian highlights of the London season. Especially effective are scenes of farriers and grooms working in the stable area at the glamorous International Horse Show at Olympia, but his sparkling composition of huntsman and hounds entering the floodlit arena with its banks of deep blue hydrangeas and 'Lordy', the Earl of Lonsdale, doyen of the show, posed in the left foreground was to become a distinctive cover of the Show Catalogue. GH could bring a touch of magic to these occasions, as in his evocation of *Epsom: Return to the Paddock* with its sunlit melée of tense galloping horses and in the foreground two lovely ladies in pretty blue dresses (*Plate 7*).

No artist could excel his skill in presenting what J.N.P. Watson so aptly describes as 'equestrian ballet' or the game of polo. Happy afternoons at Hurlingham depict in pastel and crayon the end of a chukka with relaxed players and ponies, and again a decorative girl as a salient part of the composition, with a glimpse of GH himself in his perennial soft felt hat with its black band. In contrast are exciting scenes of play in such dramatic compositions as *A Polo Match* (*32*). Equally animated is a charcoal and pastel study *Polo – In Winter or Foul Weather* of hectic play in an indoor school (*Plate 8*). These little masterpieces could only emanate from an artist who was himself an adept and perceptive horseman who understands the instinctive co-ordination of rider and mount.

Quietly informative is the pastel of *Racehorses arriving at Hampton Court for Hurst Park Races*, a reminder of the era when the railway provided transport to racemeetings. Rugged-up horses, led by lads in cloth caps and leggings, emerge from the straw-bedded trucks. But not for him the static presentation of the racing scene in saddling paddocks. Instead in tense, dramatic compositions such as *Epsom: Rounding Tattenham* and in *Becher's Brook – 1924 Grand National* executed in soft muted tones he uses impressionism, allied to acute observation, in a complete breakaway from the representational traditions of his day (*33*). These are classics of sporting art.

Gilbert Holiday also produced striking studies of gun teams and this theme of the 'battery hairies' had fascinated him from before the First World War. Snaffles considered these pictures amongst his finest achievements.

Holiday was one of the principal artists who had seen active service on the Western Front, and whose work was included in the *Royal Artillery War Commemoration Book* (1920). In addition he was a prolific illustrator for the sporting author and many of these paintings in the 1920s were reproduced in colour in *The Tatler* and the *Illustrated London News*. A number were published as prints.

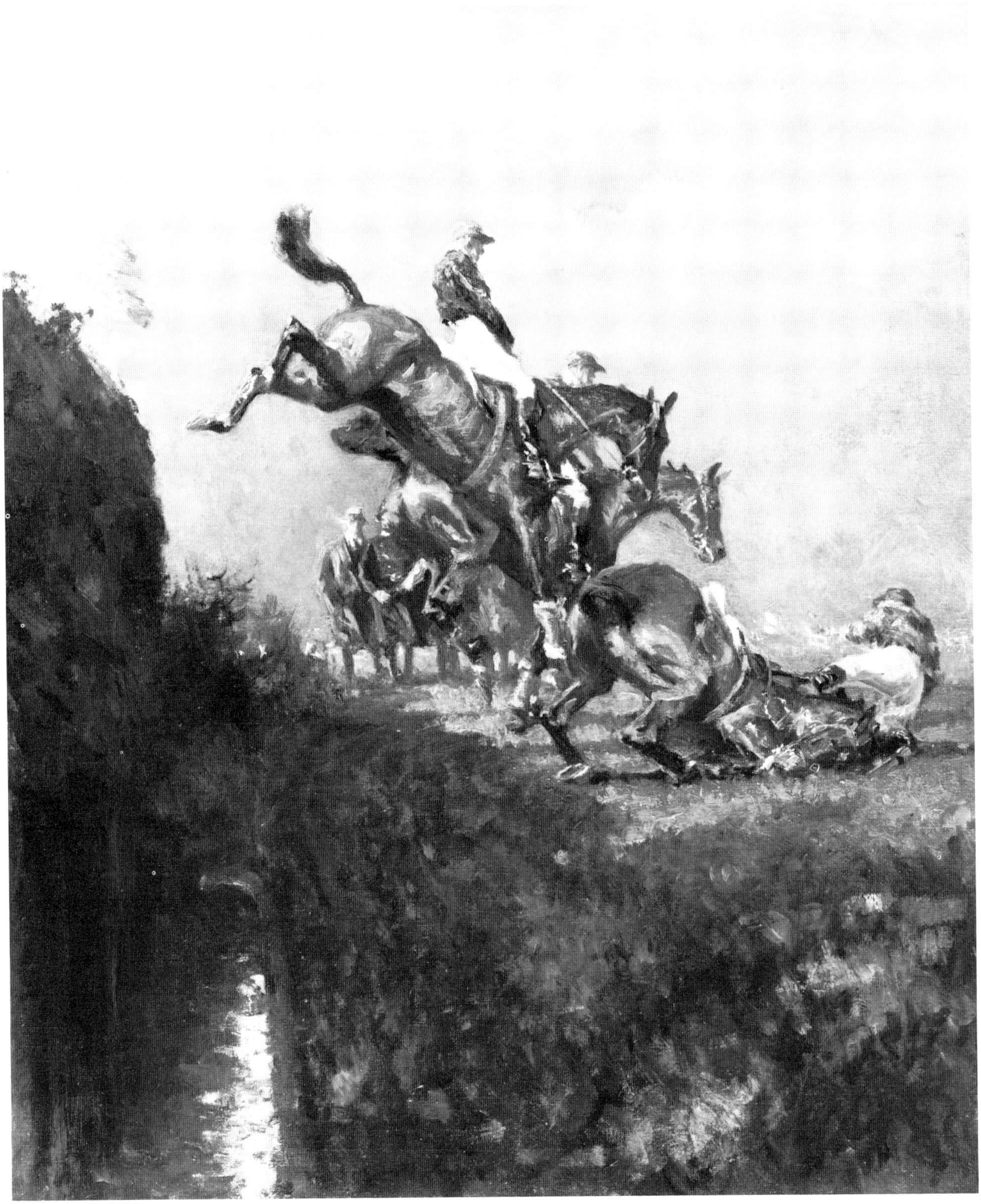

33 Gilbert Joseph Holiday, *Becher's Brook – 1924 Grand National*. Oil on canvas, 24 × 20 in (60.9 × 50.8 cm).

Though he always maintained strong links with the Army and continued to receive military commissions, basically his inspiration was found in the civilian sporting scene – race meetings, point-to-points, polo, coaching and above all hunting. His personal introduction to hounds took place during a weekend visit to Lionel Edwards who lent GH his wife's untried little horse (with a dreadful mouth!) for a day with the Old Berkshire. Both tyros finished in the middle of the Rosey Brook but Gilbert Holiday had acquired an incurable addiction. Though he never owned a horse of his own he hunted with many packs in the Shires and in Ireland, frequently, and not surprisingly, for he was a man of great charm and warmth, receiving invitations from the people who had commissioned pictures. But most of the time he followed the nearby Woolwich (Royal Artillery) Draghounds, and like most committed sporting artists, would make a swift sketch on a scrap of paper whenever activities slackened.

Deft detail abounds in his pictures of hunting; absolutely natural is the poise of his ladies side-saddle, in the relaxed quarters and lowered head of a hunter at the end of a gruelling run, the preoccupation of a huntsman casting hounds. The colours are always restrained, often only the scarlet hunt servants' coats provide definition to panoramic pastures fading into the grey distance.

Though never holding a one man exhibition, in addition to the Royal Academy, his pictures were shown at the Royal Institute of Painters in Watercolours, at the Royal Institute of Oil Painters and at the Royal Scottish Academy. But by nature he was completely uncommercial: he would sell a painting for a modest twenty pounds and considered £800–£1000 a year an adequate income; his family, his painting and hunting were the essentials of his life.

At the height of his powers in 1932, GH suffered a tragic fall over timber when out with the Woolwich Drag. Paralysed from the waist down he never walked again but he still painted from a wheel chair and with amazing courage and good humour produced *We'll All Go-a-hunting Today*, the only book written and illustrated by himself. He died from pneumonia in 1937, aged only fifty-seven, to close an important chapter in British sporting art.

John Board, equestrian correspondent of *The Times* and himself a competent sporting artist, wrote, 'Gilbert Holiday expressed almost vocally his love of sport . . . he had it all, not only can you smell them but you can feel and hear his horses . . . had he lived nobody can tell to what heights he would have attained.'

NOTES

1 Unfortunately no! The carillon of 35 bells at the parish church of St Peter and St Paul could be preset to play a number of tunes. It was destroyed by fire 15 September 1940.

2 A wellknown horse dealer and show judge living near Edenbridge, Kent.

3 Roy Heron, *Tom Firr of the Quorn*, p. 81.

4 Charles Walter Simpson with Michael Tresillian in an article 'How To Paint Horses'. *Horse & Hound*, 1965.

5 ibid.

6 Charles Walter Simpson: *Animal and Bird Painting*, 68ff.

7 Lionel Edwards, R.I., *Reminiscences of a Sporting Artist*, p. 30.

7

Lionel Edwards: The Grand Old Man of British Sporting Art

In 1947, in his seventieth year, Lionel Edwards published his autobiography *Reminiscences of a Sporting Artist* and intensely relevant to his life and work is the dedication – 'To mine own kindred' – for he added 'it is no presumption to claim kinship with all those who love similar pursuits.' Social and art historians alike must rejoice that this artist has left for posterity an incomparable record of his sporting diversions enjoyed for more than sixty years in the twentieth century.

In spite of two World Wars Lionel Edwards' long career encompassed a golden age of sporting events and activities. Nevertheless transition was on the horizon and against a varied tapestry of changing scenes and customs he lived his long life, hunting until his eighties and painting until the day before he died in 1966. With admiration and affection in his own lifetime he had become known as The Grand Old Man of British Sporting Art to rank as one of the major masters and influences of his generation.

Born at Clifton, Bristol, on 9 November 1878, just one month and a day after Munnings, Lionel Dalhousie Robertson Edwards was last of the family of eight children of Dr James Edwards, of Benarth Hall, Conway in North Wales and of his third wife, Harriet Main. Country pursuits rather than formal education directed the future artist's childhood for his father, having retired as a Chester consultant and with the tragic loss of his first wife and two children in an epidemic and then his second wife in childbirth, retreated to a new home in Wales, Benarth, in the wild picturesque country of Conway to hunt, fish, farm and start up a pack of beagles – his real inherited interests. But, as his son Lionel so neatly phrases it 'the rapid filling of the nursery emptied the stables.' [1]

After his father's death and, as the youngest of five brothers he passed a somewhat solitary childhood with little formal schooling. Destined for the Army, a brief spell with a military crammer quickly proved it was a career for which he had no aptitude. Heredity played its part, for his maternal grandmother had been a favourite and talented pupil of George Romney and, as a boy of six years old, Lionel Edwards was already drawing horses with precision. It was his mother who encouraged an artistic vocation, which followed the familiar path of his contemporaries. He studied briefly at Frank Calderon's School of Animal Painting in London and at night at Heatherley's School of Art which must be considered at this period as the more mundane equivalent of the *Atelier* Julian in Paris in the attraction it held for aspiring artists of the day. It had been established in Newman Street, London, as early as 1845 by James Leigh, and in 1860 Thomas Heatherley, a former student, became its director for the next

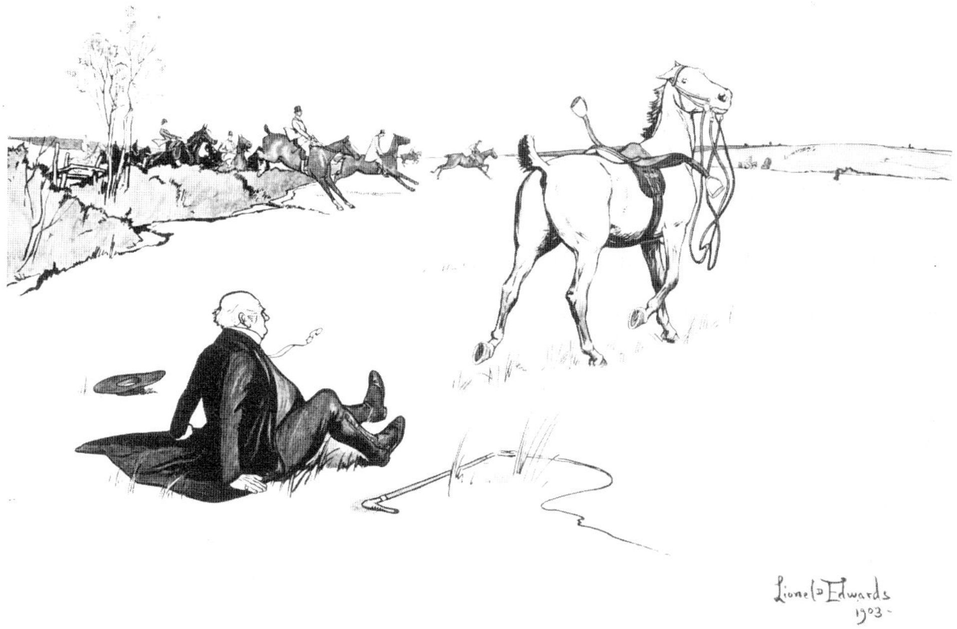

34 Lionel Dalhousie Robertson Edwards, *Canon off the White*, 1903. Print.

thirty years. It achieved great popularity being inexpensive and open to both sexes, without any preliminary test of ability. The school had a chequered and nomadic career through the two World Wars and in 1978 an appeal was launched to re-establish its finances and later, in 1986, with generous support from the Queen Mother, to purchase its Chelsea premises to assure its future.

Its influence on contemporary artists over nearly a century and a half had been impressive starting with the Pre-Raphaelites. Amongst its pupils have been numbered John Millais, D.G. Rossetti, Walter Sickert, Michael Ayrton and William Russell Flint in addition to many adherents of the school of British sporting art.

Even with scholarships Lionel Edwards' shoe-string finances allowed only very limited formal training; nevertheless he acquired a sound anatomical discipline. His first published work were drawings for *Country Life* in 1898 of the famous 'wild' white cattle at Chillingham, the beginning of a hard stint of six or seven years for popular London periodicals, only lightened by occasional days with hounds in the Home Counties on a borrowed horse, or more often a bicycle, until he acquired a one-eyed aged pony for fifteen pounds from an impoverished job-master, which he also rode three times a week in Rotten Row.

While still a student he was elected at the age of twenty to the London Sketch Club (its youngest member), where he encountered such congenial companions as Aldin and Snaffles, that generous humorist, Phil May and the President, George Haité, 'that most facile of sketchers', all to offer stimulating company and criticism.

His early studies dated from 1903, many of which are humorous simple line drawings, and strongly reminiscent of the style of Aldin and of Snaffles as in *Canon Off the White* with his Reverence on the floor (*34*). But holidays widened the artists' horizons and in 1904 he was initiated into staghunting with the Devon and Somerset Staghounds and, more importantly, began his life-long enchantment with the West Country where he painted and sold his first pictures of this subject which he admitted were 'far from good', but much encouraged he put on a small exhibition of these local scenes in the old parish hall at Porlock, hired from the local Vicar, sold every picture and paid for his hunting. In later life some of his finest work was to be inspired by the moorland scenery of sport on Exmoor, providing scope for his considerable talent for landscapes.

This modest success led to his marriage the following year to a childhood friend, Ethel Ashness Wells, daughter of a retired director of a brewery, and a union that brought no dowry but sixty years of great happiness, gave him his keenest critic and produced four sons and a daughter. Most sporting artists seem to possess a delightful knack of making successful marriages – Aldin, Armour, Snaffles, Holiday and others are all in this category. Temperamental equanimity and affection appear to be engendered by a career inspired by animals and sport; the turmoil of the religous and historic subjects of the Pre-Raphaelites and other schools rarely brought such felicity.

The couple lived on the borders of South Oxfordshire, and then moved in 1909 to Worcestershire, both hunting regularly on a slender income of £500 a year, first on loaned and later, when commissions for equestrian portraits and hunting scenes began gradually to flow in, on their own horses. Ethel was an accomplished horsewoman possessing the blessed gift of 'hands'. But Lionel Edwards with vision refused the opportunity to live in Leicestershire, realising the artist would there fight a losing battle with the foxhunter. Few artists have worked throughout their careers with greater industry and dedication; he always carried a sketchbook in the pocket of his hunting coat for, as he wrote in his autobiography 'There can be no 44 hour week or holidays with pay for the artist.'[2] He scorned recourse to photographs and to the end of his days insisted on painting out of doors, impervious to wind and weather. Sketches would be smudged by snowflakes and only in his eighties did he accept the bleak refuge of a car trailer.

In 1912 Benarth once more became his home where he kept a pack of bloodhounds and hunted 'clean boot'. Two years later through his agent, the reliable A.E. Johnson of Kingsway, he was able to put on his first one man show in London but, with the outbreak of war, entry into the Army Remount Service brought his career to a halt and he had 'four solid years of nothing but horse,'[3] an experience which inevitably educated his eye for equine conformation and afterwards he maintained that this enforced artistic abstinence had freshened his style.

After demobilisation the family moved to their permanent farmhouse home, Buckholt in Wiltshire, where Lionel Edwards became a practical farmer, for forty-three years a committee member of the Hursley Hunt, and the most popular sporting artist of his generation. A new vitality and fluency began to appear in his work and inspired (as he frankly admitted) by earlier paintings of G.D. Giles in the 1880s, he began his series of hunting countries, *Shires and Provinces*, which were also produced with success as limited edition prints. But these paintings in watercolour gouache with their delicate landscape effects and sensitive use of light and shade possessed a vibrant beauty and spontaneity far removed from the stereotyped studies of his predecessors. Often working at speed to capture swiftly changing conditions the artist would depict, as no one else, the exhilarating magic of horses and hounds streaming across country.

But nothing makes greater impact in the paintings of Lionel Edwards than his perceptive and sensitive use of climate. Not for him the clear brilliance of bright skies and vivid scarlet coats of the hunting scenes of such late Victorians as Heywood Hardy and Thomas Blinks. Sport is depicted in the soft tones of November mists, grey skies and green pastures dimmed by winter mud.

Always concerned with the problems of animal motion, of presenting the illusion of pace, Lionel Edwards had maintained that Gilbert Holiday was the first sporting artist really to master the problem of speed, but his own portrayal of movement became equally convincing – his horses and hounds cover the country at a cracking gallop. Here is the realism of a man who loved his hunting and is enchanted by the countryside whether it is the wide vales of the Bicester, the steep slopes of the Flint and Denbigh or the more vividly coloured terrain of the Emerald Isle.

Wherever the setting, and in all during his life Edwards hunted with ninety-one packs of foxhounds, five packs of staghounds, three otterhounds, two packs of beagles and one of bloodhounds – what a record – he presents the actual pursuit of hunting with verve and accuracy. Horses and hounds, huntsman and field all play their familiar parts, painted not only with lively and technical skill but with an eye that understands the hundred and one finer details of the job in hand – the huntsman's unswerving gaze on hounds as they run or pausing and feathering to recover a lost line, the confident lift of the quarters of a bold horse over post and rails. It is virtually impossible to fault Edwards in technical details, whether it is the hunt servants' buttons and bows, the fitting of a bridle or the plaits of a mane. He delights in carefully painted stone walls of the Peak country, the Irish banks of the Meath, the oxers of Leicestershire.[4] He is also a realist and his pictures often show the hunting scene as most of us have frequently experienced it, with horses and hounds ahead – a rear view with mud flying in the eye and a rider and horse coming down. A fine example of this is *High Leicestershire: The Quorn across the Queniborough Road*, with the riders taking a stake and bound fence to face delectable jumping country ahead and the famous dark dome of Billesdon Coplow away on the left (*35*).

Very beautifully the artist depicts the patchwork of English pastures in his study *The Belvoir* and also in the lovely vista in *The Beaufort: The Kill above Sodbury Vale*. Here the central figure on the tired steaming bay is the 10th Duke of Beaufort, 'Master' himself (*36*). The Duke

35 Lionel Dalhousie Robertson Edwards, *High Leicestershire: The Quorn across the Queniborough Road*, 1961. Watercolour.

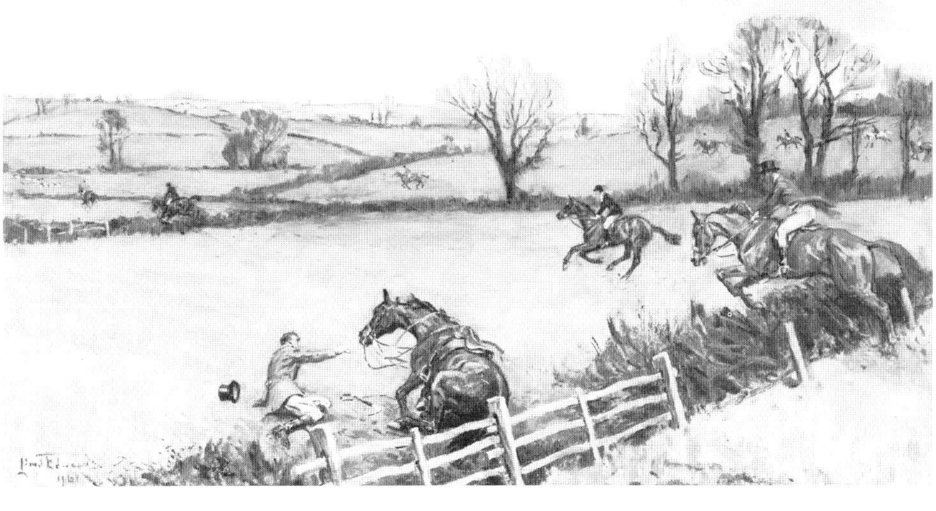

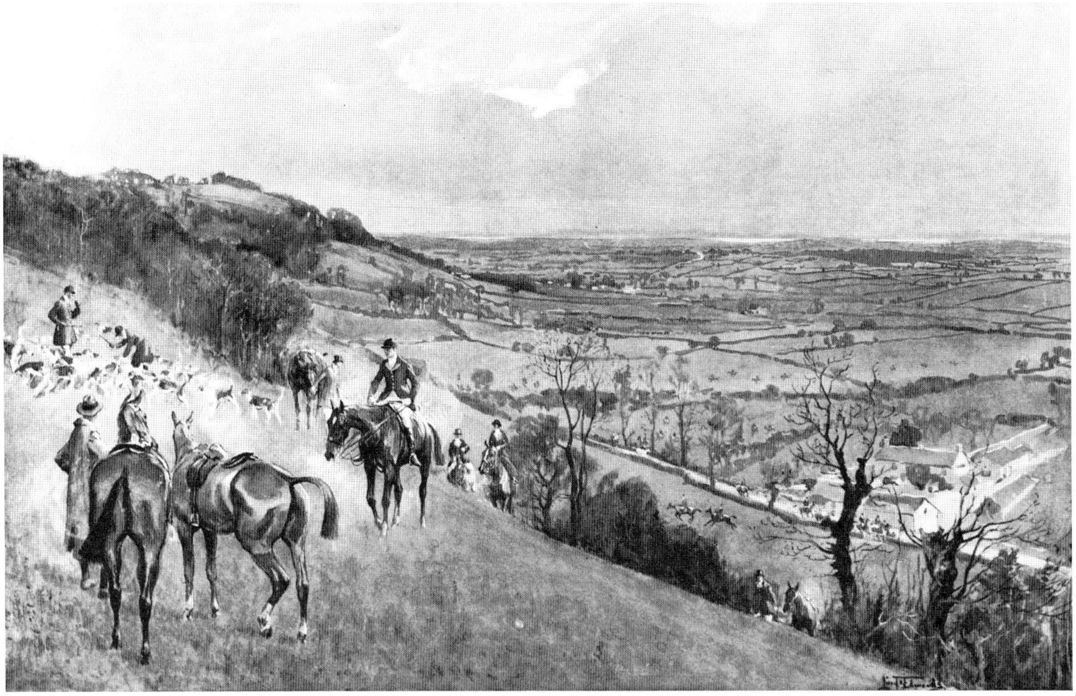

36 Lionel Dalhousie Robertson Edwards, *The Beaufort: The Kill above Sodbury Vale*. Watercolour, $12\frac{3}{4} \times 19\frac{1}{4}$ in (32.3 × 48.8 cm).

wrote in a letter in 1979, 'Of all the painters of hunting and horses he, Edwards, was and is, the man I like best and I have numerous pictures by him . . . he often came to Badminton and in the picture *The Kill above Sodbury Vale* I am the man in the Blue and Buff riding up the hill, and it is Lionel himself holding the two horses. He was actually standing there when the hounds ran up the hill and caught the fox at his feet . . . my favourite sporting artist.'[5]

And that other great sportsman of the century, Lord Daresbury, writes in the same year '. . . he is the only one that has depicted hunting as we know it, like Alken did in his day.'[6] Edwards has certainly captured for future generations the memory of an idyllic countryside with hedges and grassland undespoiled, no electric pylons and no motorways. And from his early expeditions he had a close and lifelong friendship with Denis Aldridge, wire-secretary of the South Atherstone and later of the Quorn and himself an amateur sporting artist of some merit.

Perhaps reaction to Lionel Edwards' pictures is tinged by a rosy nostalgia. But the artist is not a visionary; he painted with intense observation and he wrote, 'It should be remembered that however admirable the artistic treatment, a real understanding of what is happening is absolutely necessary . . . It is difficult to get this knowledge unless the artist is a sportsman himself.'[7] Edwards was a dedicated sportsman and a superb artist but in addition he was a countryman born and bred – the ideal combination, as vividly illustrated in *The Mockers* with Charles James being pursued by rooks against a delectable Fernie vista (*Plate 9*). Hunting became, and remained, his paramount subject; he travelled far and wide to fulfil commissions for hunt presentation pictures. In 1929 he went with Ethel to Gibraltar as the guest of General Sir Alexander Godley. With the Calpé Hunt he found foxhunting in Spain '. . . a strange experience going foxhunting in foreign soil, to ride out past the British sentry guard at Gib

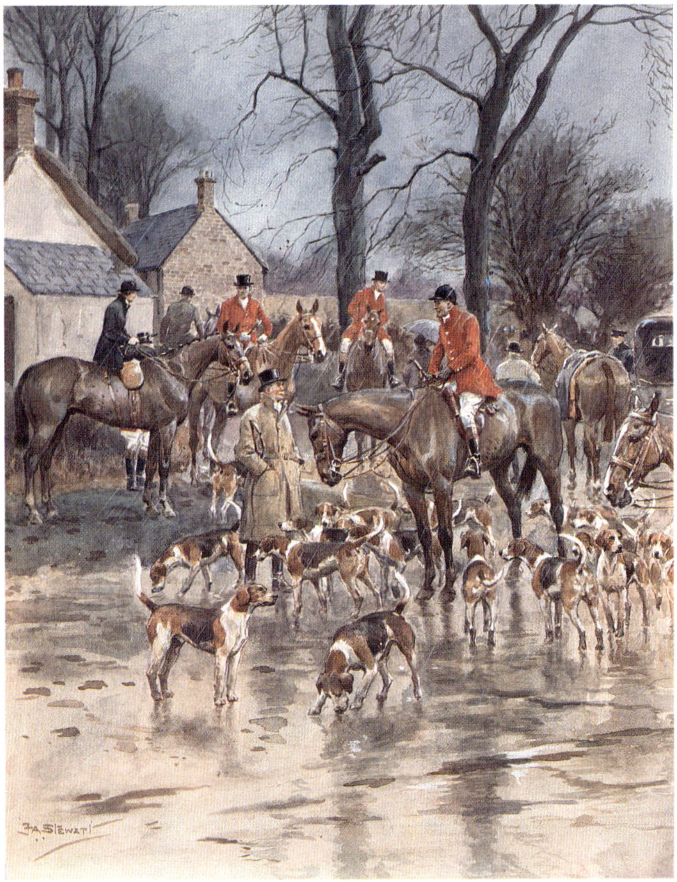

PLATE 7 (*left*) Frank Algernon Stewart, *Optimists at The Meet*, 1931. Watercolour, $11\frac{1}{4} \times 14\frac{1}{4}$ in (28.5 × 36.19 cm).

(*below*) Gilbert Joseph Holiday, *Epsom: Return to the Paddock*. Watercolour $12\frac{1}{2} \times 20$ in (31.7 × 50.8 cm).

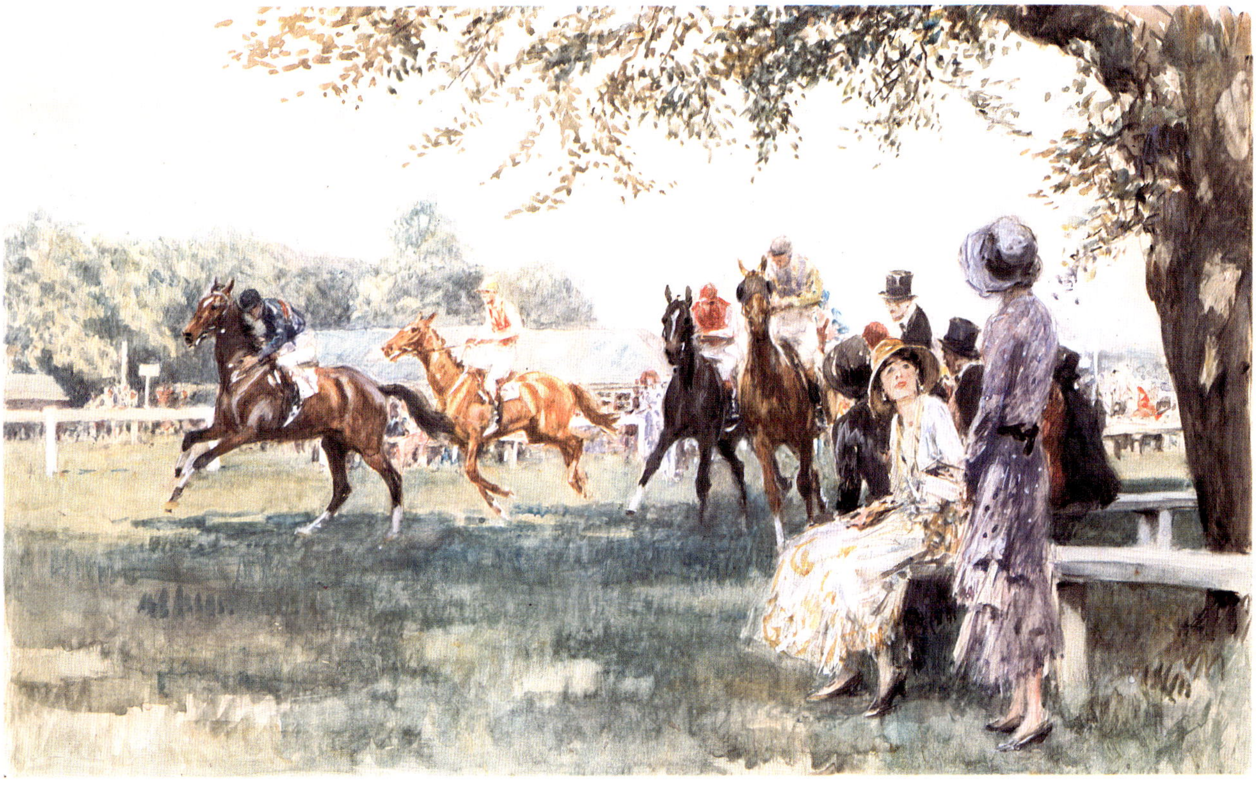

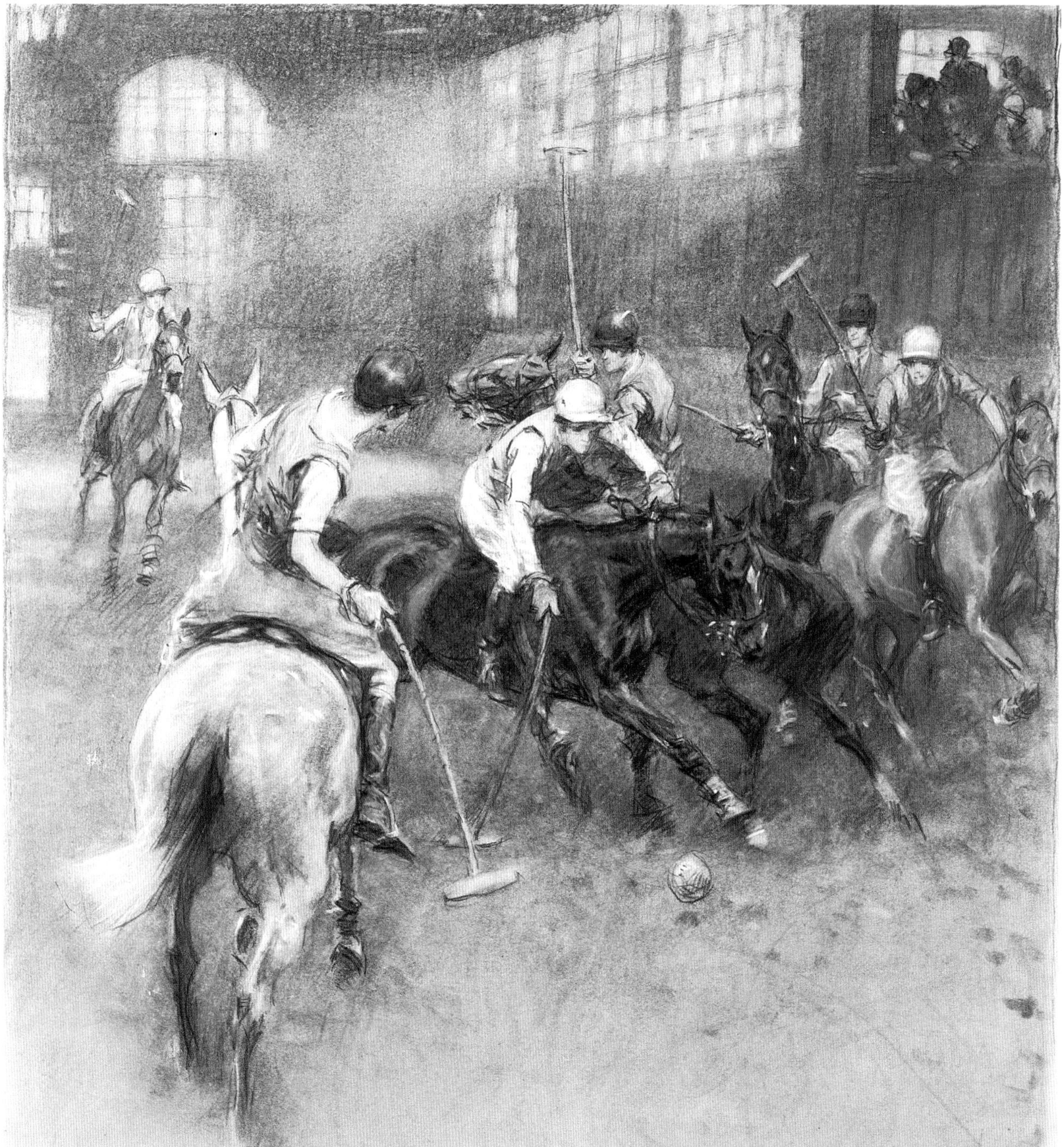

PLATE 8 Gilbert Joseph Holiday, *Polo – in Winter or Foul Weather*. Charcoal and coloured chalk, $16\frac{1}{2} \times 13\frac{7}{8}$ in (41.9×35 cm). Illustrated in *The Sketch*, 18 May 1930.

and then through the heavily guarded customs barriers at La Linea.'[8] They went on to Tangier where under the aegis of the Cosmopolitan Tent Club he enjoyed initiation into pig-sticking and wrote with some verve of its thrills in his reminiscences. He painted several convincing pictures of the sport which bore real Indian authenticity and puzzled his biographers as he never visited Asia.

Happily he possessed a versatility that covered most facets of the sporting scene. Many leading racehorse owners demanded portraits of their star performers; in 1941 for King George VI he painted Fair Glint, Sun Chariot and Fair Deal and for the Aga Khan he made a brilliant study of the 1936 Derby winner, Mahmoud, and here he suggested uncannily the Arabian blood that still infiltrates the Thoroughbred. There was a fine picture of Team Spirit, the winner of the 1964 Grand National, a horse with a wonderful front being led in his home paddock and also that other classic steeplechaser Cromwell with ill-fated Lord Mildmay to illustrate the way Edwards could put over not only the conformation but also the character of a horse; never more evident than in his study of that hero, Golden Miller, in old age – a little gaunt but still exuding the courage and wisdom of a five times winner of the Cheltenham Gold Cup. He wrote 'Racing is a branch of sporting art which seems to defeat artists. Thoroughbreds are extremely difficult to paint – or so I think, never yet having done one to my own satisfaction.'[9]

But he was always prepared to accept criticism and hints from owners and trainers, realising his own knowledge of the racing game lacked his equivalent lifelong background to hunting. Never gifted at facial likenesses Edwards would cunningly present human personality by stance and poise. A dramatic triumph for impressionism was his watercolour sketch of Pas Seul in the windswept unsaddling enclosure at Sandown Park after winning the 1960 Whitbread Gold Cup – the steaming horse, excited, alert, a blur of umbrellas and spectators and rain streaking down – an ephemeral but brilliant evocation.

His pictures of horses galloping over fences, as in the National Hunt Steeplechase at Cheltenham with the Cleeve Hills in the background (*37*) or in his many paintings of point-to-points, may lack the assured handling of that master of action, Gilbert Holiday, but lose nothing in excitement and tension, as in *The Winter Game*, with the bright colours of the jockeys and dark outline of a fence appearing through the thick flurry of snowflakes. How he loved the cold blue tones of frost and snow and he never failed to sketch out of doors in the severest weather! Typical is *String of Horses in Snow – Warren Hill*, to contrast with his fair weather picture of *Warren Hill*, 'probably the best oil I have ever done', never a medium he used with ease and confidence for his natural fluency of line and speed was inhibited (*Plate 9*).

It was not unusual for him to start a complex watercolour – four horses in a landscape – measuring 20 × 30 in and complete it in nine hours. Five minutes to study the view then a few lines and dots to mark the limits of hedge, trees and landscape; the sky was commenced and finally the horses were painted in. There is little evidence of correction. A similar picture painted in his studio in oils, would occupy five days in what he considered slow and tedious work. But the initial careful drawing sprinkled with innumerable written notes would have been made out of doors, however inclement the weather. Sometimes his watercolours combined their delicacy with such authority that they possessed the power of oil paintings.

With what brilliant effect he could use sunlight, with subtle nuances of light and shade on lithe bodies somehow to suggest the contained exuberance of two-year-olds being exercised or capture the summer racing scene of Glorious Goodwood from the Trundle (*38*). Sunshine highlights tense polo matches at Windsor and Tidworth and quiet angling landscapes on the

Test, his exciting scenes of Spanish bull-fighting and pig sticking forays in Tangier. Perhaps his most vibrant use of colour was enjoyed in his Highland stalking pictures with groups of a majestic stag and hinds against the glory of the heather.

But the artist as countryman is happily represented by scenes of ferreting, of shooting and haymaking at his home, Buckholt, not perhaps amongst his finest work but redolent of his dedication to rural England, so typical of the man. Less characteristic and hard to credit is his admission that really his greatest enjoyment was obtained from painting military subjects with a mass of uniforms and detailed accoutrements. But lack of time had precluded such fulfilment of this predilection. Nevertheless near the end of his life in 1959 he accomplished a complex commemorative composition for Lieutenant Colonel Max Gordon of the Annual Inspection of the Household Cavalry Mounted Regiment over which he expended enormous effort and energy on precision of detail.

He exhibited frequently in London, several times at Rowland Ward's Gallery where, in 1953, the Duke of Beaufort made the opening speech quoted by Lionel Edwards as . . . 'a good one . . . mine wasn't!' As an illustrator Edwards excelled and much of his best work was accomplished for his own articles and books all written in a clear readable style, the most important being, in addition to his autobiographies, *My Hunting Sketch Books*, Vols I and II, 1928 and 1930; *Famous Foxhunters*, 1932; *My Irish Sketch Book*, 1938; *Scarlet and Corduroy*, 1941 and in his seventy-fourth year *Thy Servant a Horse*, 1952, which is his tribute to generations of the willing horse. He collaborated with Frank Wallace, a fellow artist and sportsman in a joint production *A Stuart Sketch Book (1542–1746)*, in which both his love of uniforms and of the magnificent Highland scenery had full scope. He illustrated the works of virtually every leading equestrian writer of the day but reached his zenith in his inspired watercolours complementing the sporting verse of Will H. Ogilvie: here two kindred spirits fused.

All his life he retained his tall, lean horseman's figure, his appearance more of a military man than an artist. By nature modest and retiring he was generous to a degree in his advice to aspiring young painters, spicing practical tips with such admonitions as, 'Forget all about art exhibitions, art critics and, if possible your overdraft!'[10] Through pressure of commissions only Peter Biegel had the good fortune to be accepted as an actual pupil. In 1944 Major Guy Paget, the sporting art historian, was writing, 'Lionel Edwards I regard as the greatest illustrator of his day or any other. He is a landscape painter of the first class. He is a true student of nature, a good man on a bad horse to hounds, and at home with a rod or gun, but happier in the same places with neither, just looking.'[11]

Admirable was his reaction to contemporary innovations, 'I think it is unwise to condemn modern art for as one gets older and reviews the changes in art that have occurred, it is possible that that which, when it was painted, was considered outrageous, may in later years appear to be good.'[12] With regrettable results, irascible impulsive Munnings was never able to take this long term view. But Edwards did write to him after the famous Royal Academy dinner speech[13] 'Well done AJ! I was delighted you had a crack at them. The fault is not so much the young artists as the critics whose words these foolish youngsters take for gospel.'[14]

From the 1920s Lionel Edwards received acclaim and though in old age his expertise inevitably lessened, his position as the outstanding sporting artist of the day never diminished. As early as 1901 he was made an Associate of the Royal Cambrian Academy of Art, in 1926 he became a full Academician and the following year a member of the Royal Institute of Painters in Watercolour. In 1931 he exhibited at the Royal Academy *A Hunt in the Snow: The Heythrop*. He held several exhibitions in London and in 1959 the Tryon Gallery became

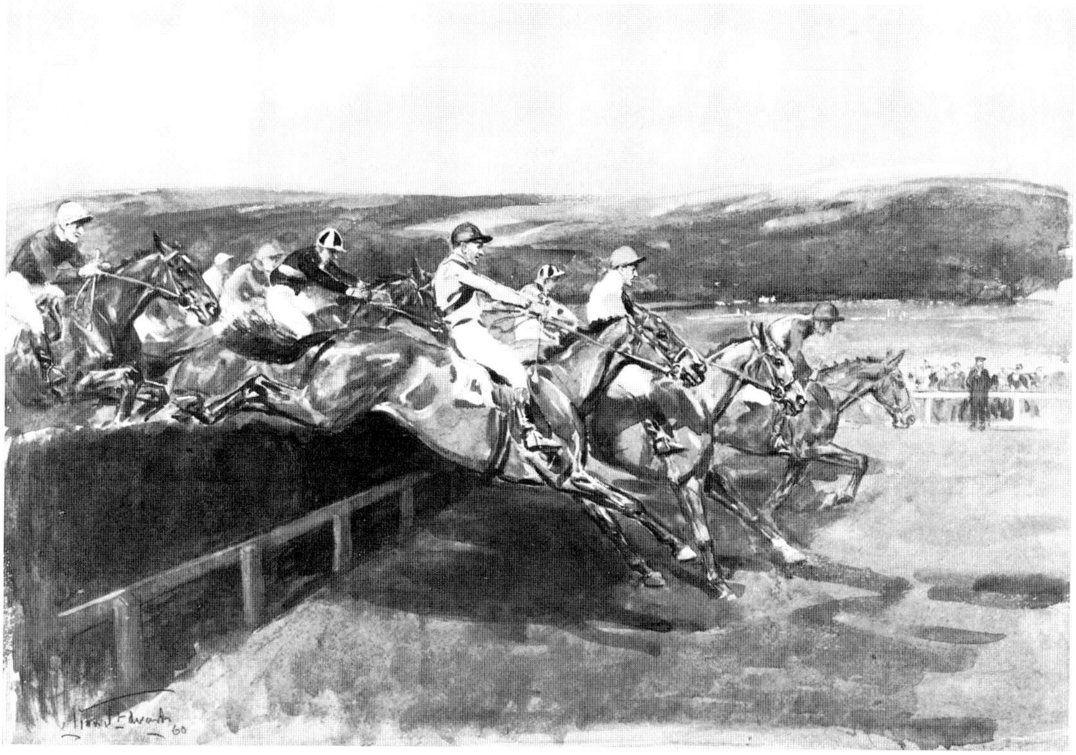

37 Lionel Dalhousie Robertson Edwards, *The Second Fence – National Hunt Steeplechase, Cheltenham*, 1960. Watercolour, $23\frac{1}{2} \times 35$ in (59.7×88.9 cm).

38 Lionel Dalhousie Robertson Edwards, *The Trundle, Goodwood*, 1950. Print, $14\frac{1}{4} \times 19\frac{3}{4}$ in (36.2×50.2 cm).

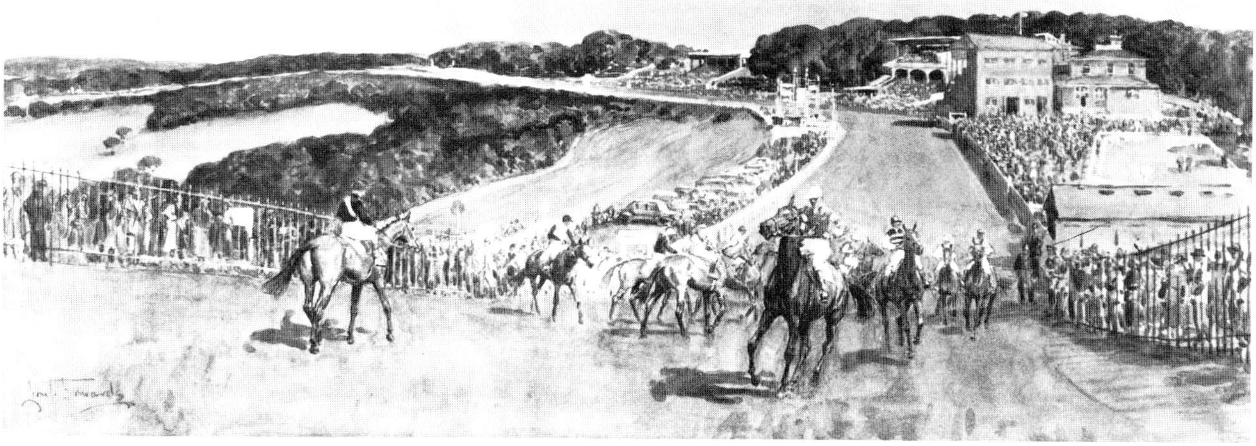

his regular venue where in 1964, in his eighty-fourth year, he exhibited a collection of over sixty works.

His style had brought fluency and credible action into the sporting school, especially the hunting scene, and had animated an awareness of landscape and climatic conditions as a vital element. This was a new approach and his assured handling of colour, light and movement owed its technique to an impressionist element which was also an exciting innovation when allied to his flair for intense observation of the rural scene. It was a precious and unique talent which he exploited to the full and which was to guide and strongly influence artists who followed after, such as Peter Biegel, Michael Lyne, John King, John Kenney and many others. And near the end of the century many newcomers, avoiding experiments in pastures new, still try to reproduce, without success, the Edwards magic.

In September 1986, twenty years after the artist's death, the British Sporting Art Trust put on at the Alpine Gallery in South Audley Street, London and later at the Leicestershire Museum and Art Gallery, a loan exhibition of works by Lionel Edwards. More than 600 pictures had been offered for the occasion and the final selection of 103 covered seventy years of the artist's working life from the early ink drawing of the *Chillingham Bulls* to a watercolour sketch of *Arkle: Cheltenham Gold Cup* dated 1966. Included were some of his finest studies of polo, racing and country scenes but the exhibitions, attended by over 12,000 members of the public, established beyond question that in the field of British sporting art Lionel Edwards remained the peerless master of the hunting picture.

With field sports in serious jeopardy the occasion was not only a tribute to a great sporting artist but a social documentary of the twentieth century sporting scene, much of which appears to be heading for extinction not only because of the ill-informed activities of the anti-blood sports factions but equally by political pressures, changing methods of agriculture and animal husbandry and by increasing urban infiltration into rural areas. In the pictures of Lionel Edwards, future generations will find realisation of a golden age that has disappeared for ever.

NOTES

1 Lionel Edwards, RI, *Reminiscences of a Sporting Artist*, p. 11.

2 ibid, p. 205.

3 ibid, p. 32.

4 Oxers, i.e., a hedge with a rail and a ditch to guard against cattle on the take-off side. A double oxer had a rail and ditch both sides of the fence. They were still being constructed in the Atherstone country in 1935 as described in Lionel Edwards' *A Leicestershire Sketchbook*, Eyre & Spottiswoode, London, 1935, p. 40.

5 Letter to the author, 2 January 1979.

6 Letter to the author, 3 January 1979.

7 Edwards, *Reminiscences*, p. 203.

8 ibid. p. 39.

9 ibid. p. 204.

10 ibid, p. 204.

11 Major Guy Paget in *The Field*, 29 April 1944, p. 450.

12 Reginald Pound, *The Englishman: A Biography of Sir Alfred Munnings*, p. 182.

13 See Appendix One, p. 207.

14 Pound, *The Englishman*, p. 182.

8

Munnings: The Master

British sporting art over the years has remained something of closed book to the average visitor to national and commercial art galleries. But various public appeals in the last two decades to prevent pictures by George Stubbs from being sold abroad, and the splendid exhibition of his works in 1984/85 at the Tate Gallery, has resulted in Stubbs being the one name that has made an impact with the man in the street. As a result the question often debated in the popular press becomes the headline 'Who is the Stubbs of the twentieth century?' A nonsensical question and unanswerable. Stubbs was unique, one of the world's greatest animal artists, who outrivalled every contemporary. Genius is not repetitive and Stubbs is incomparable.

Nevertheless modernists acclaim Alfred Munnings as the Stubbs of our day and coherent analogies can be made. Stubbs' certainty that Nature was superior to Art is equated by Munnings' inviolate conviction that 'All I've done that is any good is from Nature.'[1] Both, against their own volition and better judgement, became fashionable horse artists for the aristocratic bloodstock owners of their day. George Stubbs acquired the appellation of 'Mr Stubbs the Horse Painter' and Alfred Munnings was admiringly referred to by the Duke of Westminster as 'Mr Stubbs'.

Both artists possessed natural versatility far beyond the equestrian scene; either could have made successful careers in portraiture or as landscape painters. Stubbs also excelled as an engraver, an anatomist and in his work in ceramics; Munnings rarely ventured away from the easel and brush but he used watercolours with virtuosity, his talent as a sculptor was considerable though virtually unexploited. He was a compulsive writer with his fluent three volume autobiography a masterpiece of memory and wit. That sporting art should have been the major motivation of both these great artists has brought unequivocal distinction to the subject. Stubbs' paramount position is unassailable but Munnings will, in due time, assuredly be claimed the master of the twentieth century.

In artistic identity the artists share a common inspiration, though traits of personal character and temperament could hardly be more diverse: Stubbs, reserved, detached and with little pleasure in social participation and Munnings, convivial, the complete extrovert who, violent in his likes and dislikes, came to be regarded as the last of the English Sporting Eccentrics. He could quote at length both Byron and Surtees, compose bawdy ballads, ride cross country and mix as happily with poachers as peers. Forthright, illogical, quick tempered and often insufferably brash, conversely no man on occasions was more generous, courteous and sympathetic.

For those who knew him well he seemed to possess a dual personality occasioned almost certainly by the three tragedies in his life. When only twenty he lost the sight of his right eye; in 1912 marriage to the lovely, but mentally unstable Florence Carter-Wood, herself an artist, ended, unconsummated, less than two years later in her suicide by cyanide poisoning, and from the age of thirty he was plagued and heavily handicapped by the agonies of gout to finish his final days, his hands immobilised, unable to paint. His philosophy to eat, drink and be merry for 'art is long but life is short' was a necessary façade to mask a recurring melancholy.

Alfred James Munnings, born on 8 October 1878 at Mendham in Suffolk, was the second of four sons of a yeoman milling family with both parents of farming stock. At Mendham Mill, the largest on the Waveney, he passed his childhood in idyllic surroundings with the white weather-boarded buildings, ducks on the stream, the poplars and willows lining the river valley all as tranquil and unspoilt as in the days of Constable. From his infancy drawing was instinctive, compulsive and a constant delight with the subject inevitably equine, whether his father's 14 hh roadsters or heavy Suffolk Punches, imaginary highwaymen or Indian mustangs. Munnings had been born into a world of horses and all his long life he was himself a horseman, starting on his much loved pony Merrylegs. Years later he was still maintaining that the artist to paint horses and people must ride himself.

Education started with drawing lessons from the parson's daughter, then a spell at the village school and at Redenhall Commercial School where the headmaster encouraged him to draw, followed by four unhappy terms at Framlingham College when he was severely caned for sketching in class.

At fourteen years old, for a premium of forty pounds, he was apprenticed for six years to Page Bros & Co., a firm of Norfolk lithographers and letterpress printers. Long hours from nine until seven he remembered as engrossing and enthralling and then, with energy unabated, he would rush off to work at the Norwich School of Art for a further two hours instruction at sixpence a week. It was this training as a lithographer that developed a linear precision and accuracy which was to prove invaluable to the future artist. Fees were earned for freelance poster work and box designs for such progressive firms as Colman's Mustard (*39*), Bullard's Brewery and Caley's Chocolates for, in spite of growing enjoyment of the good things of life, for roistering pub parties and gregarious sing-songs, during his entire professional career he was a man of immense industry and application, a discipline made necessary in his youth by financial stringency.

Horizons were widened by the criticism and advice of the notable James Reeve, the curator of the Norwich Castle Art Gallery and the most informed authority on the Norfolk School of Painting. The opportunity to study Reeve's valuable private collections of pictures by Crome and Constable proved a vital influence at an impressionable age.

While still an apprentice Munnings exhibited at the Royal Institute of Watercolour Artists, and in 1899 came 'the greatest day of my life'[2] with the news that two of his paintings (executed when he was only eighteen years old) had been accepted by the Royal Academy, the first of 289 pictures to follow. Both were river scenes devoid of equestrian interest: *Stranded*, an enchanting study of two children in a boat, the little girl in a bright blue dress and *Pike-Fishing in January*, a chill winter afternoon at Lavenham Mill near Norwich with pollarded willows, dead reeds and sedges and a friend, 'Jumbo' Betts, posed with a willow pole for his rod on the bank, a foretaste of the myriad of lovely river scenes of the future. It sold for ten guineas and the celebration visit to Bungay Races became another milestone in the artist's life. The colour and exciting action in brilliant sunlight of this kaleidoscope of horse fair, races, shooting galleries, swing boats, gypsies and jockeys transfixed Munnings. It was a scene never forgotten and imaginatively recalled until his dying day, but immediately recorded in four impressionist pastel drawings that sold for twenty pounds.

With his apprenticeship finished, some financial success already achieved, half a carpenter's shop at Mendham acquired as a studio and commissions from Mr Shaw Tomkins, director of Caley's, coming in, future prosperity seemed assured. In one afternoon this golden prospect was shattered, as while he was lifting a foxhound puppy over a fence a twig rebounded and pierced Munnings' right eye. After treatment at Moorfields Hospital in London many weeks were passed in bed being professionally nursed in Norwich, half his head swathed in bandages. Fortitude, blasphemy and sympathetic visitors who read Surtees and poetry lines, to linger word perfect for life in his memory, saw him through the ordeal and then the long battle to learn to paint with monocular vision had to be won. Permanently handicapped by confused perspectives, by impaired judgment of distance and in actual application of paint, forty years later the artist still wrote 'What wouldn't I give to see with two eyes again.'[3] Finally in old age his good eye, after half a century of its double burden, began to weaken and caused him intense concern.

Though later he made his name as a painter of Thoroughbred racehorses, in the long term his enduring merit will be equally shared by his early pictures. Here his passionate love for the countryside and in particular for East Anglia provided his major inspiration. In his sensitive landscapes and river studies he reflects, with increasing talent, the traditions of Crome and Constable.

Expertise was acquired, not instinctively, but by trial and error, by struggles with composition and with constant reference to Stubbs' classic *The Anatomy of the Horse*, acquired for fifty shillings (a minor fortune for an impecunious artist in those days) and which became a landmark in his life and led to his mastery of horse structure, form and stance, to result in 1902 in such a youthful masterpiece as *The Timber Gill*, measuring 55 × 33 inches with its pair of horses, chestnut and bay, against a background of massive elms, a work considered by Munnings as one of his finest. He wrote at the age of twenty-two, 'I shall never do anything so good again' – a false prophesy of course!

During the first years of the new century Mendham village, its locals, its corners and by-lanes were his painting grounds with attendance at some of Frank Calderon's summer schools where

39 Alfred James Munnings KCVO, PRA, *Design for Colman's Mustard*, *c* 1898. Watercolour and bodycolour, 12 × 18 in (39.4 × 45.7 cm).

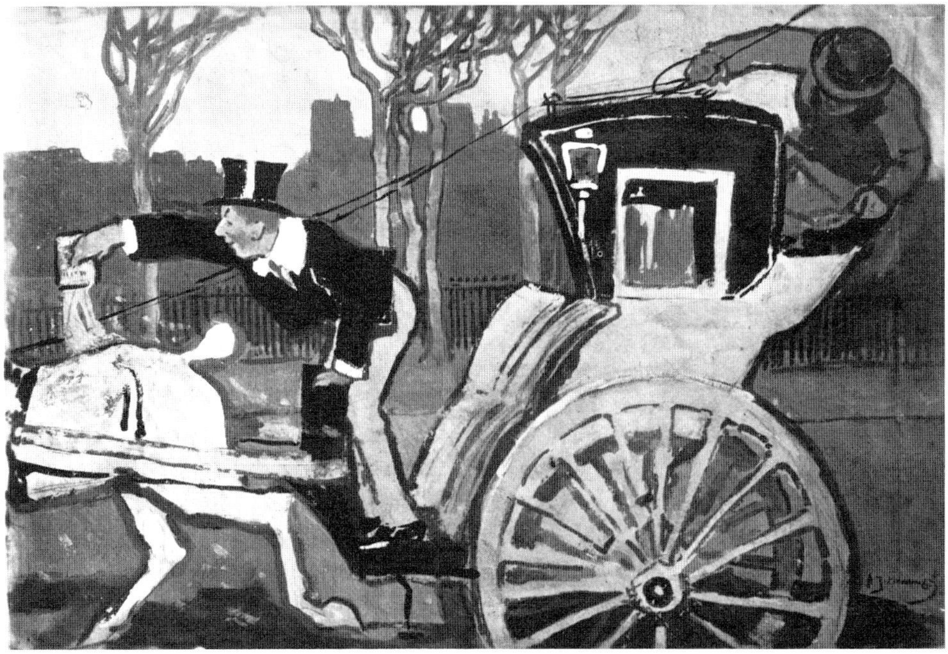

the country youth found himself not artistically, but socially, outclassed. Nevertheless friendships flourished and influential contacts were made. But Munnings never assumed the veneer of sophistication even in his days of the Presidency of the Royal Academy. The hint of the Norfolk accent with his final dropped g's always remained; pepper and salt tweeds were worn with a jaunty bow tie instead of a conventional dark suit and he was described by Laura Knight as having the airs of a poet and the looks of a stable boy.

It was Mr Shaw Tomkins, a director of Caley's and a staunch Congregationalist, but also possessed of an immense capacity for enjoyment, who widened the young Munnings' rural horizon, took him abroad as companion on several business trips and introduced him to art galleries in France, Germany and Holland. It proved an enlightening and rewarding experience and in 1902/3 and later, like many of his sporting art contemporaries, he made valuable visits to the *Atelier* Julian in Paris. Understandably this academy of art possessed an irresistible allure for young English artists. Situated in the Rue du Dragon it was the largest private art school in the city, attracting students of all nationalities and was named after its founder, an ex-prize-fighter and model. By the end of the century it was being visited by important established painters and sculptors at Julian's invitation. But the studio was noisy and cramped, caricatures and crude jokes interrupted serious work. Charles Furse described it as 'crowded with dirty brutes of every nationality, hot, filthy and revolting.'[4] Nevertheless the Bohemian atmosphere, after the narrow confines of the Norwich School of Art, proved a stimulating experience for convivial Munnings or 'AJ' as he became known. Here he painted a superb nude study of a posed girl model – an arresting change of subject to be exhibited over half a century later in the Diploma Gallery at the Royal Academy.

The impact at Versailles of the huge battle pieces by Aimé Morot left him spellbound but it was the delight and motivation experienced by the pictures in the Paris galleries that provided the real awakening. Here paintings by the French Impressionists inspired him to contrast reflected sunlight and shadow, to animate form and also to attack direct with the brush, and endowed Munnings with an artistic vision that endured all his life. An exciting spontaneity and virtuosity became the hallmark of his style and the influence of the Impressionists took over from the East Anglian School. He was to write, 'What are pictures for? To fill a man's soul with admiration and sheer joy, not to bewilder and daze him.'[5] A theme interwoven into his philosophy to his dying day and to provide the fuel for his famous Royal Academy dinner speech nearly half a century later. Gradually by sheer merit and application he achieved a wider reputation which enabled him to buy horses of his own as models and, of course, to use as hunters. Here the artist and the sportsman vied for supremacy, for the love of hunting as with Aldin, Armour and Edwards threatened his career. He hunted with the Norwich Staghounds and the Dunston Harriers, always riding with long leathers and leaning a little backwards and, according to the first-hand opinion of John Skeaping, was a poor horseman, but he walked hound puppies, haunted hunt kennels and hacked to far distant meets.

However he kept his head, painted horse portraits at ten pounds a time and for two summers he established himself with a caravanseri, travelling the countryside with a string of seven or eight horses, bays, browns and chestnuts and always including the old white Welsh mare with an Arabian profile, a donkey, dogs plus a dilapidated caravan and a flat cart in charge of a boon character, the recalcitrant gypsy lad George Fountain Page, known as 'Shrimp', who was to feature so prominently in many compositions. Here he could fulfil his destiny as a painter of the 'open air', where the influence of Claude Monet with his conviction that three strokes out of doors in front of the subject itself were better than days of application

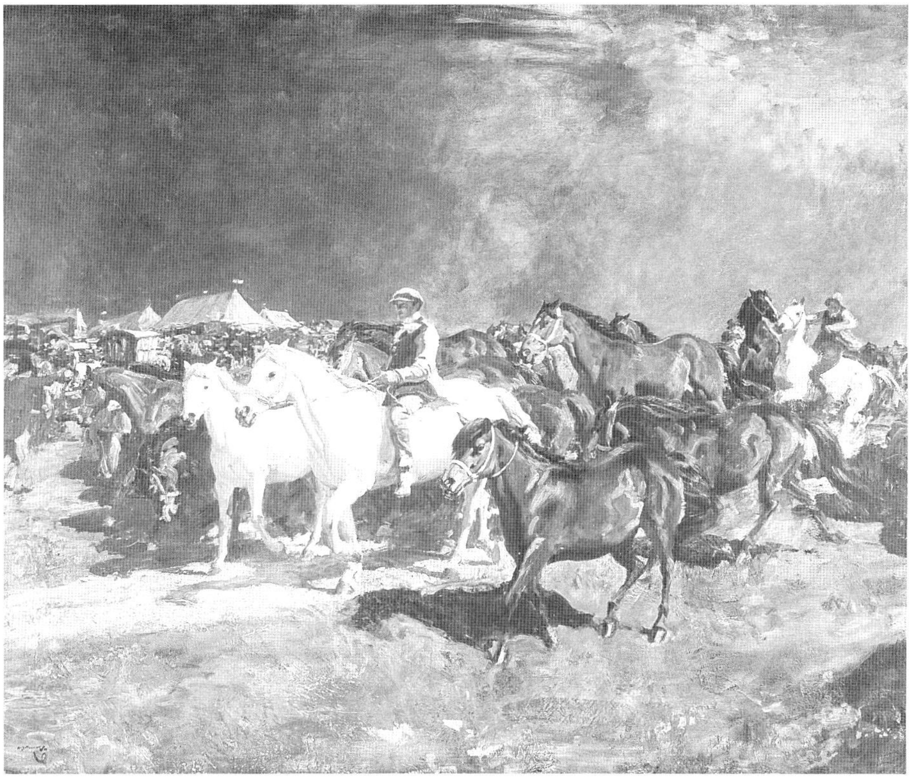

40 Alfred James Munnings KCVO, PRA, *The Coming Storm*, 1910. Oil on canvas, $58\frac{3}{4} \times 72$ in (149.2 × 182.8 cm).

in the studio, matched Munnings' own irresistible reaction to actual sunlight and country settings.

Months would be spent with Shrimp in this vagabond existence in the Ringland Hills, camping, painting, regaling at the local inns, visiting every local horse fair and farm sale. From this period came the lovely pastoral paintings of donkeys on Crostwick Common, landscapes with cows, of reed cutting by the river, of Augereau, the white pony 'that perfect model' standing in the old gravel-pit; and best of all the study of the buxom Charlotte, mother of a tinker family, leading the chestnut pony beside a well-clipped hedge. This composition of high summer, gleaming with colour, was hung on the line in 1907 in the Royal Academy. There were pictures of horse dealing, of courting couples at local fairs. His output was prodigious; he first completed several small canvases (24 × 20 in) executed on the spot, before attempting a big 40 × 50 in composition and some of the subjects were finished in half a dozen different versions wrestling with changing light and reflections. From these expeditions he produced such masterpieces as *The Coming Storm* with Shrimp riding the white mare, droving a melée of ponies against a distant background of a fair and tents and overhead the dark brooding sky (*40*). The final large version was exhibited in the Royal Academy in 1925; it was bought for the Art Gallery of New South Wales for £850. In simpler vein his small study of *A Boy in a Barn with Two Greyhounds* illustrates the artist's mastery of place, character and form which was to stamp all his work (*Plate 10*).

When autumn evenings drew in he returned to the studio and rooms rented for six years at one end of Church Farm at Swainsthorpe, bought a hunter, kept a groom and painted local hunting scenes. Though AJ loved the magic of sport with horse and hounds (though he abhorred the kill) later, in actual fact, it was as much the joy of studying the stark outlines of the countryside in winter as the excitement of the chase that proved irresistible.

In the late summer of 1910 he made his first visit to Cornwall and set up stables and studio at Lamorna. He hunted with Mr Bolitho's Hounds, painted the moorland landscape, met members of the Newlyn artists' colony, including Stanhope Forbes, Augustus John, Harold and, more especially, Laura Knight who became a lifelong friend. But though identified with the Newlyn School, as an artist Munnings had little direct connection with it. Socially, however, he was one of its leading spirits and here he encountered his future wife, the beautiful Florence Carter-Wood. The change of scenery triggered off some dramatic pictures with the rolling Atlantic and rugged boulders as background to horses and hounds; notable amongst these was *The Top of Zennor* with its dock-tailed cob dominating the horizon. A local lad, Ned Osborne, who became a useful groom, also acted as model as Munnings considerd he had the right colouring, face and figure for a scarlet coat. Painted in 1913, *Going to The Meet* ranks as one of the finest early hunting studies with Ned as huntsman on a striking big grey mare (Grey Tick, owned by a local farmer) coming directly down the hill with hounds silhouetted against a bright sky – a magical composition (*41*).

Between visits to Cornwall, Munnings began in 1913 to stay at Alton in Hampshire where 200–300 gypsies would be encamped for the hop-picking. It was a subject that was to prove one of the great inspirations of his career. AJ quickly established a rich stimulating relationship with the Romanys who appreciated his lively manner and earthy vocabulary and called him 'Mr Money' and he respected, but never romanticised, their racial mystique and importunate mode of living. Amongst them he found memoraable models and a wealth of painting material.

From these visits emerged such brilliant compositions as *Gypsy Life: The Hop-Pickers* now in the Paul Mellon Collection and *The Departure of the Hop-Pickers*, bought by the National Gallery of Victoria, Melbourne. And in later years such masterpieces as *Epsom Downs: City and Suburban Day* with its carved caravan, flamboyant gypsy woman with ostrich feathers and black ringlets, the lurcher dog and restive cob all present a contagious sense of joy and vitality (*42*). Purchased by the Chantrey Trust this picture is now in the Tate Gallery.

With the outbreak of the First World War Munnings was rejected for the Army on two occasions – there was no military future for a one-eyed soldier. But eventually service as an official war artist attached to the Canadian Cavalry Brigade brought far-reaching opportunities and was to prove a vital turning point in his career; a story to be told later.

It was in 1919, elected an ARA with a steady income and potential prosperity assured, he took a well-lit studio in Chelsea and then, in a moment of impulse, Munnings bought for £1,800 Castle House at Dedham in the heart of the Constable country. 'The house of my dreams' with its mixture of Tudor and Georgian periods, a coach house, stable, gardens and paddocks and gracious bow windows opening on to a distant view of the river Stour. In addition there were also two cottages and thirty acres of pastures for horses and later the Swainsthorpe studio which he had uprooted and rebuilt in the grounds of his new home.

But it was to prove a love-hate relationship. Never afterwards was AJ to feel free from the responsibilities of having become a man of property and eventually the owner of thirty-three horses! It entailed painting for money and dimming of his inspiration.

But his personal star was in the ascendant and in the same year at the Richmond Horse Show he was struck by the beauty and elegance of a rider in the Ladies Hunter Class with a white gardenia in her buttonhole. This consummate horsewoman was a young widow, Mrs Violet McBride, daughter of Goldby Haines, a noted Edgware riding master who had achieved considerable success in the equestrian world. Though temperamentally unsuited to the marital state, their marriage the following March (which was childless), was to prove for the artist a halcyon haven from the practicalities of life. Violet Munnings not only recognised her husband's genius but was also an astute and clear-headed organiser and shared AJ's love of horses. He gave her a power of attorney and, allegedly, is said to have visited his bank himself only twice again in the next forty years.

Violet, by no means herself a model of tolerance, suffered his unpredictable behaviour and ill-temper with tact and understanding. She accepted the fact that AJ the dedicated countryman, was allied also to that character the obsessive clubman. His roistering evenings of lavish entertainment at the the Garrick, the Arts Club and even the Atheneum with such boon companions as Augustus John, William Orpen, William Nicholson, C.W. Nevinson and others had to be accepted along with his long absences from home fulfilling commissions. But his almost daily letters to her when away always reported progress of work in hand and scintillated with his affection and admiration. He was to write 'Your good influence and sweet kindness have been an endless source of wonder to me.'[6]

His marriage took place at a crucial moment in his career, for the exhibition of over 300 paintings and drawings of the Canadian Cavalry Brigade at the Royal Academy included forty-five works by Munnings. These, and especially the striking portrait of Major General the Rt Hon. J.E.B. Seely on Warrior, which took pride of place, had proved a catalyst to set alight his role as the equestrian artist of the day. A commissioned picture of Major General the Earl of Athlone in uniform on his charger was acclaimed a spendid likeness and brought immediate interest from leaders of high society and important bloodstock owners.

The first racehorse of popular renown he ever painted was Poethlyn, the winner of the 1919 Grand National, an evocative Aintree scene saddling up before the race, as well as another

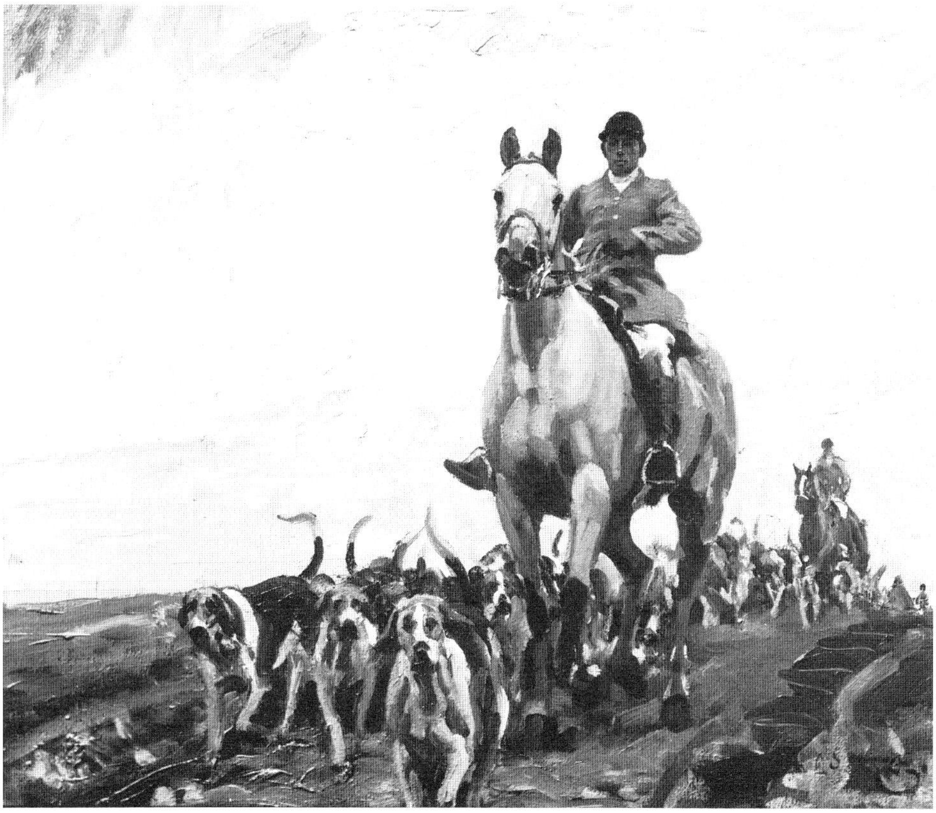

41 Alfred James Munnings KCVO, PRA, *Going to the Meet*, 1913. Oil on canvas, 20 × 24 in (50.8 × 60.9 cm).

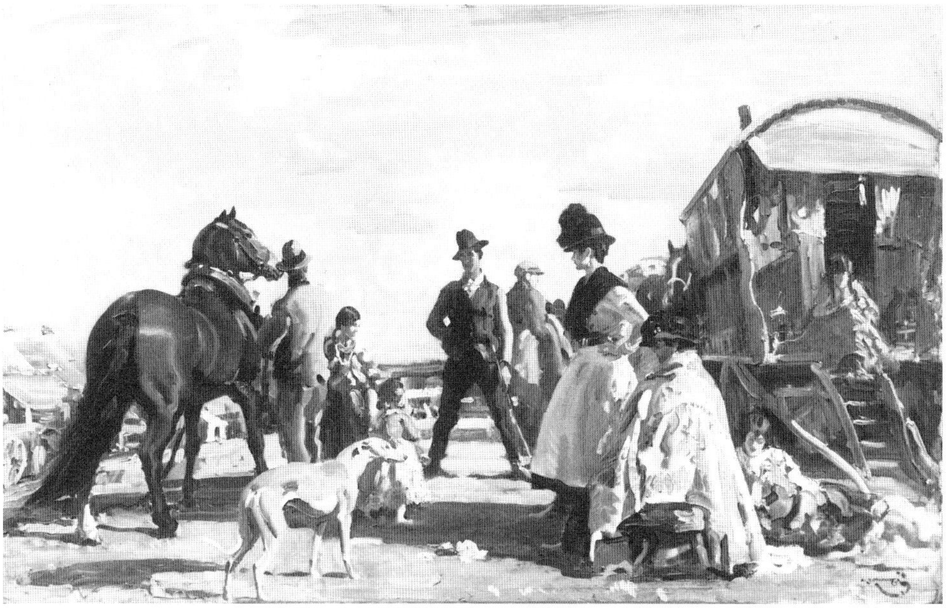

42 Alfred James Munnings KCVO, PRA, *Epsom Downs: City and Suburban Day*, 1919. Oil on canvas, $31\frac{1}{4} \times 50\frac{1}{2}$ in (79.3×127.2 cm).

study of the horse in the Peel's home paddocks at Brynpys in Flintshire with the owners, groom and greyhound. It was immediately followed by commissions from the rich Americans hunting from Melton Mowbray, from Masters of famous packs of hounds in the Shires and owners of Classic winners, all introducing him into high society and the country house atmosphere which he could never have contemplated in his bucolic Norfolk days, although these had left him devoid of pretensions and with the same free and unaffected manners for a sporting duke as for his stud groom. He would regale dinner table gossip to Violet in his letters from the Astors, from the palatial chateau of Baron Robert Rothschild 'absolutely the kindest fellow I have ever met' and then details of the St Hubert's Day Celebration with hounds received in the church at Chantilly. He dined with the Prince of Wales and his brother, Prince Henry, and 'blessed if I didn't have to do my ballad *Adrian Bell* after dinner. What a go!'

A portrait of the Prince of Wales on Forest Witch followed, commissioned by Sir Theodore Cook, editor of *The Field*, to be presented to the foxhunting heir to the Throne. Munnings ordered a six foot canvas, Sir Theodore attended every sitting, regaled His Royal Highness with vintage port and readings from Surtees. Exhibited by special permission at the Royal Academy the picture attracted great attention, but the artist himself always felt the ancient oak played too forcible a part in the composition and he deplored the current fashion of hogged manes and pulled tails that marred the beauty of the mare.

Munnings' hunting scenes possess the authority of a man who could assert 'I pride myself that I know what a well-bred weight-carrying horse should look like' and also one who understood the symmetry of a good hound. Allied to brilliant sky and landscape effects the final result, whether it is Ned, the Cornish lad jumping the hairy place in the many times reproduced picture *The Huntsman* or, in contrast, Frank Freeman on Pilot in the Pytchley country, has a touch of magic. What superb pictures he painted of the Pytchley and Belvoir Hounds in kennels and equally skilful is the portrayal of the elegant women side-saddle in the Shires in *Why Weren't You Out Yesterday?*

In later life Munnings always deplored the fact that women riding side-saddle had not more often formed the subject for his pictures. Certainly no equestrian artist, before or since, has captured more enchantingly the svelte sophistication of an attractive woman correctly turned out on a Thoroughbred horse. Beautiful Violet Munnings on one of their own hunters often provided the model. *Two Busvines and a Cutaway* compliments the expertise of the fashionable tailor of the day for no woman between the two World Wars, with any pretensions to style and form, would consider a habit made by any firm but the famous Busvine in the West End of London (*43*).[7] To accompany the two impeccable Dianas the artist presents the equivalent male foxhunter in obligatory white breeches and double-breasted swallow tail scarlet coat below which the points of the canary waistcoat are visible. This cutaway coat (or Shadbelly as it was known in the Pytchley Hunt) became almost compulsory uniform in the hunting field for any young, slim man wishing to catch the eye of the ladies and cut a dash across country. Munnings with his practical understanding of the milieu turned what might have been a mere fashion plate into a picture in which lurks a hint of flirtation allied to the keen anticipation of a day with hounds. Among successful commissions for the Royal Family was another side-saddle study with Princess Mary in 1930 on Portumna, a free-striding Irish grey horse, in the woods near Harewood House. Finished in three sittings on three consecutive balmy spring mornings AJ regarded it as 'my best equestrian open air portrait.'[8]

It was Queen Mary with typical perspicacity who suggested a picture of *The Ascot Procession Crossing Windsor Park* which resulted in 1926 in Munnings' *tour de force* – movement, portraiture, landscape and a sense of occasion brilliantly combined in a wonderful composition. In his autobiography he records in vivid prose the drama and detail of the basic preparations for the task. Crisis occurred when it was found the measurement of the canvas to include the length of the four horse equipage and cavalcade was misjudged and an extra piece was, at the crucial moment, machined on by the Windsor upholsterers for the ten foot stretcher.

Not only were astute likenesses of the King and Queen and the Princess Royal cleverly achieved but each postillion and each grey horse and scarlet coated footman assumed recognisable personality. After completion in the artist's London studio King George was immensely impressed with the picture and it was a major attraction in the Royal Academy in 1926. Munnings painted a large companion picture *Their Majesties' Return From Ascot* which was bought in 1938 for £850 through the Chantrey Bequest for the Tate Gallery where, sadly, it spends most of its time below stairs (*44*).

Elected a full Royal Academician, aptly, on Derby Day 1926, it was during the decades 1920–1940 that Munnings' career rocketed to popular fame and success with his portrayals of the Classic racehorses of the day. Commissions poured in – 'Damn it – no' was the artist's reaction but conscience prevailed, 'better men that I spent their lives in painting commissioned pictures.' A trip to the United States in 1924 resulted in many of the richest sporting Americans becoming his patrons, greatly to his financial advantage.

Stubbs' entrée into the bloodstock world resulted in some superb portraits for the ambitious aristocratic owners of the day. Munnings' pictures of twentieth century racehorses are destined to become as equally important for future generations of Thoroughbred breeders and art historians as the wonderful eighteenth and nineteenth century portrayals of Dungannon and Gimcrack by Stubbs and of Marshall's Zinganee and Mameluke and Herring's Rubini and Manuella.

Between the two World Wars racing was to soar to a zenith of popularity with enthusiastic crowds flocking to meetings. Organisation was immeasurably improved with a new type of starting gate introduced in 1929 and then three years later the Derby was the first race to be televised. Such astute owners as Lord Astor, Lord Derby, Sir Abe Bailey and the Aga Khan were all vying for Classic supremacy, and each demanding that their horses would be portrayed for posterity by the finest equestrian artist of the day. Munnings maintained that his only real happiness lay in his art but often he bemoaned the fact that painting racehorses drove him to despair: 'the difficulties and troubles of horse painting which are a hundredfold . . . But no writing can give any idea of the intricacies, the colour tones and knowledge of horse anatomy conglomerated together in the mind of one who's trying to paint a horse, I often think when looking at an old horse picture that the artist has been up against the same problem.'[9]

Swamped by commissions which, financially, he felt unable to refuse, like most prolific artists, Munnings painted too much. Nevertheless his portraits of the contemporary Thoroughbred must be considered amongst the classic works of British sporting art, and unexpectedly, in spite of desperate doubts and struggles in their execution, they brought Munnings considerable satisfaction and pleasure. He revelled in the fine conformation, exciting coat tones and varied settings of these horses: of the 1923 Grand National winner, Sergeant Murphy, with The Drifter, second the previous year turned out together against the background of dark elms and a dovecote 'such as no artist's imagination could invent', Sir Abe Bailey's Foxlaw, winner of the 1927 Ascot Gold Cup 'so dark a brown he could almost be described as black' and the Aga Khan's record breaking 1936 Derby winner, Mahmoud, with dappled quarters and Arabian head painted whilst Munnings was enduring the agonies of gout, and little Hyperion, the bright chestnut winner of the following year for Lord Derby. He was a lazy horse at home but nevertheless went on to win the St Leger and Munnings painted a wonderful picture of him silhouetted against green pastures and summer sky with his 'lad', sturdy Chinery, whose stout calves seem to be bursting out of his canvas leggings (*Plate 10*). Munnings, like Stubbs, possessed an uncanny gift for presenting the quiet dignified relationship between grooms and hunt servants with their horses and hounds.

In the scores of commissioned portraits of Thoroughbreds, by some curious alchemy, the artist avoided any repetitive monotony. The standing pose never became completely static; by the turn of a head, the pricked ears, a raised foreleg, the picture is brought to life. And never more arrestingly than in the study of *Mr Jinks, the Neighing Stallion* – with superb crest, flowing mane and tail like a plume. Munnings wrote of him – 'What more beautiful thing could there be in creation?'[10] Equally he could suggest the character of a horse as with the legendary Brown Jack, six times winner of the long distance Queen Alexandra Stakes at Ascot 1929–1934, but a kind, intelligent unassuming champion, who spent six weeks at Castle House to be painted by Munnings for his owner, Sir Harold Wernher, and also modelled in bronze for the Jockey Club, a beautiful reincarnation of a horse nationally beloved.

Munnings possessed a penetrating talent for recording movement though he only occasionally depicted pace; his picture of Viscount Astor's bay filly Saucy Sue winning the 1925 Oaks is a rare exception. His numerous scenes of starts at Newmarket scintillate with animation and with magical colour effects of vivid silks against the sky but these young excited horses are rarely seen galloping. These compositions held a wide public appeal and for him never lost a perpetual fascination. He filled scores of sketch books with drawings and notes, 'My mind was saturated with the subject', and he used one of the famous rubbing down houses on the Heath as a painting room, often working there during remissions from ever increasing attacks of gout. After his death critics during the 1970s began their denigration, dismissing these scenes as facile and slick and, certainly sometimes their impressionism verged on superficiality, but not all the examples that have begun to appear in the sale rooms with the distinctive flowing A.J. Munnings signature are authentic. It is a subject too easily reproduced but only

Munnings himself could capture convincingly the hallmark of substance in conformation and transparency in the coat of a well-groomed Thoroughbred.

In contrast to the sunlit racing days of summer were the scenes at Cheltenham of *The Saddling Paddock* and *After the Race* with grey winter skies, big horses with strong shoulders and their muffled attendants, where Munnings presented, just as confidently, that other world of racing 'over the sticks'. Steeplechasing had remained the poor relation of the turf – the pastime of the sportsman rather than of the racing man, but prestige had been achieved at Cheltenham with the inauguration of the Gold Cup in 1924 and three years later of the Champion Hurdle Race.

With the outbreak of the Second World War, Castle House was commandeered by the Army and AJ with the horses finally joined Violet in Withypool to enjoy a halcyon period. Too old for any active service, unharassed by commissions, here his passion for the English countryside took over; painting scenes of the wide sweeps of moorland, the marshes near Porlock and the groups of wandering Exmoor ponies, his days were filled with delight.

But in March 1944 Munnings was elected President of the Royal Academy, receiving twenty-four votes in the ballot against eleven for Augustus John. It was an honour accepted with pride but not without some trepidation. Violet warned him of the inevitable official ties and responsibilities but doubtless he gave a thought to the authority of office, the dignity of achievement and to his historic mentor Sir Joshua Reynolds, the very first President and then perhaps to Sir Francis Grant who took office in 1866 and had also started his career as a sporting painter. Congratulations poured in, from humble contacts of his Norfolk boyhood to some of the most illustrious figures in the world of art, politics and the judiciary.

Munnings, though cursing the duties that brought him to London so frequently, fulfilled

43 Alfred James Munnings KCVO, PRA, *Two Busvines and a Cutaway.* Oil on canvas, 25 × 29 in (63.5 × 73.6 cm).

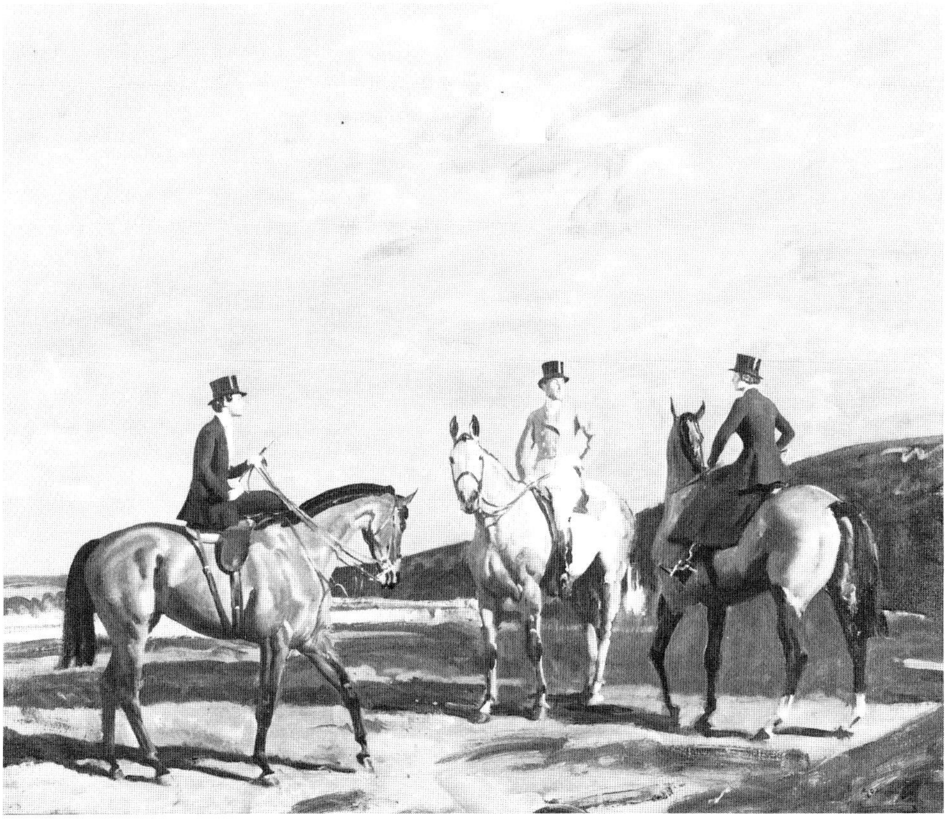

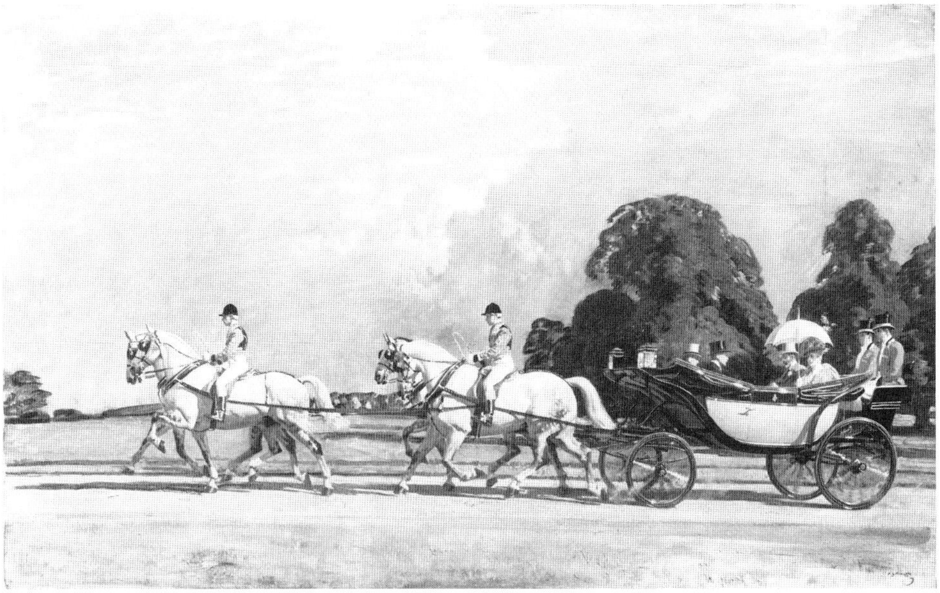

44 Alfred James Munnings KCVO, PRA, *Their Majesties' Return from Ascot*, 1925. Oil on canvas, 30 × 40 in (76.2 × 101.6 cm).

his official position with diligence for five years. He enjoyed, of course, the historic traditions and revelled in the camaraderie of the Royal Academy dining club. He received with a suitable display of reluctance and modesty, though with inward pride the insignia of the KCVO from the King, but lied about his swollen hand in a sling – 'a sprained wrist, sir,' too embarrassed to admit to the wretched gout. With even greater pleasure and gratification he became a Freeman of the City of Norwich for his 'service to culture' – here, indeed, he was the local boy made good.

But inevitably it was a Presidency fraught by problems. Munnings, with a total lack of administrative ability added to his explosive temper and exaggerated prejudices, was temperamently unsuited to the diplomatic demands of the position. He carried his intolerance of all modern art to the point of obsession and never failed to voice his opinion. For him, basically, art was sacrosanct and should not suffer the whims of fashion or unschooled innovation. New liberal policies being put forward by the Council infuriated him, his reactions possibly ascerbated by increasing ill-health and attacks of gout.

At the Royal Academy Banquet on 18 April 1949, the first for ten years, in the presence of the Duke of Gloucester, the Archbishop of Canterbury, Winston Churchill and Lord Montgomery, Munnings, now seventy-one, made his famous speech which has reverberated into history.[11] Speaking from the heart, forthright and honest but tactless, arrogant and transgressing all the rules of good taste for such a formal occasion, Munnings pursued the theme that modern art was 'foolish drolleries' being foisted on a gullible public. Picasso and Matisse were dismissed as daubers and he brought under vicious attack contemporary critics, the Arts Council, the Tate Gallery and accused his fellow Royal Academicians of 'shilly shallying' and defiling tradition. 'If you paint a tree for God's sake try and make it look like a tree, and if you paint a sky, try and make it look like a sky.' It was an occasion never to be forgiven or forgotten by the Establishment and as a live broadcast achieved major publicity. Any official support for a future National Gallery of Sporting Art was killed. In mitigation it was suggested that the President had dined not wisely but too well; in actual fact he was recovering from an attack of gout and had for once been completely abstemious.[12]

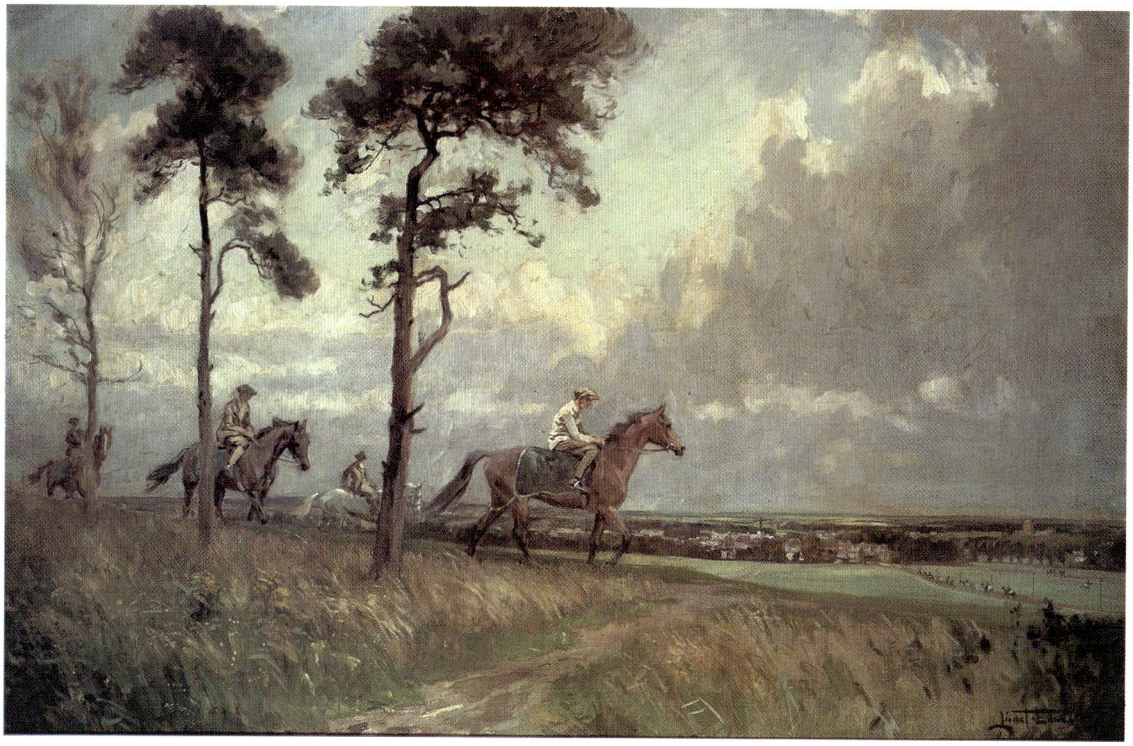

PLATE 9 (*above*) Lionel Dalhousie Robertson Edwards, *Newmarket: Warren Hill*, 1932. Oil on canvas, $19\frac{1}{2} \times 29$ in (49.5×73.6 cm). Photo lithograph. (*below*) Lionel Dalhousie Robertson Edwards, *The Mockers*, *c* 1925. Gouache, $13\frac{3}{4} \times 20$ in (34.9×50.8 cm).

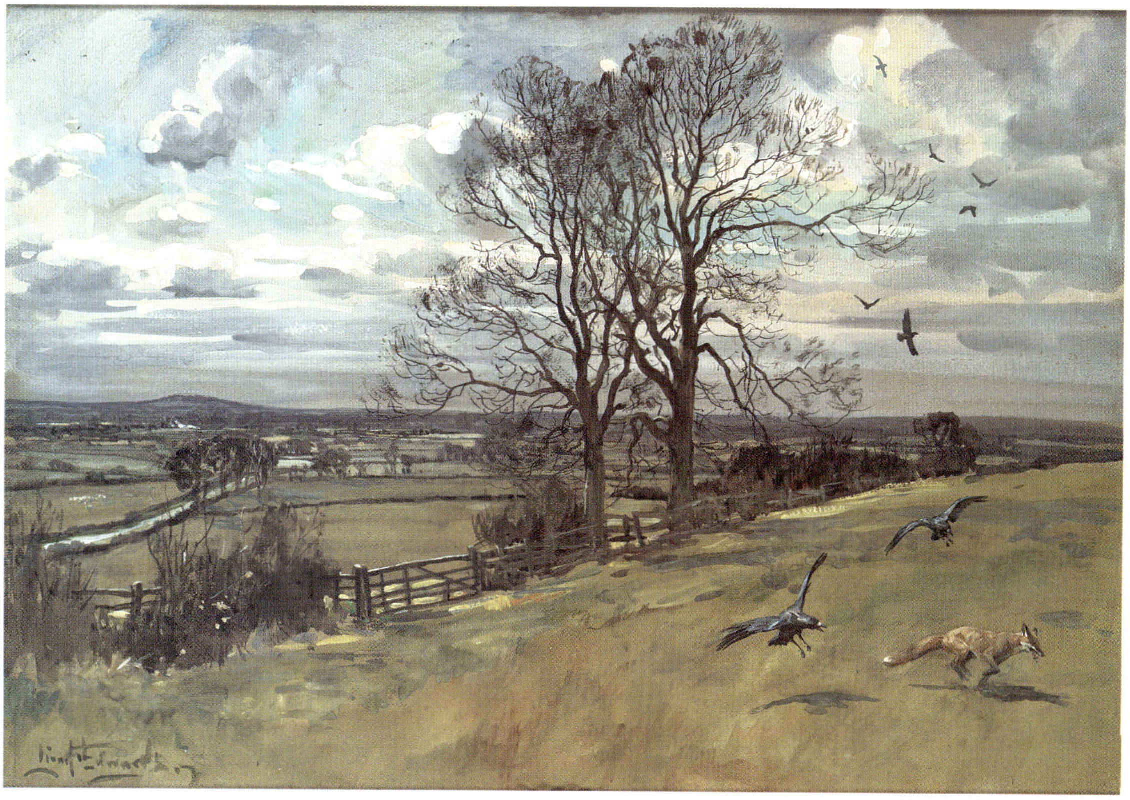

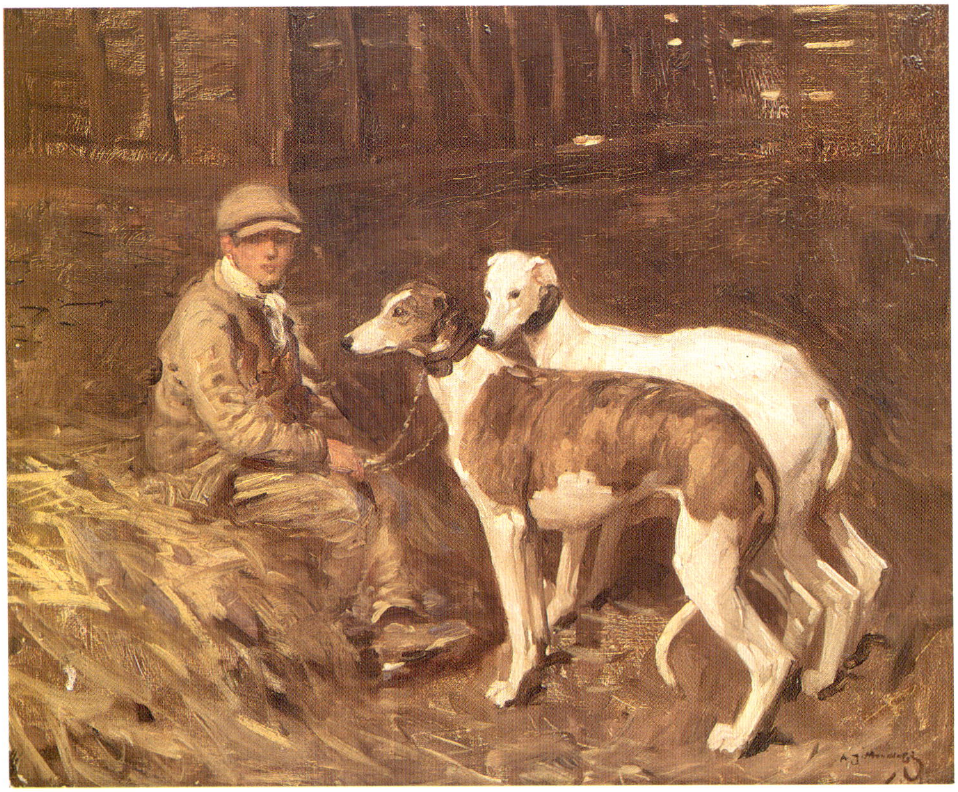

PLATE 10 (*left*) Alfred James Munnings, KCVO, PRA, *A Boy in a Barn with Two Greyhounds*. Oil on canvas, 20 × 24 in (50.8 × 60.9 cm).

(*right*) Alfred James Munnings, KCVO, PRA, *Hyperion*, 1937. Oil on canvas, 20 × 24 in (50.8 × 60.9 cm).

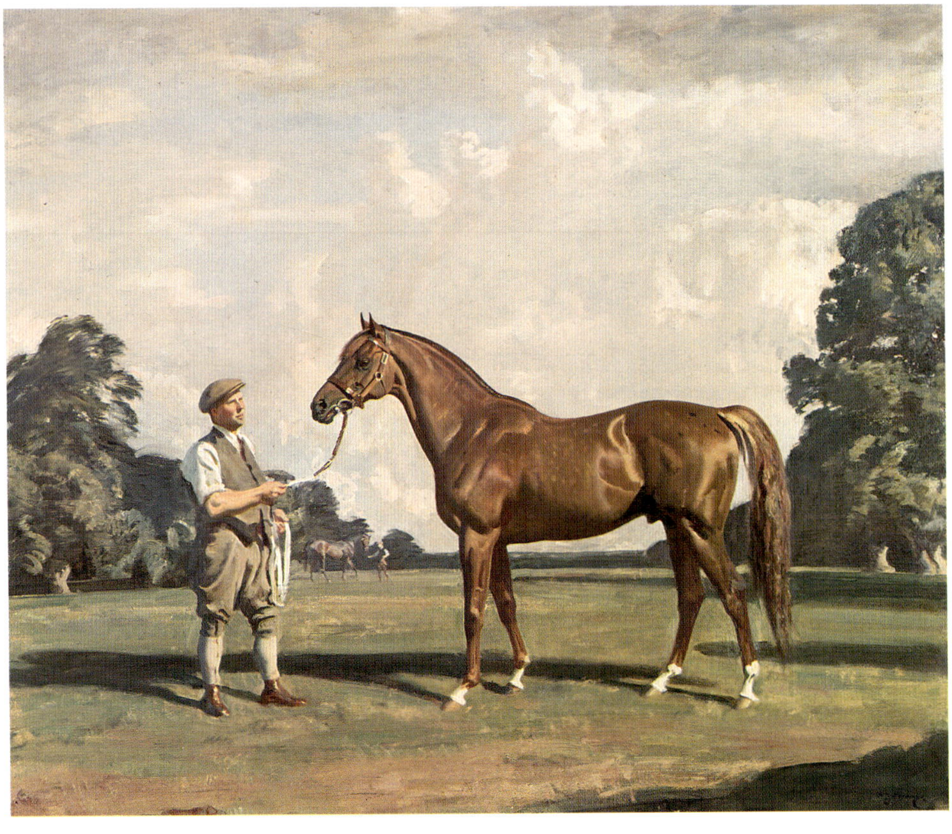

His speech not only created a sensation within the hallowed walls of Burlington House but by the following day had achieved headline priority in both the national and international press, as far afield as the United States and South Africa. Munnings himself was swamped by letters and telegrams of approbation and congratulations which continued for the next month. He had expressed much of the feelings of the common man recently confronted by a spate of complex abstract pictures which he could neither enjoy or understand. Housewives, hoteliers, doctors, clergymen, octogenarians, students and even the Secretary of the Transport Workers Union (sic) wrote to praise him for his 'blasts of clean fresh air'.[13] Many letters were reprinted in his autobiography including a half dozen in strident disagreement.

At the end of 1949 he resigned from the Presidency with relief on both sides and immersed himself in the writing of his autobiography in three successive volumes – *An Artist's Life*, *The Second Burst* and *The Finish* – determined to forestall all those who might distort facts about him after his death. From youth he had always been a compulsive writer and fluent versifier, keeping an erratic journal of lively comment, regularly corresponding copiously with his wife and friends, so rich material was available. Against his lyrical, vivid powers of description of people and scenes his total lack of literary discipline and sense of chronology ranked of minimal importance. But it is temperamentally indicative perhaps that AJ confided to his friend and mentor, Guy Schofield, editor of the *Evening News*, 'I cannot tell all.' There were hidden depths of melancholy in his character under the façade of bravado. Reginald Pound in his perceptive biography of Munnings, *The Englishman*, wrote, 'His imagination unfolded only in the aura of a past . . . to physically realised experience. It made for readability if for no more than surface truth.'[14] Nevertheless as a feat of memory, as an incomparable social record of the first half of the twentieth century and as a boisterous self portrait of the travails and triumphs of a great artist, the autobiography is a triumph. It won enthusiastic reviews and Munnings delighted in his acclaim as an author with a packed postbag of praise from friends and strangers, a party by the Times Book Club and a Foyles Literary Luncheon.

No more big pictures were attempted in his last years. After some final bitter skirmishes with the Royal Academy over his active antipathy to the works of Stanley Spencer amity was finally restored.[15] In the winter of 1951–1952 the Council invited him to give two lectures, one on Stubbs and the other on Constable. Both were an enormous success with over 600 tickets being sold in advance and each lasted two hours, double the traditional allotted time, but, as might be expected, not a dull moment! Final recognition of his national status was handsomely accorded in 1956 by a retrospective exhibition of 309 of his works in the Diploma Gallery at Burlington House.

Exhibitions of his pictures had not been numerous, though as long ago as 1921 the art critic, Paul Konody, had drawn attention to the quality of his work exhibited at the Alpine Gallery and in 1928, the civic authorities of Norwich had put on a collection of his paintings which had brought long queues of sightseers. Ten years later an exhibition at the Leicester Galleries in London had achieved social, but small financial, success in contrast to his show there in 1947 which broke all previous records in its volume of sales for any exhibition of a living artist in this country and earned him £20,788. In 1955 at the Russell Cotes Gallery at Bournemouth a retrospective exhibition proved a popular forerunner of the triumph at the Diploma Gallery.

In 1956 this last illuminating exhibition with over 300 pictures ranging from his first Royal Academy exhibit *Stranded*, painted in 1898 with the two children in their boat amongst the reeds of the Waveney river, to Augereau the white cob in the sandpit, the massive Friesian

Bull, (the splendid picture no one would buy), Canadian soldiers in Flanders, the Ascot cavalcade, gypsy scenes and glamorous hunting personalities in the Shires. In addition there were many tranquil landscapes such as *Winter at Flatford* and *May Blossom on Exmoor*. It covered a career that had lasted sixty years, and these pictures, with their penetrating observation and assured technique, also engaged the emotions with their remarkable impact. The flair of the equestrian scene allied to the poetic observation of the English country landscape left no doubt in the eye of the beholder that Munnings was a great artist.

Words in the catalogue Preface written by Anthony Devas, ARA, must have brought delight to AJ: 'Now that for the first time a big retrospective exhibition of his work has been arranged in London, it would be a beneficial thing there if all the artist students were encouraged to go and see it . . . For this is the real world – this delighted response to life, this love of simple and ordinary things, and the enormous skill and technical accomplishment displayed in the more elaborate commissioned works – that too is the real world for painters, for that craftsmanship is the backbone of the masterpieces of artists as diverse as Stubbs and Botticelli, Rembrandt and Degas.'

Professional criticism of the exhibition was mixed, an opportunity to pay off old scores was not to be resisted. But the public flocked to the Diploma Gallery, prices for his pictures soared and though none of the exhibits there was officially for sale several racing scenes privately fetched high prices (for those days) – *Coming Off the Heath*, £1000 and *Under Starter's Orders*, £1200. His last important racing portrait, painted later in the year, was of Her Majesty's chestnut Aureole, son of Hyperion, being saddled in the Paddock at Epsom before the 1955 Derby in which he ran second. Included, in the Ben Marshall tradition, are the royal owner, Captain Boyd Rochfort the trainer, and Willie Carr the jockey. Not, perhaps, one of the artist's most deft and fluent compositions but with failing health as cardiac symptoms become more serious, for Munnings, predictably a non-cooperative patient, time was short. He filled the summer driving to Newmarket, making new studies at the starting gate. He was still able to ride a horse and revel in the country scenes of the Stour Valley but by April 1959 again totally stricken by gout, his hands bound in flannel, utterly immobilised, he was never to paint again. Three months later on July 17th he died in his sleep in his eighty-first year.

In accordance with the artist's wishes his estate and the pictures currently in his possession at his death were left to the nation. Lady Munnings, with admirable initiative, established Castle House, Dedham as the Sir Alfred Munnings Art Museum with its original furnishings, studios and pictures. A Trust was formed and the house in its charming setting is open to the public and provides a fitting memorial.

In 1972 an exhibition of his work, selected by Humphrey Brooke, Secretary of the Royal Academy, was put on at The Minories, Colchester. Six years later in 1978, the centenary year of the artist's birth, a commemorative exhibition lasting five months was displayed at the Sir Alfred Munnings Art Museum; included were many early posters, portraits and work as an official War Artist.

At the end of 1986 when his pictures were already selling for six figures the Manchester City Art Gallery in conjunction with the Sir Alfred Munnings Art Museum put on an exhibition of over eighty pictures and drawings and the bronze of Brown Jack, which then travelled to York and Bath during the following six months. In complementary display, with the title 'Munnings v the Moderns' was a collection of non-representational works executed in the 1940s and 1950s by contemporary artists (all unrelated to sporting art) with a catalogue which included the famous Presidential Dinner Speech.

Nearly forty years on a new generation was still not ready to forget past indignities and, almost with one accord, the art critics of the leading national newspapers made this Munnings exhibition an occasion to denigrate not only the artist's work and technique, but his character and antecedents. *The Times* considered that '. . . at his best he seems more like a very fair magazine illustrator.'[16] The *Sunday Times* referred to his work as '. . . almost dazzling in mediocrity.'[17] The *Guardian* acclaimed him as 'boorish, arrogant, arriviste.'[18] Obviously sporting art was an abhorent concept but these reviews exhibited a total lack of comprehension of the subject and of the time and place of Munnings' inspiration. Not only was the considerable expertise of the artist dismissed as negligible but also the incomparable pictorial appeal of these scenes of the English way of life. In the next century those reviews will inevitably be dismissed as misguided.

Munnings takes his place as the quintessential English artist, who brought sporting art into the modern idiom with a brilliance and vigour not seen since the epoch of Stubbs, and who in his instinct for natural beauty, inherited something of the magic of Constable and Crome. As Christopher Neve wrote so appropriately, 'He painted his own version of the English idyll.'[19]

His ashes were laid in the Crypt of St Paul's Cathedral with a memorial tablet next to that of Constable's. How AJ would have rejoiced in its inscription of the lines by John Masefield the Poet Laureate, 'O friend how lovely are the things you helped us to perceive.' And how, inevitably, he would have remarked 'What a go!'

NOTES

1 Reginald Pound, *The Englishman: A Biography of Sir Alfred Munnings,* p. 210.

2 Sir Alfred Munnings, KCVO, PPRA, *An Artist's Life*, p. 64.

3 ibid, p. 103.

4 In a letter to his father, the Ven. Charles Wellington Furse, Archdeacon of Westminster, *Illustrated Memoirs of Charles Wellington Furse,* ARA, 1908, p. 3.

5 Stanley Booth, *Sir Alfred Munnings 1878–1959*, p. 23.

6 Pound, *The Englishman*, p. 129.

7 The firm of Busvine was founded in 1871 by the inventor of a side-saddle safety skirt and finally closed in 1951.

8 Munnings, *The Second Burst*, p. 225.

9 Munnings, *The Finish*, p. 44.

10 Munnings, *The Second Burst*, p. 267.

11 See Appendix One, p. 207.

12 Munnings, as a generous host, had somewhat unfairly acquired an intemperate reputation. Humphrey Brooke, who, as Secretary of the Royal Academy, was often with him and in their ten years' association and friendship stated he had never seen him the worse for drink, (Pound, *The Englishman*.)

13 Munnings, *The Finish*, p. 165.

14 Pound, *The Englishman*, p. 190.

15 Impulsive AJ had denounced as pornographic, pictures on exhibition by Stanley Spencer and quite unforgiveably informed the police.

16 John Russell Taylor, *The Times*, 16 December 1986.

17 Marina Vaizey, *Sunday Times*, 18 January 1987.

18 Waldimar Januszczak, *Guardian*, 21 December 1986.

19 Christopher Neve, *Country Life*, 21 September 1978.

9

Women Make Their Mark

Before the beginning of the twentieth century the school of British sporting art was dominated by the male artist. It is not difficult to assemble a list of 300 or more named sporting painters working between 1650–1900 but feminine equivalents of Francis Barlow, John Wootton and Henry Alken are remarkably absent.

Admittedly Joan Carlile, born in the early seventeenth century, was an amateur animal painter of some distinction and about 1653 she moved to Covent Garden 'resolved to use her skill for something more than empty fame'.[1] For posterity she has left a huge staghunting scene in which she and her family are also portrayed. There was also Judith Lewis working in the mid-eighteenth century in a continental style and with considerable elegance that suggests she might have been a pupil of John Wootton. After the death of her husband she lived with her artist brother, Stephen Slaughter, in Kensington and her bas reliefs attracted the attention of Walpole. Two examples of her sporting conversation pieces which had been for many years in a private American collection, came on to the British market in the 1980s; but these two names are feminine exceptions in the sporting sphere.

Women artists in Britain play virtually no part in the hunting, shooting and fishing milieu until Sarah Ferneley engraved some of her father's works in the mid nineteenth century and also painted some sporting scenes and landscapes. It would have been a minor miracle if they had, for women's participation in the actual sporting world was the exception rather than the rule. Early Victorian propriety forbade well-bred daughters from taking an active part in the Golden Age of Foxhunting from Melton Mowbray (that was left to such delectable *demi-mondaines* as the famous Skittles, 'Mrs' Nelly Holmes and the pianist Clari) so, understandably, in the hunting pictures of Alken and Ferneley women play little part, though allegedly Mr Assheton Smith, the famous MFH of the Quorn, had once given his hunt button to a redoubtable Mrs Turner Farley of Leicestershire, an inveterate foxhunter.

Of course sketching and painting, like riding, had always been a part of a young lady's education, but artistic subjects seldom seem to have stretched as far as field sports. In fact, until nearly the end of the nineteenth century the only women artists who immediately come to mind in connection with horses are Vigée le Brun from across the Channel with her striking portrait of Marie Antoinette riding astride, and Rosa Bonheur, who disguised herself as a man to frequent fairs and markets to make sketches for her famous horse pictures. In justice, perhaps, should be mentioned Miss Ainslie, who exhibited sporting pictures at the Royal Academy when Queen Victoria first came to the throne, but, like both Miss Charlotte Hardcastle and Miss Ella Brown later in that era, she seems to have specialised in game and not bloodstock. Women were not even admitted into the Royal Academy Schools until 1860 and not into the actual life school until 1893 when, after much discussion, a separate class was set up for

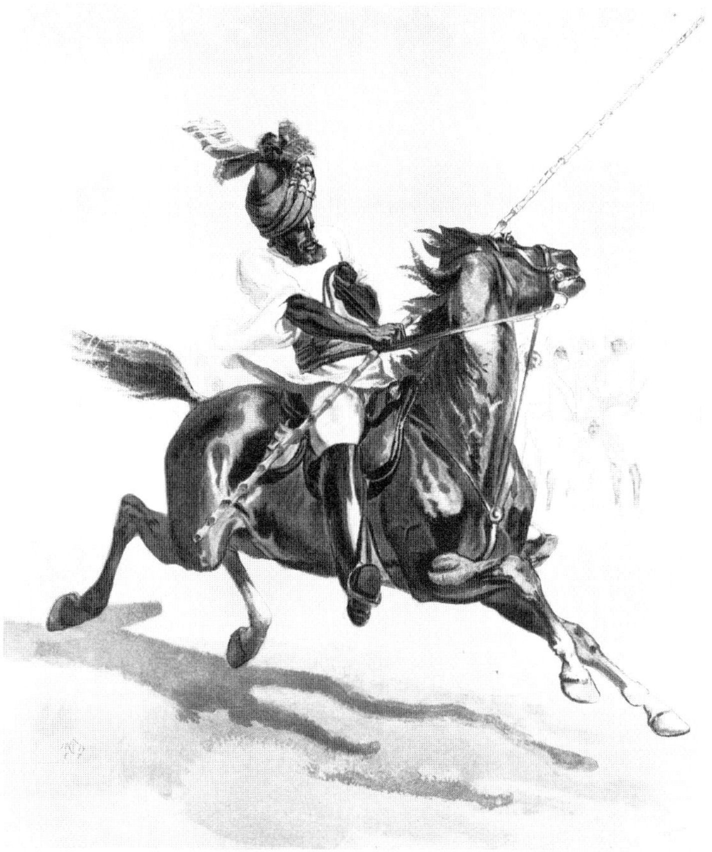

45 Lady Butler (Elizabeth Thompson), *'Missed!' A Bengal Lancer at the Game of Tent-Pegging*, 1873. Chromolithograph from a watercolour, $18\frac{3}{4} \times 33\frac{1}{2}$ in (47.5 × 85 cm).

them and models had to be appropriately draped – the proprieties still had to be observed!

It was with the arrival in the Shires of the Empress of Austria in the late 1870s that hunting became very much *à la mode* for young women, often with the ultimate quarry being wealthy husbands rather than the fox. As a result by the turn of the century a handful of women painters eventually started to make some impact in the world of equestrian art – and not merely as amateurs. It was an epoch also when women were shaking off the shackles of restrictive practices in more ways than one. In the hunting field the 'safety' skirt had superseded the enveloping folds of the Victorian habit to be followed by the even less constricting 'apron', and bloomers, much featured in *Punch*, were approved for the fashionable pastime of cycling. But more indicative of feminine revolt was the militant Suffragette movement which culminated in 1913 with Miss Emily Davidson trying to seize the reins of the King's horse, Anmer, in the melée at Tattenham Corner in the Derby and which resulted in her death.

Women were ready to make their mark in many spheres and certainly with distinction as animal artists. First in the field was Elizabeth Thompson, born of cultured English parents in 1846 near Lausanne, but her inclusion amongst British sporting artists *per se* may be considered unjustified for though her major subject was certainly equestrian her inspiration, however, was predominantly martial. In the masculine verve and strength of her battle scenes of death and glory her influence in revealing alternative subjects for the late Victorian woman artist to paint, other than the usual delicate flower studies and playful pussycats, was considerable.

Early girlish watercolours illustrate Elizabeth Thompson's autobiography *From my Sketch Book and Diary* with ponies in Western Ireland and, in travels in Italy, of the start of the traditional riderless horse race in Rome, but these give little indication of her flair for brilliant draughtsmanship and her ability to endow galloping cavalry with power and action. She studied at the Female School of Art in South Kensington and under Giuseppe Bellucci in Florence and by 1873 her dramatic oil painting *Missing*, exhibited at the Royal Academy, had created a great sensation and the following year *The Roll Call* was purchased by Queen Victoria. Elizabeth Thompson's masterpiece, '*Scotland Forever*' of the onrushing cavalry in the final charge of the Scots Greys at Waterloo, painted as an antidote to the Grosvenor Gallery aesthetes, achieved fame that endured until the First World War when both the British and German armies (the latter with suitable alteration) used the scene for propaganda. Her pictures, some of the first to reveal the grim realities of war, received the approbation of Ruskin who considered nothing comparable for power and colour had been seen since the death of Turner. The woman artist had achieved status!

In the sporting idiom an early fluent watercolour *Missed! A Bengal Lancer at the Game of Tent-Pegging* illustrates her undoubted skill in capturing a dramatic moment of truth – a Sowar has missed his aim, fury is suggested in the angry features of the rider, also speed and tension in his backward seat as he fights to control the careering black horse – brilliantly effective in its economy of detail (45).

Elizabeth Thompson (better known after her marriage in 1877 as Lady Butler) in subject matter may be somewhat remote from the school of British sporting art, but her pictures nevertheless certainly herald the first liberation of the Victorian woman artist and inspired a few brave spirits to attempt important extrovert compositions in the animal sphere. The first, and unquestionably the most important, of these was Lucy Kemp-Welch. Born in 1868 she was a regular exhibitor at the Royal Academy between 1896–1949 and her first pictures in their strength and panache inherited the style of the French animal artist, Rosa Bonheur, and in a personal idiom they possessed a realism and trained understanding of anatomy and conformation. In addition the popularity and acclaim received by the large sensational cavalry scenes of her contemporary, Elizabeth Thompson, must also have made considerable impact on her early professional career.

Lucy Kemp-Welch's childhood was spent in Malvern where an ability for sketching and painting was encouraged by an artistic mother and her innate dedication to animal life nurtured by her solicitor father, a keen amateur naturalist. With her sister, Edith, frequent visits were made to the New Forest and drawing books were filled with studies of insects and ponies, recording in detail eyes, ears, heads and legs, a habit that never left her. In addition she became a first class horsewoman, an ability that brought a convincing comprehension of the subtle relationship between mount and rider.

She was privileged to receive her artistic training at the Bushey School of Painting under the inspired guidance of Sir Hubert von Herkomer, RA. Bavarian by birth, he had established the art school in 1883 and quickly acquired a reputation for endowing his students with sound draughtsmanship and an ability to exploit their own natural talents. In 1885 he was appointed Slade Professor of Art and in some years as many as fifty to sixty works by his pupils would be accepted for exhibition at the Royal Academy.

Without doubt the paramount influence and authority of Lucy Kemp-Welch's career came from Herkomer who could impart his knowledge in an attractive and dramatic way. With her sister she arrived at the school in 1891 having initially been refused entrance because of her poor drawing. Both sisters were inordinately shy and introverted, having recently lost both their parents, and both seemed devoid of any remarkable talent. They settled in Bushey, which under the impact of Herkomer and his wife, had become a thriving art colony and gradually they entered into the generous and lively activities put on by the Herkomers for the students and their adherents. Correct draughtsmanship and life drawing formed the fundamental training at the school – animal form and action had to be shelved until complete mastery of the human figure merited promotion to the next class. It was a discipline never to be forgotten or ignored by Lucy Kemp-Welch.

But animals, and especially horses, were always her persistent inspiration and, by chance, seeing gypsies driving a group of ponies and cobs through the village on the way to Barnet Fair, on immediate impulse she bought an 8 ft canvas and started work on an immense painting of the scene. This addiction to grandiose compositions with horses approaching life size appears curious in an artist herself remarkably small and slight, perhaps it expressed an innate conviction in her own outstanding ability. Herkomer himself was astounded by his first viewing of the half finished picture. In only six months this unassuming girl had acquired technique, expertise and a confidence that this experienced teacher had never remotely suspected possible. From that moment he devoted energy and enthusiasm to launching the career of this woman animal painter who had emerged so unexpectedly from his school. *The Gypsy Drovers* was hung in a premier position in the 1895 exhibition at the Royal Academy and for the next twenty-six years she was to exhibit annually at Burlington House, adding up to forty-four pictures in all.

As early as 1896 press art critics had been writing 'Miss Kemp-Welch has developed a talent such as is common in man and quite rare in a woman for animal painting,'[2] and 'She is now regarded as one of the best painters of the horse the century has ever seen.'[3] Nevertheless though she became the first and very active President of the Society of Animal Painters which numbered Alfred Munnings, Frank Calderon, H.W.B. Davis and Lionel Edwards amongst its members and her artistic prestige was widely recognised, she never received election to the Royal Academy – male chauvinism prevented that due accolade – a slight on his favourite pupil that never ceased to rankle with Herkomer.

In 1897 she had consolidated her popularity and success with the huge composition *Colt Hunting in the New Forest*, later to be purchased by the Chantrey Bequest for the Tate Gallery for the then considerable sum of £525 (*Plate 11*). Lacking personal height, painting these enormous canvases imposed practical problems but Lucy Kemp-Welch firmly believed, like Manet, Munnings and Lionel Edwards, that a convincing composition of an outdoor subject merited the *plein air* treatment. This picture was actually painted on a site in a woodland clearing where a big wooden case was constructed around the canvas with doors opening outwards. Here for three months she worked daily in all weathers, often on a ladder.

This official rounding-up is organised by the Verderers' Agisters five times a year to coincide with the sales of ponies at Beaulieu Road Station. Though known as colt-hunting, ponies of both sexes are branded with the owners' individual mark, and the tails are cut to specific patterns for different areas of the Forest to prove the annual turning-out fee has been paid. Lucy Kemp-Welch, being a courageous and able rider, had personally taken part in these rough rodeos which enabled her to stamp her work with an exciting authenticity.

In this spectacular composition with trees and undergrowth in mellow autumn colouring, the peaceful landscape contrasts and merges with the brown, chestnut and grey tones of the leading ponies. The artist's photographic eye for movement has recorded the helter skelter tension of the occasion with wonderful veracity – the shouting encouragement of the galloping forest agister seems almost audible.

A study of *Hunters in the Orchard at Bushey with 'Trust'* painted in 1902 shows her in different vein, but the real Thoroughbred scene held little appeal for her and the few racing pictures such as *Start at Goodwood* and *Going Strong* in watercolours fail to suggest the quality, elegance and speed of the blood horse. She considered the breed had been evolved by man and not fashioned by nature, lacking the faults of native ponies which were 'variable and lovable beyond words'.

Particularly spectacular and effective, inspired by Robert Browning's poem '*The Last Ride*

Together,' was her equestrian study *The Riders* exhibited at the Royal Academy in 1911. Ridden by the beautiful girl is the handsome Black Prince, the horse presented to Lord Baden Powell after Mafeking and frequently loaned as a model to the artist. In its free style of painting and theatrical vigour one feels that the influence of ill-fated Charles Wellington Furse had played its part.

But Lucy Kemp-Welch's real artistic dedication appears to have been given primarily to the heavy working horse (*46*) and her most impressive pictures are of farming and forestry activities. In her painting of greys there is real mastery and here, one feels, she has learnt much from Bevan and Crawhall. A subtle impressionism takes over from her early realism with delicate colour tones from silver, blue and cream to a fleck of white to make these studies of grey horses a delight. Here was an artist who obviously loved the pastoral scene and undoubtedly some of her finest work is found among the farm horses.

In 1905 she held her first personal exhibition at the Fine Art Society and a book on her work, *The Open Country*, was published by Hodder and Stoughton with a foreword by Hubert Herkomer. He, unfortunately, had become chronically ill and too incapacitated in 1907 to accept the Presidency of the Royal Academy. As an act of kindness his former pupil purchased the art school, which became the Lucy Kemp-Welch School for Drawing and Painting and though she attempted to follow his traditions her own artistic commitments elsewhere necessitated much delegation. Herkomer died in 1914 and the war brought important Government commissions for Lucy Kemp-Welch. The school finally closed in 1926 and for many seasons she took to the road with car and caravan with Lord John Sangster's Circus and produced a rich harvest of scenes of the sawdust ring with such effective studies as *Elephants and the Big Top*.

She possessed an observant and accurate eye for all animal portraiture and though the highest public acclaim was reserved for her big important pictures such as *Titans*, the shunting horses at Euston Station and the dramatic *Launching the Lifeboat*, much of her true talent also lay in such sensitive portrayals as *Trust a Terrier* and an *Alsatian Dog*, studies of donkeys in woodland and tranquil swans on limpid lakes. It was this artist's undeniable dedication to animal compositions great and small and to the country way of life that encouraged her women contemporaries to take their place in the school of British sporting art.

Lucy Kemp-Welch lived until 1958 and twenty-seven of her pictures hang in public galleries, but for more than a couple of decades her name passed into oblivion until

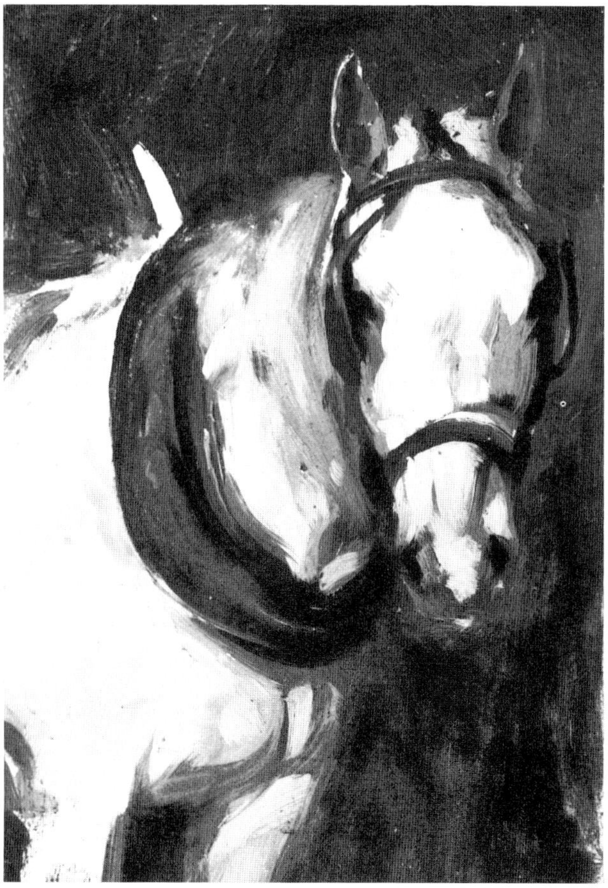

46 Lucy Kemp-Welch, *Head of a Carthorse*. Oil on canvas, $9 \times 6\frac{1}{2}$ in (22.8×16.5 cm).

in 1976 David Messum, a West End art dealer, seized an unexpected opportunity to buy the contents of the artist's old studio at Bushey which for years had remained neglected and forgotten. With admirable initiative he put on exhibitions of her work in London and Beaconsfield and produced a finely illustrated biographical catalogue and thus a new generation became aware of the merit of one of the country's most talented women animal artists.

But few of Lucy Kemp-Welch's contemporaries shared her ambitions and ability for the grandiose and Maud Earl, who was working at the turn of the century and died in 1943 (with feminine ambiguity she appears never to have revealed the date of her birth) virtually confined her artistic career to portraits of dogs. But her father, George Earl, a sporting painter whose work included some admirable polo and shooting scenes, and her uncle Thomas Percy Earl, and another relative, Percy Earl, all contributed to a wider sphere of sporting activities.

With the constant royal commissions from the Queen and the acclaimed expertise of Edwin Landseer, canine portraiture had attained a peak of popularity in the Victorian era. This interest, of course, was no new facet of British sporting art for the aristocracy and wealthy had always demanded artistic immortality for their canine friends. Horace Walpole's favourite Patapan was painted by John Wootton whose delectable portrait also of Muff, a dog of obscure breeding but immense charm, was included in the Paul Mellon gift in 1977 to the Tate Gallery (through the British Sporting Art Trust). Stubbs' many studies of poodles, pointers, spaniels and foxhounds followed by such classic portraits as Landseer's Bashaw, Lord Dudley's Newfoundland, Mustard, favourite of Sir Francis Chantrey all followed this tradition; so Maud Earl was conforming to a wellworn convention in her choice of subject.

By 1859, also, the first dog show had been held in the Town Hall of Newcastle-upon-Tyne and in 1873 the Kennel Club was founded to formulate rules and regulations. Eight years later Charles Cruft, son of a jeweller, organised the first of his series of dog shows at the Royal Agricultural Hall, Islington. These were to become an annual event, internationally famous and today, run by the Kennel Club, rank as the major canine event of the year.

By the beginning of the century dog ownership had almost developed into a cult. For leaders of fashion the pedigree 'pooch' decked in bejewelled collar parading at stylish resorts complemented the *haute couture* of beautiful owners. Breeds of foreign extraction had always been popular; spitz and Pomeranians appear in several of Stubbs' pictures but, by the end of the nineteenth century, the oriental Pekinese and the Japanese spaniel became the spoiled family pets. The more serious interest in pedigree breeding of sporting dogs, initiated by the Kennel Club and the Crufts Show, resulted in important commissions for portraits of spaniels and setters, champions of the show bench and the sporting arena.

During her career Maud Earl had to contend with the growing success of photography but her sound anatomical knowledge, allied to her spontaneity of style, enabled her triumphantly to over-ride this challenge. She broke away from the contemporary stereotyped and often saccharine presentations of the dog world. Naturalism and vitality hallmark her work, whether she was painting the portrait of a much loved family pet or a working gun dog as in the splendid study of the liver and white champion setter, Dabchick, with her companion Dear in the background (47).

Royalty and the aristocracy provided a steady flow of commissions. King Edward's French bulldog, Peter, his Irish terrier, Jack, and his successor, the faithful wire-haired fox terrier, Caesar, all sat for Maud Earl. On the King's death *Silent Sorrow* was painted for the *Illustrated London News*, showing Caesar bereaved and inconsolable, a moving study but skilfully devoid of sentimentality. A conventional portrait of *St Hubert's Peter*, a yellow Russian retriever belonging to King George V was exhibited in the 1914 exhibition of the Royal Academy. One of the artist's most important patrons was the Duchess of Newcastle, a successful breeder of fox terriers, borzois and clumber spaniels.

Before the outbreak of the First World War she held several London Exhibitions with such titles as 'Canine Celebrations', 'British Hounds and Dogs', 'The Power of the Dog' and 'Whose Dogs are Those?' Many engravings were published after her paintings and she was much in demand as an illustrator of authoritative works by such canine experts as William Arkwright and Harding Cox.

In 1916 she emigrated to New York where her flair for the dog domain was transformed into a decorative idiom for houses and even hotels with modish designs of Pekinese and Japanese spaniels providing the motif of Oriental panels and screens.

But in her own country Maud Earl will always be acclaimed for her splendid portrayals of the sporting dog. In a fine picture of greyhounds, *Straining at the Leash*, and a bull terrier seizing a water rat, in studies of foxhounds, of clumber spaniels, active and in repose, her intuitive understanding of canine character is allied to brilliant brushwork that in the years to follow was to inspire many women animal artists. Few, however, have matched her aptitude in this canine subject.

In retrospect it is possible to realise that the first woman who conformed to the accepted traditional role of the sporting artist, travelling, as in the eighteenth and nineteenth centuries, all over the country, was certainly Florence Mabel Hollams, who, in her working career of over sixty years, fulfilled over 1740 commissioned portraits of horses and almost as many of dogs. Born in 1877 at Deene Park in Kent her artistic talent was possibly derived from her direct ancestor, John Hamilton Mortimer, painter of conversation pieces and historical scenes, who was elected an ARA in 1778. She studied not only at Frank Calderon's school but also, with surprising initiative for a Victorian young lady of the day, went to Julian's studio in Paris like so many of her male contemporaries.

Determined on a career in art, in which marriage was to play no part, by the age of eighteen she exhibited at the Royal Academy her picture *Rounding up Mares and Foals on Exmoor*. Such compositions and landscapes were briefly her major subject and many of these went to America. In 1903 however, she married Charles Lionel Fox, the land agent for the Cazalet family of the Fairlawne estate in Kent, the successful racehorse breeders and trainers. She lived for many years at Puttenden Manor near Tonbridge, hunted enthusiastically with the West Kent of which her husband was the Honorary Secretary, produced two sons and late in life moved to Somerset.

Early in her long and active career (she died only in 1963) she ceased painting compositions and turned to the simpler aspects of equestrian portraiture. Most of the influential sportsmen of the day became her patrons including the Duke of Norfolk, Earl Sefton, Earl Beatty, Lord Cornwallis – in fact Debrett could have been her address book.

Always a lightning artist, after looking at a horse for only five minutes and making a few sketches on pieces of wood in her paint box, she would herself take the wheel of her large car, putting the chauffeur in the back (his duties incidentally had been to remove samples of the horses's mane and coat for reference). Returning home, after seeing perhaps ten horses on the trip, the first picture would be completed at the end of another week. On collection, allegedly, the invariable fee of twenty-five guineas was placed in cash on a silver salver held by the butler in the hall. Though never under any financial pressure Mabel Hollams must be considered a compulsive painter, for her capacity for work was prodigious but her methods inevitably resulted in a repetitive quality in her style (*48*). Nevertheless she painted some admirable portraits of well-known sportsmen and sportswomen on their favourite hunters and she could produce a convincing likeness. Many commissions came from the world of steeplechasing and especially notable were her commemorative portraits of the Grand National winners, Master Robert and Reynoldstown.

Some of her most attractive subjects derived from the canine field with her studies of hounds and working terriers and pictures exist of an occasional coursing scene. The Hunt staff of the West Kent and local subscribers were portrayed in local settings and she often painted direct on to wooden panel with the grain forming the background pattern of many horse portraits.

In 1934 Ackermann's put on a loan exhibition of Mabel Hollam's work and here it was possible to assess her merit as one of the most popular equestrian artists of the day. Unfortunately she had to compete with such outstanding exponents as Munnings and Lionel Edwards and her own undoubted talent was diminished by her urge to paint too much too quickly, but in country houses all over the British Isles her pictures of favourite horses and dogs fill pride of place. Her portrait of Her Majesty The Queen's Aureole was, like Munnings', almost her last equestrian painting; today it hangs at the top of the visitors' staircase at Sandringham. Indisputably her industry and initiative were a major influence in establishing the status of the professional woman painter in the male dominated world of British sporting art.

An artist working in the same period but in a different context was Edith Oenone Somerville, born in 1858, whose artistic talents are frequently ignored. Her literary collaboration with her cousin Violet Martin Ross in the foxhunting classic *Some Experiences of an Irish R.M.*, its

47 Maud Earl, *Dear and Dabchick, Champion Setters, the property of Colonel Cotes*, 1912. Oil on canvas, 25 × 32 in (63.5 × 81.2 cm).

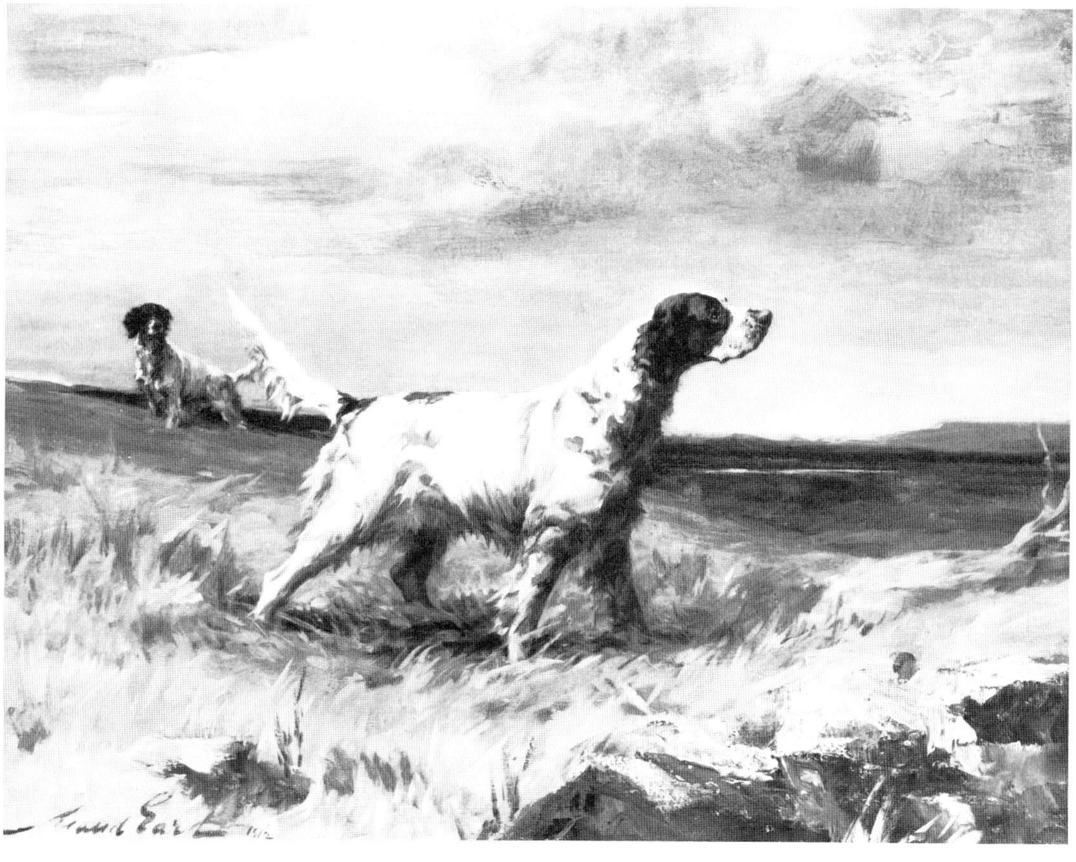

48 Florence Mabel Hollams, *A Grey Hunter*. Oil on canvas, 16 × 20 in (40.6 × 50.8 cm).

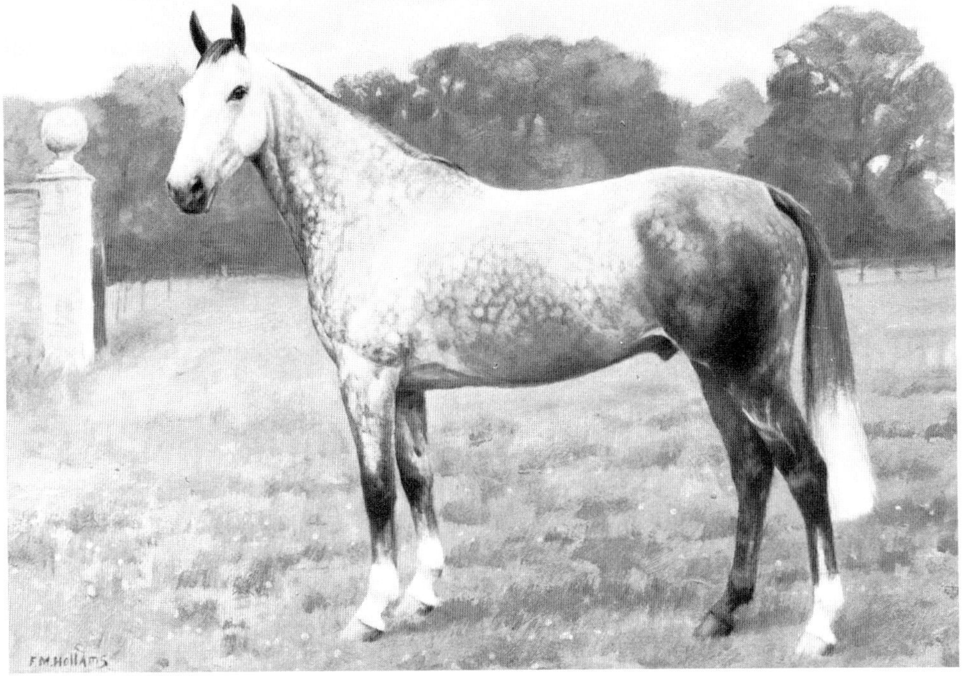

sequel and other works has assured them both a status in sporting literature only surpassed by Surtees himself. But many of these books were also illustrated by Edith Oenone Somerville and initially she had studied art seriously in Paris under Colarossi and Delecluse and also at the Westminster School of Art.

But she returned to live in Ireland, sharing a home with Violet Ross and, as Master of the Carbery Foxhounds, background for the books and their pictures was never lacking. Her subjects and artistic style reflected admirably the quirks and contrasts of life in rural Ireland. The context was often comic but she possessed an astute understanding, not only of horse and hound, but also of the complexities of local loyalties and jealousies. She exhibited with the Fine Art Society, the Royal Hibernian Society and held one man shows at the Goupil and Walker Galleries in London in 1920 and 1923.

It is interesting to find that almost without exception these women artists working at the beginning of the twentieth century had experienced professional art training. None could glibly (and sometimes proudly!) admit, as their sisters fifty years later, that they had never had a lesson in their lives!

Nina Colmore, only eleven years old at the birth of the new century, must perhaps be considered the transitional woman artist who was to use, like the male painters of the era, the accepted contemporary approach to the sporting scene. In childhood, spent at Hounslow, the family horses and ponies became her earliest subjects for drawings and she received much encouragement from her mother, an amateur watercolourist of ability who, fortunately, appreciated the value of sound teaching. As a result Nina Murray (as she then was) went to Heatherley's and then enjoyed valuable continental training at Julian's, Cabanes and Colarossi in Paris, and also with Constant Janvier in Brittany. But continental tuition, whilst improving her technique and stimulating her love of travel, still left her dominant motivation with the racecourse and the hunting field. She herself was always a dedicated sportswoman and keen foxhunter and she married in 1916 Captain H. Colmore, an active polo player, so her artistic future became predictable.

Between the two World Wars her prestige as a competent animal artist was firmly established. In travels abroad a stay in Austria resulted in finely observed studies of the Lipizzaner stallions performing the various 'airs' – the Levade, Piaffe, Capriole and Spanish Walk of the Spanish Riding School at Wels in the days before their activities were centred in Vienna. In Egypt, for King Fuad, she painted studies of local scenes and characters and these pictures can now be seen in the Cairo Museum.

At home commissions came from such distinguished owners as the Duke of Windsor, the Aga Khan and the Duchess of Westminster. For Lord Astor she painted a fine portrait of his big bay Craig an Eran, emphasising his strong front and intelligent head. A quarter of a century on Mr F.C. Ferguson's 1946 Derby winner Airborne, a lovely grey colt, made an arresting subject and five years later she was portraying the chestnut Ki Ming, winner of the 1951 Two Thousand Guineas for Mr Ley On, a Chinese restauranteur (*49*). Again she was another woman artist whose real ability in the sporting field was dimmed by comparison with the incomparable pictures of the Thoroughbred by Alfred Munnings, but Nina Colmore in her equestrian portraits achieved an excellent likeness and firm definition establishing form and character. Any subtleties of landscape effects however tended to escape her brush though she produced some pleasing presentation hunting pictures such as *Miss Guest with her Hounds*, with the hound portraiture effectively sustained.

Her actual dog studies always exhibited an uncanny talent for characterisation and nowhere more strikingly than with the watercolour of *Terriers* – little Cairns, the essence of alert intelli-

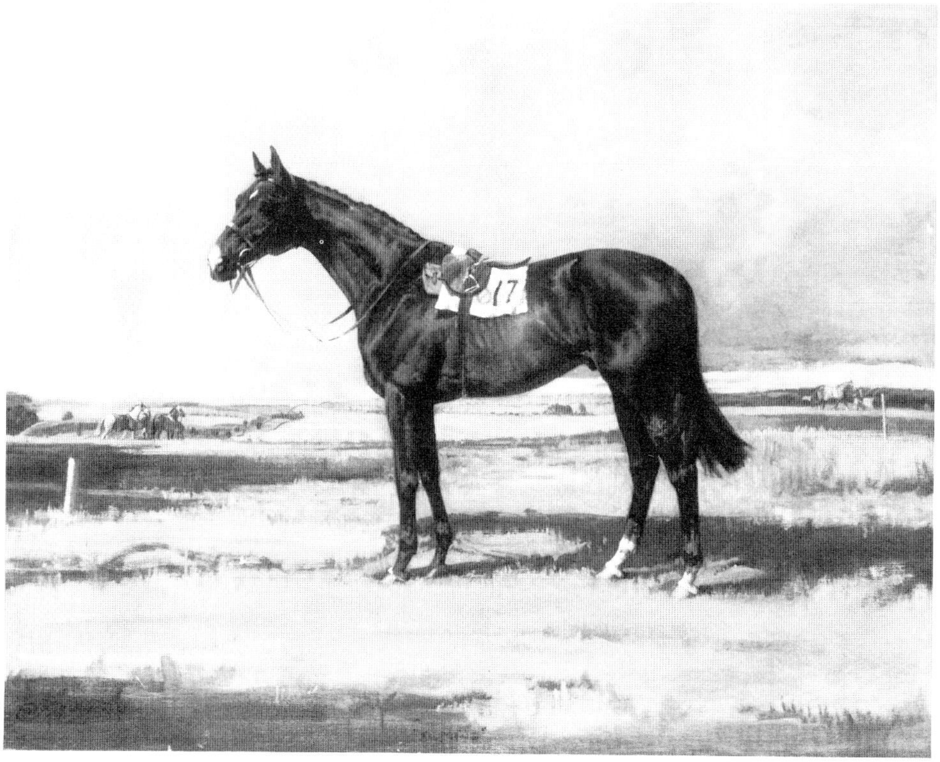

49 Nina Colmore, *Mr Ley On's Ki Ming: Winner of the 1951 Two Thousand Guineas*. Oil on canvas, 28 × 36 in (71.1 × 91.4 cm).

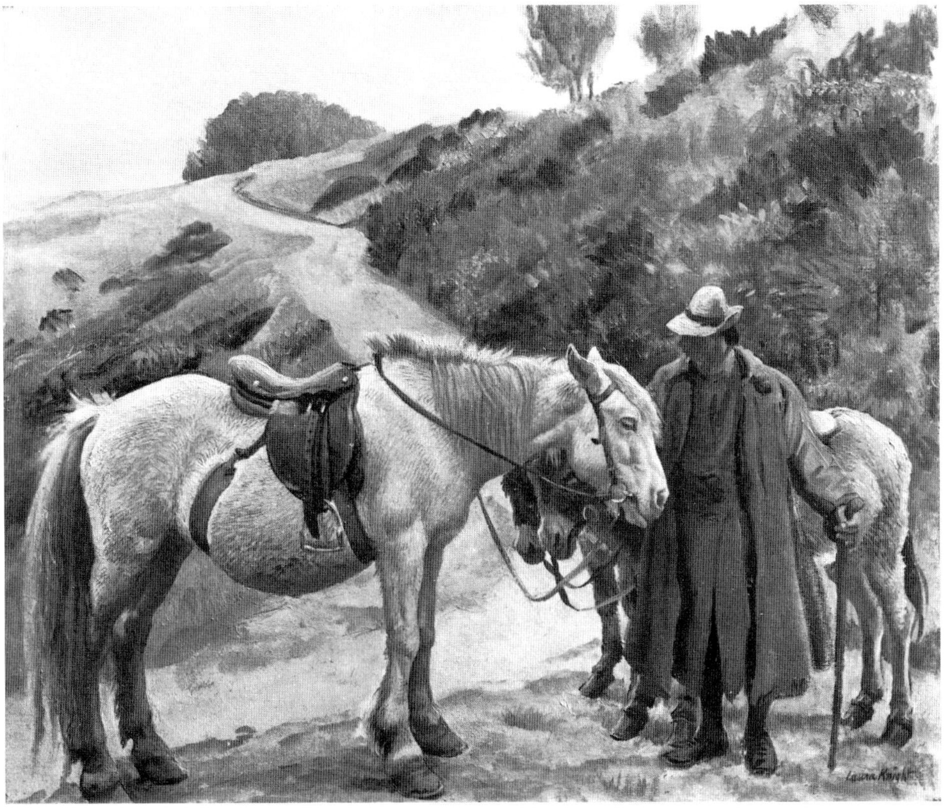

50 Laura Knight, DBE, RA, *Kitty*, *c* 1937. Oil on canvas, 25 × 30 in (63.5 × 76.2 cm).

gence. Inn signs were also amongst her activities and splendid examples enlivened the Horse & Jockey at Romsey and the Waggon & Horses at Stockbridge.

Late in her life her expertise appeared undimmed in a commission she fulfilled with splendid confidence of the champion team of Shire Horses of Young's Brewery in action in Windsor Park. A woman of great personal charm, energy and courage and an inveterate traveller in many parts of the world, Nina Colmore received the MBE for her services as a driver in Italy and the Middle East in the Second World War and in 1956 she was awarded the Diploma of the Paris Salon. In her own country she must be valued as the forerunner of the spate of women artists in the second half of the twentieth century who, with male dominance finally vanquished, fulfilled with equal competence the demands of the growing market for sporting art.

But contemporary with Nina Colmore, one of the great women artists of the century who must be included is Dame Laura Knight, born in 1877. Never, of course, to be considered an artist of the British Sporting School yet, indirectly, her influence initiated some important innovations amongst its traditionalists.

In 1965 Laura Knight, DBE, RA, then in her eightieth year, was honoured with a retrospective exhibition in the Diploma Gallery at Burlington House. She had sat on the Academy Council under three Presidents: Sir William Llewellyn, Sir Alfred Munnings and Sir Gerald Kelly and, as one of this century's most distinguished artists, had triumphantly surmounted and outlived the establishment's earlier prejudice against the feminine sex. Women had at last been accepted on equal terms, talent was the only criterion and Laura Knight had certainly never been lacking in this commodity. Of Midland yeoman stock her early childhood had been spent in Nottingham, sustained by her mother's unshakeable determination that this third daughter should become an artist, a pipe dream that was to be richly fulfilled.

Russell Flint in his introduction to the Catalogue of the Exhibition wrote, 'If we consider the careers of women artists throughout the centuries it soon becomes plain that Laura Knight surpasses them all in sheer variety of achievement. Where, in the boundless field of art, has any woman – or how many men – shown such a wide range?'[4]

Amongst an infinity of subjects ballet, gypsy life and the circus have made her name famous, but the art of the circus is a genre of its own. In her studies of liberty horses and rosenbacks, whether in the highlights of the sawdust ring or in the shadows of the tented stalls, realism and glamour vie for supremacy and Laura Knight's skilled draughtsmanship bring authority and strength to all her animal studies.

Nevertheless also in the sphere of sporting art Laura Knight unexpectedly fulfils a small but important role. Her interest in racing dates from childhood visits to the Nottingham meetings and was certainly encouraged by the friendship of her husband and herself with Munnings. When she was immobilised with a broken ankle it was AJ who beguiled the tedium with his inimitable readings from Surtees and later enthused her with the joys of the turf. Visits to the races resulted in more than sixty paintings and here she brought an original approach with such impressionist compositions as *Showers at Ascot*, painted in 1936, with its pattern of umbrellas and elegant gowns sweeping damp grass to bely the popular supposition of perpetual sunshine in those halcyon pre-war summers (*Plate 11*). Often painting from the top of a car (a Rolls Royce) at Tattenham Corner, it was character and atmosphere that engaged her attentions – the bookies, the Cockney crowd and above all, the gypsies, not the horses and jockeys. A splendid study *c* 1938 of that dramatic tipster in theatrical costume, 'I've Got an 'Orse' *Prince Ras Monolulu at Epsom*, evokes memories and in her *Derby Day* a Rolls Royce

51 Laura Knight, DBE, RA, *Boxing Study*, *c* 1917. Pencil drawing, $9\frac{1}{2} \times 9\frac{1}{2}$ in (24.1 × 24.1 cm).

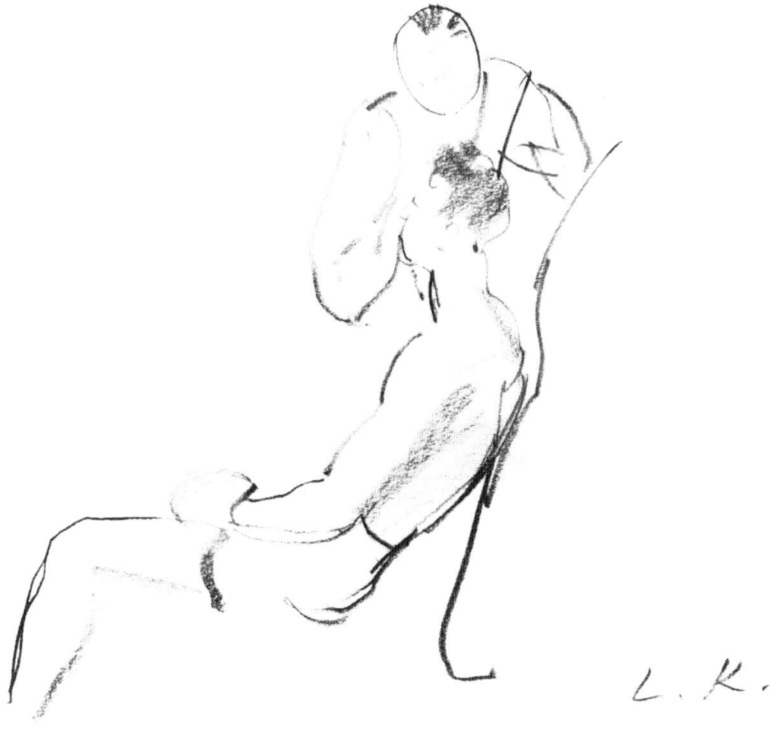

fills the foreground and spectators, perched high, survey the undepicted horses against a background of the distant grandstand.

In actual fact she had passed her fiftieth birthday and been elected an ARA before she ever really studied the horse. It was the heavy horse that won her attention; for her the Thoroughbred as a subject brought little appeal, though the second Viscount Astor in the 1930s did persuade the artist to paint portraits of his 1936 Two Thousand Guineas winner, Pay-Out, and also of his unbeaten Mannamead then stabled near Winchester.

From this period date unsophisticated studies in the Malvern Hills of Mrs Betteridge's 21-year-old white pony *Kitty* with large belly and stay girth, and the accompanying donkeys that became subjects (*50*). In 1937 Laura Knight's genius for the balletic image of Pavlova and Karsavina was transposed to the boxing ring at Blackfriars with fluent drawings illustrating a contrasting lightness of foot allied to the power of the punch. These were the legacy of many pictures of pugilism she had made twenty years earlier at the Canadian Forces Training Camp at Whitley during the First World War (*51*). She wrote, 'Here was a subject at last with a vengeance! The gymnasium became my studio.'[5]

Her versatility was inexhaustible; her studies of heavy farm horses ploughing possess remarkable power and authority, a winter scene of youngsters sliding and skating on a frozen lake exudes merriment in freezing cold. In a charcoal sketch of *Sleeping Greyhounds* animal form is portrayed with an intense observation rare amongst the conventional animal artists of the day.

In 1965 Laura Knight was writing, 'Even today, a female artist is considered more or less a freak, and may either be undervalued or overpraised . . . from babyhood, the horizon of womenkind has been confined to the four walls of a home . . . Now that womenkind are no longer born to hold a needle in one hand and a scrubbing brush in the other, what great things may not happen?'[6]

Dame Laura Knight gave to British sporting art, in her infrequent examples of the subject, the important lesson that experiment is a necessity of creation if tradition, and accepted background of sporting compositions, is not to breed repetition and monotony. By the first half of the twentieth century the woman sporting artist had certainly made her mark and the flair and originality of Laura Knight had left the door wider open for an exciting future for a flood of successors.

NOTES

1 Exhibition catalogue, 'British Sporting Paintings 1650–1850', The Arts Council of Great Britain at the Hayward Gallery, 1974, p. 33.

2 *Bazaar*, 1 May 1896.

3 *Dublin Herald*, 5 August 1896.

4 Catalogue introduction by William Russell Flint, RA, 'Exhibition of Painting and Drawings by Laura Knight, DBE, RA', Royal Academy of Arts Diploma Gallery, London, 1965.

5 Laura Knight, DBE, RA, *Oil Paint and Grease Paint*, p. 212.

6 Laura Knight, DBE, RA, *The Magic of a Line*, p. 307.

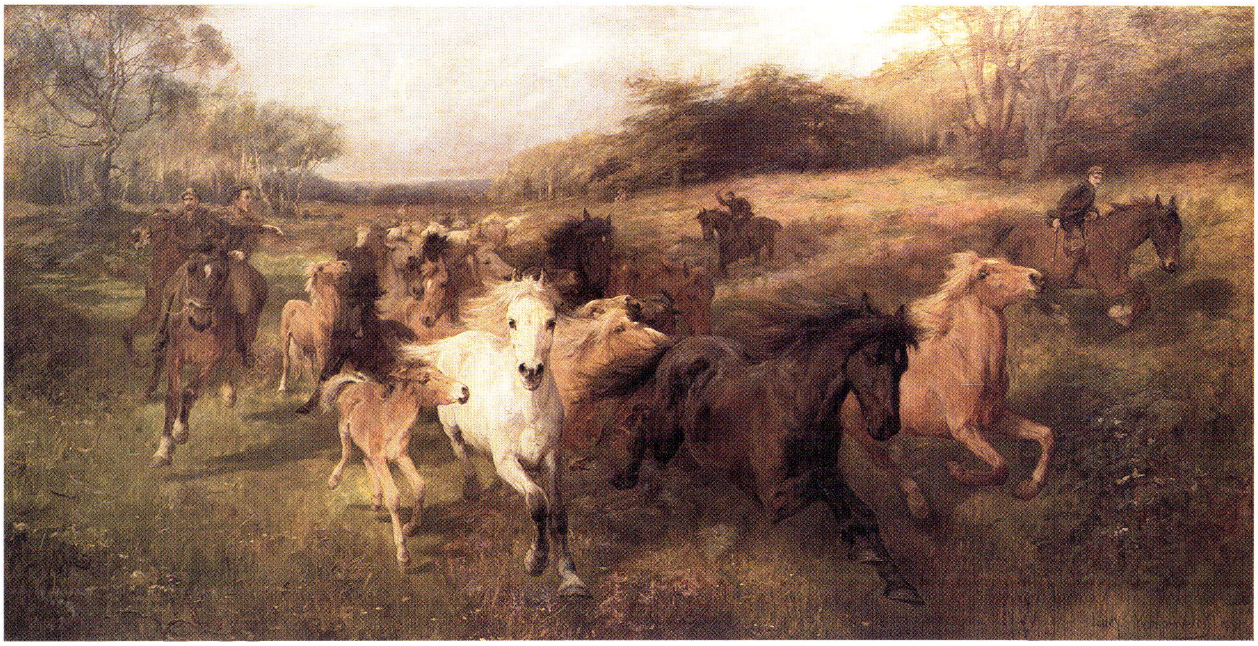

PLATE 11 (*above*) Lucy Kemp-Welch, *Colt Hunting in the New Forest*, 1897. Oil on canvas, 10 × 5 ft (305 × 152 cm). (*below*) Laura Knight, DBE, RA, *Showers at Ascot*, 1936. Oil on canvas, 25 × 30 in (63.5 × 76.2 cm).

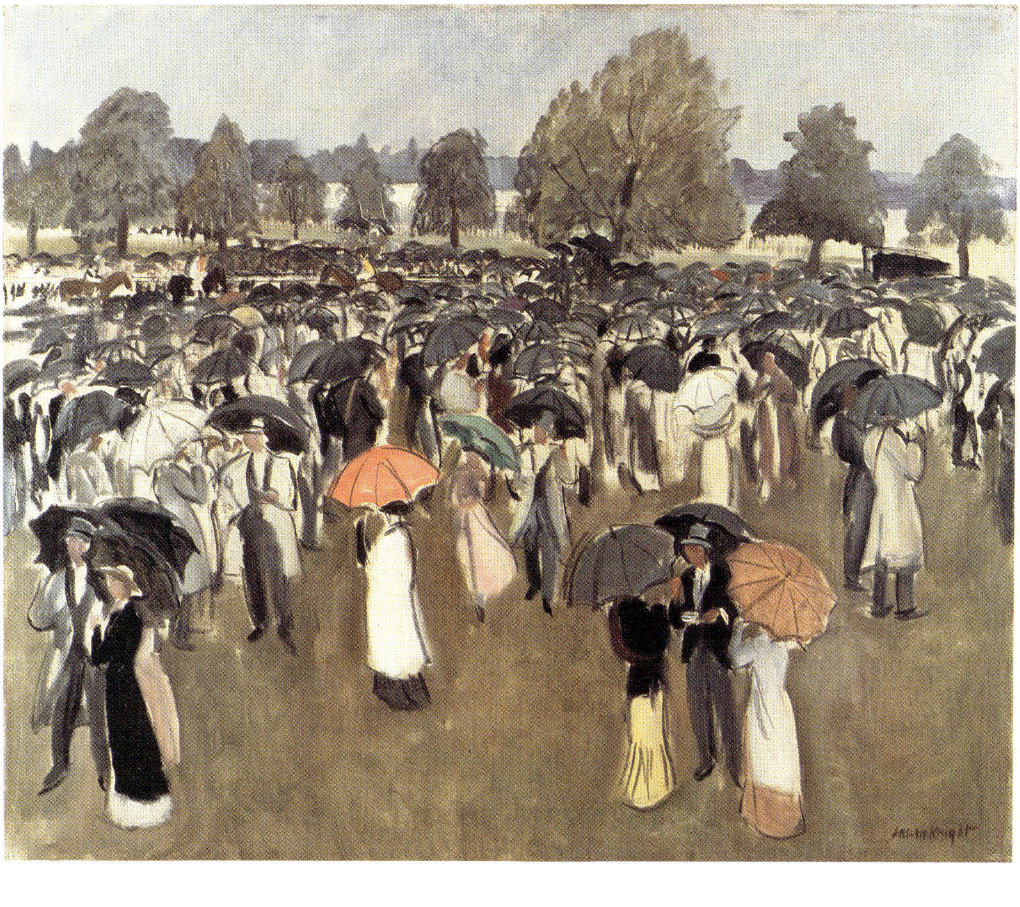

PLATE 12 (*left*) Snaffles (Charlie Johnson Payne), *The Season 1939–40*, 1940. Print, $19\frac{1}{2} \times 28\frac{1}{4}$ in (49.5×71.7 cm).

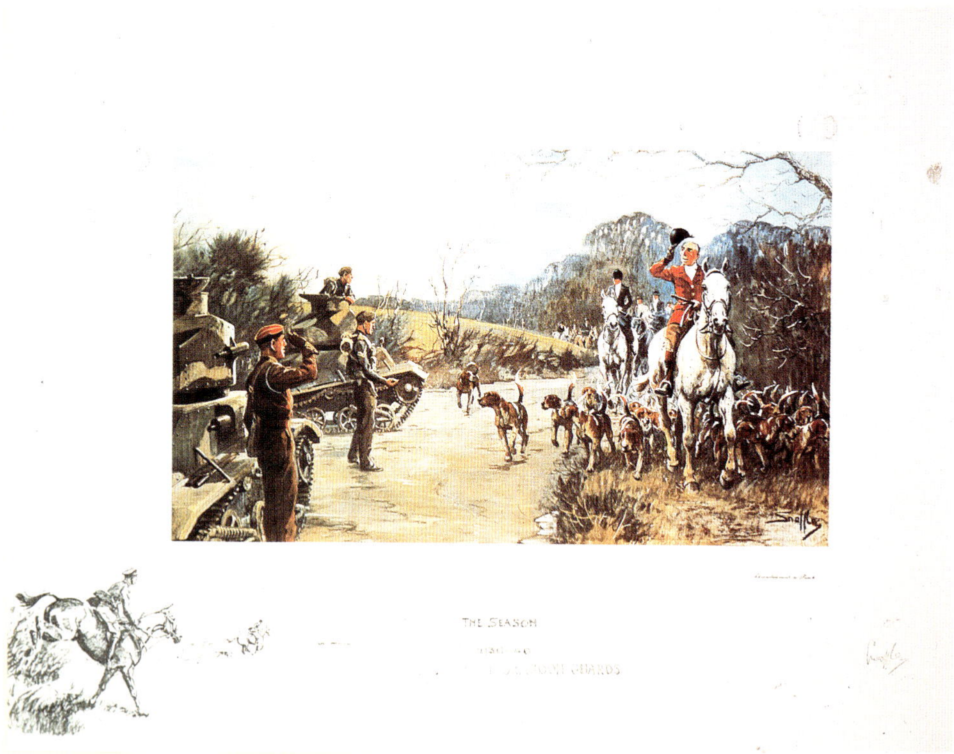

(*right*) Alfred James Munnings, KCVO, PRA, *A Halt on the March by a Stream at Neslé*, 1918. Oil on canvas, 20×24 in (50.8×60.9 cm).

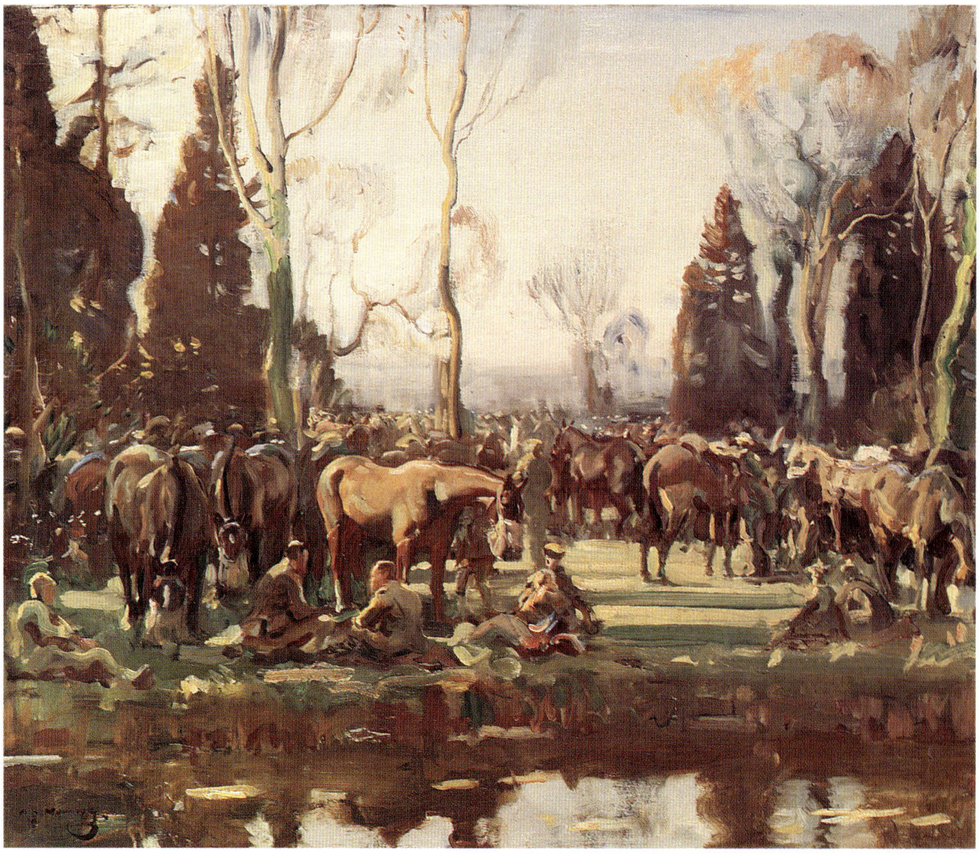

10

Sporting Artists at War

It was not until 1916 that the British Government, through the Ministry of Information, decided to form an official collection of paintings and drawings of the First World War, and a war artist department was evolved by Lord Beaverbrook.

It resulted in the recognition of young gifted artists such as Augustus John, Paul Nash, Wyndham Lewis, C.R.W. Nevinson and Stanley Spencer, all later to acquire international acclaim. In addition certain sporting artists were also given important opportunities and, in fact, whether officially commissioned or not, the catalogues of pictures at the Imperial War and the National Army Museums in London contain works by most of the leading equestrian artists of the day.

In 1914 war still held the lure of glamour and adventure and the murder of the Austrian Archduke Francis Ferdinand in June, in distant Sarajevo, with the dramatic outbreak of hostilities less than a couple of months later promised nothing more than a brief and, for many young men, welcome excitement: 'It would all be over by Christmas'. But in retrospect Lionel Edwards was to refer to the outbreak of war as the first vague hint of a catastrophe which entirely changed the world as we knew it; and G.D. Armour wrote in his autobiography that the Great War was the greatest divergence from the ordinary course of life.

Many periodicals such as *The Graphic*, the *Illustrated Sporting and Dramatic News* and *The Bystander* quickly commissioned freelance artists to depict current war incidents in Northern France.

Almost without exception every sporting artist, though many were no longer young, became involved in the national effort. Their duties in most cases made little use initially of their specific talents, and established careers, as well as the merely promising, were brought to a sudden halt. But in the midst of service duties opportunities were seized to record incidents of humour and horror, often only in a few vivid line drawings, which were to prove of infinite interest to social historians.

As the end of this mechanised twentieth century approaches, the fact can hardly be realised that the basic organisation of World War I depended almost totally on horse power. Motorised transport at that time was still erratic and virtually immobilised in wet ground conditions. Men, guns, ammunition and equipment required a limitless number of horses to keep the troops in action, and pictorially, it is the sporting artists who have most vividly and poignantly recorded the courage and stoicism of these men and their animals in action.

The outbreak of hostilities in 1914 was a bolt from the blue and overnight a supply of horses, of every type from cavalry to light draught animals, became the top priority. Remount officers were swiftly recruited from masters of hounds, racehorse trainers, riding school proprietors, in fact any experienced horseman was involved. Their job was to purchase any type of horse available to fulfil the insatiable demand until foreign importation schemes came into action. It was not an enviable duty; commercial opportunists certainly cashed in on a quick sale for crocks but innumerable devoted owners grieved to see favourite hunters being collected for cannon fodder on the Western Front.

Many contemporary artists were quickly signed on. Substituting a Bohemian life and country recreations for army discipline and tough conditions proved irksome but not without compensation. George Denholm Armour, already middle-aged, knew he had no chance of front line action but, between 1910–1914, he had visited Austria and Hungary to examine methods of supplying horses for the Yeomanry. He had written articles for *The Field* on his ideas so, when war broke out and inaction became intolerable, his offer to take charge of horses arriving by the thousand from America and Canada in batches of 300 was speedily accepted.

Requiring conditioning and schooling, most were very poor from the voyage and rough usage and many virtually unrideable. Fortunately a welcome recruit arrived in the person of Will H. Ogilvie, the well-known sporting poet, who had lived in Australia, broken in horses there and appeared well able to handle the toughest offenders. Armour relates that he only once saw him put down but the poet-horseman eventually admitted to early prowess as a buck-jump rider.

Armour went on to command a squadron in the Remount Depot at Swaythling near Southampton, through which all animals for overseas passed before issue. Good fortune never deserted him for whilst riding hundreds of these unknown horses he only sustained three falls, which suggests his horsemanship was as effective as his skill with the paint brush. His admiration of the temper and courage of the men under him was unbounded; most were utterly devoid of any equestrian background and had to learn to handle and ride horses in record time. He wrote in his autobiography, 'There were few days that the ambulance did not have to go to Netley hospital with casualties.'[1]

From this period came sketches of entraining reluctant horses, of patient heads gazing from railway wagons (*52*), a few studies of the finished article – mount and trooper, smart and secure. One of the artist's most moving compositions in beige and sepia oils shows the horse lines in Flanders in pouring rain. Today this picture hangs in the comfort of the Savage Club.

Armour many times accompanied cargoes of animals to Rouen, entailing an ill-omened channel crossing in pitch dark. After two years at Swaythling he exchanged with an officer who had a squadron in Salonika. Baggage allowance was minimal, nevertheless he managed to include a hunting saddle and gun and was promoted Lieutenant Colonel, Deputy Acting Director Remounts.

In Salonika conditions were far from pleasant with intermittent bombing and malaria but mitigated somewhat by wild fowl shooting and by polo with ponies found amongst remounts, and here also mules came into his life. Armour writes enthusiastically of the endurance and intelligence of this much maligned hybrid and made several observant sketches. (None, of course, compare with Stanley Spencer's *Travoys Arriving with Wounded at a Dressing Station at Smol, Macedonia.*) He wrote movingly of the sufferings of horses living in winter blizzards, denied any chance of finding shelter 'they looked the picture of misery . . . But I never saw a single one the worse of it; no colds, coughs or any evidence of illness!'[2] Orders for the disposal of the horses and mules in Macedonia at the end of the war caused him acute distress. Any over fifteen years of age were to be destroyed and the rest sold into virtual slavery; the largest block of animals being bought by the Greek Government and 10,000 went to Romania.

Shortly before the Armistice a mixed pack of hounds, imported originally to the Western

52 George Denholm Armour, *The Great War: Entraining Horses*, c 1914. Drawing from *Bridle and Brush*.

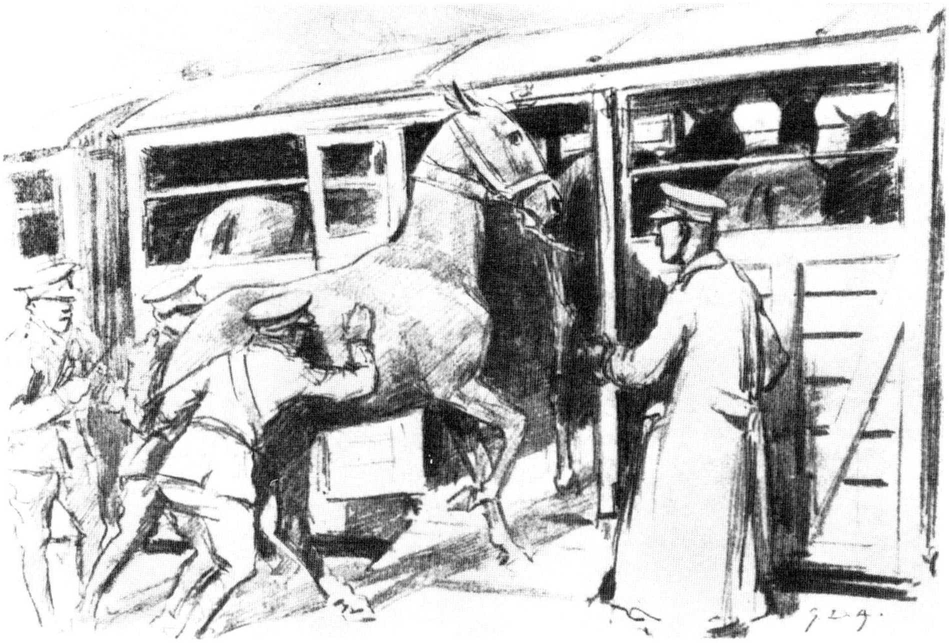

Front, arrived in charge of a former whipper-in of the VWH (Cricklade) Hounds. Hares were hunted in rough country of rocks and precipices and Armour's sketches of a dedicated band of sportsmen provided a cheerful record of these diversions.

After four years service on army pay, Armour finished his military career as a Colonel and was awarded an OBE, but beginning again in his fifties his professional life as an artist entailed a hard struggle. Though he had sold a few drawings during the war and *Punch* had paid him a small regular fee for work as opportunity offered, he returned to a meagre bank balance and after having hundreds of horses under his command, for a couple of years as a civilian, he found the ownership of even one hunter beyond his finances.

The outbreak of hostilities in 1914 was bitterly regretted by Cecil Aldin who had just attained the peak of ambition and become an MFH as Joint Master of the South Berkshire Hunt and soon took over single-handed. The War Office asked Masters to carry on, so somehow he managed to hold together a reduced pack till the Armistice. But, like G.D. Armour, he quickly found himself in charge of a Remount Depot, and eventually became official Remount Officer for Berkshire with 300 horses at a time stabled at Purley, near Pangbourne, and other centres.

As Remount Officer for the entire county and with only a small company of men unfit for active service (Munnings was to come under this listing) and all virtually completely inexperienced with horses, staff problems became insuperable. Aldin made an extraordinary innovation which received small encouragement from the War Office, by deciding to enlist the services of women from those with a background of the hunting field and horse ownership. From the beginning their appointment as stablehands and riders proved an oustanding success and he was able to set up the first all-woman remount depot at Purley, soon to be copied in many other areas in the country.

All social classes were involved, daughters and wives from stately homes, farms, hunt kennels and riding schools, including Aldin's own daughter. Some of the teenage girls were so small that they used boxes and upturned buckets as stands for grooming. A splendid picture by Aldin shows horses tied up in a big beamed barn being tended by a bevy of women in khaki breeches and overalls (53). Another of his successful wartime compositions was *A Landgirl Ploughing* with a team. Both these works were officially purchased for the Imperial War Museum. He admitted however, that between 1914–1917 he barely touched pencil or brush but that this change of occupation was a good thing for the artist, as also experienced by Lionel Edwards, and brought unexpected improvement to his work.

At this same period Lynwood Palmer, being too old for active service, organised in the City the 750 horses of the Royal Mail and, appreciating the feminine potential, enlisted women as drivers and trained them himself.

From childhood the military occasion had always engrossed Snaffles and after his brief early career in the Royal Garrison Artillery and, later, a year in the Leicestershire Yeomanry, it was predictable that in 1914 he would immediately demand to be involved in active service. However, rejection on medical grounds proved a bitter disappointment and, as an acceptable alternative, he joined the staff of *The Graphic* and was sent to Northern France to depict front line action for its readers at first-hand. His first picture '*Lieu at'em My Lads*' appeared on 24 October 1914 and four other wartime studies were published in the *Illustrated Sporting and Dramatic News* and three of these, *Hit* (*c* 1915), *Gunners* (*c* 1915) and *Whoo-Whoop* (*c* 1918) were to achieve great popularity as prints.

Many drawings, mostly in pencil and ink, of the gunner teams, exhausted, soaked in mud and rain brought to those at home realisation of the ghastly hardships being experienced by the troops. The detail was extraordinary considering that sketch books were banned in the battle area and work had to be produced from memory in appalling conditions. Some poignant examples of these can be seen in the Imperial War Museum.

But dissatisfied amid the carnage with his own relatively safe and privileged position as an artist, and perhaps because in between he fell in love, he returned to marry the charming,

53 Cecil Charles Windsor Aldin, *Women employed in the Remount Depot. 'The Kennels', Pangbourne*, *c* 1917. Pastel, $34 \times 51\frac{1}{2}$ in (86.3 × 130.8 cm).

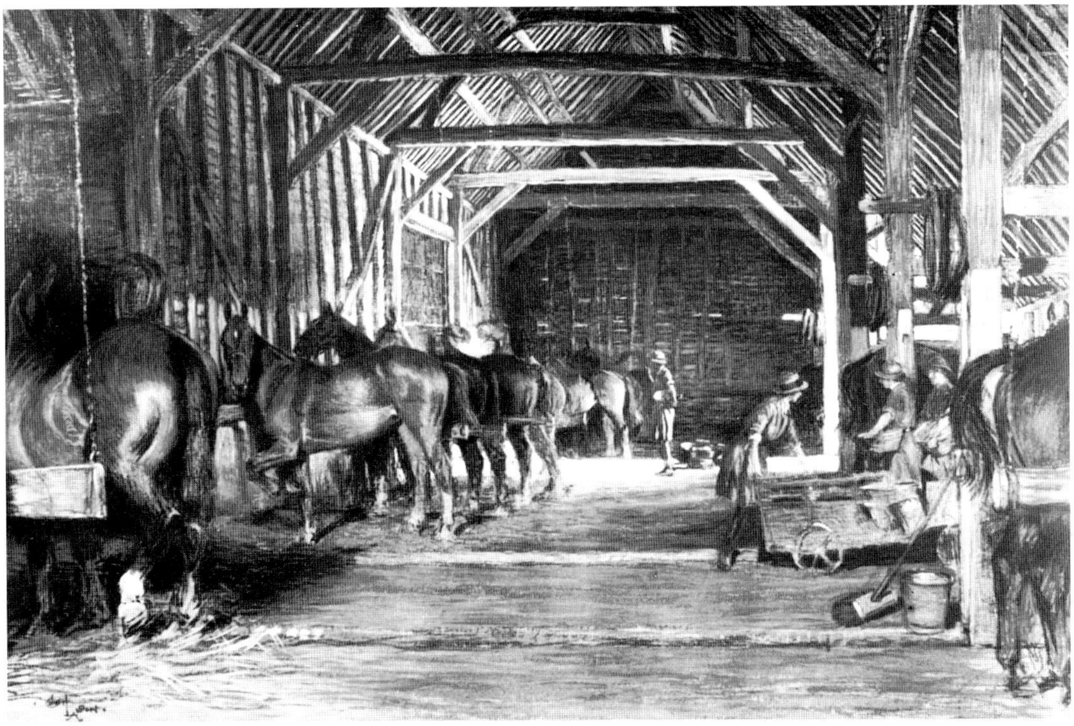

54 Snaffles – Charlie Johnson Payne, *'Forrard on me lads and hit 'em – 'ard'*, *c* 1941. Print, $9\frac{1}{2} \times 23\frac{1}{2}$ in (24.1 × 59.6 cm).

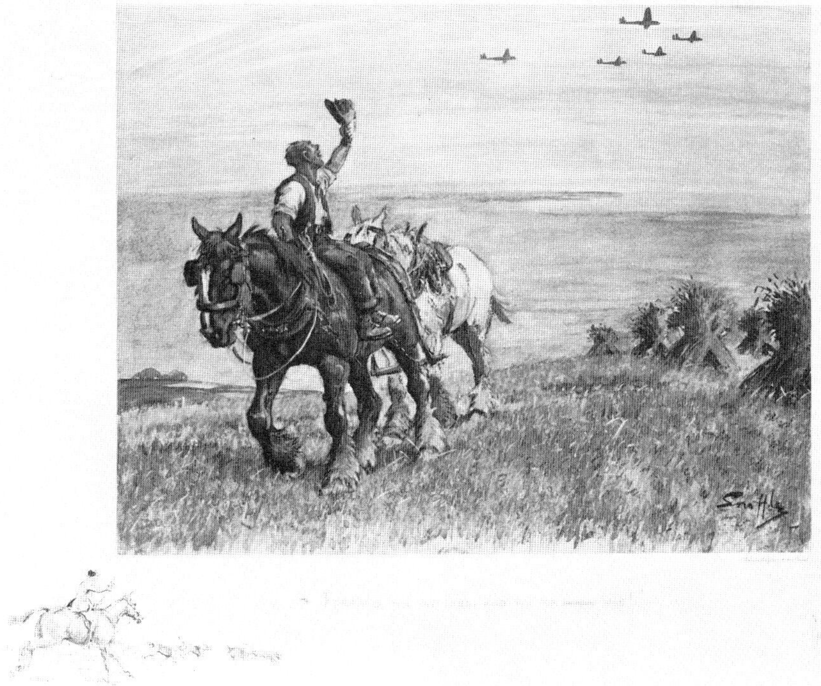

sensible Lucy Georgina Lewin. Born in Australia, daughter of a retired captain of a merchant fishing fleet, she was for the rest of her life to influence his impractical ways by sound guidance.

In 1916 Snaffles enlisted as a mechanic in the Royal Naval Auxiliary Motor Launches but later, much to his delight, was commissioned as a lieutenant in the RNVR and posted to HMS *President* in the Thames to join Norman Wilkinson, the marine and angling painter, in the 'Dazzle' camouflage section with its headquarters in Burlington House. Never entirely convinced that his new innovation proved a really effective protection for factories and buildings (in 1945 he alleged artists selected designs in their favourite racing colours!), nevertheless for ships at sea he was dedicated to the value of 'Dazzle' and over 2,700 ships of all types were painted with confusing patterns. Two years after the Armistice he was somewhat surprised to receive the Order of the Crown of Belgium. The reason for the award remains obscure but Snaffles suggests he had helped camouflage safe transport for King Albert.

In the final years of the war he was attached to the Northern Patrol and went as far afield as Poland to gain first-hand experience for camouflage technique and conditions for paintings and prints on Royal Naval Reserve subjects. These resulted in such dramatic scenes as *Watching the Sweep* RNRT and TBD's[3] *Shepherding a Convoy*. He was one of the very few sporting artists to record the war at sea and he produced a surprising flair for depicting vessels in storm conditions with men struggling in oil-skins.

In the Second World War, Snaffles though nearly sixty, nevertheless for a short time was camouflaging aerodromes but then joined the Home Guard and worked on the land until overtaken by ill-health – but from this rural background some striking pictures and prints emerged. Three that achieved enormous popularity and were originally published in *Punch* show a ploughman returning home with his heavy horses waving to a squadron of our bombers overhead, *'Forrard on me Lads and Hit Them – Hard!'*, (54) and the scene in the dusk *'Pass*

Friend' as a fox slinks by Charlie White of the Home Guard, and *The Season 1939–40* with the hunt passing two parked 4/7th tanks in a country lane (*Plate 12*). This records that strange early phase – 'The Phoney War' – when active hostilities seemed waiting for 'the off'. In two World Wars Snaffles caught much of the essence of England in danger with the same truth and facility of his inimitable studies of hunting and racing in the halcyon days of peace.

Lionel Edwards was yet another established artist engulfed by the Army Remount Service in various depots and was to finish up as a Sales Officer at the demobilisation. From August 1914 he spent most of his time in London trying to join up – worried that activities might cease before he had an opportunity to play a part. In actual fact whilst pestering the War Office as early as August and October he was contributing drawings to *The Graphic*. One shows horses in an inn yard being commandeered for military service, others drawn from the description of an officer serving on the Western Front includes a night scene of a Pickford removal van, requisitioned for overseas provisions delivery, charging a mounted party of Uhlans.[4] *Country Life* published his studies of horses, gaunt and unkempt, after the voyage from America to contrast with the same animals sleek and glossy later at the Remount Depot. Eventually in March 1915, through the influence of Lord Charles Bentinck, he was appointed Second Assistant Superintendent with the temporary rank of Captain to the Remount Depot at Romsey. Here he formed many friendships amongst the congenial company which abounded, elderly cavalry officers, masters of hounds, racehorse trainers and 'other ranks' jockeys, grooms and even a couple of Canadian cowboys.

There was no opportunity for serious painting and throughout the war for some reason he never applied to be appointed an official war artist, but he earned commendation for a series of watercolour drawings of details of some equine skin infection which received the personal thanks of Major General F. Smith, DD, DVS Southern Command and the request 'I hope Captain Edwards will allow me to retain this beautiful work'. Edwards himself considered that the mule was the most useful of 'His Majesty's four-footed soldiers' and, like Armour, thought their evil reputation was due to poor handling and lack of understanding. A vivid line drawing published in *The Field* early in 1918 depicts a soldier being adroitly bucked off an army mule. Trips to France with troop horses were a welcome diversion from everlasting stable duties, produced a few moving studies of horses, cold and dejected, huddling together in wind and rain; one bears the title '*And Some There Be That Have Left No Memorial*'. In February 1919 he sent two coloured Remount sketches to his agent, A.E. Johnson, with the titles *The Docks* and *Evening Stables*. Though he writes wisely and entertainingly of his experiences in the Remount Depot in his autobiography *Scarlet and Corduroy* he also records the devastating fact that 377,312 horses and mules were sent from the United Kingdom to France between 1914–1918.

More than twenty years later he produced a dramatic oil painting of the *Charge of the 3rd Dragoon Guards at Honnechy in 1918*, their last action in which two officers and ninety men were lost. Curiously enough this picture first began on canvas as a hunting scene, but now forms a valued item of the collection of the Royal Scots Dragoon Guards.

Four years of military life in a world of horses was for Lionel Edwards never dull (55) and, unconsciously, his eye became educated to every detail of equine conformation, an artistic bonus for a lifetime – though he admitted that schooling rogue remounts for a period broke his nerve. Immediately after the Armistice sales of horses at the Depots took place all over England. He escorted hundreds sold in lots at such centres as Birmingham, Bicester, Leamington and Oxford. He himself bought four, a mixed bag, which included a lovely hack for Ethel and an ugly American horse which became a first class hunter.

In Hitler's war, Lionel Edwards, then in his sixties, found his niche when asked to form and command a mounted unit of the Home Guard, a duty which he fulfilled seriously and usefully, whilst increasing farm production at Buckholt. At the same time he continued to write illustrated articles for *Country Life* on such subjects as hunting in war conditions.

Though blind in one eye, Alfred Munnings made persistent efforts to enlist but inevitably received rejection papers. Nevertheless, at an ultimate examination at Bodmin he was graded C3. Determined to find a place with the Remounts he wrote to Cecil Aldin and by return received a letter, 'Come at once', and was immediately immersed in the care of thousands of horses then arriving from Canada, proving himself particularly adept at the filthy and evil smelling job of treating mange.

Predictably AJ also found means of enlivening the daily round and was occasionally permitted to take a Canadian charger out with Aldin and hounds; Aldin, as Munnings writes in his autobiography, proved a good amateur huntsman. Much to Aldin's regret, at the end of a year Paul Konody, the art critic, arranged for the appointment of Munnings as an official war artist under the new Ministry of Information, to be attached to the Canadian Cavalry Brigade to make official pictorial records. Augustus John and William Orpen had already been sent to France with the rank of major but AJ turned up at the Headquarters of the commander of the Brigade, General J.B. Seely (later Lord Mottistone) as a civilian; though later he borrowed a tunic and Sam Browne and became what he described as an 'imitation captain'.

Artist and General struck up an immediate rapport for both were dedicated horsemen and also appreciated the good things of life, which included champagne. Munnings' first subject was Seely himself on his renowned horse, Warrior, which went through the war with him and returned home to win the Isle of Wight Point-to-Point. Painted to the accompaniment of enemy gunfire the portrait proved to be an outstanding likeness of the General, informally wearing a long woollen scarf for comfort; it now hangs in the National Gallery at Ottawa.

Munnings with his easel and canvases travelled with the Brigade baggage, constant danger

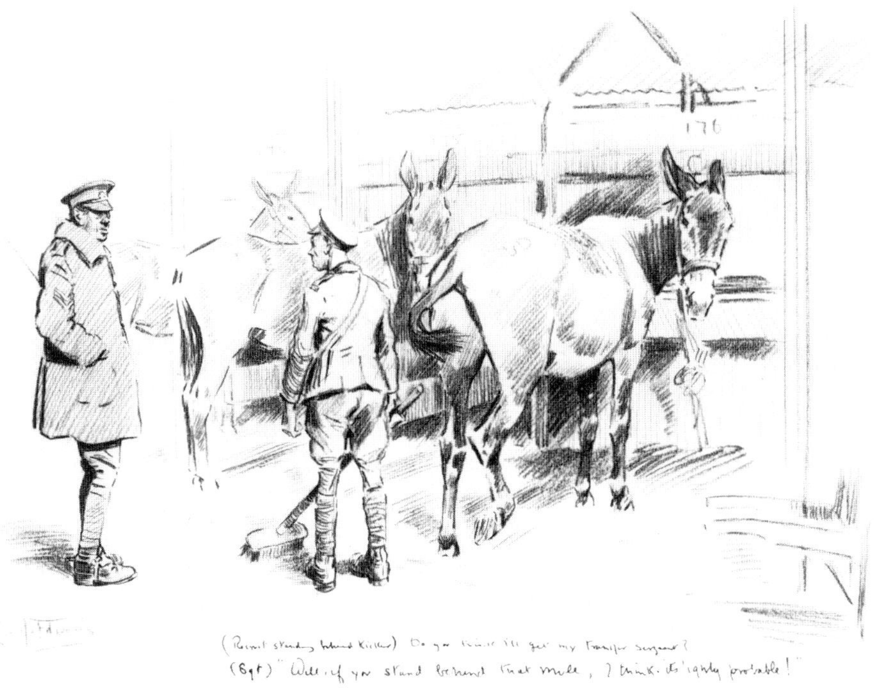

55 Lionel Dalhousie Robertson Edwards, *The Kicker*, *c* 1917. Pencil drawing, $9\frac{1}{2} \times 13\frac{3}{4}$ in (24.1 × 34.9 cm).

never daunted him and a myriad of subjects inspired a huge collection of admirable paintings and scores of crammed sketch books. 'What a chance for an artist' he wrote.[5] The military motivation proved the turning point in Munnings' career. His deep admiration for the officers and men of the Canadian troops and his determination to record scenes under fire with sincerity and discernment resulted in dramatic and moving pictures.

Eventually returning to England laden with canvases, some rolled up in a golf bag, over forty works provided, in 1919, the focal point of the Canadian War Records Exhibition at the Royal Academy. At once his reputation as an artist was assured, both nationally and internationally, and he was suddenly precipitated into the fashionable sporting world of the Thoroughbred, for as peace was declared racing and hunting soared to popularity. Owners of Classic and other important winners, masters of renowned packs of hounds, royalty and the aristocracy all demanded equestrian portraits by Munnings. His future prosperity was never again in doubt and he himself stated 'I have often wondered had there been no 1914–1918 War whether painting people on horseback would have absorbed the greater parts of my efforts in the years that followed.'[6]

But no more perceptive pictures appeared from the tragedy of the First World War than such masterpieces as Munnings' *Strathcona's Horse on the March* with its troop in full marching order, and the moving study of *A Halt on the March by a Stream at Neslé* with men dipping canvas buckets into a river against a sombre landscape (*Plate 12*). Particularly evocative are his vivid sketches of tired horses and memorable is a picture of stalls covered by tattered tarpaulin, with drowsy heads basking in the sunshine. Munnings, more than any of his contemporaries has left for posterity a remarkable and moving record of equestrian life in the desolation of the Somme.

Later he accepted commissions for an equestrian bronze to stand in the Horner Chapel in the village church of St Andrews at Mells in Somerset as a memorial to young Edward Horner, the last direct male heir to the Horner estate, killed in action in November 1917 on the Western Front. He made two small sketches in clay for Lady Horner's approval and then used photographs to obtain a likeness. The high stone plinth was designed by Sir Edward Lutyens but it was the Dedham blacksmith who made the armature for the model and the work was completed at Castle House, actually being cast there. Though the cramped proportions of the chapel were to inhibit the full impact of this superb figure (about two-thirds lifesize) of the cavalry officer, it illustrates the fact that Munnings possessed a mastery of three dimensional form that could have led him to great distinction as a sculptor. Careful and correct detail of uniform and military accoutrements complement and never diminish the poignancy and dignity of the figure. This masterpiece has failed to receive the publicity and acclaim it deserves.

As soon as the war broke out Gilbert Holiday was determined to become personally involved in activities with no waste of time and almost immediately went to France as an unofficial war artist. William Marler suggests this was probably at the suggestion of *The Graphic*. As early as August and September 1914 he was sending vivid drawings to this periodical of the British cavalry going into action near Lille, wounded soldiers on the seafront at Dinard and a page of sketches of Tommies in lighter mood on horseback laden with French loaves; sometimes these would be accompanied by brief articles written by himself. *The Graphic* published his full page colour drawing *Keeping Their Hand In* of sword exercises and cavalry drill behind the lines in sight and sound of gunfire. Without any permits or passes his itinerant life on the war front was full of incident. Arrested at one time by the British as a spy, on release he was soon apprehended again by the French authorities and only saved from the firing squad by the completely fortuitous intervention of a French acquaintance.

In 1915, after lying about his age (he was thirty-five years old and the limit at that time was thirty), he was commissioned into the Royal Field Artillery VIII Corps and his artistic ability, allied to a complete disregard for danger, found him being employed as a Forward Observation Officer to produce panoramic maps of the German skyline to facilitate the strategic laying of British gun emplacements. It entailed crawling out into No Man's Land at dawn to spend hours of the day making accurate sketches from the doubtful protection of a shellhole or ruined tree; later in his dugout he would complete the required maps. It was a hair-raising occupation and he escaped snipers' bullets by inches on many occasions. He was finally reported dead when a shell brought down an entire building on top of him but, protected by a falling cupboard, he was rescued, bruised but otherwise uninjured. Fortunately the official tragic communiqué to his family was intercepted.

A guardian angel seemed to have cared for GH as he worked through some of the fiercest hostilities at Arras and Passchendaele. But in all his official duties a sketch book was his constant companion and no opportunity was lost to record every aspect of life and death at the Front and to Gilbert Holiday we owe some of the most accurate evidence of the endurance and sufferings of men and horses at war. His family possess brilliant sketches of gun teams under bombardment, men and officers in action and repose, braw Scots in kilts, devastated village streets lined with troops.

In time of peace he had always been fascinated by the skill and panache of the Gunner Teams of the Royal Artillery. Snaffles had referred to these pictures as beyond criticism by art critic or soldier and Holiday's painting in 1914 of *The Musical Ride of the King's Troop Royal Horse Artillery at Olympia* was one fine example. This same expertise he brought to

56 Brian Hatton, *An Advance Guard patrolling a Road*, 1915. Charcoal and white paint on brown paper, 22 × 16½ in (55.8 × 41.9 cm).

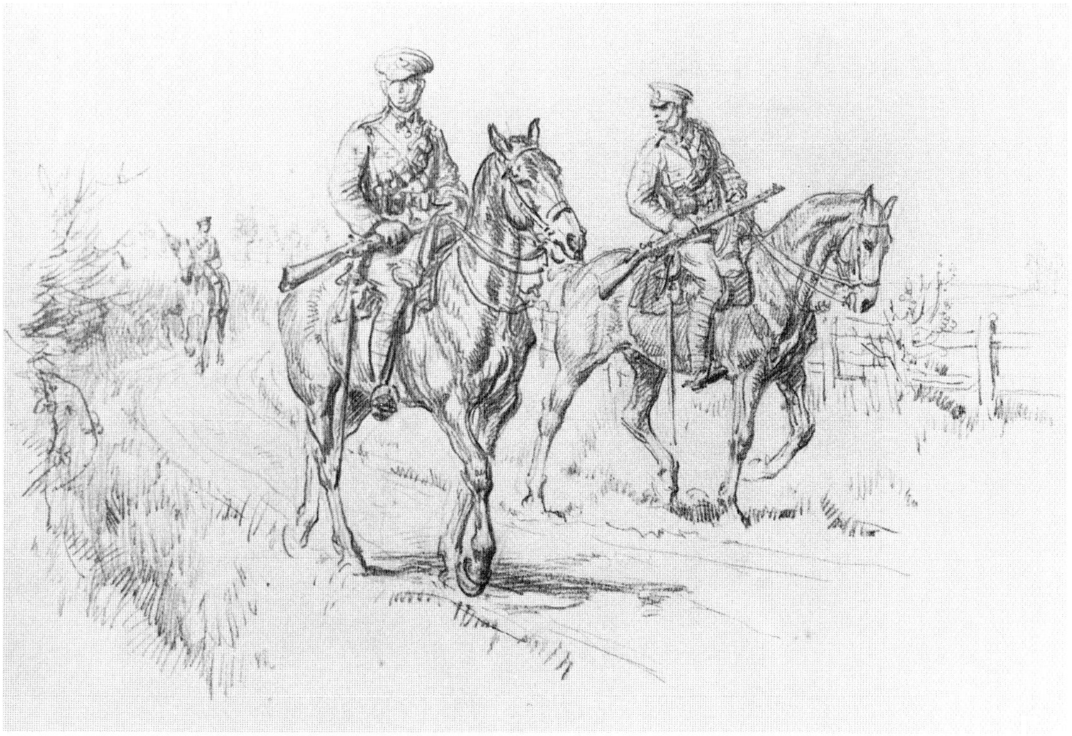

these studies of the Gunners in live action in France. Many were reproduced in *The Graphic* as half page illustrations as what GH called his 'on the spot studies'.

In 1917 during the Third Battle of Ypres he accomplished some of his most vivid and important work as an official artist. At the Imperial War Museum can be seen several drawings in coloured chalks such as *The Battery Wagon Line*, *The Ammunition Column* and also *Ypres Christmas 1917*. The latter was a study for his important oil painting of the subject with the ruined Square and Cloth Hall of Ypres – a scene of haunting devastation.

Before demobilisation in 1919 Gilbert Holiday served with the Army of Occupation in Germany and later in that year exhibited in the Royal Academy a striking picture of the 29th Division of Gunnery crossing the Hohenzollern Bridge, with the salute being taken by General Plumer standing under the statue of the Kaiser. Many works by the artist are today included in the *Royal Artillery War Commemoration Book*, known as 'The Gunner Bible'. Munnings and Holiday must be recognised as the two artists who more, perhaps than any of their contemporaries contributed records of the First World War which can be acclaimed as pictorially accurate and also as important works of art. In addition Brian Hatton also left a few moving drawings of his service with the Worcestershire Yeomanry. A study in charcoal and white paint on brown paper of *An Advance Guard Patrolling*, (56) and *Civilisation 1915* in charcoal wash – a heap of dying men and horses – give some indication of the calibre of this brilliant artist who was himself killed fighting in Egypt the following year.

By 1914 the equestrian studies of Lowes Dalbiac Luard had achieved recognition and considerable prestige in France and England. At the outbreak of war the artist was already forty-two years old but faithful to the traditions of his family (his grandfather Lt Col Lowes Luard had served with distinction in the Peninsular Wars in the 4th Light Dragoons) he enlisted at once and with his bilingual abilities was quickly attached to the RASC. Later, however, his outstanding gifts for organisation and capacity for hard work resulted in his appointment as Supply Officer and the rank of Lieutenant Colonel.

From this active service in France he left some striking studies of gun teams bogged down in mud as the poignant drawing *French Gun Team* with horses in utter extremity (57). But

57 Lowes Dalbiac Luard, *French Gun Team*, *c* 1916. Drawing, 12 × 17½ in (30.5 × 44.4 cm).

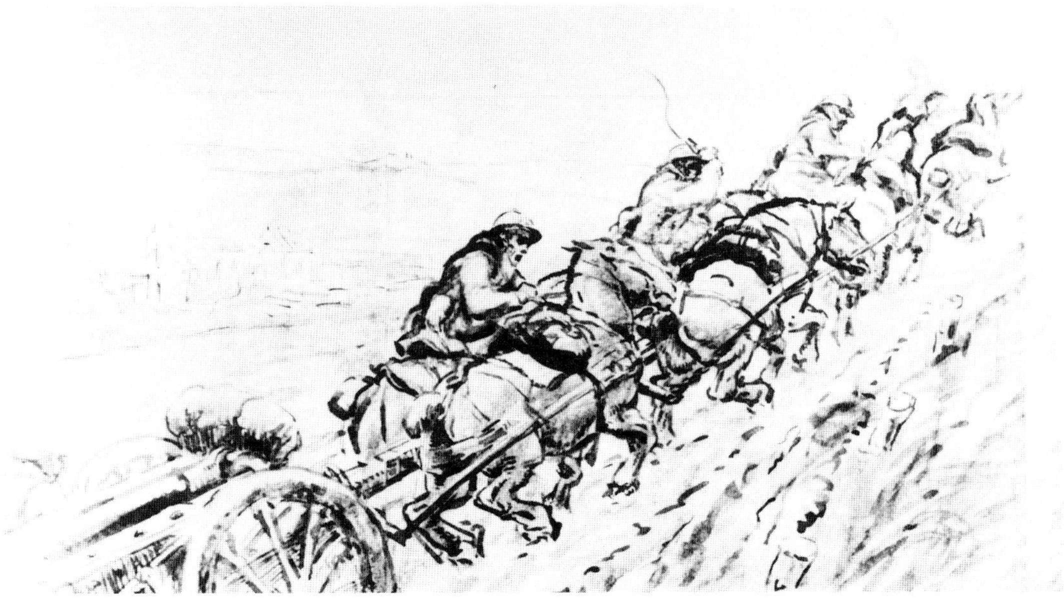

in spite of the pervading death and desolation letters home were embellished by humorous sketches of army life. It is regrettable that the all-enveloping war effort left no time for Luard to work seriously with pencil and brush, but for outstanding services in the Army he was awarded the Croix de Guerre avec Palmes and was mentioned five times in Despatches.

In the Second World War he was head of the ARP in St John's Wood but also produced a few topical drawings in pen and pastel for the War Artists' Commission under the aegis of Sir Kenneth Clark. Half a dozen of these including a *Mule Battery in Wales* are in the Imperial War Museum. He also played a part in a popular series of lectures on 'War and the Artist' given at the National Gallery.

A woman artist who made an important contribution to the pictorial scene of the First World War was Lucy Kemp-Welch. In 1915 when it was obvious that a long bitter struggle lay ahead with an insatiable demand for ever more manpower she was approached by the Parliamentary Recruiting Committee for a relevant poster. Her first sketch of charging horse and rider was approved and, working from photographs of actual uniforms and equipment, her final completed design with the one word 'Forward' in large black letters proved dramatically effective. After the war all remaining copies were quickly bought up.

Early in 1916 she worked with the Red Cross, learning to drive, but failed to achieve posting abroad and spent much of her time filing papers at the London headquarters. Fortunately opportunities to paint were not lost and her true calibre as an artist was revealed in the striking composition *Forward the Guns!* which was eventually bought for the Tate Gallery by the Chantrey Bequest (but unfortunately reproducing inadequately.) Measuring five by ten feet the picture was painted in the autumn of the year at Bulford Camp on Salisbury Plain where the Royal Horse Artillery had their barracks. Her diary records incidents of progress with details of the problems of combining accuracy and action. Her untiring dedication made possible a demanding task, for many days were handicapped by poor weather; nevertheless she would return home with a mass of working sketches. She made numerous drawings of tack and equipment as authenticity of every belt and buckle had importance. But in the completed picture it is speed, danger and sheer physical panache of horses and riders that come over with amazing vitality.

It was after the Armistice that Lucy Kemp-Welch received two of her most important war commissions. In February 1919 Lady Normanton, a Trustee of the Imperial War Museum, asked the artist for a picture commemorating the work of the sixteen women working at the Russley Park Remount Depot in Wiltshire. It was to rank as an overall tribute to more than 200 women whose war effort in twenty-one similar centres had been the demanding and often dangerous task of training and caring for horses of the Army. Lucy Kemp-Welch asked £1000 for this commission but agreed to a lower fee if she could make extra studies at Russley on her own behalf.

Work had to be commenced at speed as the Depot was due for closure in June 1919 but owing to illness the picture, of course of huge dimensions, was not completed until 1920. Another painting of Russley exhibited at the Royal Academy, *The Straw Ride*, a brilliant evocation of girls riding and leading in pairs restive horses, all silhouetted against a wide vista through the open school doors, was preferred by the Trustees to the more stereotyped commissioned work and in 1922 the artist herself presented it to the Imperial War Museum (*58*).

Another important war composition was executed by Lucy Kemp-Welch for the Royal Exchange, subscribed by her fellow members of the Empress Club in Dover Street; the theme illustrated was *Women's Work in the Great War 1914–1918*. The first design was turned down

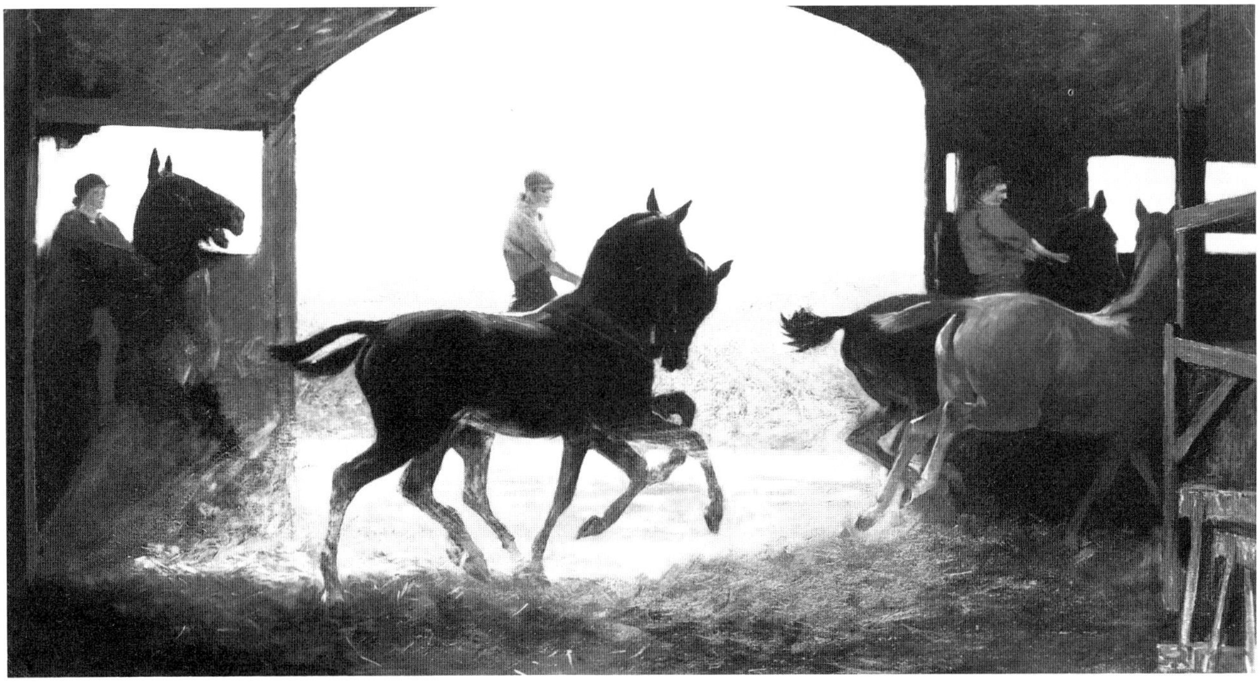

58 Lucy Kemp-Welch, *The Straw Ride. Russley Park Remount Depot*, *c* 1918. Oil on canvas, 44 × 58½ in (111.7 × 148.5 cm).

by the Gresham Selection Committee and it was not until April 1942 that the final large panel was unveiled by HRH Princess Mary and a large replica was also painted for the Empress Club. Without any equestrian content the mood is quiet, of concentrated effort in various spheres all executed in soft pleasing colour tones.

Lucy Kemp-Welch's last commission was a posthumous action portrait of Captain the Hon. Elydir Herbert, son of Lord and Lady Treowen, killed at Huj in November 1917 fighting his way across No Man's Land to capture an enemy machine gun – a work the artist fulfilled movingly and dramatically, even going to the lengths of having loads of concrete and rubble dumped by her studio to achieve realism of battlefield desolation.

Some of Maud Earl's work for the war effort centred round full page advertisements in *The Graphic* for Buchanan's Scotch Whisky – a series of brisk canine studies with Irish and Highland terriers and other breeds with such topical titles as *Dublin Fusiliers* and *Highland Light Infantry*.

In the historic records of Hitler's war, Laura Knight must be considered amongst the most valuable contributors but in no way can these sketches be equated with her animal or equestrian scenes. Paramount amongst this work is her commission in 1946 from the British Government to record the Nuremberg Trials. Her arresting oil painting of the scene now hangs in the Imperial War Museum but also in existence are numerous portrait sketches of such leading figures as Mr Justice Lawrence, Norman Birkett, KC, as well as such villains of the piece as Ribbentrop and Goering.

In the First World War she had received assignments from Lord Beaverbrook to paint a picture fourteen feet long of Scottish Canadian soldiers bathing nude in a river. Conventions of the day substituted these soldiers washing their knees before the kilted Saturday evening relaxation with the girls. But out of this commission sporting art received a bonus, for Laura Knight had the good fortune to see Joe Shears, Bantamweight Champion of the day, emerging from a barber's shed, 'I followed his bruised and purple face, cauliflower ears and broken nose to the gymnasium.'[7] From this chance encounter the sporting scene was to be enriched by some splendid boxing studies over the years in which the artist skilfully captures the nimble split-second reactions of muscled contestants.

From 1914–1918 many portraits and landscape artists of distinction produced valuable and enduring records of various spheres of national service. Occasionally the equestrian factor played a small part; Orpen amongst his 138 works in the Imperial War Museum includes a few isolated studies of the Household Brigade and horse lines in France. Equally John S. Sargent in 1915 provides a watercolour of horses in welcome contrast to his studies of damaged tanks.

Total mechanisation of service techniques and equipment in the Second World War provided small scope for the talents of any sporting artist but Terence Cuneo, in between his numerous drawings and paintings of tanks and aeroplanes, also included some retrospective work of former hostilities such as the dynamic *Saving the Guns at Le Cateau*.

John Kenney left a collection of fine action drawings from Normandy to the Baltic, made during his service with the 121st Light Royal Artillery Regiment after D-Day. These have been accepted for the official regimental records at the Royal Army Museum at Woolwich but they give little indication of his future as an outstandingly successful artist of the hunting scene.

Also, in the book by Lt Col G.E. Bouskell Wade MB, TD, DL, published in 1948 '*There is an Honour Likewise . . .' The Story of the 154 (Leicestershire Yeomanry) Field Regiment R.A.* are some splendid horse drawings by Kenney illustrating life before and during the Second World War. Some between 1939–45 are humorous, with recruits attempting to establish relationships with reluctant remounts. Several are more serious studies in Syria and Palestine; and later in Italy, a few are poignant, depicting the patient endurance of the few horses and mules still used in military service in the Second World War.

Blessedly, with the end of World War I, the horse had, at last, played its final active service role on the actual battlefield. Perhaps this is the only redeeming feature to emerge from the general slaughter and devastation of that terrible 'War to End War!'

NOTES

1 G.D. Armour, *Bridle and Brush*, p. 255.

2 ibid, p. 354.

3 RNRT = Royal Naval Reserve Trawler; TBD = Torpedo Boat Destroyer.

4 *The Graphic*, 15 August and 24 October 1914.

5 Reginald Pound, *The Englishman: A Biography of Sir Alfred Munnings*, p. 65.

6 Stanley Booth, *Sir Afred Munnings 1878–1959*, p. 18.

7 Laura Knight, DBE, RA, *The Magic of a Line*, p. 150.

11

Peace and a Changing World

After the four years of hostilities and deprivations of the First World War, by 1919 people of every class turned with relief to normal life. Many tragic memories had to be obliterated and those of the younger generation who survived (and casualties amongst the British alone had been nearly three million) were more than ready for a new golden age of sport, though practical problems certainly lay ahead which were to become more complex with the passing years. Fruitless but serious attempts, even before the war, were made to curtail blood sports. A bill in 1908 by militants of the Humanitarian League was followed, in 1915, by an indictment *Killing for Sport*, edited by H.G. Salt with a biting preface by G. Bernard Shaw and, as late as 1949, by a private members' Bill which met with defeat; but the controversy was to reappear and by the 1980s to become a political issue and a positive threat to foxhunting and coursing.

Nevertheless, after the First World War, splendid sport continued to be enjoyed in the hunting field, and the popularity of shooting and coursing remained unabated. Racing, which from 1914 had suffered almost total eclipse (by 1918 it had been restricted solely to Newmarket), attracted huge enthusiastic crowds as soon as peace was declared. The Derby's return to Epsom in 1919 was advertised by a lively poster by that brilliant star of design, Dudley Hardy, RBA, showing the world and his wife en route to the races (*59*). The steady growth of the popularity of racing was also to be indicated later by Charles Cundall in his crowded canvas *Derby Day – 1933*, a panorama of the Downs and the old stands packed with humanity. This artist might be considered perhaps the William Frith of his day. With such influential owners and breeders as the Lords Derby and Woolavington, the Aga Khan and also the King (who won the 1928 One Thousand Guineas with Scuttle) proving important patrons for contemporary sporting artists – Lynwood Palmer, Aldin and Armour were still only in their fifties – commissions were not lacking.

It should be remembered, however, that before the First World War the country had been still, in rural terms, a coherent unit; landlords played their part in seeing that tenant farmers welcomed hounds and kept wire to a minimum. A certain panache had still existed; in 1912 Lord Lonsdale entertained 200 Masters of Foxhounds to dinner at the Peterborough Show. Liveried second horsemen in white cords, black coat and cockaded top hats still rode hunters to meets (recorded for posterity by Munnings' study of *Dale, Mr Robert Bolitho's Groom*); motor horse boxes were not popular, they cost all of £450 but grooms were still cheap, with wages at only £2. 10s per week plus cottage and livery.

All sport was in the ascendant; attendance at football matches soared and the Cup Final was to become a national event. Fishing and polo, though minority activities, also received ever increasing support and most field sports were now less restricted by social status. Many of the landed gentry were impoverished and wealthy war manufacturers had become country

59 Dudley Hardy, *On the Road to the Derby*, 1919. Poster: 'Peace', $84\frac{1}{4} \times 39$ in (213.9×99 cm).

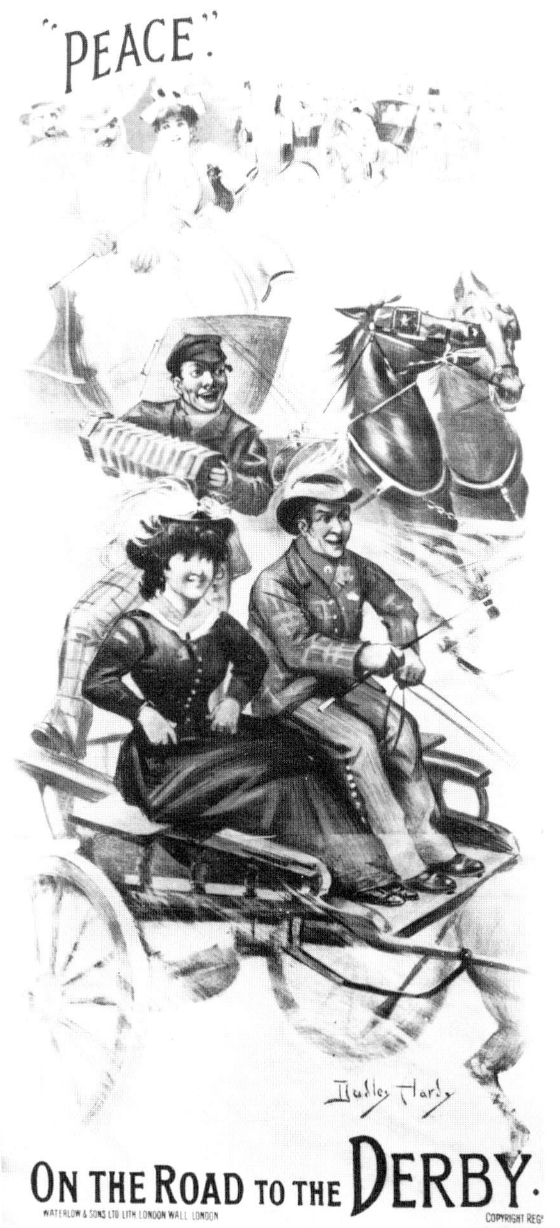

gentlemen. Some had received titles for their diligent services and though a few found difficulty in comprehending the subtle relationship of rural landowner and tenant, their generosity to hunt funds, and their boost to local employment, brought welcome financial impetus to the countryside. With the onset of peace, however, British agriculture was once again devalued politically and entered a period of acute depression – a bonus, of course, for the foxhunters as acres of arable land enforced by war stringencies swiftly reverted to grass, as seen in the studies of hunting countries by both Lionel Edwards and F.A. Stewart and virtually every Midland hunt became a galloping paradise.

The enthusiasm of the Prince of Wales (later Edward VIII and Duke of Windsor) for foxhunting and, in lesser degree, of his three brothers, was to bring a social glamour to the Shires not enjoyed in such excess since the halcyon days a century earlier and recorded so memorably by John Ferneley Snr. The Prince with his ADC, the sporting Major 'Fruity' Metcalfe, established a stud of hunters at Melton Mowbray and made himself immensely popular with yeomen farmers and socialites alike. Being a fearless, but rash, horseman, and lacking something of the experience and finesse necessary to control fresh and over-corned Thoroughbreds, he suffered his share of falls. Ill-informed publicity followed and when he took to riding in point-to-points concern was voiced by Parliament of the danger to life and limb of the heir to the Throne. For many artists of the day such as A.J. Munnings, Charles Simpson, William Orpen and others the dashing Prince provided a glamorous and popular subject.

A feature of this period was the arrival of foxhunting Americans who found the attraction of sport with the leading English packs irresistible. Between the wars many such enthusiasts as Ambrose Clark, Victor Emmanual, the young Paul Mellon and others spent their winters in Leicestershire, returning across the Atlantic with astutely selected pictures by Ben Marshall, John Ferneley and Henry Alken as mementoes of wonderful days with horse and hound in England. This was the beginning of the exodus of eighteenth and nineteenth century British sporting pictures to the United States which escalated in greater degree with the purchases by Paul Mellon and Jack Dick in the 1960s and which was to have long term repercussions on British sporting art in this country.

The impact of Hitler's war with its total mobilisation of all resources had a much greater effect on national sporting activities. As before, hunting was allowed to continue on strictly limited food rations for a nucleus of packs of hounds and a few hunt horses. Colin Ellis wrote, 'In its blackest days there was comfort in knowing that if England came through it and if we came through it . . . we could go back to Leicestershire and find the Quorn Hounds waiting for us.'[1] All racing was cancelled in 1939 but after one or two false starts was permitted to continue on a very reduced scale for the sake of British bloodstock breeding, but most courses had been ploughed up and buildings requisitioned. Though food rationing and strict agricultural direction continued until 1954, the capitulation of Germany in 1945 brought again an overwhelming resurgence of every form of sporting interest, but with the implementation of the Beveridge Plan a classless society, backed by social security, emerged. Recreational activities, including field sports, were now enjoyed by all members of the community led at the top by the Royal Family, with the Queen herself an active horsewoman and a knowledgeable and astute breeder of bloodstock and the Queen Mother keenly and successfully involved in steeplechasing. But equally motivated were myriads of new enthusiasts, many of them women and the majority lacking any traditional rural background. Amongst them could be found mechanics, bank managers and shopkeepers all keen to enjoy an active role in rural and animal sports, ranging from hunting to shooting, beagling to steeplechasing.

With the victory parades over, intensive farming became no longer a top priority and British agriculture once again faced the possibility of a gradual depression except in the hands of the grain entrepreneurs in East Anglia; though at the end of the 1980s even the viability of cereal crops was threatened. Many big and small landowners, sensing a bleak future, sold out and the country received again a new population composed predominantly of company directors and business magnates who, however, once installed in their rural homes, learnt to play the role of squire with generosity and good humoured energy. Big shoots were lavishly organised, maybe a couple of 'chasers put in training, wives were soon in the saddle and their sons and daughters joined farmers' children to become the enthusiasts of the Pony Club, mounted on smart ponies.

Many of the great landed estates, of course, still existed after the Second World War but, in general, the traditionalists gave way to a new order. With the popularity of the Hunt Supporters Clubs, car followers, in some cases, outnumbered mounted foxhunters. Motor horse boxes and trailers tended to block the roads and to antagonise folk on ordinary workaday affairs, as predicted thirty years earlier by Lionel Edwards. Syndicated shoots sold their game to West End poulterers, eventually even helicopters were to bring millionaire foxhunters, strangers to the local farmers, from the metropolis to the meet. But sport still flourished though, as wages increased, few riders in the Provinces brought out a second horse and many lacked a groom (by the sixties 90% of grooms were girls). More often the tired foxhunter drove the tired hunter home himself (or herself) and then conscientiously attended to stable duties before enjoying whisky and bath. But as Foxford was to write in *Horse & Hound* in 1986, 'It is useless to look back to the "good old days". The best of times is now.'[2]

The two World Wars had finally destroyed the privileges of landed society but had not endangered the enjoyment of sport which, in all its spheres, continued to grow in popularity. A significant sign of the times as early as 1945 had been the organisation in South Wales by the Banwen Miners of their own hunt, officially recognised and still flourishing today. But

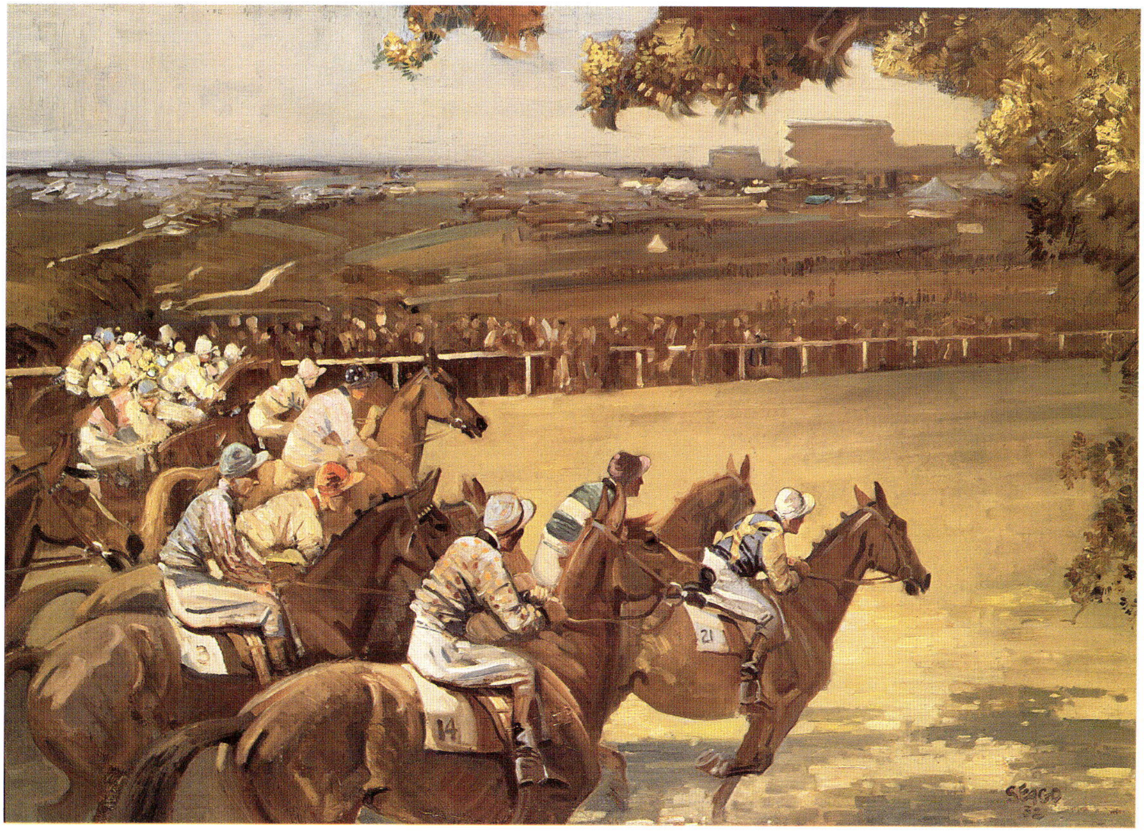

PLATE 13 (*above*) Edward Brian Seago, *Line up for the Start at Epsom*, 1938. Oil on board, $21\frac{1}{2} \times 30$ in (54.6×76.2 cm). (*below*) Peter Biegel, *Champion Hurdle at Cheltenham: Bula beats Persian War – 1971*. Oil on canvas.

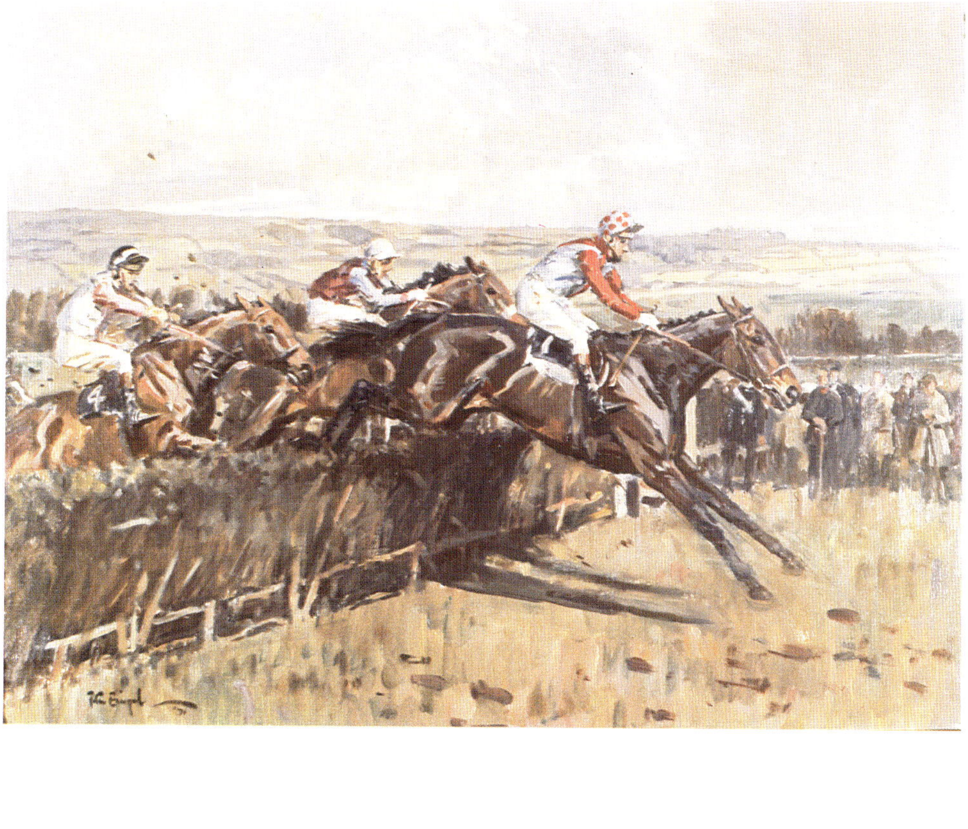

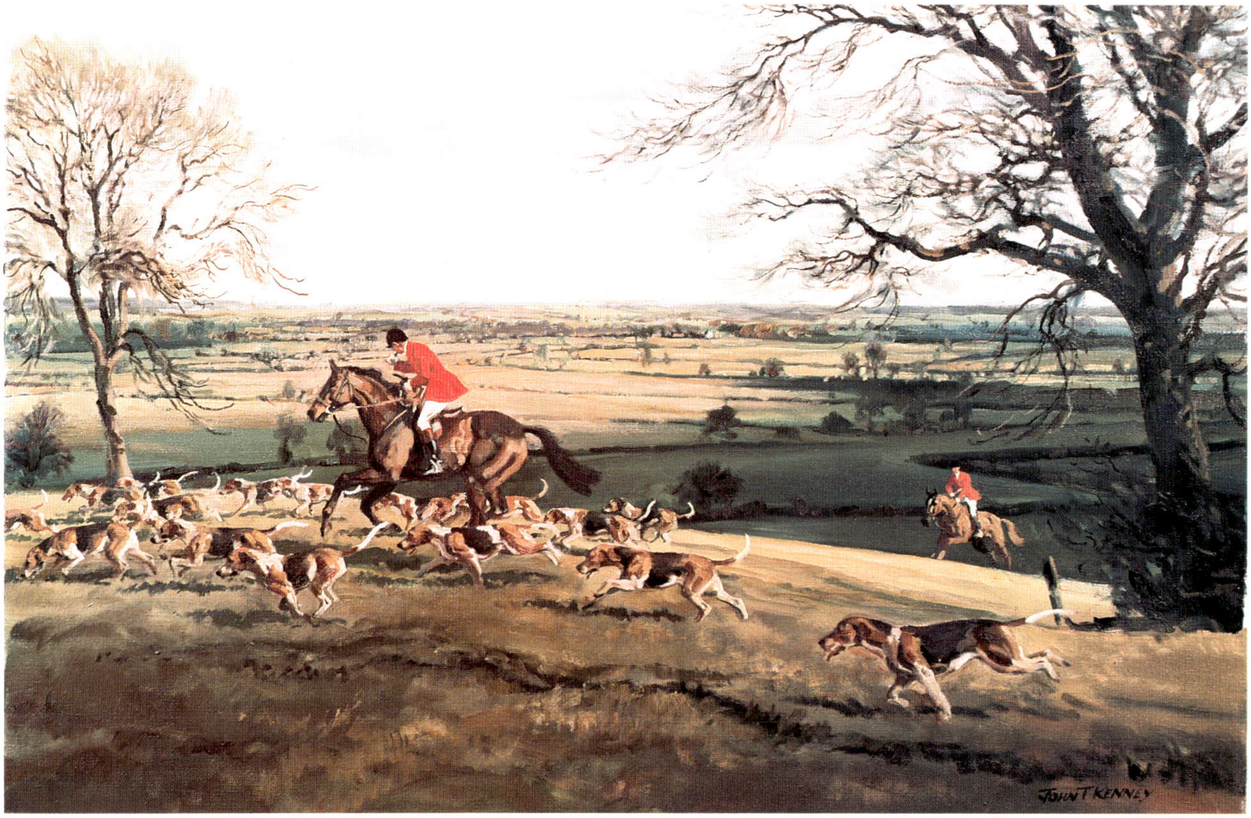

PLATE 14 (*above*) John Theodore Eardley Kenney, *The Fernie – Away from Bunkers Hill*, *c* 1963. Oil on canvas, 18 × 30 in (45.7 × 76.2 cm). (*below*) John Theodore Eardley Kenney, *Hounds on the Road*, 1970. Oil on canvas, 15 × 20 in (38.1 × 50.8 cm).

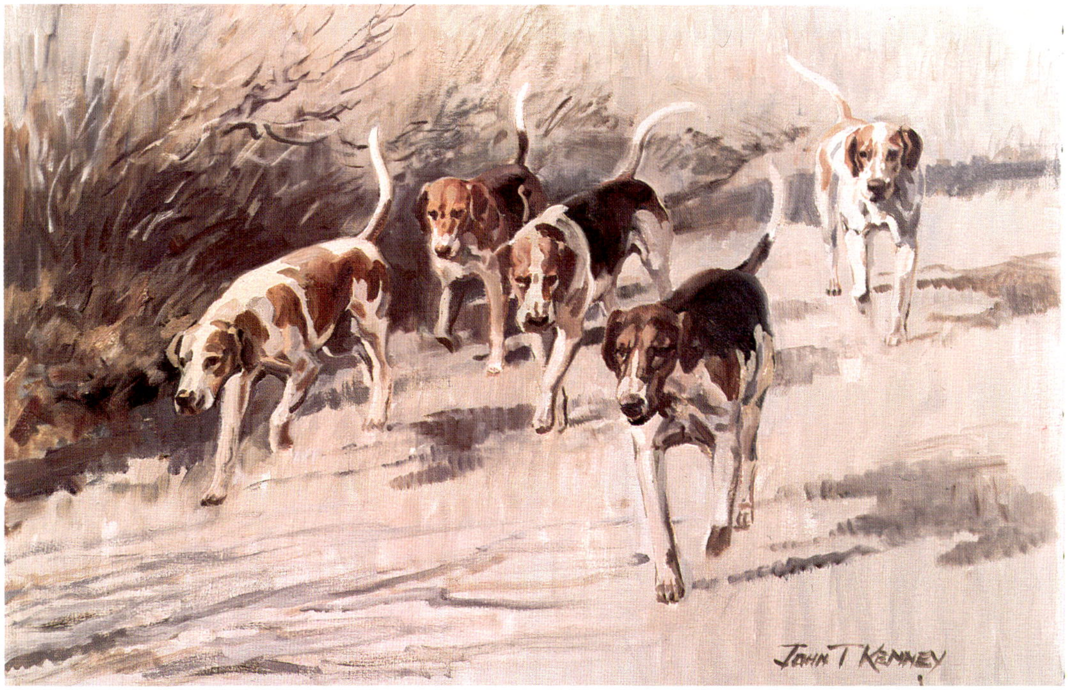

since the days of Osbaldeston the Leicestershire miners had been staunch supporters of the Quorn.

In spite of the incomplete recovery of the country from the ravages of a six years' war the world of sport was given an enormous boost in 1948 by the holding of the Olympic Games in Great Britain. The major equestrian event 'The Military' or 'Championnat Equestre' aroused such interest that the Duke of Beaufort was inspired the following year to initiate an annual equivalent competition at Badminton which now attracts thousands of spectators, and these Three Day Events are being held at national and international level in various parts of the world. At the same time show-jumping under the aegis of Major 'Mike' Ansell (later Colonel Sir Michael Ansell, CBE, DSO) who returned almost totally blind from a prisoner of war camp, became a highly organised activity attracting an ever increasing public. Polo was to become gradually re-established both at prestige level at Smith's Lawn and Cowdray and at more modest clubs in various parts of the country. Dressage was no longer an esoteric exercise reserved for the continentals and, most surprising of all, in a world where motorised transport reigned supreme, harness interests were to become a popular diversion under the organisation of the British Driving Society and also were to develop some exciting and somewhat dangerous competitive events avidly supported by HRH The Duke of Edinburgh.

Allied to the hunts the Pony Club soared in membership until the early 1980s and was to be the training ground of many future British Olympic riders. But equally important in its long term implication was the enormous popularity of riding clubs all over the country, a movement initially started by R.S. Summerhays in 1936 in Eastbourne. These were to provide for a modest outlay participation and instruction in riding activities for a completely new public.

Thus for the generation of sporting artists recently demobilised from active service the mid-century brought promise of a stimulating future with unexplored subjects to exploit against a changing background.

Commercial galleries such as Ackermann's, Fores and Frost & Reed, dealers for over a century and a half in sporting pictures, were ready to welcome young and competent artists and later in 1950 the Richard Green Gallery and, in 1959 the Moorland and Tryon Galleries also opened in the West End to make their own considerable impact in the same field. Prints in colour, signed in limited editions, were published after the most popular works and were to prove a lucrative income for the sporting artist with such equine stars as Arkle, Brown Jack, Mill Reef and Red Rum becoming public heroes.

But perhaps the most significant event for British sporting art after the war was the opening in 1949 and brief survival of a National Gallery of British Sports and Pastimes at Derby House, Stratford Place, W1 by Walter Hutchinson, Chairman of Hutchinson and Co., Publishers Ltd, under the guidance of Jack Ellis, the art dealer. Unfortunately Hutchinson's untimely death only two years later brought the swift dispersal of the entire collection by Christie's for derisory sums. It was to lead to the disappearance of many of the finest sporting pictures overseas, eventual soaring prices and ultimately to the formation of the British Sporting Art Trust.[3]

NOTES

1 Colin D.B. Ellis, *Leicestershire and the Quorn Hunt*, p. 187.

2 *Horse & Hound*, 12 December 1986.

3 See Chapter 18, page 197.

12

Mid-Century and New Names

By the mid-century several gifted and ambitious young artists, frustrated by the six years' creative negation of Hitler's war, were eager to renew their careers in this changed England, but in the school of British sporting art, inevitably motivated by such influences of the past as Ward, Marshall, Ferneley, Alken and the more recent late Victorians, breaks with tradition evolved only gradually. Munnings and Edwards, though both by now senior citizens were still painting some fine pictures and from the public there was certainly no demand for, and no expectation of, a New Look in sporting art, though Dior had achieved a spectacular metamorphasis in the world of feminine *haute couture*. Nearly a couple of decades and more were to pass before any innovative approach to the sporting subject became apparent.

The influence of Lionel Edwards appeared inescapable for he still reigned as the doyen of the hunting scene and ambitious youngsters were only too happy to make their name in his shadow. Perhaps, fortunately, these new aspiring painters missed comparison with brilliant Edward Seago, born in Norfolk in 1910, who had for a time appeared likely to vie with Munnings in his pictures of East Anglian rural and sporting scenes, and in portraits of Derby and Ascot Gold Cup winners, and such equestrian highlights as *Line Up for the Start at Epsom* (*Plate 13*). But Seago, early in his career, became obsessed by the world of circus and ballet, and later succumbed to the lure of landscape painting. A fine artist was lost to British sporting art and most of his work in this field has received little acclaim as it remains in private collections.

Lionel Edwards, though ever generous with advice to aspiring artists, amongst whom must be included Eric Meade-King, Denis Aldridge and John King, in all his long career, however, had through lack of time, only ever accepted one pupil. As a boy at school Peter Biegel had corresponded with his hero Lionel Edwards, and by fortunate chance happened to be in the right place at the right time – in a railway carriage *en route* from Salisbury to London.

After the Normandy landings in 1944 Biegel had been invalided out of the Army. The following year travelling to a medical board he was able to offer a share of his sandwiches to a tall spare man in a bowler hat with a ring in the back, Lionel Edwards himself! Before the train had reached Woking an assignation was made for the following Sunday when Peter Biegel was accepted to work as a pupil at Buckholt, living at the Black Horse in the village, after spending two terms at the Bournemouth School of Art studying figure drawing. The agreed time came to an end but the pupil stayed on 'learning my trade and hunting' to become almost a member of the family.

Born in 1913, Peter Biegel, son of a naturalised Dutchman (a keen hunting man) and an Irish mother also had for an ancestor Frederic Sang, a French artist and architect of distinction who had been responsible in the 1850s for frescoes in the now demolished Coal Exchange and ceilings at the Royal Exchange. In addition an Irish great-grandfather was killed in a steeplechase at the age of twenty-one so hereditary background was propitious. By the age of twenty Peter Biegel had actually received his first commission from an Irish priest, friend of the family, later Group Captain Monsignor H. Beauchamp, MC, for a painting of his little horse winning a steeplechase at Towcester, ridden by young Gerry Wilson. It was that famous National Hunt jockey's first ride in public, and he wore black and white colours made out of a silk evening dress belonging to the artist's mother. After education at Downside, Biegel had endured five years in the City but with some determination abandoned a business career and in 1938 became a student at Lucy Kemp-Welch's School of Art at Bushey. Progress was soon interrupted by war service with a Territorial Army commission in the 4th Battalion Wiltshire Regiment.

Early demobilisation made him among the first of the new generation of sporting artists to make his name and with time and experience his tendency to reflect the style of his master diminished and eventually a stamp of personal authority appeared in his pictures. From his own considerable ability as a rider he always possessed a flair for capturing the likeness of a horse. His Thoroughbreds show bone and breeding; variations in the angle of the rider's seat at different paces is cleverly co-ordinated as in his study of *The Immortals: Golden Miller, Easter Hero and Arkle* and in the fine watercolour of Golden Miller with Gerry Wilson in the saddle, in the blue with yellow hoop colours of Miss Dorothy Paget (*60*).

Several trips were made to the States for commissioned pictures, where he had the opportunity of hunting over the big timber country in Pennsylvania. Two of his most interesting portraits were of the English-bred Ludham at Belmont Park and the other of Quick Pitch, the American Champion Hurdler. The press on the other side of the Atlantic reported with surprise, 'Unlike many equine painters on this side of the ocean he works without photographs, preferring to have the horse posed and work from life.'[1]

His racing paintings are always stamped with pace and spontaneity as in his study of the Champion Hurdle at Cheltenham in 1971 with Bula beating Persian War (*Plate 13*). Later

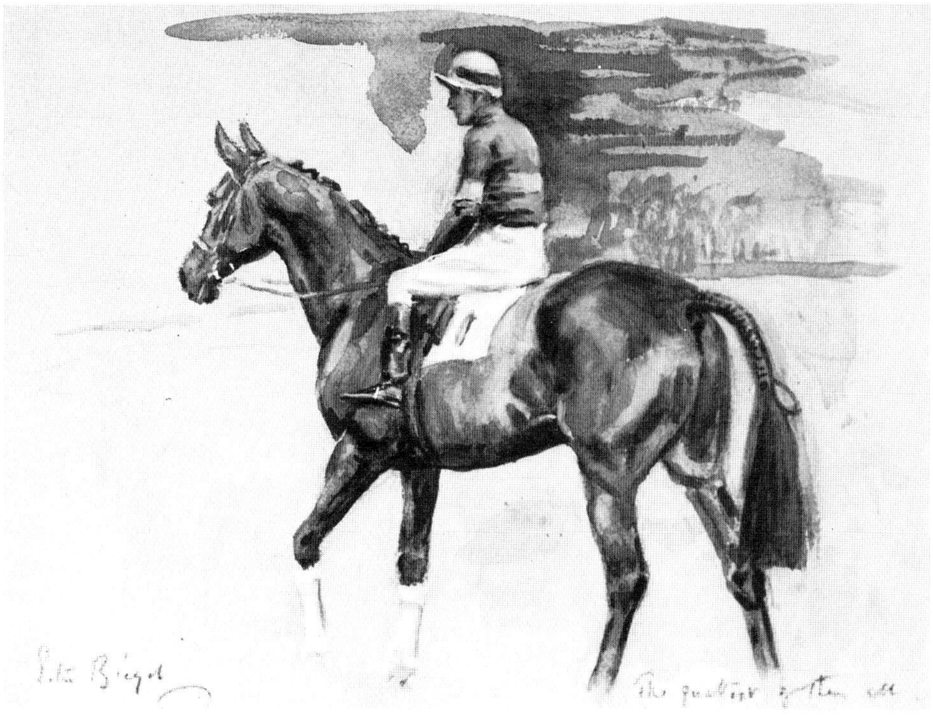

60 Peter Biegel, *Golden Miller – The Greatest of Them All.* Watercolour.

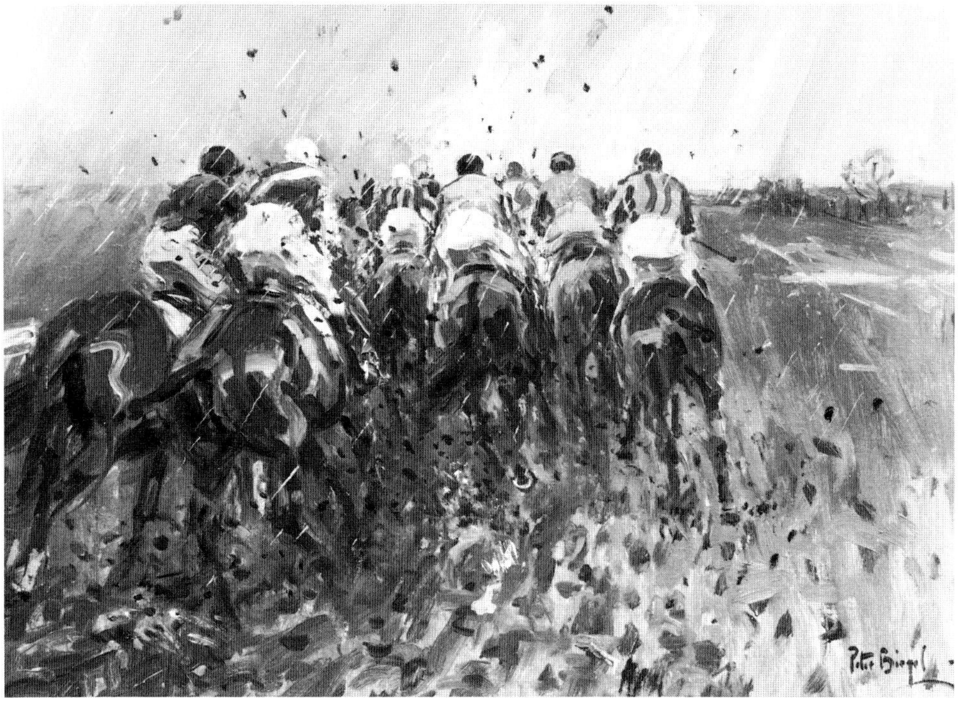

61 Peter Biegel, *Mud in Your Eye*. Watercolour.

in his career, Impressionism effectively took over dramatic moments in some 'chasing scenes and is especially effective in the blurred melée of disaster at the fatal twenty-third fence in the 1967 Grand National, which led to the victory of the outsider Foinavon, at the price of 444-1 on the Tote. This provocative technique also admirably records jockeys' vicissitudes in *Mud in Your Eye*!, (*61*).

Predictably his own obvious enthusiasm for hunting and racing in all weathers gives Biegel's work a refreshing factual integrity. From Lionel Edwards he inherited the same appreciation of the country scene in winter, often stark and bitter but, under snow, enchantingly beautiful. Hounds were also sensitively observed whether working a line or individually portrayed at the Peterborough Show. His versatile talent also included studies of brewery Shire teams, Exmoor ponies, mares and foals in summer meadows and stalking on the Scottish moors. His work was exhibited at Combridges in Dublin, and in 1950 at Rowland Ward's Gallery in London and in the 1960s three exhibitions at the Tryon Gallery in the West End proved convincingly Peter Biegel's ranking as one of the most popular and gifted sporting artists of the day.

In this post-war period the name of Michael Lyne was also to make considerable impact. Born in 1912 at Upton Bishop in Herefordshire the son of a parson, as a child he was remarkably precocious and by the age of four he had dictated and illustrated two little books on a rabbit and a dog. Totally dedicated to the country way of life and field sports (a fox's brush decorated the seat of his infant trousers), education at Rossall brought little scholastic success. As a great-great grandson of John Bacon, RA, the eighteenth century sculptor who was responsible for the monuments to Samuel Johnson in St Paul's and the Earl of Chatham in the Guildhall, hereditary talent doubtless played its part, for art early in his life was the paramount interest allied to hunting.

Lacking the academic qualifications for a possible veterinary career, brief training at the

Cheltenham School of Art decided his future as a professional artist. His knowledge of anatomy was acquired at first hand, skinning and dissecting animal carcases, expecially horses, to feed beagles, a task even that perfectionist, Munnings, had not been able to stomach.

For two years he painted and occasionally managed to hunt and his first pictures, watercolour drawings of the Ledbury, began to sell at Mr Rutland's Gallery (Whitcombe's) in Cheltenham. Constant attendance at meets, at the kennels, where the huntsman, Bob Champion proved patient and informative and commissions, encouraged by such local sportsmen as Sir Jocelyn Lucas and Captain H.A. Clive, Secretary of the Ledbury Hunt, enabled him to start his own pack of beagles.

In 1938, at the age of twenty-six, Lyne published the first of five books, *Horses, Hounds and Country* and in the Foreword 'Dalesman' (C.N. de Courcy Parry) wrote of it, '. . . send this sketchbook around the world for wherever there is an English home there it will be welcome . . .'[2] Certainly the keenly observed illustrations and wise text corroborate this opinion. Many show his first hand experience of beagling and otterhunting.

War service in the Royal Armoured Tank Corps swallowed valuable years but peace brought immediate commissions and in 1946, 1947 and 1951 exhibitions at Ackermann's. Michael Lyne was by nature prolific as well as talented (in his heyday he averaged over a period of twelve years a picture a week) and patrons soon included such star sportsmen of the hunting field as the Duke of Beaufort and Lord Knutsford.

Happily married, he settled permanently in Gloucestershire but travelled far afield. He made nine trips to America, the first time in 1949 through the auspices of Mr Frederick Warburg who had admired a picture by the artist in the United States Embassy in London. With immediate enthusiasm a comprehensive tour of the leading American packs was arranged. The artist filled a portfolio of sketches and returned home to finish two dozen works for such sporting connoisseurs as Fred Monticue of Millbrook, George Ohstrom Snr, Russell Arundel Snr, and others and, most gratifyingly, for Paul Mellon, whose incomparable collection of British sporting art now includes ten watercolours by Michael Lyne. Exhibitions in New York and elsewhere were to widen his diversity of subjects for they included studies of harness teams (*62*),

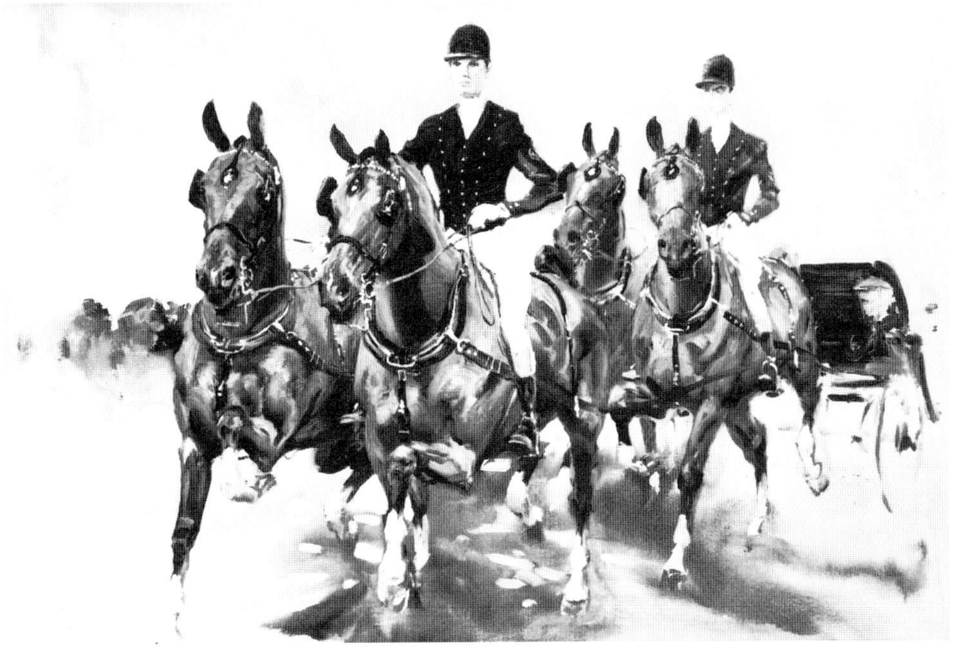

62 Michael Lyne, *Mr Chauncey Stillman's Hackneys and Postillions*, 1927. Oil on canvas, 24 × 36 in (61 × 91.4 cm).

three day event competitions, basset hounds and of the Maryland Hunt Cup, with two fine paintings of the 1963 and 1964 winner, Jay Trump, at Fences 3 and 11.

Michael Lyne frankly admits in his own books that Munnings and Lionel Edwards were major influences early in his career. Munnings is reflected in such studies as *The Whipper-In* and *The Huntsman* and Lionel Edwards in scenes with the Quorn from Ella's Gorse and other highlights of the Shires. But engagingly he also states, 'I have great delight in my work and do not take whatever talent I may have for granted and frequently feel the gift may completely disappear – this makes any successful painting more of a wonderful joy.'[3] But he had wise thoughts to record on the problems facing the painter of the hunting scenes. Perfection of draughtsmanship was an essential but of the conflicting demands of the artist and the sportsman he wrote , '. . . the former must arrange the interests of the latter upon his canvas and must be cautious indeed with regard to artistic licence. Composition plays little part in the life of a sportsman, but it is all important to the painter. A moment of time must be captured, and the arrested figures shown must convey a clear history of what is happening – it must have the atmosphere of the moment, it must be composed as a picture should be and yet not a sporting detail must be missed.'[4]

From 1965–1976 Michael Lyne was exhibiting regularly at the galleries of Frost and Reed and later at their subsidiary Christopher Wade in the West End. Hunting provided the major theme with pleasing compositions evoking both Shires and Provinces or contrasting scenes in Ireland with the Black and Tan hounds of the Scarteen and its daunting hairy banks. Hounds were portrayed with uncanny perception whether in full cry or, as in John Masefield's words, 'a flock of shaking feather' milling around hunt servants at a meet.[5] But in these collections also would be contrasting scenes in watercolours of hunter mares and foals in green meadows, of racing at Newmarket, and 'chasing at Cheltenham with a subtle sketch in oils after the 1964 Gold Cup, where the personality of the two tired heroes, Arkle and Millhouse came over with striking spontaneity.

In Michael Lyne's pictures, especially in watercolours, landscape effects were rarely ignored and intense observation, allied to fluent brushwork, sometimes resulted in a familiar sporting occasion becoming an important work of art. His studies of stalking in the Highlands in rich contrasting colour tones, Gallic ceremonies of venery in the Forest of Compiègne, or the Berkeley Hounds with the hunt servants in their chrome livery against the Castle background exhibit the artist's impressive versatility which hallmark his career.

Always fascinated by the galloping horse (in 1945 he had illustrated Henry Wynmalen's book *The Horse in Action*), his racing studies capture zest and excitement but lack the authority of his hunting scenes. As with Peter Biegel, the 1967 Grand National disaster at that fence after Becher's also resulted in an impressionist approach (*Plate 15*), but even more dramatic were a couple of pictures in Lyne's 1967 London Exhibition. The art critic of *Horse and Hound* had written somewhat despairingly earlier in the year '. . . Sporting art appears to be in the doldrums . . . where is originality – does each one of our popular artists today lack the urge or ability to experiment?'[6] Michael Lyne, spurred by this disparagement, seized brushes and palette, ignored tradition, laid paint heavily on canvas in thick texture to reflect nuances of foliage and light, producing a depth of colour and of contrast which resulted in two splendid pictures in unconventional style – *Kennel Fight*, (Plate 18) and *Marking to Ground*. The latter in its intensity evokes comparison with Sawrey Gilpin's masterpiece *The Death of a Fox* but even in its impressionist abandon each hound appears as an individual, contrasting angles of heads and bodies, with eyes impressively commanding – a real *tour de force* that stamped a fresh vision on the sporting scene.

Initiative also guided his entirely new choice of subject in several lively harness studies and in *The Demo* with its mounted police and topical street turmoil that was to foreshadow, a decade later, the appearance of the anti-blood sports activists and the soccer hooligans.

Time will confirm that Michael Lyne ranks as one of the most important artists of his generation. A fact that appears already to have been recognised in the United States by two retrospective exhibitions of his work held in 1984 and 1986 at the National Art Club (NYC) and at the Kentucky Horse Park.

Many talented sporting and animal artists spend the greater part of their working life fulfilling commissions and rarely achieve the publicity engendered by London one-man exhibitions. Though the quality of their achievements receives local appreciation from patrons their names, except to specialists in the field, remain comparatively unfamiliar. But some, by chance and endeavour, achieve a wider public and among these must be included the Cotswold artist, Thomas Sherwood La Fontaine, born in 1915 at Southborough in Kent. In his family background were some gifted artists and keen sportsmen, amongst whom should be mentioned R.S. Surtees. Like Peter Biegel and Michael Lyne, as a boy, La Fontaine was soon drawing, painting and riding horses but after education at Tonbridge School he received extensive art training. Beginning at the Regent Street Polytechnic, followed by the City and Guilds Schools, and Heatherley's, after a short spell in France he also studied under Lowes Luard in the St Johns School of Art. At a time when any teaching of animal anatomy was virtually unobtainable it is a matter of interest to find La Fontaine also worked under T.S. Tresilian with long hours spent with London Zoo animals as models. Today he still lists tigers and Sherlock Holmes as his hobbies!

Six years in the Army widened his horizons taking him from France to North Africa, Italy, Greece and Palestine with the 2nd Battalion of the Bedfordshire and Hertfordshire Regiment. On demobilisation he earned a living as a commercial illustrator and by commissioned portraits. It was not until 1962 that an exhibition of his sporting oil paintings and drawings at Ackermann's in London brought his name before a wider public with red labels quickly earmarking the pictures. Most memorable was a study in tempera of two monolithic grey cart horses against a background of Malmesbury Abbey and it was also obvious the artist not only understood equine conformation but mood and movement. Two further exhibitions followed at the same gallery in 1966 and 1973.

63 Thomas Sherwood La Fontaine, *Before the Start at Didmarton. The Beaufort Hunt Point-to-Point*, 1962. Oil on canvas, 39 × 64 in (99 × 162.5 cm).

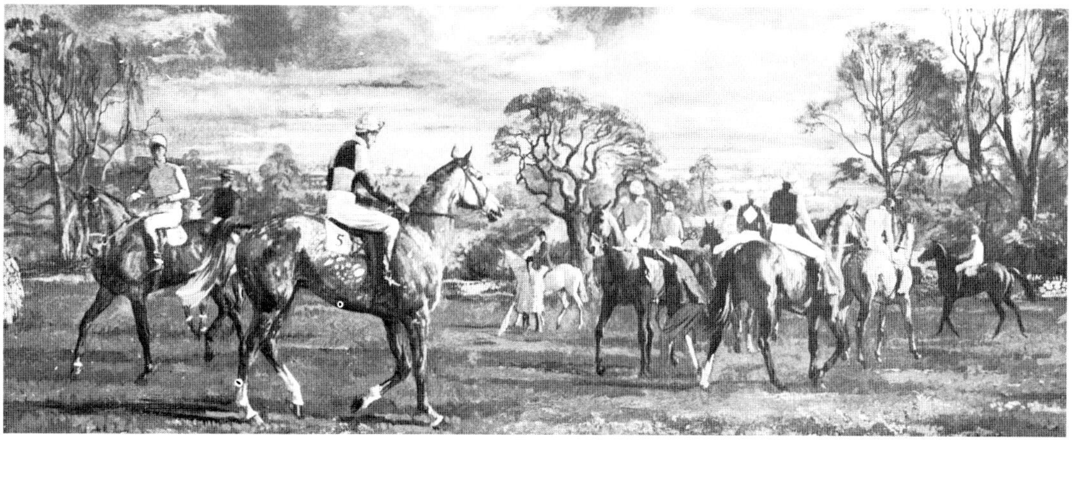

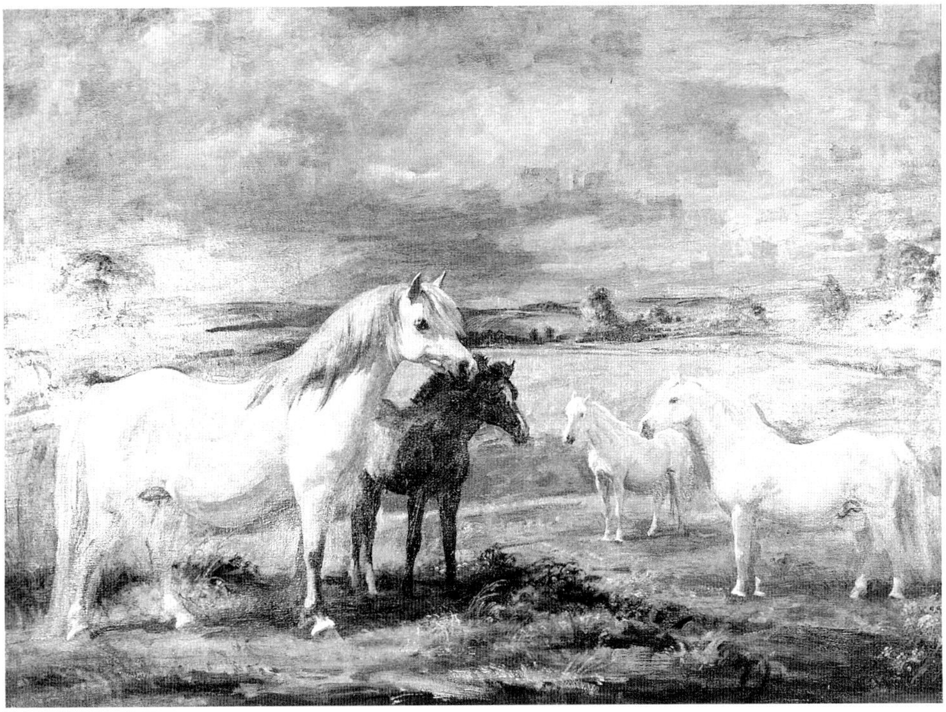

64 Thomas Sherwood La Fontaine, *Welsh Mountain Ponies at Sunwillow Stud*, 1979. Oil on canvas, 30 × 40 in (76.2 × 101.6 cm).

His subjects have varied from sunlit polo scenes at Cowdray Park, which technical purists possibly may fault but his ponies certainly gallop on and turn on the proverbial sixpence; hunting compositions which evoke memories of John Wootton with a park and stately home often the setting for hounds and horsemen, and winter vistas of rural England, with bare gaunt trees forming the background for *Before the Start at Didmarton: The Beaufort Hunt Point-to-Point*, (63).

Few artists succeed in portraying true pony conformation and character but La Fontaine excels in his group *Welsh Mountain Ponies at Sunwillow Stud*, (64). His studies of children riding possess an observation and sensitivity which make them a joy both for parents and posterity. Very pleasing in this category is *The Sumner Children at Marston House* – informal and happy – both girls sitting barebacked, together with the family dogs. Here the artist has crystallised the enchantment of English country life.

In later years as portraits became La Fontaine's major concern he ceased to consider himself a sporting artist but the rural scene often played its part in these more personal compositions. Travels to fulfil commissions took him twice a year to the States and visits have been made to Canada, South Africa and the Continent. Happily there has still been time for some racing scenes of horses on the gallops at Lambourn with also a couple of assured studies there of the successful 1983–84 bay filly, Cormorant Wood; here La Fontaine's facility for an effective scenic landscape still remains a personal hallmark of his work.

Leicestershire has been the hub of the hunting universe since the beginning of the nineteenth century – a county of famous coverts, wide pastures and stiff fences. Fortunately it produced not only great sportsmen but such local artists as Ben Marshall, John Boultbee, John Ferneley and Loraine Smith to record this early golden age of foxhunting. In the mid-twentieth century the name of John Kenney was to join the group for here again was a man born and bred in Leicestershire, whose first recollection was drawing a hunting scene on the nursery wallpaper and for whom the magic of horses and hounds became an obsession.

After studying at the Leicester College of Art, Kenney was destined for a career in commercial art and in actual fact he became a director at the age of 21 of a business that was to forge right ahead in this field. Nevertheless he found time to keep a hunter and snatch the odd day with the Quorn and the Fernie Hounds.

At the outbreak of war Kenney volunteered for service but with peace came chronic ill-health, which was to prove a permanent handicap, making travel far afield impossible and restricting his output. Fortunately it also caused his retirement from the world of advertising and forced him to take the plunge as a freelance artist. Becoming well known as a book illustrator, where his interest in archaeology and history proved invaluable, his talents were drawn increasingly to the sporting scenes of his own county.

Like Ferneley, who was the son of a Leicestershire wheelwright, Kenney also learnt all he could about the lore of foxhunting and steeped himself in local colour. He followed hounds by car with a sketchbook, noting the particular line a fox would take from a certain covert, observing the ways of individual hounds, recording the typical ridge and furrow contours of old pastures, visiting kennels and stables.

This factual knowledge gave his work immense authority, for his artistic compositions never ignored logical hunting procedure. Initially an over enthusiasm for hunting scarlet marred some works but influenced by the muted effects of Lionel Edwards' palette the fault was soon to disappear, although the magnetism of the old master inhibited any spontaneous innovation in Kenny's hunting scenes.

The artist lived at Smeeton Westerby, in the heart of the Fernie country, and his pictures of this pack in High Leicestershire possess not only vigour and charm but are remarkable for their lovely landscape effects, as in *The Fernie – Away from Bunkers Hill* overlooking the wide valley of the Welland (*Plate 14*) and in his skilful treatment of trees in such works as *A March Day Near Carlton Curlieu* with hounds in full cry and whirling rooks overhead (65).

Kenney can depict hounds on the road with particular mastery and most memorably in

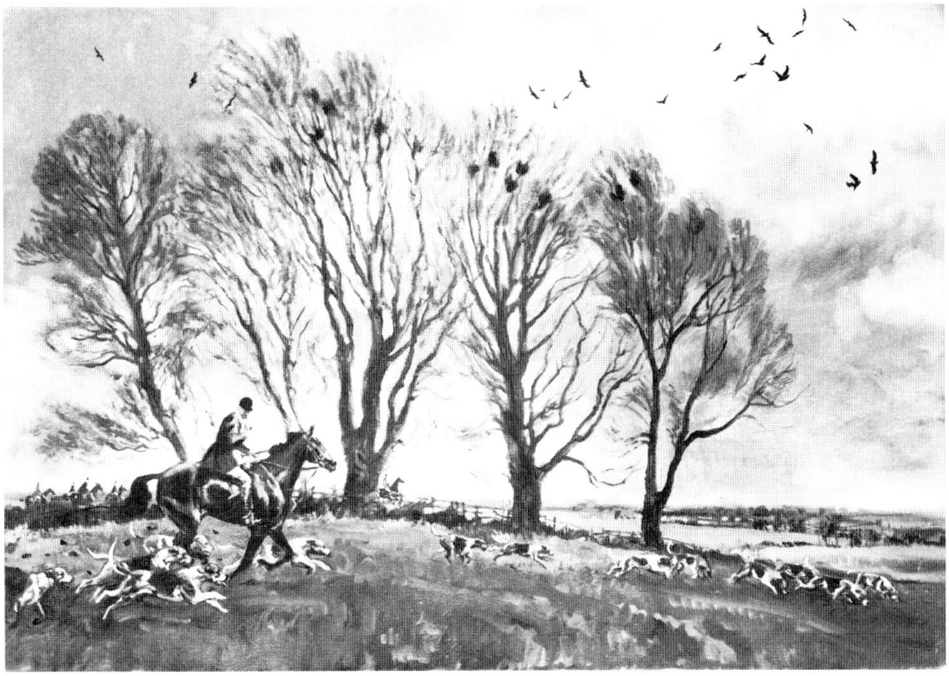

65 John Theodore Eardley Kenney, *A March Day near Carlton Curlieu*, 1970. Oil on canvas, 24 × 36 in (60.9 × 91.4 cm).

a twilight study *Hounds on the Road*, (*Plate 14*). His horsemen, too, are adroitly placed. A horse will be steadied coming into a fence, a pull is taken in a headlong downhill gallop – little touches that mean much in a hunting picture. Unusually attractive are some of his studies of foxes – vulpine Charlie in all the glory of his russet coat is set against a tangled pattern of bracken and tree stumps with remarkable effect.

An exhibition in 1963 at the Gadsby Gallery in Leicester brought numerous commissions. Ackermann's in London also showed some of his pictures of which three hunting studies and a racing scene were quickly purchased by a Senator from Georgia, USA. Tragically in 1968 Kenney lost the sight of one eye, a disaster he faced, like Munnings, with great courage and he continued to paint with unabated zest.

A charity exhibition in 1970 at Woodhouse Eaves, Leicestershire of over fifty works, in addition to local hunting scenes, included angling and racing studies, some in gouache and watercolours. Pictures of a State Landau in the Royal Mews, a fallow buck and a Welsh stallion indicated unsuspected versatility (alas never to be fully exploited as he died only two years later) when successful exhibitions of his work were held by Abercombie and Fitch in New York and Chicago. International recognition had arrived and following an impressive retrospective exhibition in 1980, again at the Gadsby Gallery, his reputation amongst knowledgeable lovers of sporting art in this country has continued to grow.

Always a man of infinite kindness and generosity to aspiring artists Kenney's four year tutelage brought recognition and success to Leicestershire born and bred Neil Cawthorne, twenty-five years his junior. Not taking to the brush professionally until his late twenties, Cawthorne quickly made his name both sides of the Atlantic and with studies of the Shires packs in action in a style, however, often repetitive of Edwards and Kenney. Later, in his skilfully painted equestrian portraits of the 10th Duke of Beaufort with hounds in Badminton Park and HRH The Prince of Wales with the Quorn Hunt at the Prince of Wales Covert

66 Neil Cawthorne, *HRH The Prince of Wales with the Quorn Hunt at The Prince of Wales Covert*, 1979. Print after original oil painting, image size 16 × 22 in (40.6 × 55.9 cm).

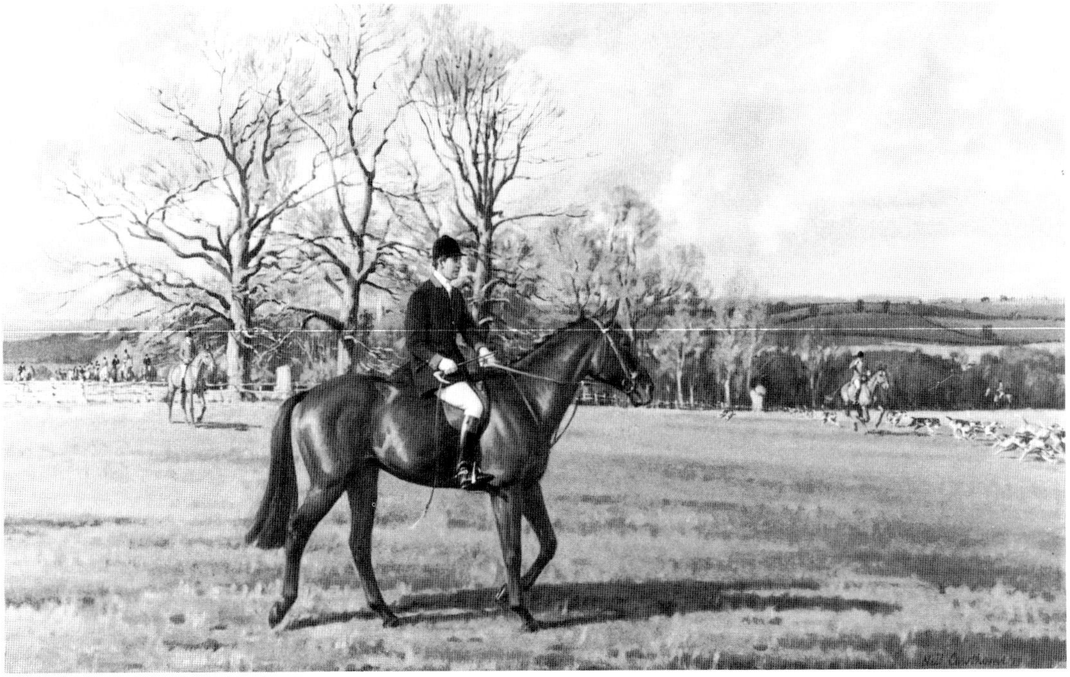

in Baggrave Park, the artist exhibits his gift for capturing the likeness of horse and rider, with the Prince on Candlewick (bred by the Queen), Michael Farrin the huntsman blowing hounds away and the Crown Equerry, Sir John Miller riding Brandy in the background (*66*). These works and others were published as limited edition prints. A study of Red Rum, ridden by Tommy Slack, clearing the water in the 1977 Grand National proved the growing versatility of the artist with commissions for two hunting series in Ireland and portraits of such Classic winners as Shirley Heights, Grundy and Bustino. Successful exhibitions of his work have been put on in Leicestershire, Newmarket and the United States.

To be painting sporting scenes after the Second World War and escape the pervading influence of Lionel Edwards certainly necessitated determination especially if the artist were an active foxhunter. Born in the new century, as early as 1901, Hesketh Raoul le Jarderay Millais (always known as Raoul) could have been totally inhibited by the Edward's style but heredity possibly played its part in establishing a personal approach to the sporting occasion. As a grandson of John Everett Millais, a founder of the Pre-Raphaelite Brotherhood who, in 1896, became President of the Royal Academy (he also, let it not be ignored had enjoyed foxhunting in Leicestershire with John Leech) his background was propitious. Like Michael Lyne, Peter Biegel and Tom La Fontaine, Raoul Millais as a child was determined to become an artist and after education at Winchester he went to the Glen Byam Shaw School of Art and in 1921 entered the Royal Academy Schools, and spent a summer working in Frank Calderon's studio. Horses had become his priority subject and here dissection formed part of the curriculum, Calderon's dictum was 'If you don't know what's *inside* a horse, you cannot paint what's *outside*.' Raoul then joined his father John Guille Millais, the artist, explorer and naturalist, in an African expedition, followed by a solitary visit to Angola with the sole aim of shooting a giant sable antelope for the paternal collection.

After marriage, from 1925 he went to live in the Beaufort country where he enjoyed three days hunting a week but whilst fulfilling many commissions, He eventually travelled to different parts of the country to paint equestrian portraits of Masters of hounds and favourite hunters. War years in the Scots Guards interrupted his career but later his services were much in demand to paint pictures of Classic winners such as Blue Peter, Tudor Minstrel and Nijinsky, together with Colonist II for Winston Churchill and Big Game and Sun Chariot for King George VI. Equally impressive are observant studies of hunters at grass (*67*), foxhounds and greyhounds. Intermittently he produced both authoritative line drawings and romantic compositions of fighting stallions, dramatic and exciting in the Stubbs tradition.

But particularly individual and pleasing in almost gallic vein are his evocative Edwardian harness studies such as *Sunday in the Park* with its elegant ladies and smart chaises. Future art historians will find the exact placing of Raoul Millais in the twentieth century sporting school difficult to pinpoint for in all his long career he held few exhibitions and those only late in life; one at the Grafton in London in 1962 another in New York in 1970 and in his old age at the Tryon Gallery in 1973 and 1982. In these latter it was possible to appreciate the subtleties of his style, especially in scenes of deer stalking, one of his favourite sports. In old age these assumed tiny compositions in oils on unsized paper – an innovative technique though one, perhaps, might question its long term stability. His work is rarely stereotyped and his prestige will certainly grow because he brings a personal decorative approach to the sporting subject.

Nowhere had the wind of change blown more strongly after the wars than in the feminist world. Women now not only participated in every province of the sporting field but often found there a practical livelihood. Girl grooms almost reigned supreme in the stable yard but more important they ran profitable and prestigious riding establishments; they competed in and won three day events; Pat Smythe, show jumper *par excellence*, in 1954 became the first woman to represent Great Britain in the equestrian Olympic Games. Women were welcomed as Masters of Hounds, several wore scarlet and by 1966 were permitted to train racehorses under their own names.[7] Girl jockeys were approved by 1975 as riders under both Rules, even in the Grand National.

Predictably in the sphere of sporting art the women artist was competing on equal terms for commissions and, eventually, was to outnumber her male counterpart. Amongst several new names after the Second World War a quartet of women of contrasting talents equally made their mark. In this effective vein was Juliet McLeod, born in 1917, who started riding a Shetland pony at the age of three and, as described by her husband, was 'the perfect Thelwell type'. Nevertheless she developed into a first class horsewoman, riding, shooting and schooling her own horses and also always drawing them. Wisely at sixteen years old formal schooling finished and she was sent to the Beaux-Arts Academy in Paris to study painting, but her realistic training as an equestrian artist came from Lynwood Palmer. She became his pupil and apprentice until he died in 1941. It was inspiring tuition under a hard taskmaster for, though he appreciated Juliet McLeod's extraordinary powers of visual memory and concentration, he insisted on a sound basic comprehension of anatomy. But there were compensations as she also exercised his horses and learnt from Lynwood Palmer, a superb whip, to drive a four-in-hand.

Marriage, two children and the war delayed her career but in 1947 she held her first exhibition in London at Ackermann's with the title '*Horses, Greyhounds and Cattle*', which included important portraits of the 1946 Derby winner Airborne, and Bogskar and Lovely Cottage, winners of the 1940 and 1946 Grand Nationals. In 1953 an exhibition of over eighty works at Fores Gallery included drawings, watercolours and oils with such equestrian subjects as the impecc-

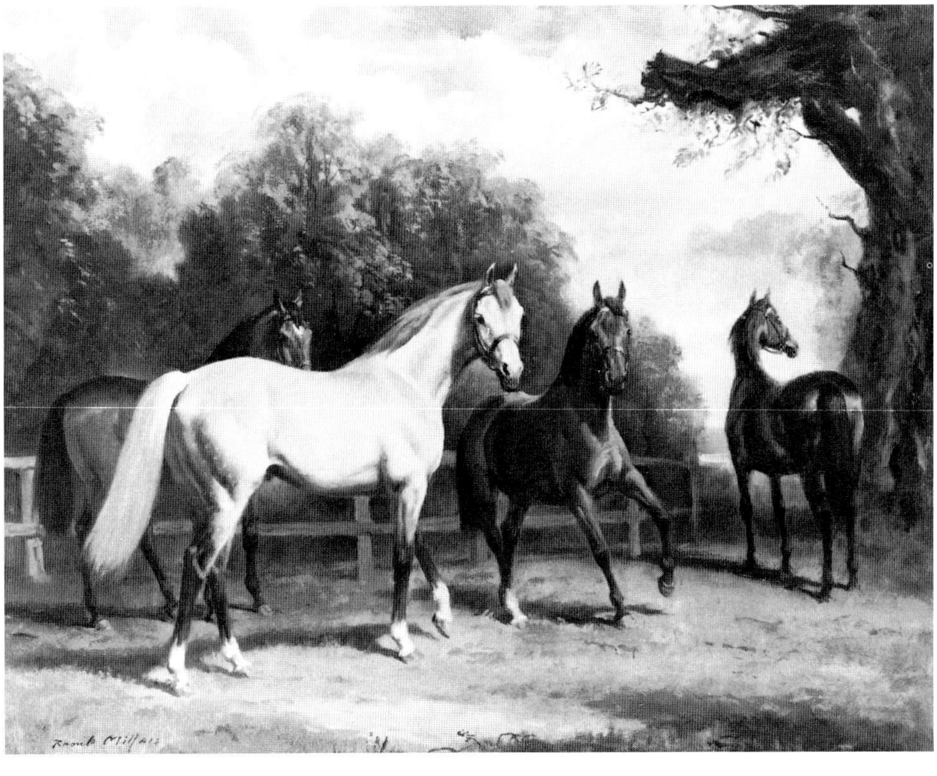

67 Raoul Millais, *Hunters at Grass*. Oil on canvas.

ably mannered Winston, the Queen's mount lent annually by the Metropolitan Mounted Police for the Trooping the Colour Ceremony, and Pompey, the stalwart skewbald drum horse of the Household Cavalry in full panoply. Constant commissions were received from leading owners and trainers of racehorses but tragically in 1954 she was stricken by multiple sclerosis. Though the disease became partially arrested, her work was limited by her physical condition and inability to travel.

A book of her paintings, *A Hundred Horses*,[8] published in 1960 records her observant and penetrating style of animal portraiture and assured handling of paint. Though the pose may be static a feeling of imminent action is apparent (*68*). Character and expression come over vividly as in a composition of *Four Polo Ponies*, none possessing any arresting markings but each an enquiring individual. She also invested such studies as *Sicilian Horses*, in a sinister storm setting, with an emotive romanticism.

Juliet McLeod painted commissions for such important patrons in the racing world as the Aga Khan, Noel Murless and Peter Burrell and particularly successful are her portraits of the 1949 and 1957 Derby winners, the big handsome bay Nimbus and Crepello, an upstanding chestnut with intelligent head. The artist was responsible for portraits of thirty-nine horses which between them had won more than fifty Classic races but most of these pictures disappeared into private ownership and so brought the artist little public renown.

Similarly the name of her contemporary, Madeleine Selfe, is better known in Newmarket than in the sporting art galleries of the West End. A talented and versatile artist, her very successful portraits of famous flat racers and 'chasers have resulted in a steady flow of Thoroughbred commissions and inevitably postponed many times her plans for a London solo exhibition, though her work has been seen there in various galleries and also in the USA.

Born before the First World War, her childhood was spent in Bedfordshire where she rode and looked after her own ponies, started drawing them as a five-year-old and illustrated her

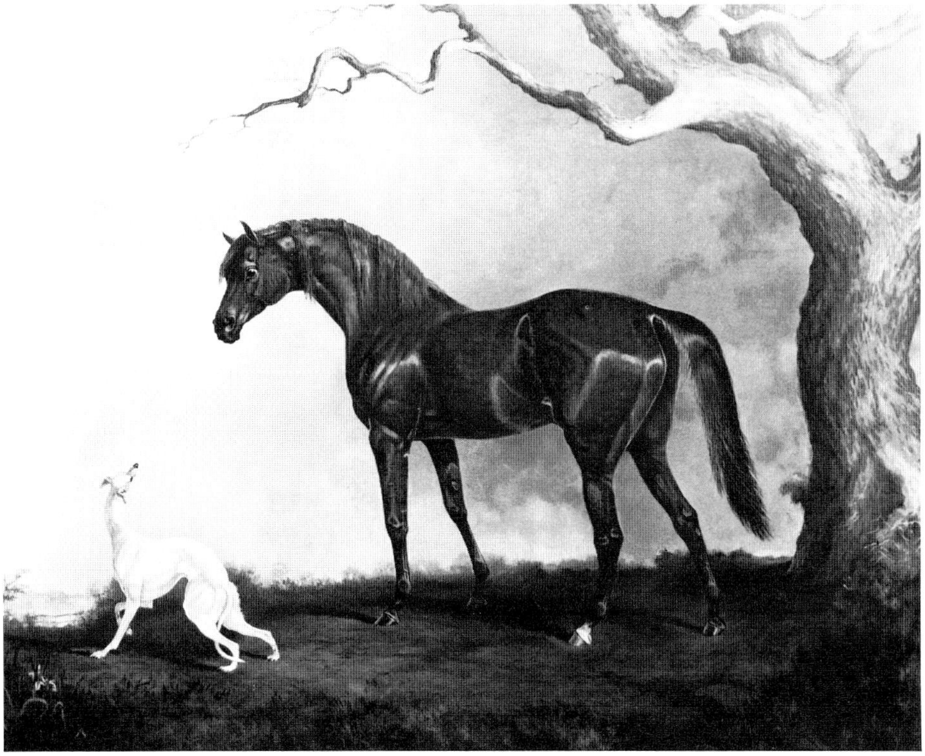

68 Juliet McLeod, *Chestnut Stallion and Greyhound.* Oil on canvas.

own stories of an imaginary mare Merango, (probably inspired by Black Beauty which she knew by heart). Madeleine Selfe was also musically gifted and *en passant* she composed an operetta, and her aim initially was to be a concert pianist for which she was professionally trained. However, hereditary factors may have played their part (both her father and paternal grandfather were amateur artists of ability and her great-uncle illustrated a standard work on human anatomy) and almost accidentally sporting art became her chosen career though without any formal teaching.

Hunting with the Oakley Hounds and interested in all field sports, private commissions for paintings of hunters and dogs soon kept her busy, but war work in the Foreign Office, marriage and two sons caused a hiatus, not entirely wasted artistically, as for two years, from 1946, she lived opposite to Sir Alfred Munnings at Withypool on Exmoor and benefited immeasurably from his help and astute advice, 'Paint what you see'. Her style, however, remained aloof from his impressionism which was a feature of his work at this period. Later, when her Army husband was stationed near Salisbury, Henry Lamb, RA, became her mentor.

Over the years she has painted portraits of many famous horses including a series of Derby winners. For HM The Queen at Sandringham she portrayed Doutelle, Aureole and a group of mares. With the immortal Arkle she cleverly captured his bold intelligent personality as well as that huge chest and the slightly ewe neck of this great horse as he went out with Pat Taaffe to win his second Cheltenham Gold Cup in 1956 (*69*). There were also studies of Aunt Edith for Noel Murless and a group for him which includes Royal Fleet and Busted; also Pia for the Countess Batthany.

Few contemporaries can equal her gift for portraying an equine likeness. Her Thoroughbreds really stand on their feet, their conformation possesses dimension and accuracy; in addition there is always a harmony in her treatment of horse and landscape. This, with a sensitive appreciation of colour values results in informative pictures of the great horses of her day.

More recently she has been painting groups of ponies and deer in the New Forest, and red deer in Scotland, with light and shade and landscape effects playing an important part in the composition, making an imaginative break from the occasional over-emphasis of the direct style of her portraits.

Two commissions which gave her immense pleasure were the Golden Wedding Aniversary present for the 10th Duke of Beaufort – much loved and esteemed 'Master' – given to him in 1953 by the Duchess. It shows the Duke with hounds in Badminton Park with the trees in the tawny glow of autumn and the distant house dimmed by mist in the background (*Plate 16*). As the Duke was also celebrating fifty years as Master of the Beaufort Hounds the work was a unique tribute.

Secondly she was commissioned to paint from life a picture recording the 200th running of The Oaks to be presented by the Jockey Club to the Order of St John in gratitude and recognition of their services with the St John's Ambulances at racecourses over the years. The painting shows the scene at the start of the race with the runners walking round and the ultimate 1978 winner, the bay filly, Fair Salinia with Greville Starkey in the saddle, standing centre, poised and alert.

Successful prints in limited editions were made after these two pictures incorporating the latest skills of colour reproduction, involving the use of eight separate printed runs to ensure accurate tonal values. Here was convincing proof that these new technical processes which, with the striking advances in colour photography, brought threatening competition to the sporting artist.

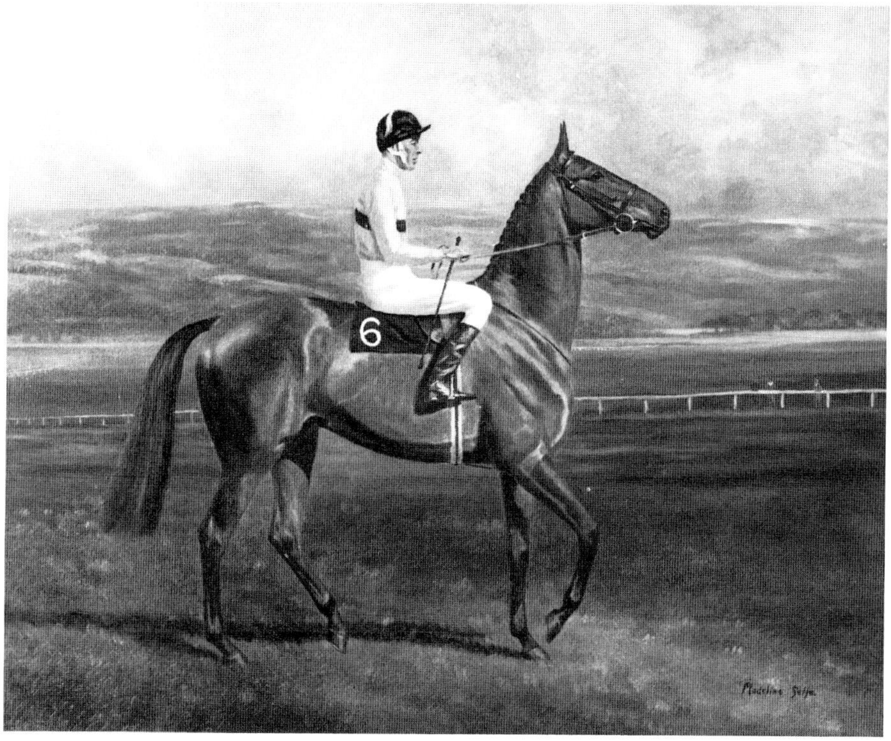

69 Madeleine Selfe, *Arkle with Pat Taaffe up at Cheltenham*, 1958. Oil on canvas, 24 × 30 in (61 × 76.2 cm).

Indicative of the changing focus of sporting activities in the second half of the century is the choice of subject of other women artists. Following the war the prestige and popularity of large horse shows, and expertly organised three-day events and horse trials spread all over the country. At most of them, trade stands were an opportune commercial feature often used by aspiring artists to put their work before a public becoming increasingly interested in sporting art.

Thousands of people must have admired the programme covers of many of these important annual equestrian events – the Badminton Horse Trials, the Ponies of Britain Shows and of the Royal International Horse Show Catalogues all with the discreet JW signature of Joan Wanklyn in the corner. Here were scenes outside the perennial hunting and racing subjects that formed the major concern of her contemporaries. The artist's childhood was spent in Cheltenham where her love of drawing and painting horses and ponies had been encouraged by frequent visits to the racecourse – entrance was free in those days – and there at an early age she learnt at first hand the way horses gallop and jump, knowledge she was to put to very good use in her future career. More conventional training followed at the Royal Drawing Society Studios, Chelsea and Central Schools of Art interrupted, of course, by the outbreak of the Second World War. Though work on portraits and landscapes played their part, animals, (with horses admitted as her main passion in life) as a subject remained a paramount interest.

Joan Wanklyn has always possessed a flair for capturing the fleeting mood of children and ponies, for she understands the stamp and style of our Mountain and Moorland breeds. But her wide appreciation of most facets of the equestrian world, whether it is the elegant movements of the dressage arena, the impulsion and muscle of an international showjumper or the alert poise of a hunter's head watching hounds, give impact and realism to her work, though often accomplished in rather slight pencil drawings and watercolours.

Some unusual commissions have made a welcome break from the sterotyped sporting scene. There was a watercolour impression of '*The Meet Up*' of the Musical Drive of the King's Troop RHA at the Windsor Horse Show at night with the floodlit castle in the background (*70*); a series of fifteen sheets of drawings of HM The Queen's horses and a striking oil painting in 1964 of *The Gallop Past of the King's Troop in Hyde Park*. Also making serious artistic demands was a set of twelve oil paintings of British Mammals, which sent her as far afield as the Larne Islands to study seals.

Unusual for a woman Joan Wanklyn finds a compelling fascination and interest in military subjects and for a number of years has studied the King's Troop RHA in action and in the daily round at its establishment in St John's Wood. Her book *Guns at the Wood* in which she is not only the illustrator but part author and editor is a valuable descriptive and pictorial record.

In the artist's 1984 exhibition of Recent and Retrospective Work at the Leighton House Art Gallery, Kensington, several commissioned studies in watercolour and oils of past historic military occasions were included to contrast with scenes of rural life in the form of *Harrowing, Four Horse teams* and *Suffolk Punches*. Late in her career Joan Wanklyn decided to forsake the sporting theme and to dedicate her talent solely to military subjects for which her precision and accuracy of detail is particularly suited.

By the end of the 1950s the school of British sporting art was being immersed, as in the mid-nineteenth century, by a spate of particularly competent animal and sporting artists. It was a repetitive situation of a hundred years earlier when Alken, Herring and Ferneley had headed a stream of talented but lesser known names such as George Henry Laporte, Harry Hall, Thomas Woodward and a myriad of others who achieved minor recognition. Now, as then, the subjects were primarily equestrian for hunting and racing were again reaching a peak of popularity but, in addition, riding instruction was being enjoyed purely as a recreation by adults as well as children which encouraged a steady demand for the horse picture. Artists

70 Joan Wanklyn, '*The Meet Up*': *The King's Troop RHA. Musical Drive, Windsor Royal Horse Show*. Watercolour and charcoal, 14 × 22 in (35.5 × 55.8 cm).

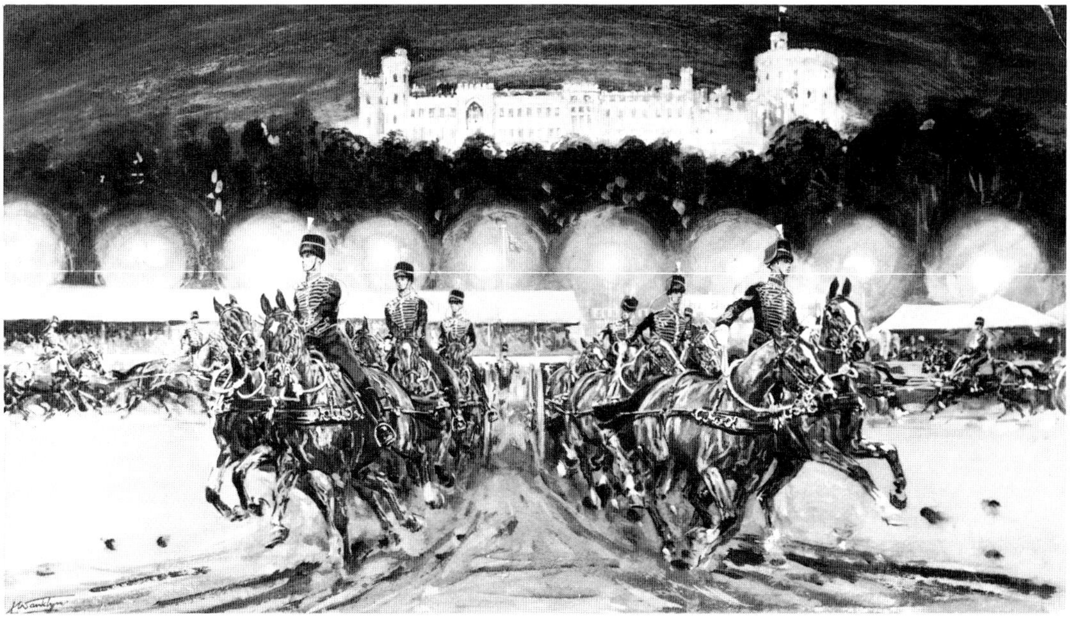

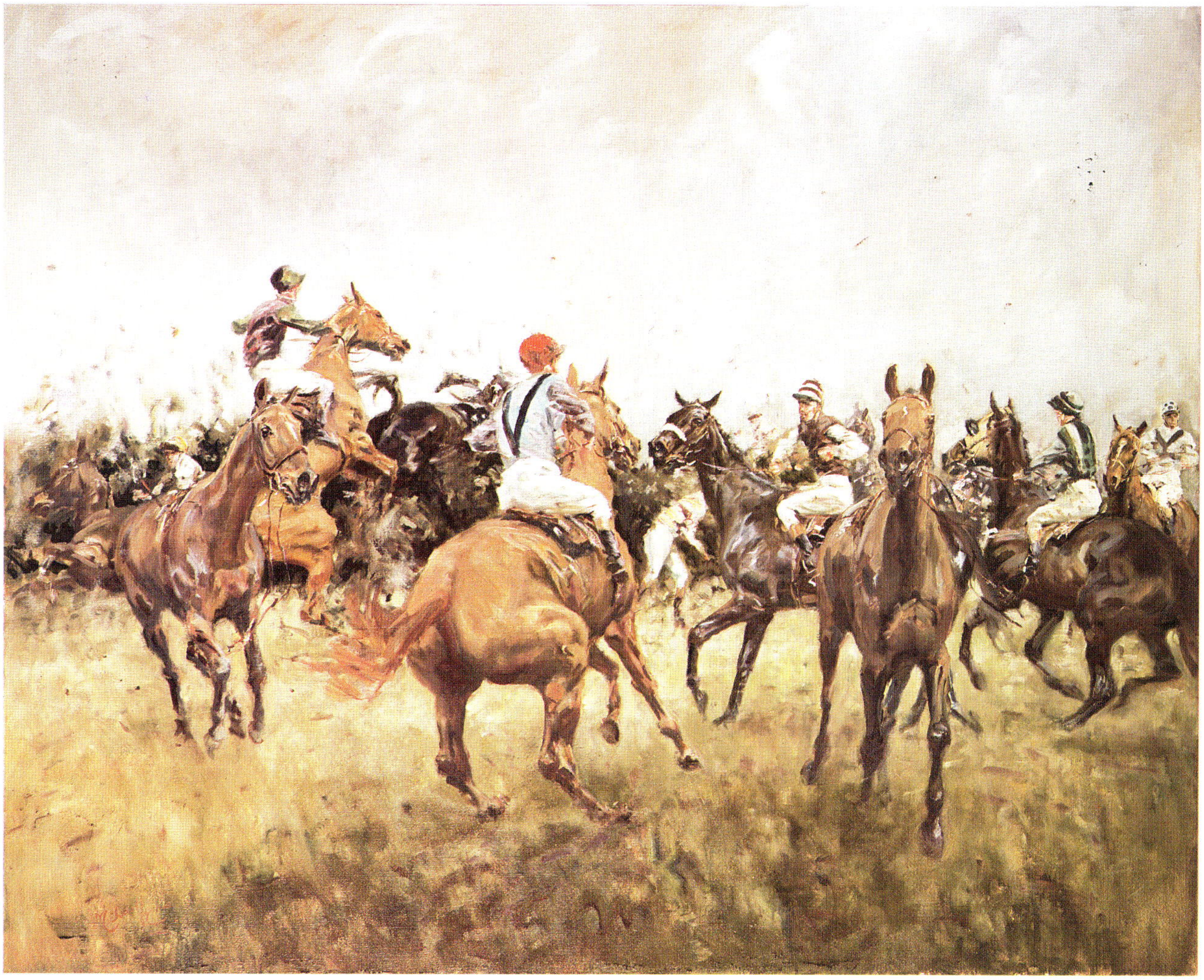

PLATE 15 Michael Lyne, *The Twenty-third Fence, 1967 Grand National*.
Oil on canvas, 40 × 50 in (101.6 × 127 cm).

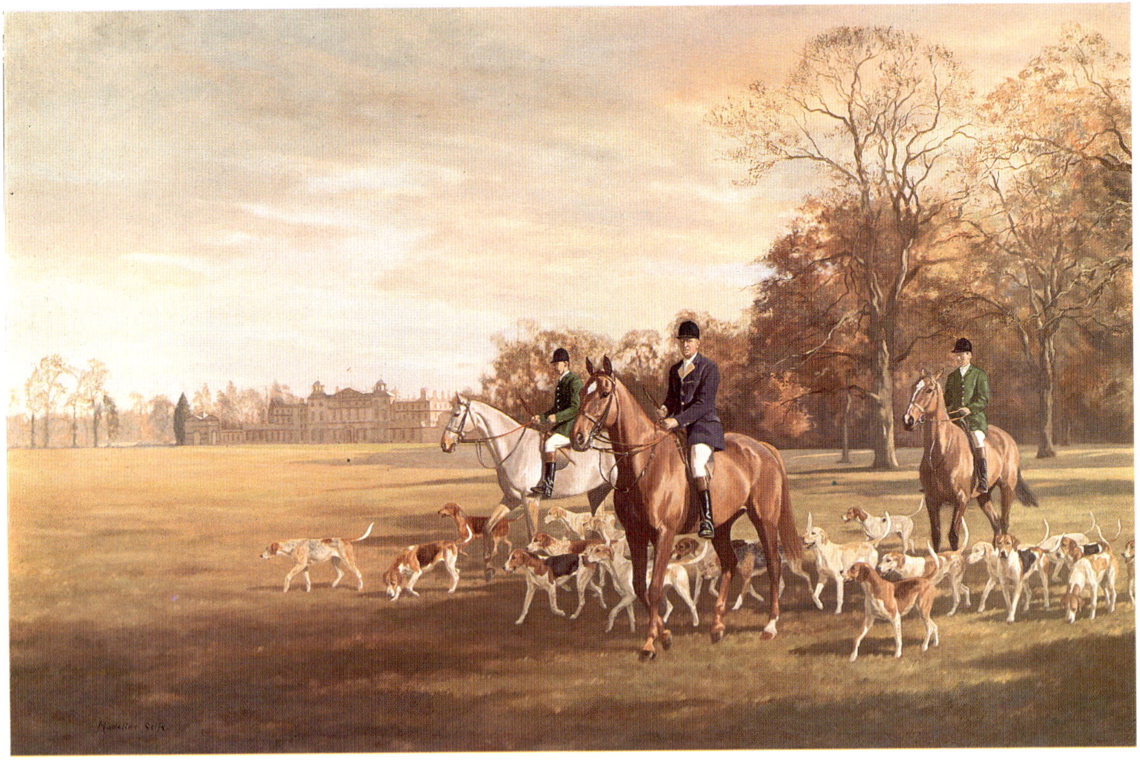

PLATE 16 (*above*) Madeline Selfe, *The Duke of Beaufort with his hounds in Badminton Park*, 1973. Print, 22 × 32 in (55.8 × 81.2 cm). (*below*) Barrie Linklater, *The Dressage Carriage: Team putting to at Windsor Castle Mews*, 1985. Oil on canvas, 24 × 46 in (60.9 × 116.8 cm).

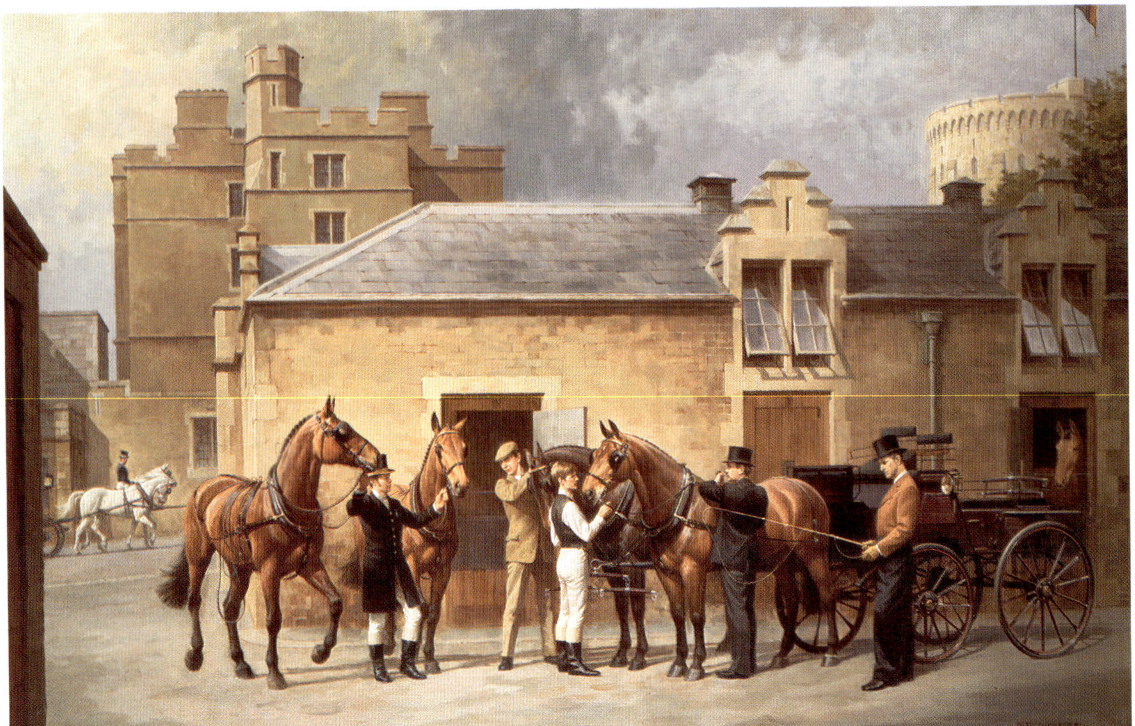

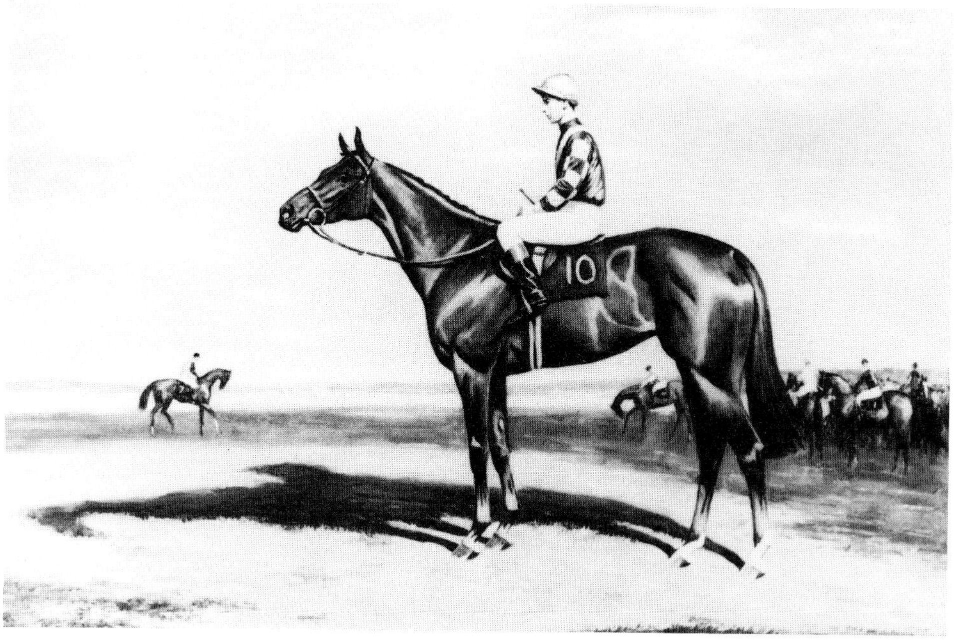

71 Lionel Hamilton-Renwick, *Glad Rags. Winner of the 1000 Guineas. Paul Cook Up – 1966*. Oil on canvas, 25 × 30 in (63.5 × 76.2 cm).

as a result rarely lacked commissions and an ever increasing number of animal painters appeared on the scene.

Amongst the most competent was Lionel Hamilton-Renwick, born in 1919, son of a well known northern sporting family, destined for a life in agriculture. He was over thirty years old when he took the plunge to study for a year at Heatherley's and later under individual artists for landscape and portraits before becoming himself a full time professional painter. Three London exhibitions followed, at the Walker Gallery, Fores and Frost & Reed. His major inspiration was the racing scene with some good portraits of leading winners of the day including the Princess Royal's (HRH Princess Mary) Red Dragon, a bay brown with high withers, the chestnut filly Glad Rags, winner of the 1966 One Thousand Guineas (*71*) and for Her Majesty The Queen a fine study of Aureole. His adept brushwork was particularly skilful in suggesting Thoroughbred quality and like Ferneley (an acknowledged but not obvious strong influence) details of conformation were cleverly observed. He portrayed several notable Masters of Hounds including Mr Dorian Williams with the Whaddon Chase and Miss Ann Bretherton with the Middleton but his eye for a background was often unexploited. A breeder and international judge of miniature Pinscher dogs and many other breeds, his canine commitments and love of travel inhibited his artistic potential. A recent successful commission has included an annual action picture of the Seagram Grand National.

His contemporary, Richard Dupont, born in 1920, from youth a dedicated foxhunter, had been accepted by the Royal Academy Schools and the Slade and, like Hamilton-Renwick, was to find his most important commissions came from the racing world. He possessed a facile talent for the bloom and gloss of the Thoroughbred and could add pleasing landscape settings but he failed when confronted by portrayal of action and accompanying owners and trainers.

After an exhibition at Ackermann's in 1960 he visited the USA and was responsible for portraits of many winners on both sides of the Atlantic to be found today in important collections. Amongst his most successful were Aureole and Pall Mall for HM The Queen. In different vein the skilful picture of Mr W.C. Saunders's team of six Suffolk Punches and happy studies of Welsh ponies provided evidence of an adept versatility which unhappily was terminated by his early death in 1977.

Ninetta Butterworth, born in Jersey in 1922, had no formal art training though both her parents painted as a hobby. Always horse obsessed, after education at the Jersey College for Girls, she worked in a local stable as a groom and during the German Occupation of the Island in the war spent six months in prison for asserting personal British priorities. Devon became her home after the liberation; she was employed in hunt stables and rode in point-to-points but eventually her natural artistic talent, allied to perseverance, led her to a career in equestrian art. From commissions for portraits of local dogs and for Christmas card firms her work by 1951 was being exhibited by Fores in London, where in 1971 she held a one man show.

The harness world proved one of her most successful subjects, often using period vehicles and scenes; and also portraits of family favourites as in the large oil painting of *'Bridget & Martini' at Willet House* for the late Eric Towler. But in addition to canine commissions she also fulfilled a steady demand for hunting pictures which have included a large painting of the Duke of Beaufort with his hounds and various members of the hunt at Boxwell in Gloucestershire and another of Major John Berkeley and his famous family pack at Berkeley Castle.

All these artists worked within the traditions of a sporting style which, in most cases, had certainly been enlivened by the fluent approach of Edwards and the stimulating use of colour and light by Munnings but basically few innovative experiments in composition or presentation had appeared. It might perhaps be considered impermissible to include the work of Doris Zinkeisen in the conventional sporting genre but the fact remains that her dramatic colourful paintings appealed to a wide picture buying public and became also much in demand as prints and several exhibitions of her work appeared at Frost & Reed and other London Galleries.

Between the two world wars many of the decorative settings and costumes of West End plays and revues produced by Nigel Playfair and Noel Coward were designed by the two sisters, Anna and Doris Zinkeisen. Born in Dumbartonshire in 1919 Doris, considerably the younger, possessed not only artistic talent but a deep interest in horses. She won a scholarship to the Royal Academy Schools but her flair for design had to be shared with her love of hunting with the Pytchley and showing her champion hack, Quaker Girl, at major shows. Nevertheless she was awarded a Silver and Gold Medal in the Paris Salon.

72 Doris Clare Zinkeisen, *Pat Smythe on Scorchin'*, 1963. Oil on canvas, 28 × 36 in (71.1 × 91.4 cm).

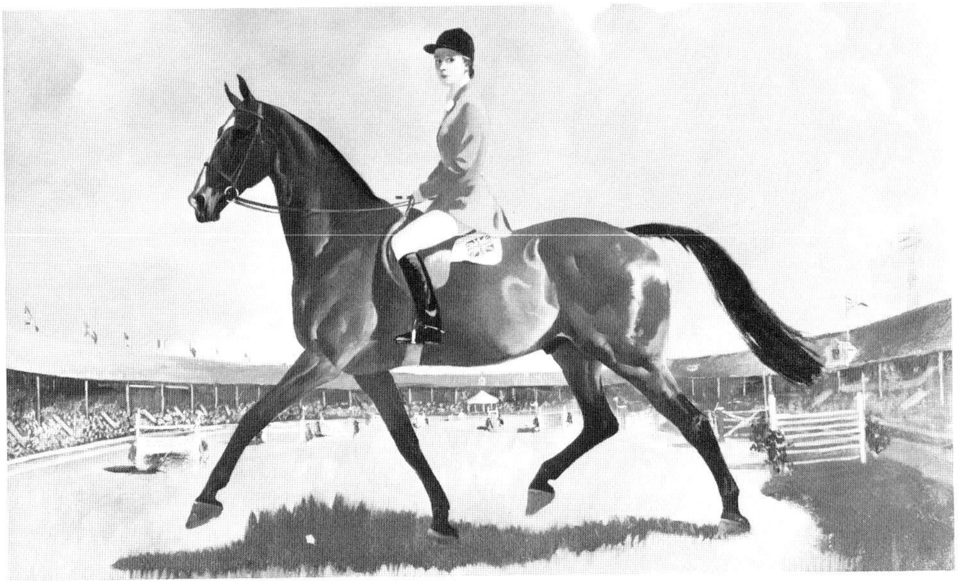

73 Vincent Haddelsey, *Meet at the Adam and Eve.*

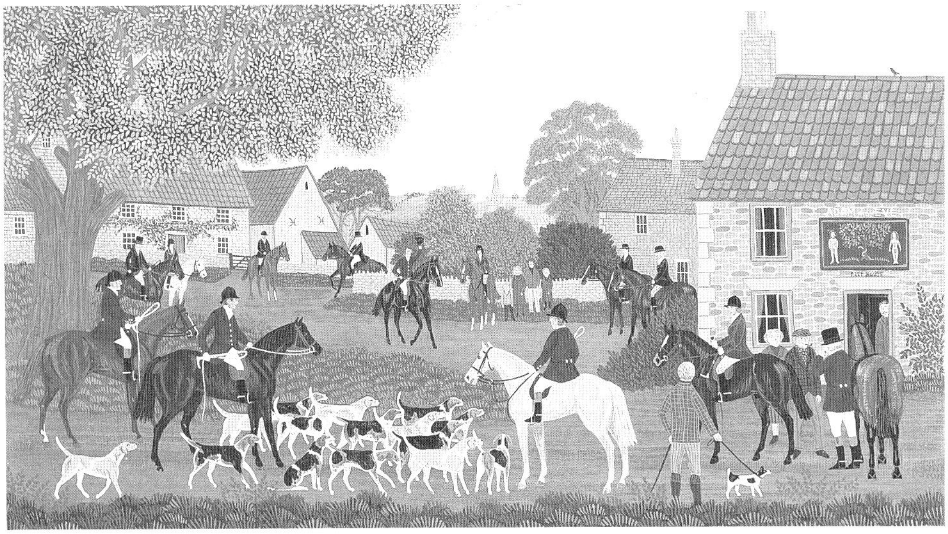

It was the horse that provided the motif for her paintings and here she established a milieu outside the school of sporting art uniquely her own, with stylised evocations of the Regency Cavalcade and other period occasions. Many were of harness scenes with the dashing Prince Regent driving Mrs Fitzherbert in his fashionable Highflyer phaeton but, whatever the elegant equipage, the teams were always precise and free-stepping, the period detail was accurate, colourful and theatrical. But Doris Zinkeisen's approach to her own contemporary sporting world lacked equivalent topical conviction. In her portrayal of *Pat Smythe on Scorchin'* posed in the arena of the White City the plain old show-jumper, hero of many international events, becomes glamourised (and very long in the back!) and the likeness of the rider herself in all the glory of scarlet coat and Harringey gold presentation spurs, also disappoints (*72*). The artist certainly captured the vitality of Mrs Glenda Spooner's famous little Thoroughbred pony stallion, Ardencaple; and perhaps reveals her real talent for the modern scene in a dignified portrait of the bay Arabian stallion General Grant, with the high set-on tail and tiny curved ears of the breed, posed against the lovely background of Lake Windermere.

Twenty years later another artist also outside the accepted genre of sporting art was to achieve considerable esteem. Vincent Haddelsey, completely self-taught, established a successful career using a formalised naive style in sporting and rural compositions. Born in 1934 in Grimsby, early peripatetic travels finally led to one man shows in New York, Paris and London. Here his own personal dedication to equestrian activity was reflected in intriguing pictures that combined primitive design and nursery accuracy with an underlying sophistication (*73*). These became much acclaimed by private collectors and many are published as lithographs.

NOTES

1 Letter to the author, 2 November 1965.

2 Michael Lyne, *Horses, Hounds and Country*, p. 31.

3 Letter to the author, 2 November 1965.

4 Lyne, *Horses, Hounds and Country*, p. 31

5 John Masefield, *Reynard the Fox*, Heinemann, 1919, p. 51.

6 Stella A. Walker, 'Sporting Art Today', *Horse & Hound*, 29 January 1967.

7 In 1986–87 of 498 Masters of Hounds listed in Baily's *Hunting Directory* 74 were women.

8 Juliet McLeod, *A Hundred Horses*, Seeley Service, 1960.

13

Breaking with Tradition

In the 1960s, exhibitions of contemporary sporting art were a regular feature of several London galleries though by then the equestrian character had become even more strongly established. Provincial dealers annually took stands at such events as Badminton and Burghley Horse Trials, the Horse of the Year Show and the Game Fair to present pictures and prints before an interested public. New names appeared and talent was not lacking but former traditions remained dominant in spite of an avant-garde Exhibition, '*The Horse by Living French Painters*' in March 1960 at the Wildenstein Gallery in New Bond Street. Strangely enough the works of these ten artists aroused little excitement and comment. Here certainly was an odd galaxy of horses which no practical horseman would covet for his stable or stud, and with no vigorous pictures of the chase to stir his blood. Instead these impressions sometimes employed the horse just to clothe an idea, contrasting the humour and spectacle of the sporting world with the serenity of pastoral France. Others, as in the studies by Claude Grosperrin, caught, with an intangible feeling for colour and form, a fleeting instant over the jumps at Vincennes, and the compelling speed and tension of the racecourse came unexpectedly to life in Cubist inspired works of Jacques Déspierre. As Colonel 'Ted' Lyon, elderly doyen of the British equestrian world, remarked, as he left the exhibition, 'I'm sure some of these pictures are *damned good* – if I could only understand them!' It is perhaps indicative to find that at this time the Tate Gallery purchases of works of contemporary life by that lively Vorticist William Roberts, had included such titles as *Cantering to the Post*, (74), and *The Horse Dealers*, as 'damned good' in their innovative mood, perhaps, as their French counterparts.

Foreign influence on British art was

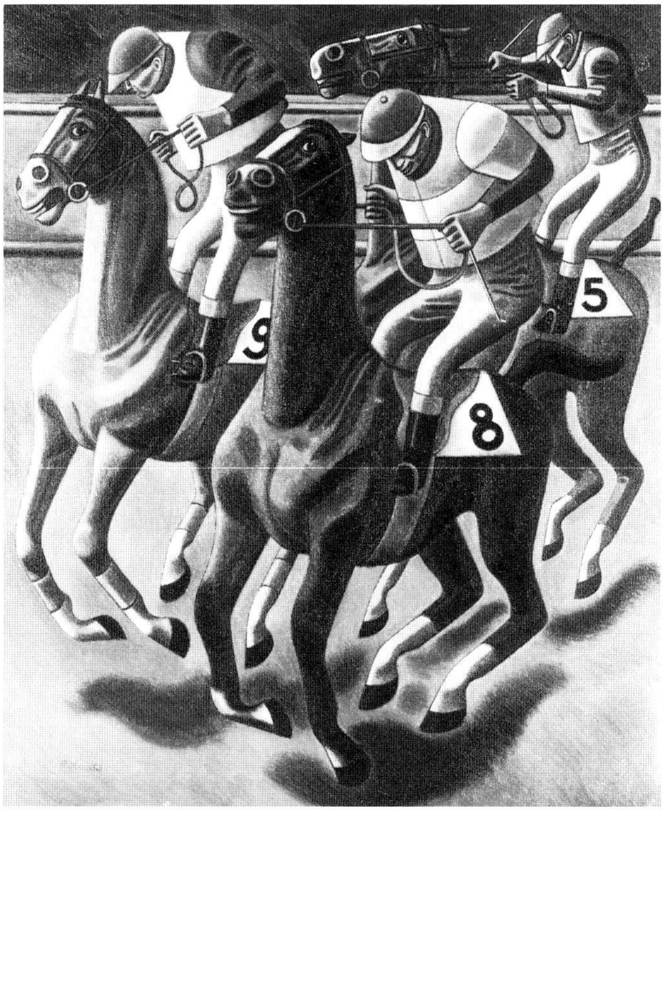

74 William Roberts, *Cantering to the Post*, 1949. Oil on canvas, 24 × 20 in (61 × 50.8 cm).

75 Tom Carr, *The Zetland*, 1953. Watercolour.

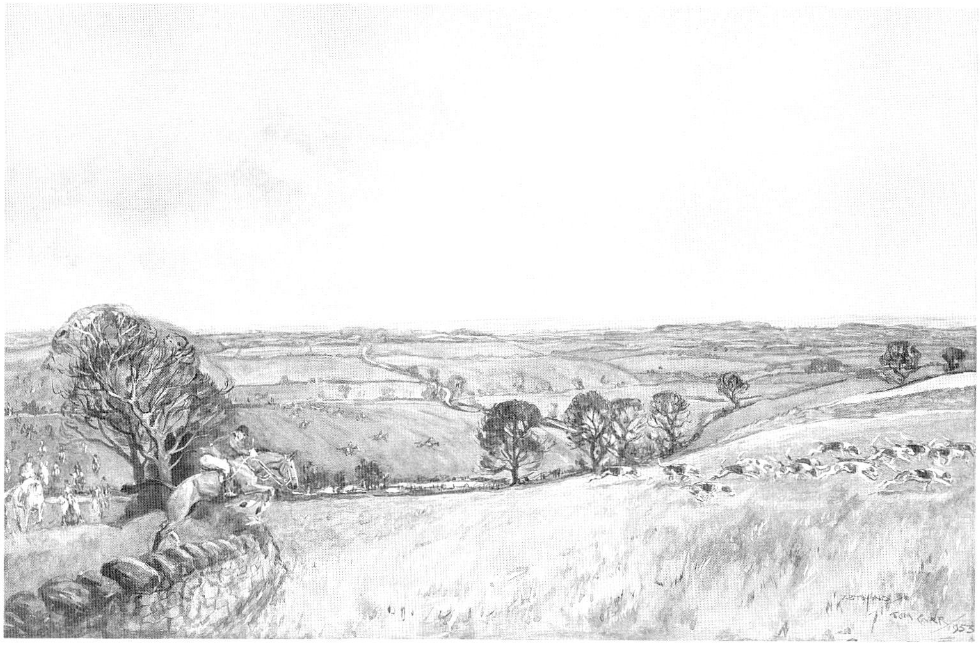

not a new phenomenon and has always been a complex issue, but this exhibition certainly made little impact on British sporting artists of the day, and predictably, the style and subject matter of Edwards and Munnings were still to be strongly reflected, with a few exceptions, until near the end of the century.

In this category must be included the pictures of Tom Carr of sporting scenes in the north which aroused loyal enthusiasm in the Border country. Most of his work has remained in private hands and has, therefore, received little recognition in southern periodicals and galleries.

Born in Durham in 1912, Tom Carr's background was unusual for he had started life as an underground blacksmith with the Priestman Collieries, and during the Second World War was making anchors for the Royal Navy. Whilst recovering from injuries and ill health, drawing and painting occupied his time and he then studied art at the King's College, Newcastle-upon-Tyne. Here in 1950 the award of a Certificate in Fine Art decided his future career, a decision requiring some initiative.

Like many pitmen Tom Carr had always been a dedicated countryman and was a keen foot follower of hounds and, in his early days, had looked after the hunt terriers of the Braes of Derwent Hunt. In addition to a natural artistic ability he was blessed with immense charm, humour and love of the sporting life and he quickly received commissions from members of the local hunts. Like Edwards he worked in oils and watercolours (more accurately gouache) and, similarly, his draughtsmanship was allied to a keen understanding of hunting lore and its technicalities which give his pictures attractive authenticity. Occasional forays into Scotland offered opportunities for contrasting subjects and scenery and also he travelled south to paint pictures in the Heythrop Country and with the Fernie, but his talent shines most brightly in his scenes with the Northern packs – the Jed Forest, the Zetland and the Percy.(75).

Tom Carr studied dry point etching in colour under G. Vernon Stokes, RBA, and this medium allowed the retention of the fine quality of his pencil sketches when they were published as prints by H.C. Dickens of London. His work as an illustrator also complemented two books by Stanislaus Lynch, *Hounds are Running* and *A Hunting Man's Rambles*.

From this same part of the world and receiving encouragement and advice from Tom Carr, comes the work of Robin Furness, (Sir Stephen Furness Bt) who has combined the roles of Joint Master of the Bedale Hunt, an active farmer and a sporting artist with success. Born in 1933, educated at Charterhouse, he then spent ten years in the Royal Navy and the Fleet Air Arm where, during that time, pictures were accepted for the Armed Forces and the National Maritime Exhibitions in London. Some professional training was received at the Goldsmiths and Carlisle Art Colleges. His hunting scenes, with convincing activity of horses and hounds, sometimes lack definition but are presented in an attractive landscape setting which is a feature of his style. His set of six studies of *Foxhunting in the Fells* gives considerable scope to this talent and these have been published as prints to make an authoritative record of sport outside the galloping Shires (76).

In contrast John Gregory King received almost an excess of media exposure, for any sporting artist who counted Lionel Edwards as a close family friend and neighbour was inevitably off to a flying start. John King was blessedly fortunate in this connection. Born in 1928, in the house he still occupies in Wiltshire, he was educated at Canford, a school with some artistic tradition – William Coldstream being for some time the art master. But the trend towards the abstract bored and baffled the future sporting artist who, from childhood, had been drawing and riding horses and going foxhunting.

On leaving school at the end of the Second World War farming became his chosen career, combined with sport with the Hursley Hunt and riding in the odd point-to-point. However, with the acquisition of some oil paints he received brief training in figure drawing at the Salisbury School of Art, intermittent advice from Lionel Edwards and finally the farmer turned professional artist. John King possesses a natural eye for a horse and a hunting country and from early days his talents, admittedly uneven in merit, were much in demand for presentation commissions for retiring Masters and for pictures of various hunts. These have frequently become successful prints with graphic remarque drawings.

Predictably the Edwards tradition is strongly evident in John King's work and his pictures inherit something of the same love of movement. His horses are rarely static, being portrayed

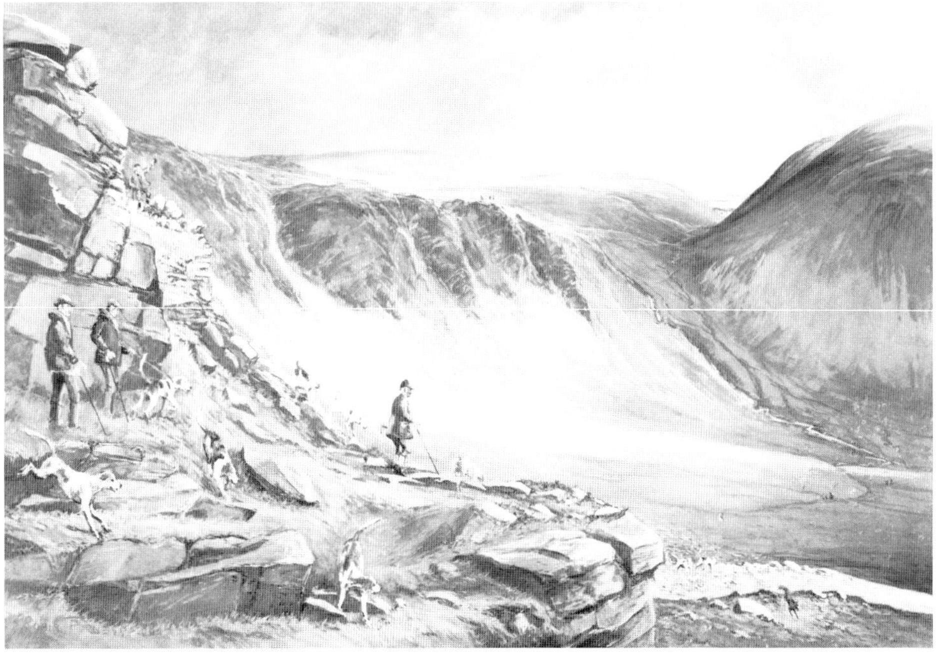

76 Robin Furness, *The Lunesdale at Cautley*. Print after the painting, 11 × 16¼ in (27.9 × 41.3 cm).

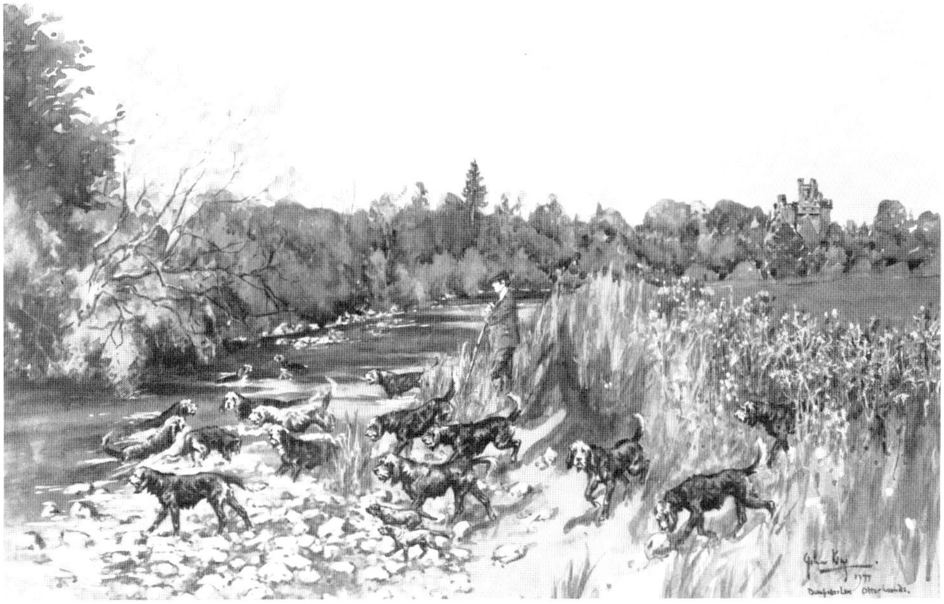

77 John King, *The Dumfriesshire Otter Hounds*, 1977. Watercolour, $21\frac{1}{2} \times 30$ in (54.6×76.3 cm).

in action, galloping and jumping (and often falling). There is emphasis on a recognisable landscape setting for, as the artist maintains, 'a hunting picture is 90% landscape' and the specific characteristics of different hunting countries form important features of his compositions – the cut and laid fences of the Shires and the contrasting water scene of the Dumfriesshire Otterhounds seen 'minking' on their way to hunt otter on the River Annan (77). Sometimes his quick, expressive brush is carried away into an excess of incident and detail and a restlessness will pervade a picture.

His line drawings have animated Foxford's hunting peregrinations in *Horse and Hound* and the same writer's book, *The Golden Thread of Foxhunting*. The speed and tension of polo matches at Cirencester, Tidworth and Windsor, young Thoroughbreds on the gallops in early morning and point-to-point scenes have also been his subjects.

In addition King displays an unexpected versatility in his clever composition of military occasions with serried ranks of uniformed cavalry and marching men; complicated by the esoteric detail of ceremonial accoutrements in such scenes as *HM The Queen Presenting New Standards to the Lifeguards on Horse Guards Parade 1974*. Several exhibitions of the artist's work have been held in London; at the Tryon Gallery in 1967, at Fores in 1972 and 1974 and the Malcolm Innes Gallery in 1984 and 1988. Commissions in the States, South Africa, Cyprus and the Continent have been fulfilled but John King's pictures provide, above all else, a lively record of hunting in this country after the 1950s.

Strangely enough it was a sculptor who was to inject fresh lifeblood into a static situation and infuse a new vitality into the sporting picture. John Rattenbury Skeaping by the end of his life was to rank amongst the nation's finest animal sculptors but it was the style of his drawings and paintings with their essential simplicity, allied to a striking impressionism, that eventually brought a transitional influence to British sporting art after the mid-century.

Born in 1901 in South Woodford, Essex, son of Kenneth Mathieson Skeaping, a competent but conservative artist, whose idea was 'to paint every conceivable detail with minute accuracy so that it looked exactly life-like. In truth he did not know the meaning of art',[1] John Skeaping received, with his brother and two sisters, no formal schooling. They lived in an unconventional family environment, where self-expression was allowed free rein, with painting, modelling, music and dancing encouraged as full time enthusiasms. Young John, an intermittent model for his father, absorbed by observation the techniques of painting whilst creatively indulging his obsession for horses – in his imagination he *was* a horse and in childhood he never drew or painted anything else.

At thirteen he became the youngest member of the Blackheath School of Art and here he quickly discovered the joys of modelling and sculpture under Frederick Halnon and on his advice moved to the better facilities of the Goldsmiths' College and later to the Central Schools and Royal Academy. Nevertheless in his early exhibitions of sculpture with his first wife, Barbara Hepworth, at the Bruton Gallery, several animal drawings, engravings and drypoint etchings of antelopes, leopards and tigers, which were inspired by visits to the London Zoo, were invariably included. Later in his career he received a commission from the publishers of the popular *How To Do It Series* to provide the text and illustrations for *Animal Drawing* (*78*), followed later by *How to Draw Horses* and *How to Draw Dogs*. Skeaping brought to these subjects not only sound technical guidance but a clarity and originality that makes these modest volumes indispensible gems for the sporting artist.

In 1951–1958 John Hislop's three books on steeplechasing and raceriding[2] with Skeaping's vigorous gouache drawings and instructional line sketches (has there ever been a better pictorial exposition on positioning the whip?) brought the artist's work before a wider public. These illustrations in their effortless spontaneity evoked the equestrian studies of Degas and Crawhall or, perhaps indirectly, the pre-historic cave paintings of Altamira.

Between 1962–1978 Ackerman's held six important exhibitions of Skeaping's drawings and paintings (and in 1981 and 1984 two posthumous exhibitions) which created intense interest in sporting circles. In these, and also in an exhibition put on by Frank Partridge Inc., in New York in 1966, amongst a variety of subjects, the racing theme was always dominant, for the artist had never escaped his childhood ambition to become a jockey. His immediate concern was with mobility, pace and rhythm, achieved with a brilliant economy of line that verges on genius.

The artist also understood intimately the relationship of man and horse for he had received rigorous riding instruction from a rough rider Bombardier of the King's Troop, he had regularly ridden work for trainers, as an amateur in Ireland he had won a few 'bumper' races, had whipped-in for the Essex and Suffolk Hunt and, in addition, with heavy horses he had as a boy learnt to plough the land; but the conviction of his drawings rests on his complete mastery of animal anatomy. This, by the angle of a pastern, the flexion of a hock or the poise of the head the artist can suggest the split second impetus of a fighting finish or the hazards of jockeying for position. His manipulation of his favourite gouache medium is masterly and the use of colour always exciting and subtle. Brilliant characterisation also excelled in his striking studies of the flamboyant

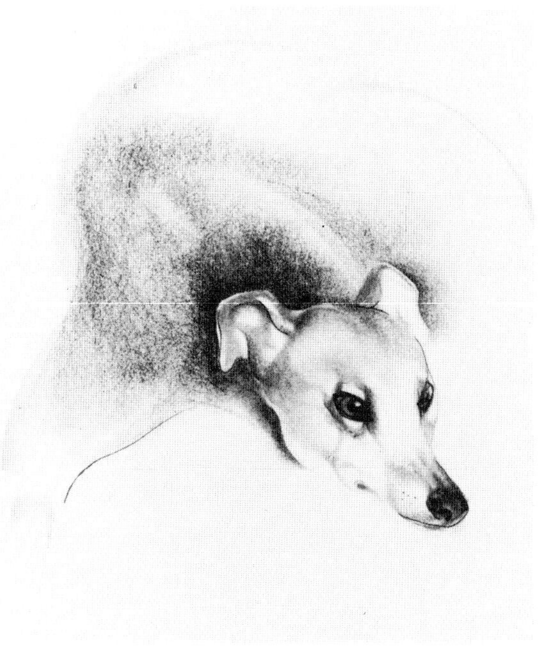

78 John Rattenbury Skeaping, RA, *Greyhound, Portrait*, 1936. Drawing, pencil and coloured chalk, from *Animal Drawing*.

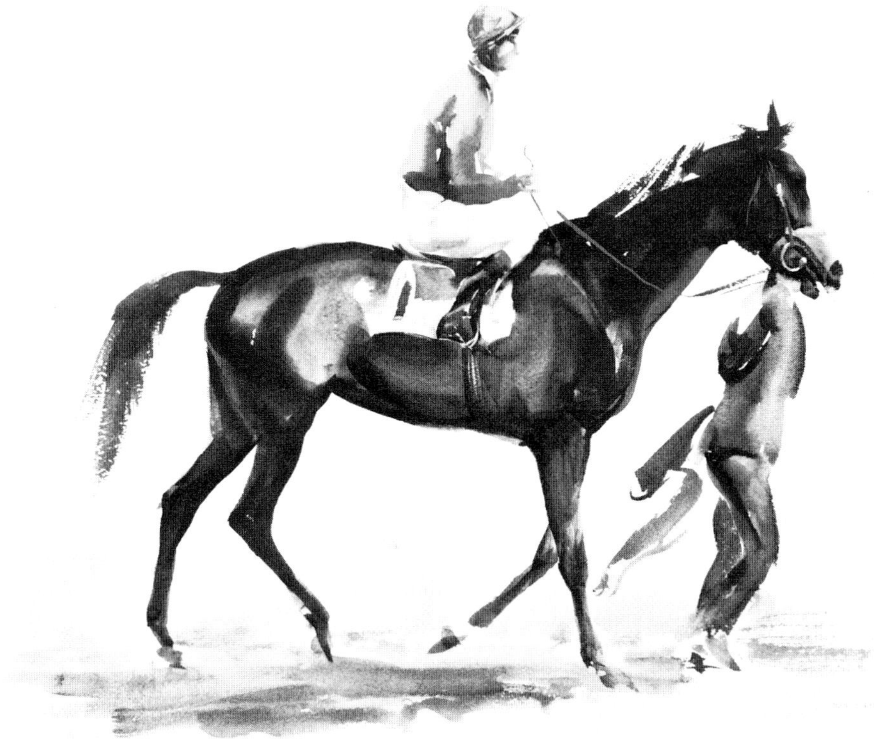

79 John Rattenbury Skeaping, RA, *Two year old Filly*, 1964. Gouache, 18 × 22½ in (45.7 × 57.1 cm).

rejoneadors of the Portuguese bull fighting ring, also with the white-grey horses of the Camargue where he spent the last years of his life and, above all, his striking studies of greyhounds, racing and in repose. In Ireland he had for a spell been a professional trainer and sport with greyhounds always remained an intense pleasure; eventually he was appointed a steward of the National Greyhound Racing Club.

For a decade or more Skeaping's creative energy was, to a serious degree, diverted from sculpture to be much absorbed by painting and though his fluent impressionist style suggests a deceptive ease and facility the personal approach of this extrovert artist to this work was that of the dedicated perfectionist. Encountered one day, gloomy and despondent in Ackermann's gallery during a highly successful exhibition, he was questioned, 'What's the matter, John?' – the reply 'I've just torn up seventy drawings.' – 'You've *what* – why?' – 'They weren't good enough!'

When working in oils his verve and immediacy became diminished. Action and pace are presented skilfully but the style becomes mundane. In such portraits as of Royal Palace, the 1967 Derby winner, the likeness is excellent, pose and conformation convincing but the impact is insignificant. In comparison Skeaping's gouache drawings brought a dramatic and individual approach to the sporting scene but received little immediate innovative reaction from contemporary artists (*79*, *Plate 19*). Time was to elapse before infiltration of this spontaneity gradually appeared during the next decade (sometimes with little success when slick impressionism was based on anatomical ignorance) but sporting compositions were gradually to become less stereotyped with contrasting styles and techniques.

This trend, however, was not to be adopted by two long established and distinguished painters for whom the sporting subject had rarely offered inspiration though later in their careers they too were strongly attracted to the equestrian scene. Terence Cuneo was born in 1907, the son of Cyrus Cuneo, a Garibaldi by descent and a talented illustrator studying in Paris under Whistler. His mother was also an artist, an exhibitor at the Royal Academy, and these parental influences led to their son's career in art studying at the Chelsea Polytechnic and the Slade School.

Naturally prolific and incredibly versatile his artistic innovations accepted no limits. After appointment as an official war artist, when he was both the author and illustrator of *How to Draw Tanks* he became a leading industrial artist, then an obsessive railway enthusiast, a master of ceremonial function, including an official composition of *The Coronation Ceremony in Westminster Abbey*. With skill, observation and brilliant technique he painted military commissions, numerous regimental and battle scenes, studies of aircraft in action, an admirable selection of portraits and landscapes, even a Crucifixion. Amongst his galaxy of subjects the world of sport began eventually to play its part, ranging from polo at Cirencester Park (*80*), a detailed study of a meet in 1970 of *The Eastern Counties Otterhounds* at Guist Bridge, River Wensum and Chester Races; and most effective of all, for the bi-centenary of the race, *Derby Day 1979*, a massed scene of crowded detail in the William Frith tradition.

He was responsible in 1964 for the fine painting of the Duke of Beaufort in full ceremonial uniform on his grey charger, commissioned by Her Majesty the Queen to celebrate the fortieth anniversary of her Master of the Horse. An equestrian portrait only surpassed, though in simpler form, fourteen years later by the picture of Lord Daresbury on his favourite grey hunter presented to commemorate his forty-one years as Master of the County Limerick Hounds and posed against galloping Irish pastures. It showed, to Lord Daresbury's great delight, the first bank he ever jumped in Ireland.

The artist also excelled in lively studies of the Calgary Rodeo and also of the white-grey horses of the Camargue and their *gardiens*. Awarded an OBE for his services to art in the 1987 New Year's Honours, Terence Cuneo, one of the more stimulating artists of the century certainly brought, late in life, a sense of occasion to the British equestrian scene.

His contemporary, Frank Wootton, started his career at the Eastbourne School of Art and

80 Terence Cuneo, *Ponies in the Lines – Cirencester Park*, 1972. Oil on canvas, 24 × 41 in (60.9 × 104.1 cm).

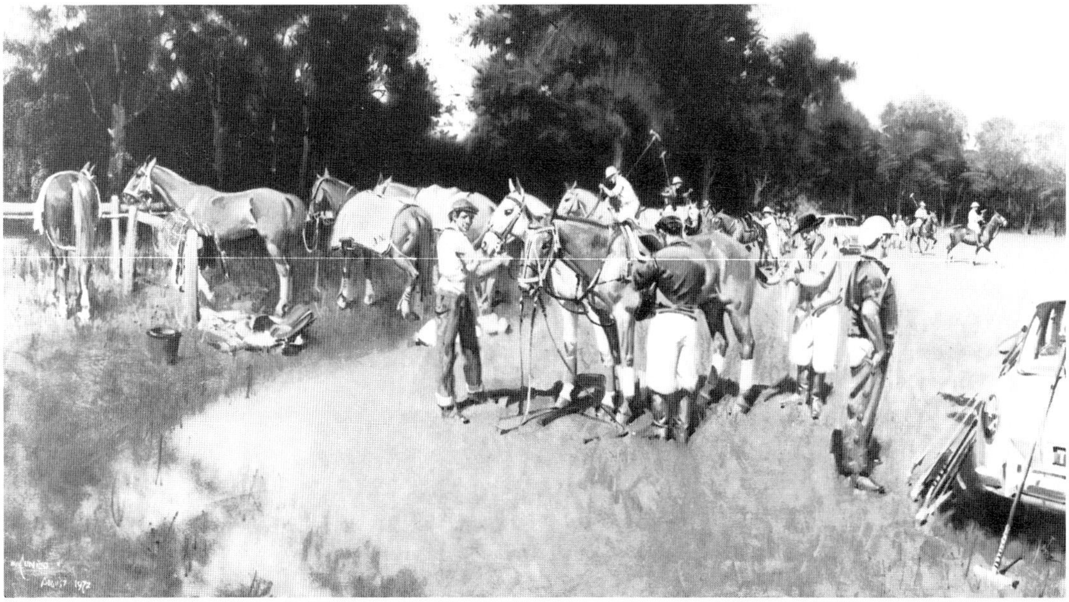

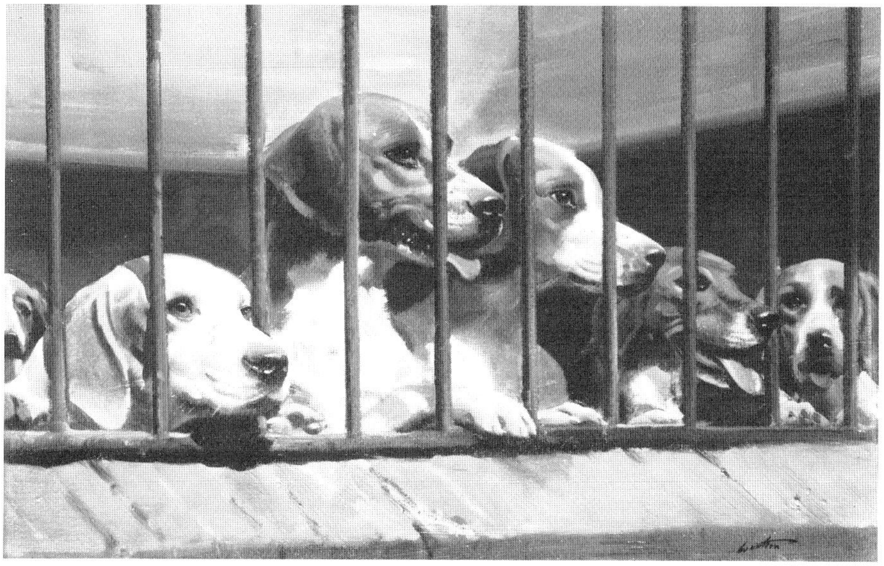

81 Frank Wootton, *Left Behind*, 1969. Oil on canvas, 16 × 21 in (40.6 × 53.3 cm).

gained the travelling scholarship and the Gold Medal. In the Second World War he was appointed an official war artist attached to the Royal Air Force. Never without commissions he has painted in all six continents and in more than fifty different countries. It was, however, his very fine landscapes of Sussex and the South Downs that won him his greatest acclaim and popularity. Later he devoted much of his time to sporting art with exhibitions at Ackermann's in 1964, the Tryon Gallery in 1974 and also in New York. He uses a rich diversity of subjects, though his hunting scenes such as *Going Out* and *Huntsman Returning – South Downs* still tend to suggest the talents of the landscape and not the sporting painter.

But his studies of foals, Arabians, Thoroughbreds and Shires are cleverly differentiated and if such works as *The Trumpeter: The Household Cavalry* and *Alexander The Drum Horse* are familiar repetitive themes, in his study of hounds, *Left Behind*, any foxhunter will appreciate his sensitive observation of canine character (*81*).

Almost as a second thought Barrie Linklater also turned his considerable artistic talents to sporting art. Born in 1931 in Birmingham he studied at the Woolwich Polytechnic School of Art and worked as a freelance illustrator. With sound draughtsmanship he soon received commissions for views of such picturesque venues as Oxford, Cambridge and Windsor but then found his metier in portraiture in which a pleasing sensitivity distilled his defined realism.

His entry into equestrian art occurred at high level with the commission of a painting of HM The Queen's mares and foals as a Jubilee present from HRH Prince Philip. Achieved in a cleverly designed composition, executed in the Stubbs tradition, Barrie Linklater began steadily to make his name with some distinction in the world of sporting art. Today there are ten pictures in the Royal Collection.

Amongst his portraits, landscapes and pictures of military occasions, at an exhibition at the Newbury Spring Festival in 1986 impressive oil paintings of Shirley Heights and Bustino made their mark, and most pleasing were his watercolours of the Derby winner and his studies of hounds. Also included was an interesting commission for HRH The Duke of Edinburgh with the scene in Windsor Castle Mews of the royal dressage Carriage Team 'putting to', which again illustrates Linklater's calculated skill in composition with its background of the distant castle tower and a glimpse of two Windsor greys with postillion, all perhaps slightly inhibited by a disappointing stiffness of pose and a flatness of tone in the buildings (*Plate 16*). But very evident is the artist's flair of portraiture, as not only the Duke himself but each groom and horse exude personality; it is a fascinating facet of an unusual subject. A later study of the jockey Keith Mooney also illustrated this gift and an exhibition in 1988 at the H.C. Dickens Gallery in London further showed his keen eye for the equestrian scene.

Certainly the early sporting pictures of Cuneo and Linklater showed little hint of the liberating influence of Skeaping, but this influence became more clearly apparent with younger artists for whom the Sport of Kings was a major subject. In the works of Peter Howell the derivative source from Skeaping's studies cannot be directly indentified but this artist certainly broke new ground in his free and unconventional style, in which the soft muted tones often evoke Robert Bevan's sensitive feeling for the equestrian world.

In 1972 Peter Howell held his first one man exhibition at Ackermann's. Its title 'The Racing Scene' aptly emphasised the artist's dedication to the turf as his source of inspiration. It was also obvious that his approach was stamped with professional understanding though his artistic execution was subtle and original in concept. Venues are identified as *Horses Returning from Work: Crossing the Moulton Road, Newmarket* and *Returning from Exercise: Winter Scene, Shrewton*, but individual portraiture of horses and riders are not specifically intended (*Plate 17*). It is the essence of the sporting scene that breathes conviction and today this has become the hallmark of Peter Howell's work. Observed in delicate tones against the faint mist that haunts English horizons many of these pictures possess an insubstantial quality but simultaneously excite by their latent realism and authority. Equine action and conformation are rarely distorted though impressionism prevails.

Born in 1932 in Caernarvon in North Wales, Peter Howell, son of an Army captain, was the youngest of nine children. Early in life he was introduced to racing by his father and, with singular good fortune, spent most of his school holidays in Newmarket in the yard of that king of trainers, the Hon. George Lambton, where he rode the hacks. It was a wonderful initiation into the world of horses that was to become a lifelong obsession.

Education at St Joseph's College, Ipswich, brought little scholastic success and only his flair for drawing put him top of the art class. This, with a strong aversion to team games, especially Rugby, provided small impetus towards a conventional livelihood. It had, therefore, to be art or horses. Those vacations in Newmarket had worked their spell, so he began his career in the racing world as a lad at Major McNee's stable in Lambourn and during the next years he worked with such notable trainers as Toby Balding, Dick Thrale, Fulke Walwyn and others in various capacities – rider, box driver, travelling lad, head lad, assistant trainer and, finally, was himself to hold a National Hunt trainer's licence.

The tough work and long hours in racing stables, however, never dimmed Peter Howell's enthusiasm for drawing. During trips to various courses all over the country he widened his artistic horizons by visits to public galleries and on spare days would frequent exhibitions in London. Though he recognised the quality of such masters of the British school as Marshall, Herring and Ferneley they made little impact and it was the French Impressionists, especially Toulouse-Lautrec, Manet and Degas, who had used the racing and equestrian scene with imaginative colour and fluency, that were to prove the dominant influence.

Marriage in 1964 to Joanna Smith, herself a talented artist in watercolours, with horses also playing an important part in her life, provided the ultimate stimulus. The following year racing was abandoned for painting.

Though never actually starving in a garret, there followed some stark struggling years in a cottage in Cornwall when, in order to live, Peter Howell had to paint full time, to learn quickly, to improve and sell his work. It was a formidable proposition. But after a first small exhibition in 1969 with his wife in Wadebridge, followed by a more ambitious display in Newmarket during the December sales, he never looked back.

To the knowledgeable it was at once apparent that here was an artist whose style attractively diverged from the traditional but, nevertheless, captured with authenticity the excitement and fascination of the racing world, whether it was the tension of a close finish at Fontwell or exercising in the morning frost on the wide expanse of the Marlborough Downs.

Three successful exhibitions between 1971–75 followed at Ackermann's, which led to commissions and exhibitions in the States where the Thoroughbred scene in Saratoga and South Carolina provided inspiring subjects. Such American sporting connoisseurs as Mr William du Pont, Mr Bert Firestone and others quickly recognised this new talent and acquired considerable collections of Howell pictures.

It is an amazing success story for a self-taught artist, culminating in 1981 in his most important commission for seven pictures for the new 'largest hotel in the world', Le Pavilion in Miami. For a fee of 120,000 dollars the theme was racing around the world; predictably, a stirring Grand National represents England.

Today the artist and his wife live in Kirkcudbrightshire where there is a yard of family Thoroughbreds all at hand to provide convenient models. Peter Howell, lean and trim, totally devoid of Bohemian excess, rides out every morning and appears more likely to be schooling hurdlers than tackling a daunting expanse of canvas. But nothing is allowed to interfere with regular concentrated hours in the studio where he works almost exclusively in oils. His paintings can vary from a modest 14 × 18 in to a stunning 6 × 8 ft and several preliminary sketches are tried out before the final composition is attempted. Though Thoroughbreds provide the focal point it is his subtle colouring, allied to skilful use of reflected light and appreciation of landscape effects, that make his work outstanding, an idiom that was to be copied in the future by lesser talents. Regular trips to the training areas of England, France and the United States provide constant commissions with exhibitions regularly in New York, Saratoga, California and in Toronto, Canada.

Another new arrival, Peter Curling, was only twenty-one when his first exhibition of racing pictures was put on by the Tryon Gallery in 1976. Born in Waterford in Ireland he was educated at Stoneyhurst and then at Millfield where he was awarded an art scholarship. He also studied with the renowned Signorina Simi in Florence, the inspired and guiding light for several British sporting artists. A short period with John Skeaping proved very valuable at a formative age and to him he owes his liberating presentation of the galloping horse. However, Peter Curling's own active contact with the Thoroughbred racehorse, riding work on the Berkshire Downs and Newmarket, gives his pictures a personal authority and from early days he was not afraid to use a large canvas showing 'chasers at speed over jumps, jockeys cleverly poised at the moment of truth. Impressionism becomes effective in a fine study *Two Furlongs Out* where he cleverly blends the brilliance of racing colours into a rhythmic harmony. In 1976 Curling's first one-man show in London was at the Tryon Gallery and in 1980 he shared a second exhibition there with Alison Guest and Sarah Ponsonby when the young artist was still feeling his way. There was some distortion of form but also welcome originality in the way jockeys, and not horses, would take command of a canvas.

In 1986 at the same venue it was interesting to see in his collection of over fifty pictures that youthful exuberance had developed into serious achievement with improving technique

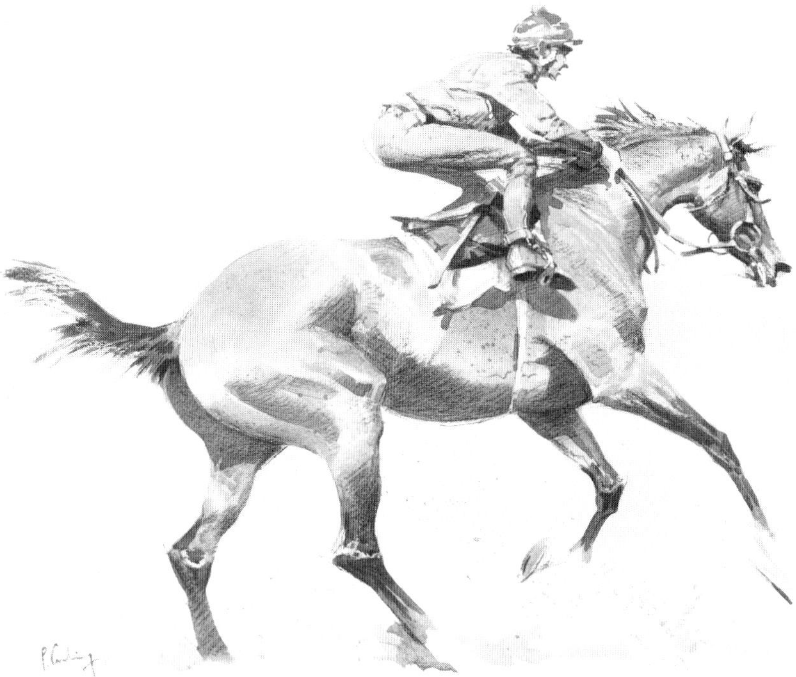

82 Peter Curling, *Daft as a Brush*. Watercolour, 15 × 20½ in (38.1 × 52 cm).

and keen observation. Now married and living permanently in Ireland, Peter Curling's former potential had reached fulfilment in a striking composition, the large *Sprint Finish*, with impetus and tension splendidly conveyed and also in a lively watercolour *Daft as a Brush* indicating that the artist understands the wiles of young Thoroughbreds at first hand (*82*). His talent was apparent not only in the racing scene for there was brilliance and subtlety in studies of the Tipperary Hounds against a backcloth of cloud-swept Slievenamon, and in his happy groups of browsing mares in lush meadows.

Today the racecourse has become the contemporary sporting artist's major inspiration and, thirty years after those first innovative gouache drawings by John Skeaping, it is clearly obvious that their influence has permanently enlivened current sporting art in the twentieth century. It has been an age of great horses such as Brigadier Gerard, Mill Reef, Arkle and Red Rum whose exploits have stirred the imagination of the public and provided inspiring commissions for countless artists. Racing, therefore, became established as the popular subject with several new names whose work began to appear at the end of the 1970s. Among the most interesting of these were Tod Ramos, Roy Miller and Nicholas Tolley, each of whom had benifited by personal and practical experience in the stables and in the saddle.

Adrian Ramos, known as 'Tod', born in 1956, the son of the portrait artist, Theodore Ramos, as a boy and while at the Brighton School of Art had worked for the trainer, Gordon Smyth, and later rode out every morning for 'Frenchie' Nicholson before attending the Gloucester College of Art and Design at Cheltenham. He then went for three years to the Royal Academy Schools.

His first London exhibition was held at the Richmond Gallery with a miscellany of pictures under the title of *The Racing Year 1985*. Venue and mood were effective in his studies of paddock and bar, whether at Royal Ascot or the Grand National, and also in the immediacy of scenes at the start and by the saddling boxes with clever characterisation of owners and trainers. The artist possessed an observant eye for detail, for accurate racing colours which he cleverly allies to pleasing tonal values but his galloping horses lacked authority and substance.

The following year forty pictures provided a second kaleidescope of current turf occasions with such convivial scenes as the Arkle Bar at the Cheltenham Festival and informed gossiping groups in the paddocks and in 1988 the third exhibition again covered 'The Racing Year'. In his exaggerated use of light and shade on equine form the artist has not yet mastered the Munnings expertise, nevertheless 'Tod' Ramos puts over the essence of the racing world with engaging verve. But a tendency for an over facile escape into impressionism, especially obvious in his 1988 exhibition, must not be allowed to flaw this fresh approach to familiar scenes.

Roy Miller began his career as a commerical artist in his fifteenth year, at the same time studying at evening classes at the Manchester Regional College of Art and then at Farnham College of Art, and exhibited his first picture in the Royal Academy in 1961. It was not until twelve years later that the sporting scene became his subject. In 1977 his handsome study in oils of Prince Philip driving a team of Thoroughbred/Cleveland Bays to a private drag, with Windsor Castle in the background, was presented by the Coaching Club to the Queen and Prince Philip to mark the Silver Jubilee. He has painted portraits of over a dozen Classic winners and there have been effective pictures of 'chasers in a snow blizzard and in contrast mares and foals in pleasant pastures with leafy trees which was used as a Christmas Card for the Injured Jockeys Fund.

Nicholas Tolley, born in 1958, obtained a BA in Fine Art in 1980 and has since used the racecourse as inspiration; in crowded spectator scenes he cleverly generates tension and excitement. People, not horses, would appear to be the more successful focus of his talent and amongst the most interesting of these is a tiny portrait of Lester Piggott in the saddle in the colours of Mr F.B. Moller (*83*). Other studies in caricature of such personalities as Lord Porchester and Major Dick Hern suggest that in this currently unexploited field he may find his ultimate niche.

Further names abound – but none of these young artists of the turf have, as yet, recaptured the ebullient *joie de vivre* of *Derby Day 1966* by John Gilroy, the portrait artist and poster specialist born in 1898, with his rollicking scene of members of the Garrick Club enjoying their sporting outing to Epsom (*131, page 204*).

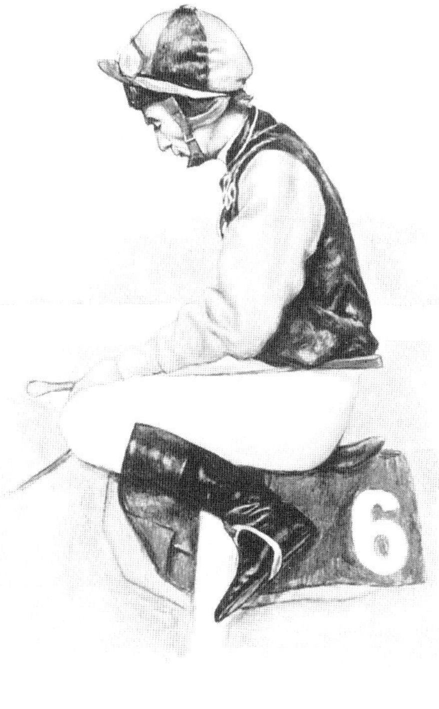

NOTES

1 John Skeaping, *Drawn from Life*, p. 25.

2 John Hislop, *Steeplechasing*, 1961; *Racing Reflections*, 1955; *From Start to Finish*, 1958.

83 Nicholas Tolley, *Lester Piggott in the colours of Mr E.B. Moller*, 1984. Colour, oil on card, $5\frac{1}{8} \times 7\frac{1}{8}$ in (12.7 × 17.7 cm).

14

Women in the Ascendant

After the mid-century the dominance of the woman artist gained considerable impetus. It reflected, of course, the enthusiasm of feminine participation in almost every sporting activity, but never anywhere more strongly than in the equestrian field. It would appear that, second only to most small girl's ambition to emulate Pat Smythe as an international show jumper, was the desire to become a horse artist. Many of them with little ability and less training, unfortunately, succeeded and, in the provinces amongst their friends, became busily engaged optimistically fulfilling commissions to depict family ponies and bogus hunting scenes.

In this century examples of mediocre amateur sporting art by both sexes abound, in which the basic principles of composition, animal anatomy, and even the competent application of paint are absent and unmitigated by any hint of originality. Edwards and Munnings have been diluted and distorted with results that are insignificant and bad.

Equally, of course, in the eighteenth and nineteenth centuries, many artists of poor talent up and down the country were also painting portaits of favourite hunters, famous racehorses and important local occasions. Every market town possessed its native sporting artists whose names have passed into obscurity and never earned a mention in Walter Shaw Sparrow's comprehensive books on the subject. Occasionally dusty and discoloured pictures emerge from family attics, amusingly naïve and a little grotesque, but, nevertheless, in their way relevant as a minor contribution to sporting history. Today's mediocrity may become tomorrow's documentary so, in this context, denigration should be modified.

Aspiring animal artists of the 1960s, however, faced daunting handicaps for representational art had ceased to be taught at virtually all the accredited art schools, and anatomy was a subject that rarely figured in the curriculum. It was commendable, therefore, that some of the young women artists working at this period produced sporting pictures with an appreciable degree of talent and significance. Though no startling innovations or originality of style were to stimulate the critics there was often a pleasing understanding of rural and sporting life. The theme, nevertheless, remained almost entirely equine, not surprisingly in the pervading atmosphere of horse-obsessed femininity.

Joy Stanley Ricketts appeared on this sporting scene after a decade or more spent as a stage designer and cartoonist of theatrical and film personalities for the national press. She had gained an art teachers' degree at the Birmingham School of Art but, as her own interest in horses and riding grew, a change in inspiration was to include equine portraiture, family scenes of ponies and children, military figures and Olympic riders. Her pictures combine a first class likeness in a pleasing landscape setting, attributes appreciated by the public in her collections presented at the Royal Windsor Horse Show and at the Badminton Horse Trials. In 1972 she was commissioned to paint the British Olympic Team Dressage horse, Kadette with Jennie

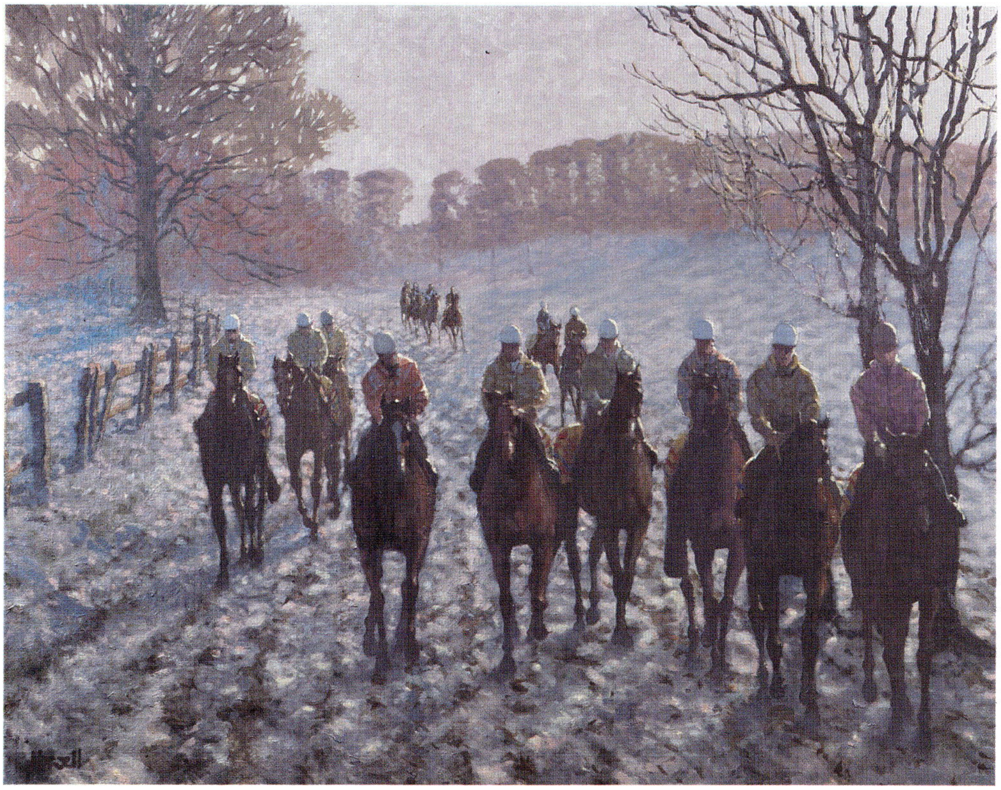

PLATE 17 (*left*) Peter Howell, *Horses returning from exercise: Winter Scene, Shrewton*. Oil on canvas, 24 × 30 in (60.9 × 76.2 cm).

(*right*) Peter Howell, *Horses returning from work: Crossing the Moulton Road, Newmarket*. Oil on canvas, 24 × 30 in (60.9 × 76.2 cm).

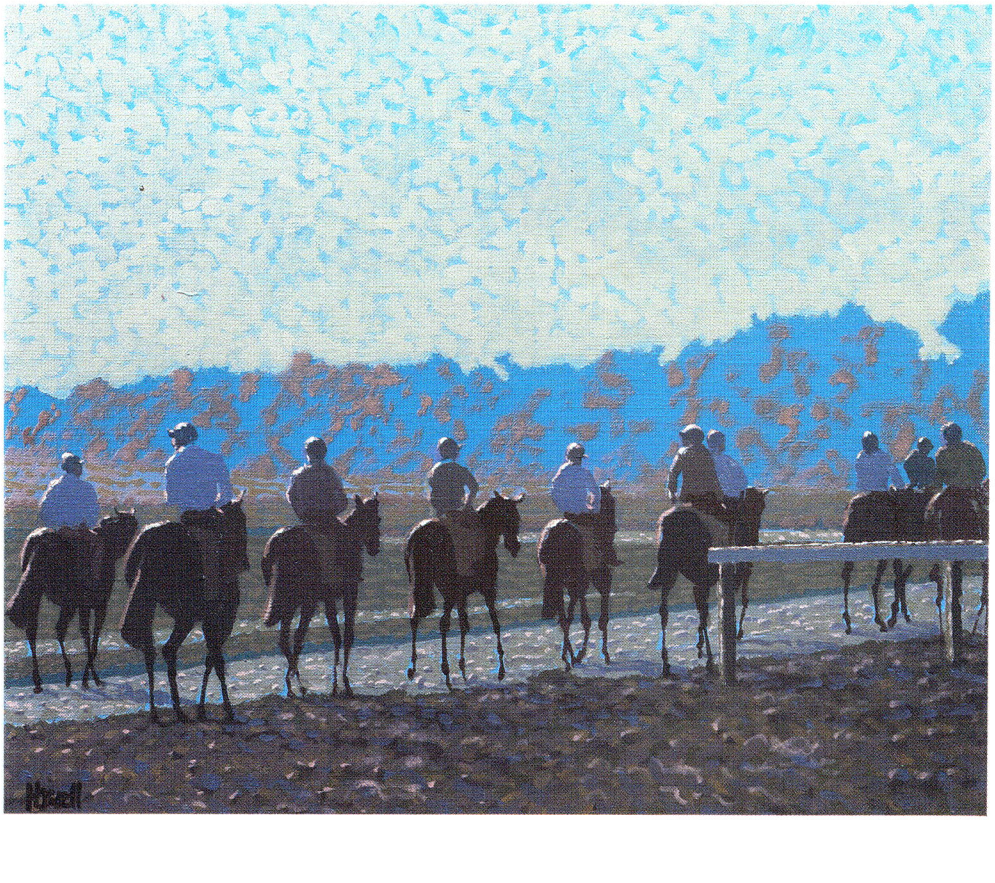

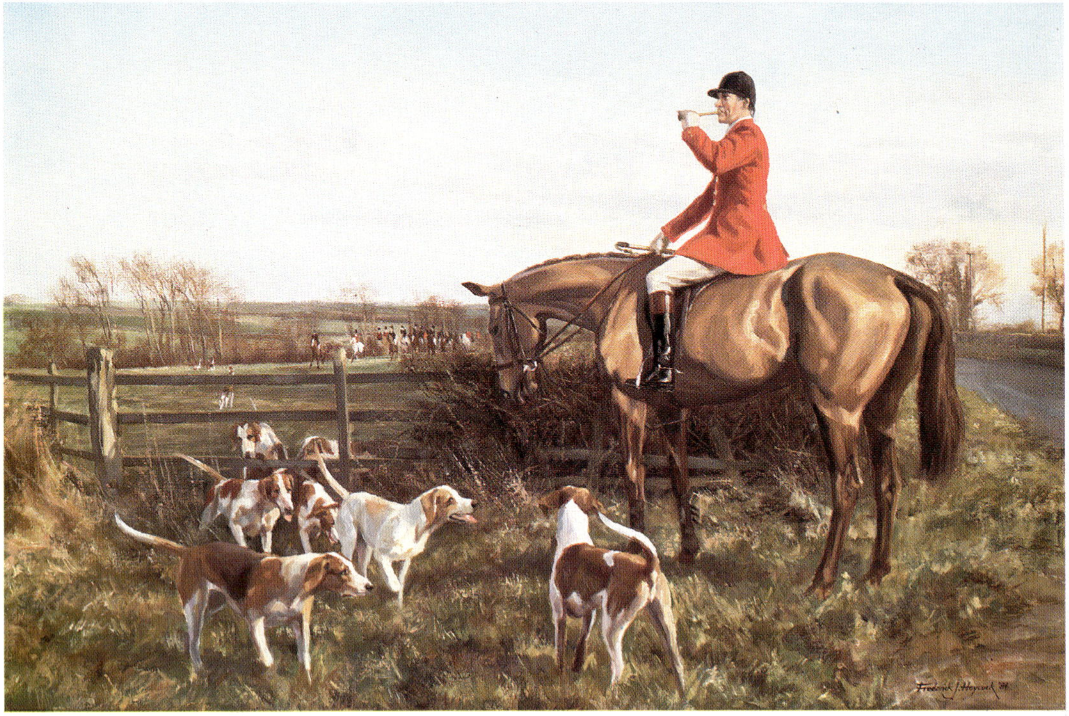

PLATE 18 (*above*) Frederick W. Haycock, *One Draw More: The Quorn at Ashby Pastures*, 1984. Oil on canvas, 20 × 30 in (50.8 × 76.2 cm). (*below*) Michael Lyne, *Kennel Fight*, 1967. Oil on canvas, 40 × 50 in (101.5 × 127 cm).

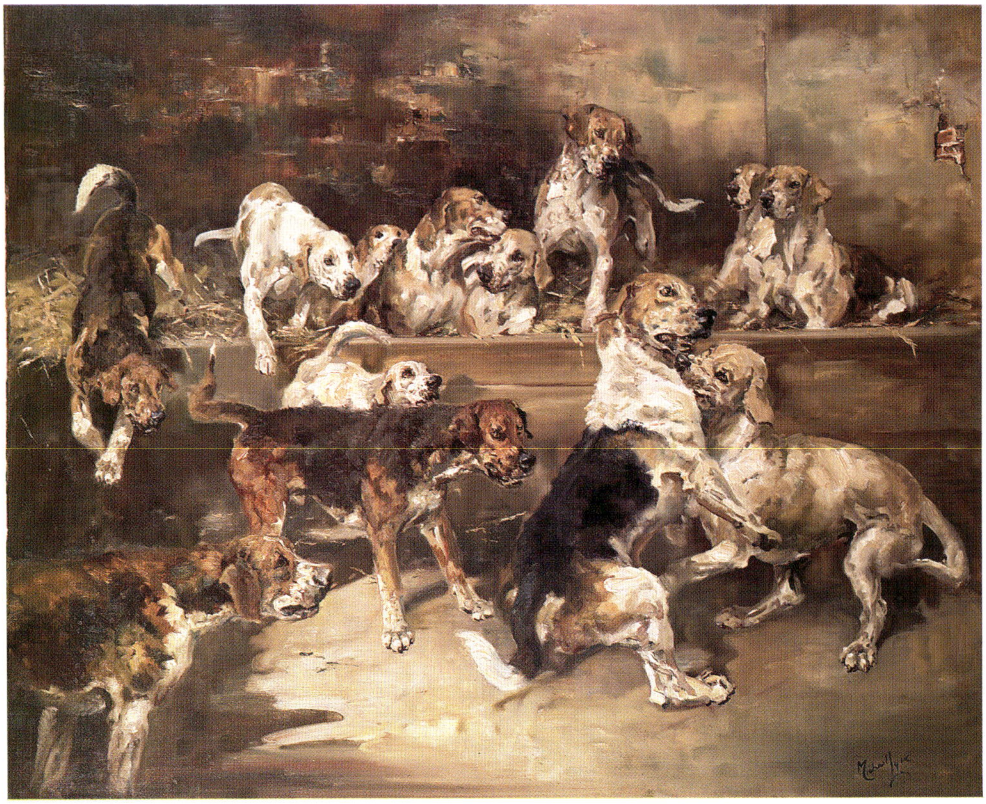

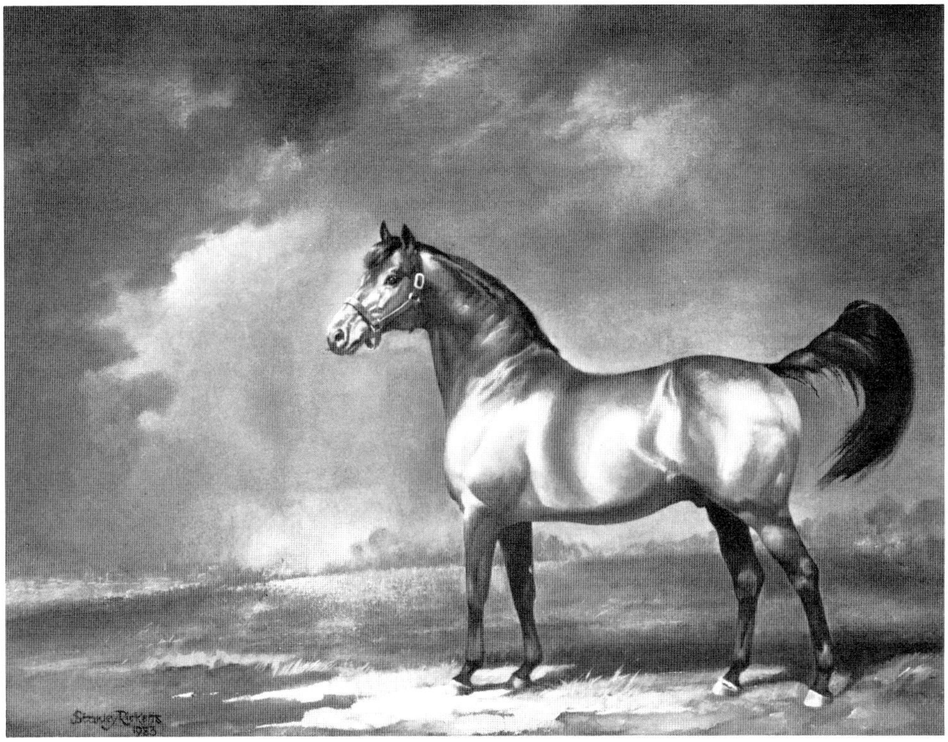

84 Joy Stanley Ricketts, *Study for portrait of 'Current Magic'*, 1983. Oil on canvas, 25 × 30 in (63.5 × 76.2 cm).

Loriston-Clarke, and also portraits of Captain Mark Phillips with his international event horses, Rock-On and Great Ovation. The 1978 Derby winner Shirley Heights was amongst her studies of Classic winners and in 1984, for the celebration of the centenary of the National Light Horse Breeding Society (HIS), her portrait of Mr T. Max Abram's Current Magic, thrice winner of the King George V Champion Cup at the HIS Stallion Show, surrounded by six vignettes of various activities of HIS horses, illustrates her authorative formal style (*84*). More recently she has been painting miniature equestrian portraits measuring only $2\frac{1}{2} \times 1\frac{1}{2}$ in in oils on panel which have proved highly attractive to sporting visitors from the States.

It is to the Hon. Aylmer Tryon, who first established the Tryon Gallery in Dover Street and later with the Moorland Gallery in Cork Street, W1, that so many young women artists of the day owed their opportunity to exhibit work before a wider public. He had a percipient eye for talent and gave sympathetic guidance to potential development and was to launch the careers of a notable bevy of women painters. Amongst the most important was Leesa Sandy-Lumsdaine, born in 1936 in India, where she passed an idyllic childhood in the hills before being educated in Gloucestershire and Lausanne. She studied at the Gloucestershire School of Art but her time was also dedicated to hunting with the Cotswold, winning several ladies races and owning and training her own horses for point-to-points and hunter 'chases. But though her life was much engulfed by these sporting activities, which also included breeding and working greyhounds and whippets, (the latter she considered 'a walking lesson in anatomy') her ambition to become a successful artist was paramount. At her early exhibitions at the Tryon Gallery in 1967 and 1969 her keen appreciation of form and discriminating colour sense in animal studies and hunting scenes were obvious but it was some time before an inherent stiffness and inability to introduce free action and complementary landscape details were overcome. Happily, in 1971, in a joint exhibition with Sarah Ponsonby her pictures of ponies, dogs and foxes, and especially her stalking scenes in the Highlands, pleasing backgrounds and movement began to play an important part in her compositions.

It was in her portraits of Thoroughbreds that she began to excel, in fine paintings of Nijinsky and Blakeney. It was in a real *tour de force*, *Immortals of the Turf*, a composite study ranging from Mill Reef to the Flying Childers, posed chronologically, and including also Diomed, St Simon, The Tetrarch and Hyperion that her full potential appeared. Horses and jockeys are presented with telling detail of stance and colour, most sensitively painted is the stormy sky, casting deep shadows. Trips to the States and East Africa brought commissions and varied experience.

Leesa Sandys-Lumsdaine introduced humour as well as observation in her hunting and racing scenes, often in dual compositions such as *Saturday Night* with the led, lame hunter, tired and muddy in pouring rain (*85*), to contrast with its fellow picture *Sunday Morning* of the same grey walked out in winter sunshine, comfortably rugged up with bandaged off hind and accompanying terriers (*86*), and another pair – *Winter Woollies* with its flaked out 'chasers and jockeys at the end of a hard race to pair with *Summer Silks* a couple of keen, shining Thoroughbreds going down to the post. Such attractive subjects became popular as limited edition prints.

In later exhibitions in her career the artist had found opportunities to forsake the sophisticated equestrian scene to exploit her talent for the simpler characters and pleasures of the country way of life, with such paintable subjects as roving foxes, badgers and her own long-dogs. Trips to Southern Ireland resulted in the classic *The Bride* with the tinker taking his sow in the pony-drawn shandrydan to a marital assignation.

The humble moke also produced some of the artist's most engaging work, for she subtly suggests that there is more to an ass than long ears. An artist who can paint both Thoroughbred

85 Leesa Sandys-Lumsdaine, *Saturday Night*, 1969. Print after oil painting, 16 × 20 in (40.6 × 50.8 cm).

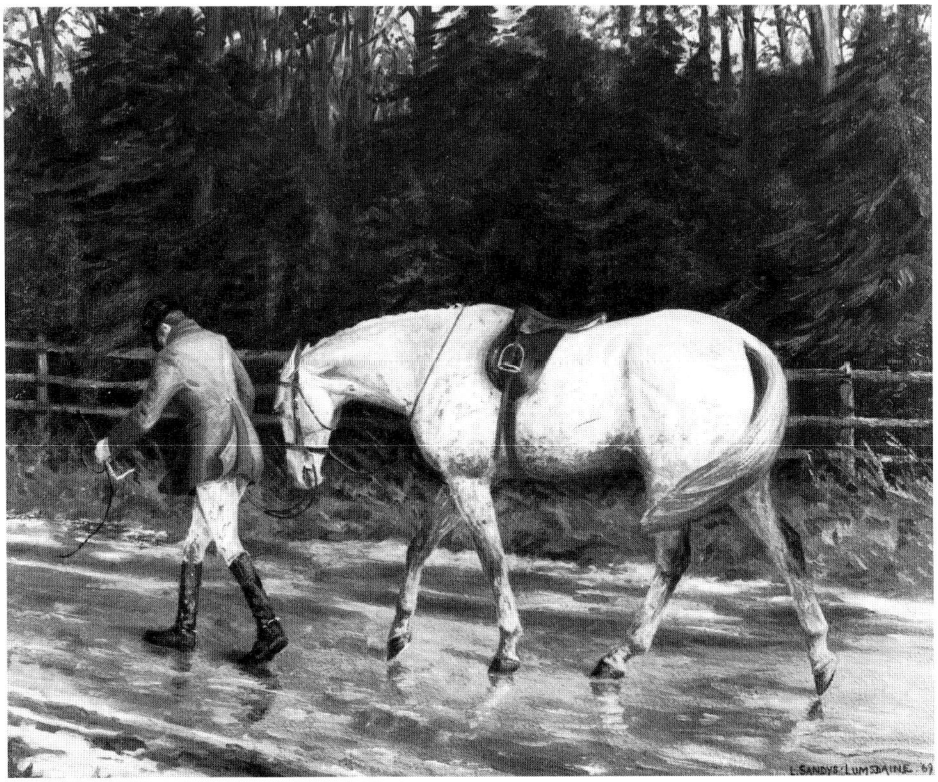

and donkey with such keen observation and understanding certainly made a memorable place for herself in the annals of twentieth century sporting art before her early death in 1985.

Another young artist, Sarah Ponsonby, sharing exhibitions at the Tryon Gallery in 1967 and 1971, was making a new impact on the scene. Irish by birth with a childhood spent in a world of horses in Co. Kerry, she studied at Signorina Simi's *Accademia della Bella Artii* in Florence and later at the Brera in Milan. After a brief affiliation with the abstract which, if nothing else, enhanced her colour sense and which she never totally abandoned, she returned for inspiration to the equestrian world. Vitality and mobility dominated her horse pictures and her racing studies brought her commissions from Virginia, California and also Canada, where in Montreal in 1969 she received the important Elizabeth T. Greenshields Memorial Award for her striking painting *Night Racing*, an impression of speed and contrasting light and colour (*87*).

She made these racing impressions of galloping Thoroughbreds at full stretch her special theme in a vigorous style instinctively derived from those early gouache sketches by John Skeaping. As youthful exuberance was adjusting to more sober discipline, painting took second place in Sarah Ponsonby's career when she began to concentrate on sculpture. In her exhibition at the Tryon Gallery in 1971 the major work included was a set of seven related bronze models including *The Wild Horse Fight*, zest and animation were their keynote but a lack of substance and definition had yet to be overcome.

In quieter vein the work of Alison Guest, a Sussex girl born in 1951, also appeared at the Tryon Gallery. She started drawing and painting horses in her Pony Club days and held modest exhibitions at Battle and Tunbridge Wells before she was twenty-one. Self-taught, apart from a brief spell in the Hastings School of Art, and spending much of her time following hounds

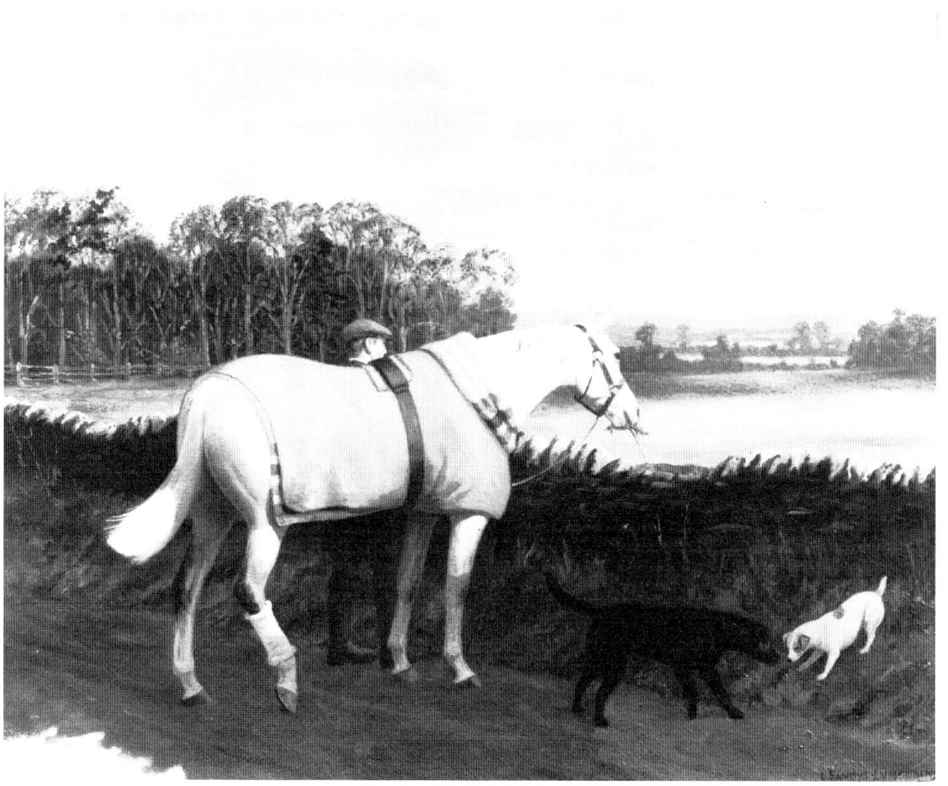

86 Leesa Sandys-Lumsdaine, *Sunday Morning*, 1969. Print after oil painting, 16 × 20 in (40.6 × 50.8 cm).

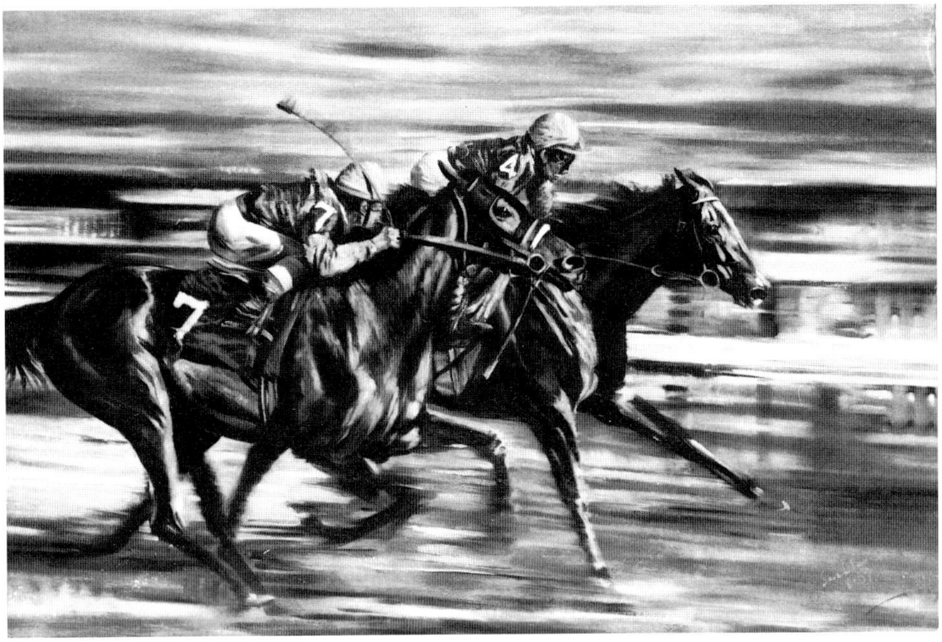

87 Sarah Ponsonby, *Night Racing* (detail), 1969. Oil on canvas, 24 × 36 in (60.9 × 91.4 cm).

in the New Forest and the West Country, either on a borrowed horse or in a Land Rover with the terriers, she learnt to understand the subtleties of sport and the joys of rural life. Here she acquired an observant eye for a country as well as for its animals, her hunting scenes such as *Drawing the Gorse* and *Blowing for Home*, painted in restrained tones, possess a pleasing authenticity.

It was a period when exhibitions of British sporting art at commercial galleries received regular reviews in such periodicals as *Country Life* and *The Field*. *The British Racehorse* always included an article on a sporting artist ranging from masters of the eighteenth or nineteenth century to established exponents of the contemporary scene. *Horse & Hound* in the early 1960s began to include frequent features on sporting art and, though the quality of the printing paper mitigated against realistic reproductions, the subject matter seems to have been read by readers with surprising interest.

In 1982, Michael Clayton, the editor of *Horse & Hound*, celebrated the centenary of the Masters of Foxhounds Association by initiating an art competition 'to encourage younger artists in the great tradition of British sporting art.' Entrants had to be under forty years of age and the subject chosen was a contemporary hunting scene, to be judged by Captain Ronnie Wallace, Chairman of the Association, and the Hon. Aylmer Tryon, Director of the Tryon Gallery and *Horse & Hound*'s own art correspondent. From over 130 entries the three winning paintings were all by women. The first prize of £600 was awarded to Alison Guest for *The Four o'Clock Fox: Long Holcombe, Exmoor, December 1981*, evoking the winter tones of the moor as evening draws on with the huntsman, adroitly placed, watching the hounds below in a rippling stream (*88*). Inspired, however, was the introduction of the white patches of lingering snowdrifts to give contrast and pattern.

Hounds are complex subjects for the artist to put on canvas, with canine intelligence and sentiment ready to ensnare. But the second prize winner, twenty-one-year-old Heather Budgett, who had also studied with Signorina Simi in Florence, had triumphantly avoided all hazards in *The Following Morning: Bitches in Bicester Hunt Kennels 1981*. Skilful grouping and keen perception of hound character ensured maximum effect.

In third place was a small attractive scene by twenty-five-year-old Susie Whitcombe, *The Puckeridge and Thurlow, Hatfield Forest, Noon 1981*, with a galloping field against a background of trees, still carrying the dark green and golden foliage of autumn.

The judges were impressed by the highly competent standard of the twenty-four pictures selected for final appraisal but once again the *Horse & Hound*'s art correspondent was writing (perhaps unfairly in view of the Editor's briefing for the competition) '. . . it was disappointing that no one brought a completely original approach to the world of scarlet and ratcatcher – Isn't it about time for the appearance of a "new look?"'[1] Nevertheless, encouraged by the great interest aroused by this practical foray into the world of sporting art, two years later the jaunts and jollities of *Horse & Hound*'s own centenary celebrations were much enlivened by a second art competition again initiated by the editor with prize money of £3000. Being based on a theme of 'The World of Horse and Hound' and with no age limitation artists found scope for individual inspiration and the results, by any criterion, were a resounding success, providing a kaleidescope of the modern sporting scene.

Each entrant was permitted to send in a maximum of three pictures and two of the same judges were involved with the place of Captain Ronnie Wallace being taken by Mr Dorian Williams, President of the British Horse Society and a keen collector of sporting works.

With nearly 200 paintings received it was a daunting task to equate flair with draughtsmanship, composition with conformation and landscape effect with sporting technique. Once again feminine talent overshadowed the results. Of the thirty-four pictures selected for final placing, twenty-three were by women who were awarded four of the six prizes. There was no controversy in placing Leesa Sandys-Lumsdaine's *Echoes from the Past* as the first prize winner – a work of imagination suggesting romantically the intangible enchantment of the world of horses and hunting (*Plate 21*). But there was nothing tentative about her authoratively painted hunts-

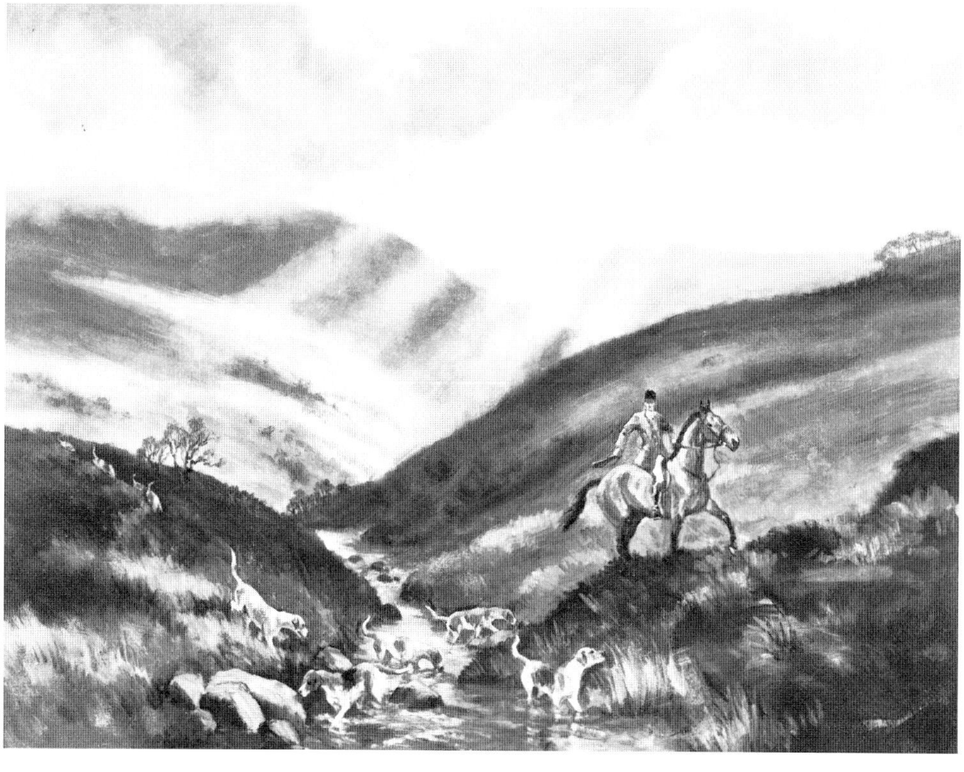

88 Alison Guest, *The Four o'clock Fox: Long Holcombe, Exmoor, December 1981*. Oil on canvas, 20 × 24 in (50.3 × 60.9 cm).

man on his sensible bay horse – a splendid type with intelligent head and strong quarters enhanced cleverly by diluted light and shadow. The knowledgeable could appreciate the artistry of the cunning evocation of foxhunters of a bygone age as depicted by Wootton, Stubbs and Ferneley. Brilliantly posed and deftly painted are the six foxhounds in the foreground, their raised heads subtly linking the huntsman of today with the haunting figures of the past. Typically Leesa Sandys-Lumsdaine had been rescuing lambs in a winter blizzard for a neighbouring farmer so last hours at the easel had been curtailed and the picture arrived bereft of final detail. But in its understatement and sense of space lay its magic – anything more could have been too much! It was to be the artist's last important work, and her finest, before her tragic death from cancer the following year.

The men certainly came into their own with two spendid hunting scenes by the unknown Frederick Haycock, an artist from Warwickshire. His painting *One Draw More: The Quorn at Ashby Pastures* with Michael Farrin (a good likeness) blowing his horn, the chestnut horse shrewdly posed with lowered head, hounds individually assiduous and the mounted field making a distant focal point, possessed a Munnings quality in its approach and technique (*Plate 18*). Traditional, of course, but immensely pleasing and painted with observation and skill – attributes that equally relate to his other work depicting *The Fernie at Peatling Parva*.

Born in 1948 and having lived and worked in the sporting world of Warwickshire (apart from two years in London) all his life, first as an illustrator and then fulfilling commissions of hunting scenes and gun dogs, Haycock's talent had not been recognised further afield in this country though three of his paintings had been sold to an enthusiast from Maryland USA.

In this competition again taking third place (and the award for the best entry by an artist under thirty) was Susie Whitcombe, with her deceptively simple study of *Royal Winner – Willie Carson* riding Milord at a swinging walk. The picture pleases by its sense of fluent movement and delicate delineation of muscles and veins achieved by the clever manipulation of thin oil paint on vellum.

Susie Whitcombe studied for a time at Heatherley's but her own addiction to equestrian activities, which included hunting, polo, dressage, riding work on racehorses (she holds an amateur jockey's permit and, incidentally, a private pilot's licence) stamps her significantly individual style with truth. In 1988 her growing reputation in the sporting field was to be boosted by an exhibition at the Malcolm Innes Gallery. Here a lively little study of *Parade for the 3.45 at Epsom* typified her observant approach to a topical scene (*Plate 19*).

Ability and observation were certainly apparent in the *Horse & Hound* Centenary exhibition. There was a pleasing composite scene by Joy Hawken of *The World of Horses* and also several fine hound studies with a skilfully painted head of *Sandhurst Viscount* in the Landseer tradition by Rosemary McMullen, *Hounds in Bracken* by Heather Budgett and Samuel Barnett's decorative *Ten o'Clock in Kennels*, all suggesting that future commissions would not be lacking.

From this competition some unfamiliar names received a welcome boost and included in these were Angela Webber; also Ruth Gibbons and Joy Hawken, both amongst the finalists and who shared a combined exhibition at the Tryon Gallery the following year with the intriguing title 'The Turf, The Field and The Farm.' Though completely diverse in style both these artists present the sporting and rural scene with confidence and ability and each possesses a happy flair for animal characterisation.

Ruth Gibbons, who studied at the Southport School of Art and was, early in her career, a full time illustrator in the Royal Ordnance Factory, has painted portraits of many of the leading Classic winners, including Grundy, Shirley Heights and, of course Red Rum. One of

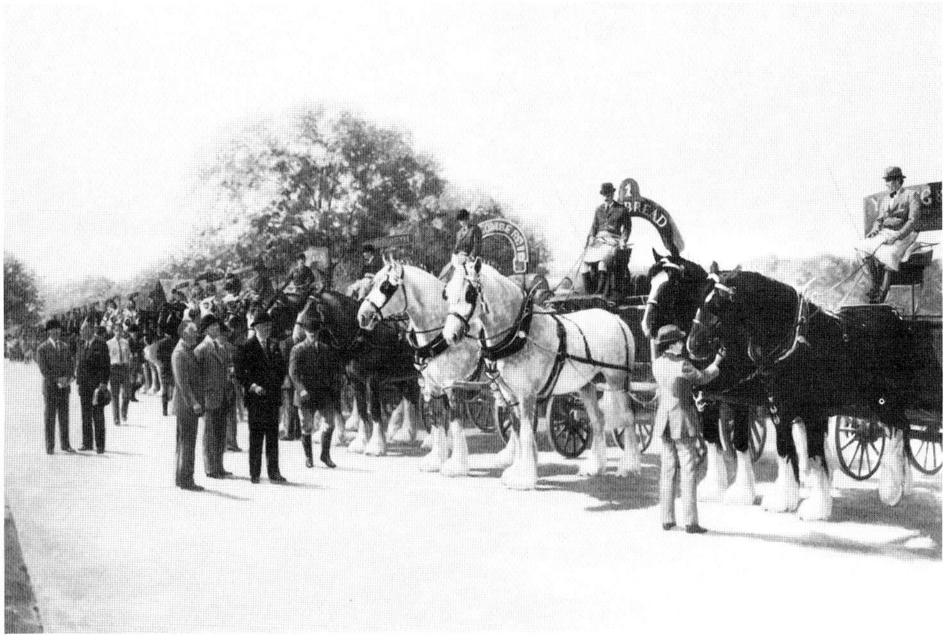

89 Ruth Gibbons, *European Brewery Covention 1983. Heavy Horse Turnout of British Brewers in Hyde Park.* Oil on canvas, 36 × 48 in (91.4 × 121.9 cm).

her most successful works was her commission for the 1983 Brewers Convention showing the Crown Equerry, Colonel Sir John Miller, KCVO, DSO, MC, inspecting the teams of heavy horses, where she combines a sense of occasion with decorative design (*89*). In different vein she evokes hunting pleasures in *Not a Ploughed Field in Sight* with both horses and riders coming over as individuals.

Born in the Shires, Joy Hawken's choice of watercolours and pencil drawings provide a particularly apt medium for her sensitive studies of horses, hounds and farm. She is at her best in such fluent paintings as *Foals at Newmarket*, the main focal point of the lovely bay youngsters being further embellished by lively pencil sketches.

Among a steady sequence of young women who continued to paint equestrian subjects some were blessed with natural ability, but many, unfortunately, lacked adequate basic and vital skills in draughtsmanship and, indeed, no compensating spark of originality. Frank Calderon stated that 'everything we see, everthing we paint, has some shape, some boundary, some form, and it is the faculty of drawing alone that enables the artist to depict it'[2] and from this threat of mediocrity the arrival of an exceptional talent was to bring new lustre and distinction to the scene.

Attractive, dark, Susan Crawford, born in 1941, daughter of a trainer of 'chasers in East Scotland worked in the 1960s in a studio in Chelsea. She first exhibited with Leesa Sandys-Lumsdaine and Sarah Ponsonby in 1969 at the Tryon Gallery when her strikingly confident approach to sporting art resulted in a sell out of her paintings on the opening days. This break-through was to herald a spate of commissions that has never diminished. But she has never rested on her laurels or modified her innate modesty; she maintains: 'I'm not as good as people think – it's just that, sadly, there are no Munnings about!'[3]

Riding, hunting and racing had always been a way of life for this artist but even as a small child (and ranking even more important than the highlight of the annual Pony Club Camp) was the urge to make pictures of horses. After school days in Surrey and Switzerland she worked in the studio of Signorina Simi in Florence, where she learnt to draw and, as she

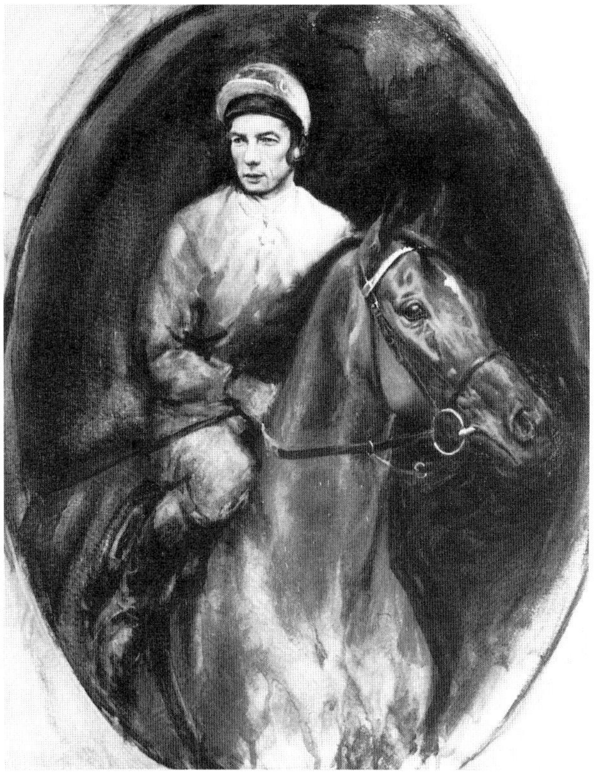

90 Susan Crawford, *Assessing the Field – the Mare, Park Top, with Lester Piggott*, 1970. Oil on canvas, oval, $19\frac{1}{2} \times 15\frac{1}{2}$ in (49.5 × 39.4 cm).

says 'to observe'. Here also she received advice from Annigoni, who deplored that so much talent should be 'wasted on horses'! But her sensitive nudes, portraits of Italian peasants and detailed studies of animal movement illustrate a rich diversity of accomplishment. Painting, in actual fact, never formed part of her training but she has found excitement and fulfilment in the medium of oils and her technique, especially on wooden panel has a smoothness of texture and graduation of colour tones that have stamped her pictures with the inimitable 'Crawford' style, at times, perhaps, used with an excess of precision.

It was her racing studies that made immediate pictorial impact and in an early exhibition Mrs Lester Piggott, confronted with the portrait *Assessing the Field* of the Champion jockey and the Duke of Devonshire's mare, Park Top, exclaimed 'It's marvellous! The best thing I've ever seen!' and Lester had surely been portrayed by every sporting artist of the day; but this was certainly a perceptive and brilliant likeness of both horses and rider (*90*). The painting was purchased by the Duke and included in 1977 with the great masters of the Chatsworth House Collection exhibited at the Royal Academy.

From the striking cover of the catalogue of her first 'one-woman' show in 1972 at the Tryon Gallery with dramatic impressionist line-drawings of a rearing horse and jockey it was obvious that an unusual talent had arrived that could animate the existing confines of sporting art (in fact she has exhibited at the National Portrait Gallery and the Royal Scottish Art Gallery). In Susan Crawford's earliest collection most impressive was a small study painted on copper of *Horses in a Storm*, reminiscent of Sawrey Gilpin's Diploma work presented in 1797 to the Royal Academy, and a striking oils of *A Grey Mare and Foal* in a landscape of romantic beauty emphasized the exciting potential of this young artist.

Most arresting were her animal compositions in which conformation and action are sensitively identified with animal character. There is a poetic maternal harmony in her large picture of a pale grey Lipizzaner mare, grazing under flowering cherry trees at the Piber Stud in Austria to contrast with her study of a young stallion under training at the Spanish School in Vienna, which conveys the tentative acceptance of restraint and obedience. But, conversely, in *Equine Loose* a powerful chestnut is shown at the moment of truth when animal assertion has triumphed. The dynamic painting of Whistlejacket comes to mind, but the genius of Stubbs' has been the artist's constant inspiration and like him, she paints animals with something of the same absorbing passion and integrity. Pictures of cheetah, zebra, and buck share pride of place with whippets, Jersey calves and a Charollais cow. A racing Saluki by some alchemy evokes its desert heritage but equally convincing is a superb portrait of *Kilkenny Famous*, champion bitch hound at the Peterborough Show.

Susan Crawford has never lacked commissions. Amongst several for the Royal Family have been an official portrait of the Queen Mother (not entirely successful), a happy picture of the Queen riding the free striding ex-hurdler Wocan in Windsor Great Park and a debonair likeness of the Prince of Wales in his blue Windsor coat on the dark brown Candlewick. This was presented as a Jubilee gift to the Queen by the Masters of Foxhounds Association. In addition there is *Special Treat*, the informal painting of the Queen Mother offering a titbit to Bustino, and studies of the royal family event horses, Goodwill and Columbus, not forgetting lively portrayals of the Corgis, alert and endearing, to rank as little canine masterpieces.

Further generations could label the artist with some justification as the John F. Herring of her day for, like the nineteenth century master, she has fulfilled a documentary function with her fine portraits of the leading contemporary Thoroughbreds including fourteen winners of the Derby. In addition numerous commissions from the United States, Canada and the Continent have added to the list which has, in its length, proved a definite detriment to the fulfillment of Susan Crawford's true potential.

But racing historians will forever be in her debt for convincing portraits of such stars of the turf as Nijinsky, Mill Reef, Ela-Mana-Mou, Shirley Heights and the much lamented Troy. Her studies of Red Rum galloping on the Southport sands suggest not only his stamina and courage but also the extrovert personality of this wonder horse. A superlative picture of two Derby winners of 1969 and 1973, *Blakeney and Morston*, together in a fenced paddock (both incidentally bred, owned and trained by the late Mr Arthur Budgett) and the 1983 Oaks and St Leger winner, the elegant filly, *Sun Princess*, epitomise the beauty and quality of the modern Thoroughbred (*Plate 21*).

Her portrayal of *The Mighty Ribot* and his dusky groom and of Lord Howard de Walden's champion miler, *Kris*, ridden at full gallop by Joe Mercer indicate that though most commissions demand an acceptable likeness in the conventional 'facing left' pose, opportunities for an alternative approach bring stimulating interpretations (*91*).

Competence and expertise were required to undertake successfully the important portrait of HM The Sultan of Brunei playing polo. Undaunted by the long journey, the brevity of the visit and a large canvas of 60 × 54 in Susan Crawford produced *The Winning Goal*, a real *tour de force* made spectacularly decorative by the skewbald markings of the galloping pony with its scarlet leg bandages (*Plate 20*).

Like most sporting artists after the mid-century, academic study of anatomy played no part in Susan Crawford's career. She realised, however, that the structure of a horse can assume curious anomolies when reproduced on canvas, but she never uses a specific pose to hide any deficiencies in her ability – she attempts to solve the problem, not always with complete success.

Her numerous commissions for impatient patrons have meant that a possible gift for landscapes, apparent in her early work, has remained unexploited and, on occasion has proved disappointingly mundane as in the backgrounds in some of her Thoroughbred portraits, but never have observation and perception of the horse itself been lacking. Her detailed observation of specific conformation, allied to stance and equine character, hallmark these portraits.

Recently her concern has been for a deeper attention to the head and eye of the horse, illustrated in the striking study of *Hot Foot*, a successful sire standing at Newmarket. The painting of the actual head-collar is as remarkable as the delicate detail of the head but the artist explains 'I love leather!'

During this more recent feminine domination of the scene of British sporting art, Susan

91 Susan Crawford, *Kris and Joe Mercer*. Oil on canvas, 24 × 30 in (60.0 × 76.2 cm).

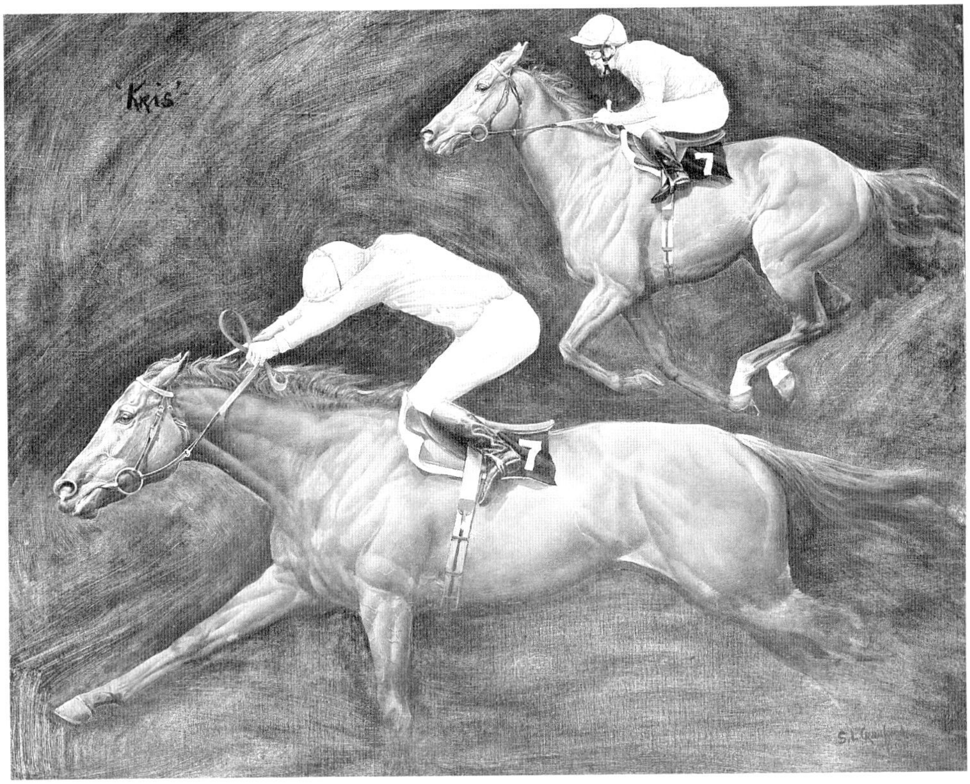

Crawford, in a strictly representational sphere, has reigned supreme. The quality and distinction of her work, effectively reflecting the influence of Stubbs, has assured her recognition as one of the most accomplished sporting artists of her era. Her ultimate status rests with future opportunities in which her talent can be allied to her imaginative flair and divorced from the conventional approach to the equine subject. The result could be spectacular.

But feminine talent continued to arrive. Amongst newcomers in the 1980s was Claire Eva Booth whose early sketches of local point-to-points led to full-time study at the Medway College of Art. With the modern trend for the racing scene and her own predilection for the racing Thoroughbred, she started riding work for a time with the trainers Mick Haynes and Tommy Gosling at Epsom. She visits race meetings and sketches relevant incidents and then plans and completes her compositions in her Kent studio. Working in oils, pastel and watercolours, her scenes certainly express impetus and excitement with close-ups of rival jockeys nearing the winning post. Impressionist in style, her blurred harmonious colour tones were initially curiously effective. It is an interesting talent that has already brought important commissions, including twelve racing scenes for HM The Queen Mother's private box at Cheltenham. A solo exhibition in 1986 at the Court Gallery in London led to the publication of fourteen limited edition prints after her works by Felix Rosenstiel's Widow & Son, but over-exuberance and a lack of artistic discipline in later exhibitions could threaten the promising potential of this artist.

NOTES

1 Stella A. Walker, *Horse & Hound*, 28 February 1982.
2 William Frank Calderon, *Animal Painting and Anatomy*, Seeley Service, 1936, p. 17.
3 Letter to the author, 22 November 1973.

15

Field Sports and the Naturalist Artist

In the school of British sporting art such rural pastimes as shooting, angling and coursing have never fulfilled a major role. Certainly Stubbs left us a few incomparable shooting pictures and later James Ward, Dean Wolstenholme and Abraham Cooper all recorded the sport with verve, though infrequently. To George Morland and James Pollard we owe some happy studies of the more tranquil pastime of angling; and coursing afforded an occasional subject for John Wootton, John Nost Sartorius, George Garrard and others. But hunting and racing always provided the most constant pictorial stimulation and in the twentieth century the equestrian theme has still dominated the scene.

Other field sports, though enjoyed by thousands of keen sportsmen, rarely produce major works of art. In fact it has been the naturalist to whom we owe some of our most constant records of these other activities, though more specifically within the range of the ornithological and piscatorial expert than in actual participation. In the terms of British sporting art problems also exist in defining the dividing line between the naturalist and the sporting artist. Much of the best work of the exponents in each category has been as illustrators for lavishly published books on their specialised topics. In this century there is a wealth of literature available on shooting and fishing but comparatively few important artists have painted these subjects outside a literary background.

Winners of Classic races and portraits of favourite hunters have always, and still do, command commissions; a successful day with rod or the triumph of a right and left with gun seldom seem to merit artistic evidence. As already seen in the Edwardian era, Archibald Thorburn, Heywood Hardy, Thomas Blinks and others gave us pictures of the shooting scene but ever more frequently these occasions were to be recorded by photographers which were later inserted in those neatly detailed game books of the country estates. Mand Earl and Arthur Wardle tended to concentrate more on the working of gun dogs than in the actual sport in hand. Perhaps this dearth of first class pictures of guns in action is explained by the fact that many of the best sporting artists were themselves dedicated hunting men.

Though the important seasons of partridge and pheasant shooting coincide with England's autumnal months of mellow colouring and diffused sunlight, even Lionel Edwards has given us only occasional examples of sport with gun and dogs in a few pleasing scenes at Buckholt, painted especially as an antidote to the stress of war pressures (*92*). But a feature of this period were the humorous shooting drawings, scenes to be found in *Punch* from such illustrators as G.D. Armour. The *nouveaux riches* tyros are not spared in his five sketches *Old Dogs & New Masters.* Snaffles in some line drawings also reflected the eccentric humour of the shooting scene but he would also depict the quiet pleasures enjoyed by an individual sportsman and his dog (*100, page 165*). Though Munnings never carried a gun himself, in his youth he spent

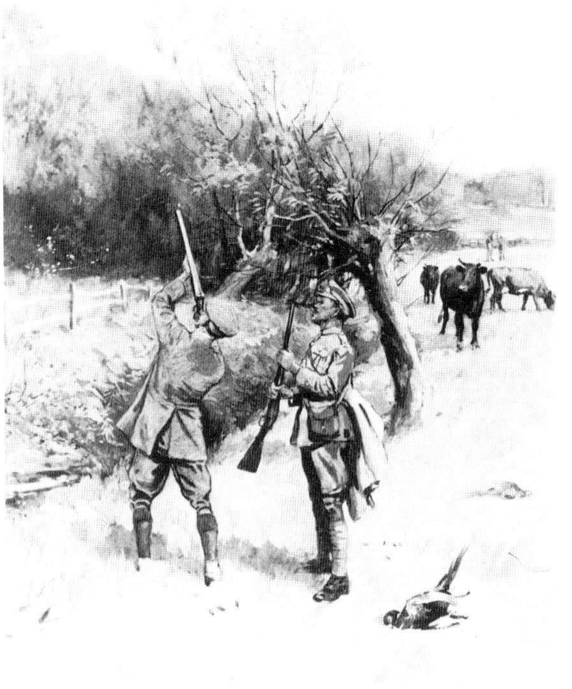

92 Lionel Robertson Dalhousie Edwards, *The High Shot*, 1915. Watercolour, 21½ × 13 in (54.6 × 33 cm).

some happy days as beater enjoying the scenery and the company. His cheerful study, *The Shooting Party*, dated 1901 (*93*), tramping through a field of swedes after lunch suggests, with a touch of caricature, the unsophisticated pleasures of sport with friends and, as he admitted, it was not only the mellow light of the October sun that gave the glow!

In contrast and most evocative of solitary aspects of the sport is Brian Hatton's observant composition, dated 1910, *Man Duck-Shooting with Dog on Lugg* (sometimes known as *The Gamekeeper*), of the alert sturdy countryman in worn corduroys with his spaniel by an old pollarded willow – a magical picture by this young artist (*Plate 22*).

Charles Simpson displayed his keen appreciation of the wildfowling scene and occasion in his huge painting *The Punt Gunner* with its chaotic rising duck, which was awarded a Gold Medal in the sporting art exhibition for the Olympics in Paris in 1924 – a striking contrast to his illustrations of hounds and field streaming across the Shires. Thirty years later, in 1967, John King was painting an informal shooting picture for the tenants of South Manor Estate to present to Lord and Lady Rank on the occasion of their Golden Wedding – showing the two leading characters, their retrievers and beaters on the stubble – but these are isolated examples.

In the 1970s John Trickett, born in Sheffield, and first studying accountancy before becoming a professional footballer, finally fulfilled his early artistic ambitions as a sporting artist and especially in the shooting scene. His realistic studies of gun dogs – spaniels, labradors and retrievers – and exhibitions in London and Nottinghamshire brought recognition and success (*94*); later he developed his talent into effective shooting compositions in woodland and open country. Several of his works have been reproduced as limited edition prints.

Early in the century a certain vogue for humour in the shooting world was to be met by caricatures by such exponents as Charles Hope and H.N. Bateman, but a draughtsman in the John Leech category has yet to appear to exploit fully the comic dilemmas of the tyro confronted with the formal rituals of the big syndicate.

Though shooting in the twentieth century has inspired only limited artistic representation, in the sport of deerstalking many leading artists have found its setting in the Scottish Highland an irresistible attraction. As already indicated it was only in the late Victorian era that the sport in its modern form attained popularity, recorded on large canvases by Landseer and Ansdell when Balmoral, John Brown and the craze for tartan had established a northern royal pilgrimage every August. Today the sport holds the same appeal for a dedicated minority and the necessity for a controlled culling of old, diseased and an excessive number of deer is being recognised even by the avid anti-blood sports fraternity. Venison has become a viable food product and provides an alternative source of income for farmers forced to diversify.

At the turn of the century John Guille Millais, born in 1865, son of Sir John Everett Millais, RA, brought observation and talent to the stalking scene. From childhood Scotland's flora and fauna had been his constant attraction; in addition he had become a keen and proficient stalker and also a sporting naturalist in his own right. A popular illustrator of many books on wildfowl and mammals, his most important work was the classic *British Deer and Their Horns*, published in 1897, and here his excellence as a draughtsman shows his intimate knowledge of indigenous and imported deer. His paintings capture not only the action and spirit of the sport of stalking but the glories of the Highland environment.

This inheritance he bestowed on his younger son, Raoul Millais, the third generation of the family to find a favourite subject in fine paintings of deer. Late in his career in the 1980s he reduced these studies to tiny dimensions, in a style that brought a romantic aura to both the sport and setting.

Born in 1880 and also as much naturalist as sportsman, Vincent Balfour-Browne was destined for the Bar but abandoned a legal career before the First World War to study painting and drawing under George Lodge. Later stalking and the red deer took command of his life and his own love of the sport and the Highlands gave his work perception and authority. His brilliant series of paintings on deer stalking with his writings on the subject quickly attracted a wide public. Several works of basic information followed such as *How to Stalk* and *The Life of the Stag* and the lavish publication late in his life, in 1977, of *The Stalking Letters and Sketches of V.R. Balfour-Browne* emphasised the fact that his observant talent had recorded the sport in the twentieth century with incomparable vision and flair.

Lionel Edwards in his *Scottish Sketch Book* showed himself as deft with Highland mountain mists and deer as in his paintings of the winter mud and grey clouds of the hunting field but he wrote that 'no animal so utterly defeats the artist as the deer tribe,'[1] but he conceded

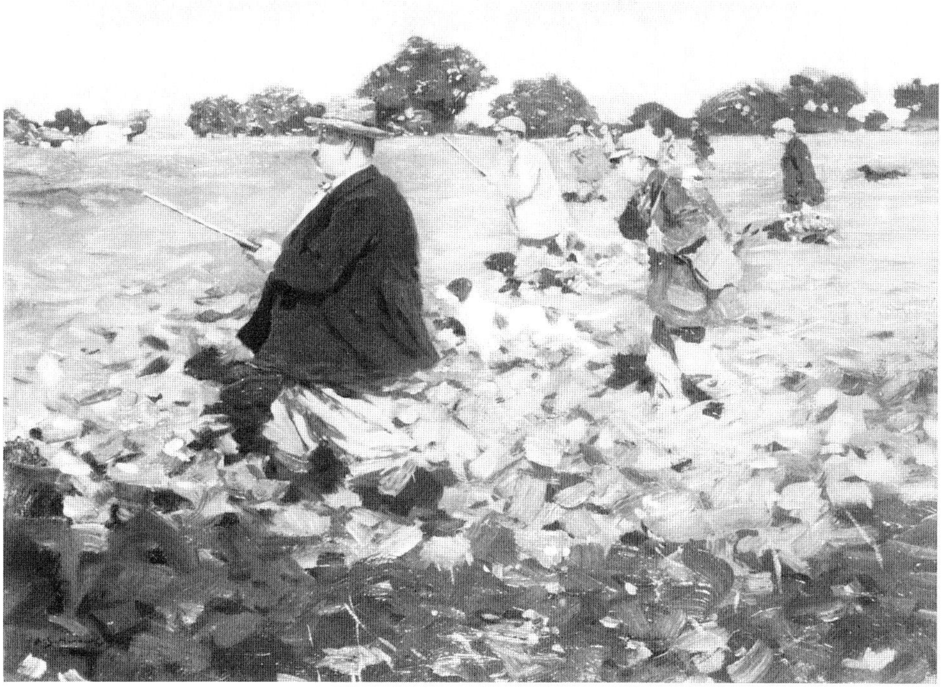

93 Alfred James Munnings, KCVO, PRA, *The Shooting Party*, *c* 1901. Oil on canvas, $16\frac{1}{2} \times 22$ in (41.9×55.8 cm).

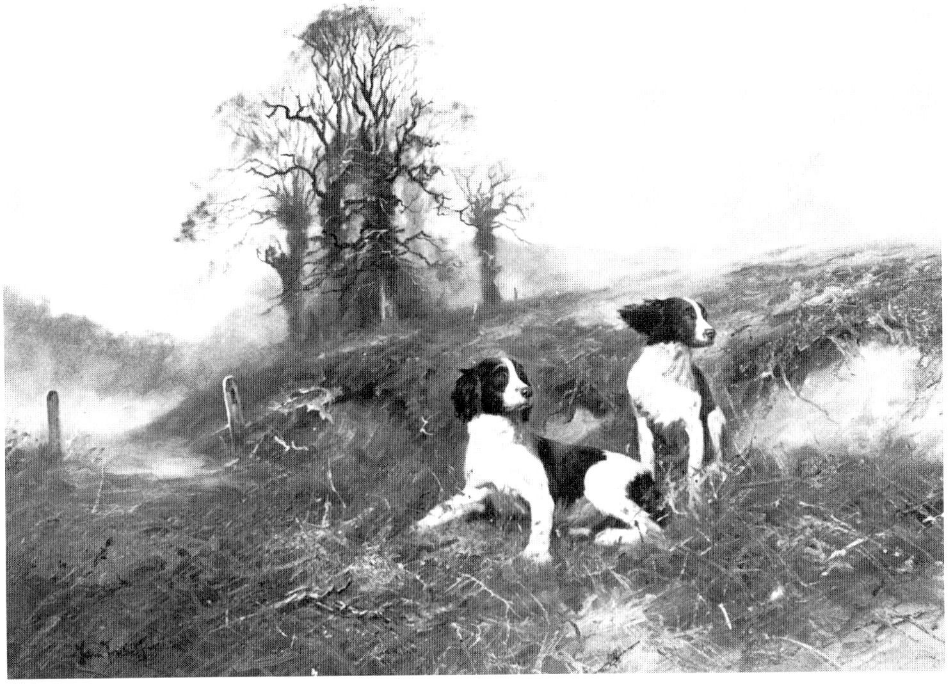

94 John Trickett, *Springer Spaniels*, 1987. Oil on canvas, 24 × 30 in (60.9 × 76.2 cm).

success to his close friend Frank Wallace. Born in 1881, from childhood, animals and especially deer stalking had aroused the youthful imaginaton of Wallace. Inherited artistic talent from his mother's family led to a period of study at the Calderon School and a lifelong association with Lionel Edwards provided constant encouragement and advice. He wrote regular articles on deerstalking for *Country Life* illustrated by his fine studies of stags and hinds, and living the greater part of his life in Scotland, contact with John Guille Millais also proved a great inspiration. Working most frequently in gouache and acquiring a sure eye for composition he could relate deer coherently to magnificent Highland scenery. There was no dichotomy between the naturalist and the sporting artist.

By the mid-century many young sporting painters were drawn irresistibly to the stalking scene. Michael Lyne in his autobiographical work *A Parson's Son*, relates in vivid prose the thrill of his first stalk and the kill of an eleven pointer, and his painting of *Stalking at Black Corries* with its garron, ghillies and distant loch possesses the same verve and factual impact. In his many exhibitions stalking regularly played a colourful role.

John King also with success devotes part of his time to pictures of deerstalking and Susan Crawford, in her painting in oils, completed in three days in Invernesshire, of *The Stalking Pony* – a sturdy light grey Highland laden with the inert body of the stag, brings home the reality of death on the moors (95).

In the 1980s the Sports Council reported that of all our national activities fishing was the most popular, and assessed the number of active fishermen at around $3\frac{3}{4}$ million. It certainly must be accepted as one of the most ancient for men have fished as long as men have hunted. Before the seventeenth century fishing provided a welcome source of alternative protein (especially on Fridays), so its status was primarily practical rather than sporting. However by the next century Gervase Markham was referring to angling as 'The Sport and Recreation of Gods and Saints'. Today 'the gentle art' is enjoyed by sportsmen of every persuasion, whether believers or heathens; of all social categories from artisans to poets, but oddly enough in this feminist age amongst its devotees only five per cent are women.

Its tranquil joys have been invaded by the formal organisation of clubs and associations for both coarse and fly fishing (the Flyfishers' Club celebrated its centenary in 1984). More recently a sponsored competitive element has been introduced with big money to be won. Passionate articles in the press have discussed the moral issues involved. Angling magazines in great number appear regularly and tastefully illustrated books (though often using colour photography) on matters piscatorial flood the literary lists. But this sophistication has in no way dampened the ardour of the dedicated for whom the ancient craft of angling is not merely a sporting pastime but a private adventure and way of life.

Virtually no historic stately home possesses collections of angling pictures and this popular sport has never founded an artistic school of its own like racing and hunting. The detailed technical knowledge of the pastime is extremely difficult to apply pictorially and in the twentieth century, as in the past, few artists have appeared with the expertise and eye to produce pleasing and credible pictures of this most engrossing activity.

In the first decade the careers of such noted Victorian exponents as J.C. Hook, William MacTaggart and John Macwhirter were nearing their end, but occasionally Archibald Thorburn would divert his ornithological talent to a scene such as *Landing a Salmon* – a pleasant painting of two anglers and a dog, or to such studies as *A Sea Trout*, (*96*). Happily Ernest E. Briggs was at the height of his powers and in Walter Shaw Sparrow's words could 'make lyrics in colour and particularly in watercolours.'[2] Born in 1876 in Dundee of Yorkshire parents he was intended for a career as a mining engineer, but precarious health influenced a switch to art with study at the Slade School, Heatherley's and later in Italy. In 1899 when only twenty-

95 Susan Crawford, *The Stalking Pony*, 1978. Oil on canvas, 24 × 30 in (60.9 × 76.2 cm).

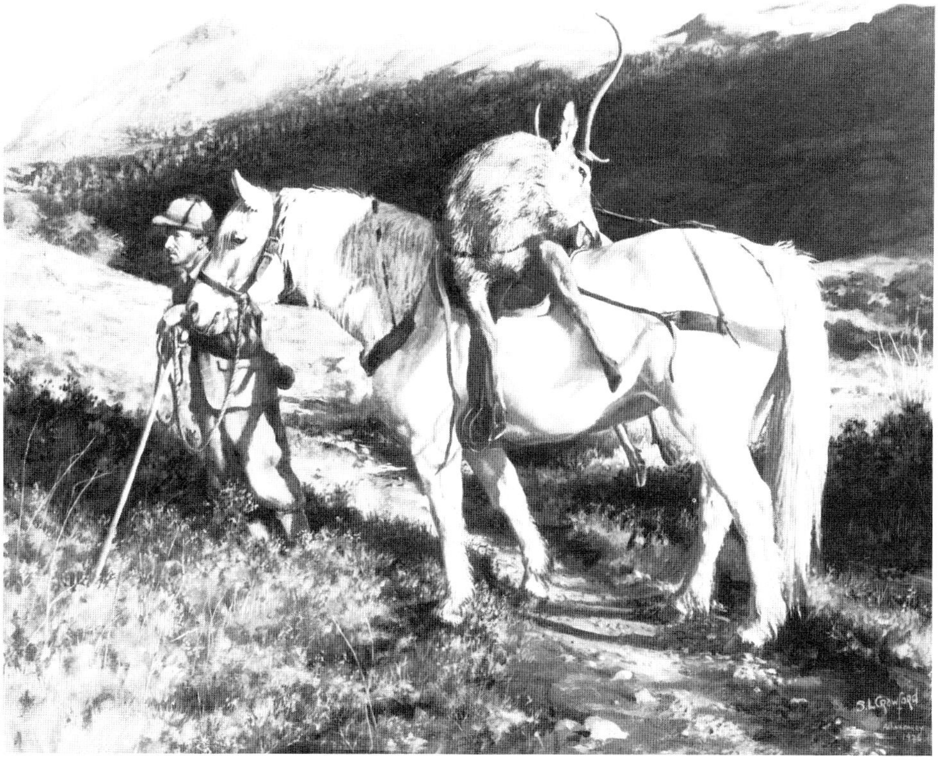

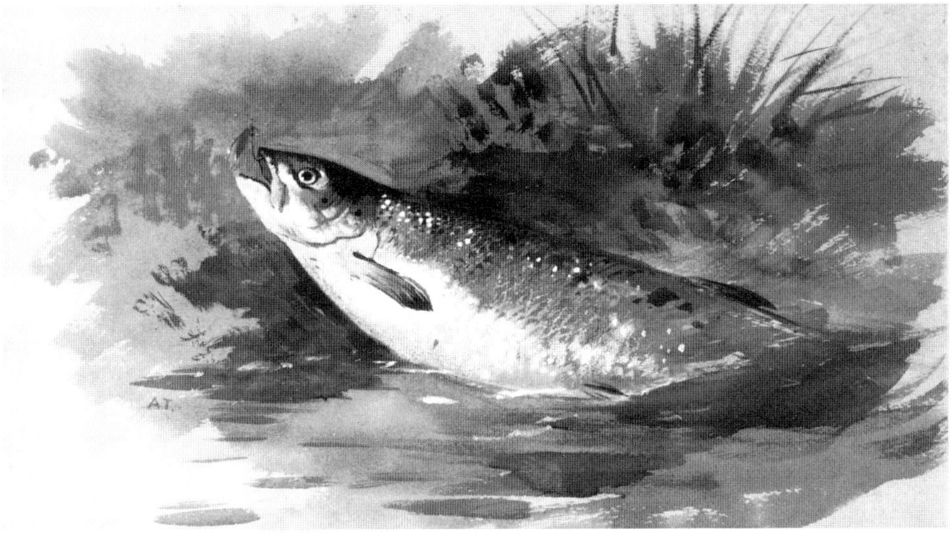

96 Archibald Thorburn, *A Sea Trout.* Watercolour, $10\frac{1}{2} \times 14\frac{1}{2}$ in (26.6 × 36.8 cm).

three he started exhibiting regularly at the Royal Academy, continuing until his death in 1913.

Ernest Briggs must be considered one of the finest British artists of the angling scene (*Plate 24*). His handling of running water, with the transitory shadows of a variable sky, resulted in landscapes of great beauty which, allied to his outstanding draughtsmanship and his own personal mastery of the actual sport, assured that an individual fisherman's style of casting and stance in the river were immediately recognisable. In his classic book *Angling and Art in Scotland* published in 1908, with his fine illustrations of gentle vistas of lochs and mountains he wrote in the Preface a nice explanation of the split loyalties of painter and sportsman: 'when the fish are inclined to rise it is not upon the scenery that the fisherman casts his eye; nor at such moments does the artist angler think of pigments and brushes but rather does his fancy lightly turn to thought of flies and the varied colours displayed in his fly book.' [3]

Contrasting in style, the splendid picture in oils of *Mr and Mrs F.S. Oliver Angling in Norway* painted in 1903 by Charles Furse must be considered a *tour de force* unequalled, perhaps, in characterisation and panache unless one includes in the British school American-born John S. Sargent, RA, with his wonderful *Portrait of a Young Salmon Fisher: Alec McCullough* of the same period, with its comparable fluent brushwork and exciting composition.

In different vein Norman Wilkinson, born in 1878, a friend and near contemporary of Ernest Briggs, began a career in marine painting and posters and became official Marine Painter to the Royal Yacht Squadron. But from boyhood he had been an ardent flyfisher and eventually his sport became his primary subject and in 1920, after his innovative camouflage work for the Royal Navy in the First World War, he took up the mantle of Briggs and began working in watercolours and later oils in the angling scene.

The following year an exhibition of these works in the Dunthorne Gallery in London established his success and, until his death in 1971, his sensitive gentle paintings of angling, especially in Scotland, achieved unbroken popularity. Much of his work was also effectively executed in drypoint in a style that Walter Shaw Sparrow referred to as 'an adventure in drypoint impressionism'. *Spring Fishing on the Spey*, with a fish fresh taken and the rod bending to its weight, the critics selected as one of his finest examples in this medium. In oils his work was enriched by a broader sense of light and shade though his colour sense always remained subtle and pleasing.

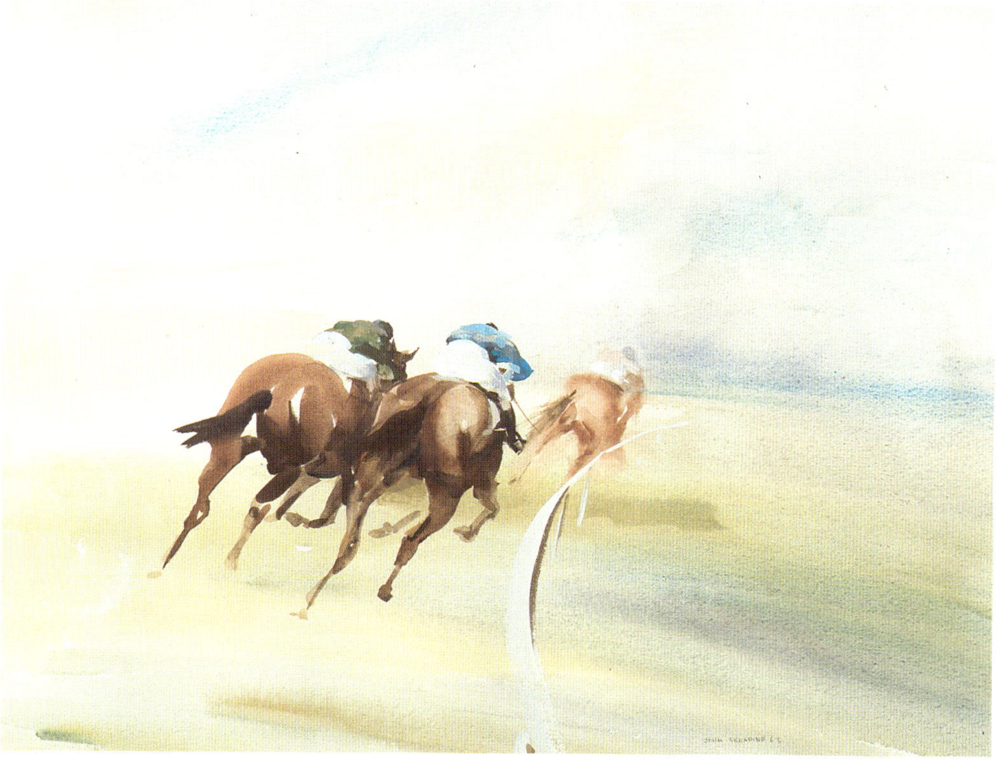

PLATE 19 (*above*) John Rattenbury Skeaping, RA, *Turning for Home*, 1963. Watercolour on paper, $17\frac{3}{4} \times 22\frac{7}{8}$ in (45×58 cm). (*below*) Susie Whitcombe, *Parade for the 3.45 at Epsom*, 1988. Oil on canvas, $11\frac{1}{2} \times 15\frac{1}{2}$ in (29.2×39.3 cm).

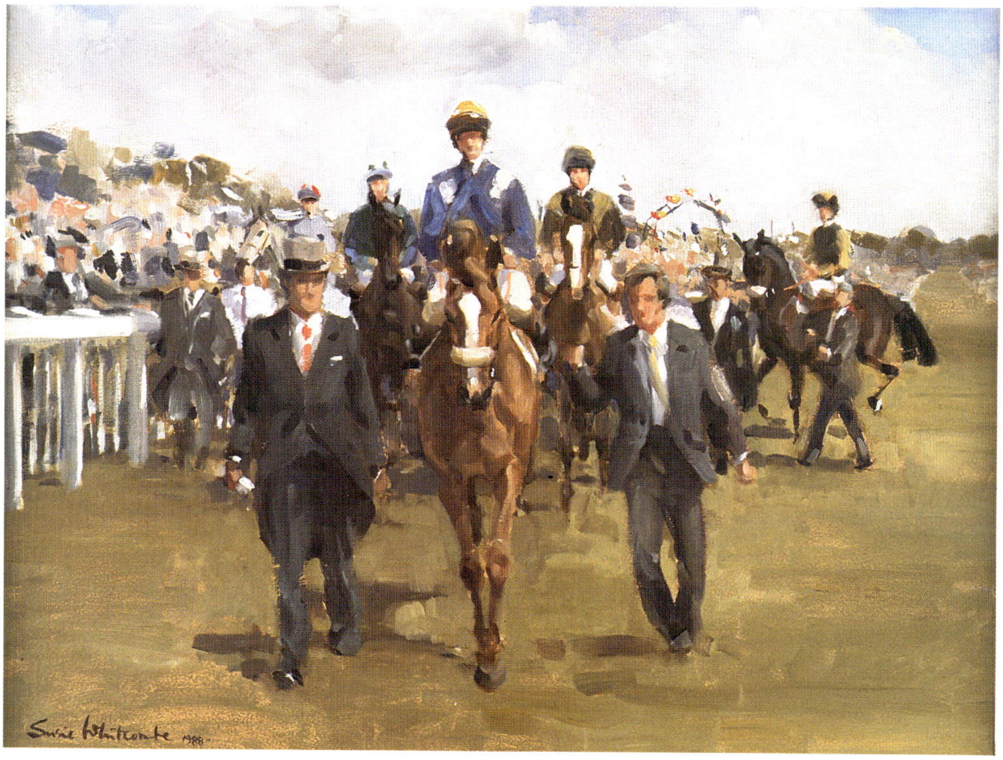

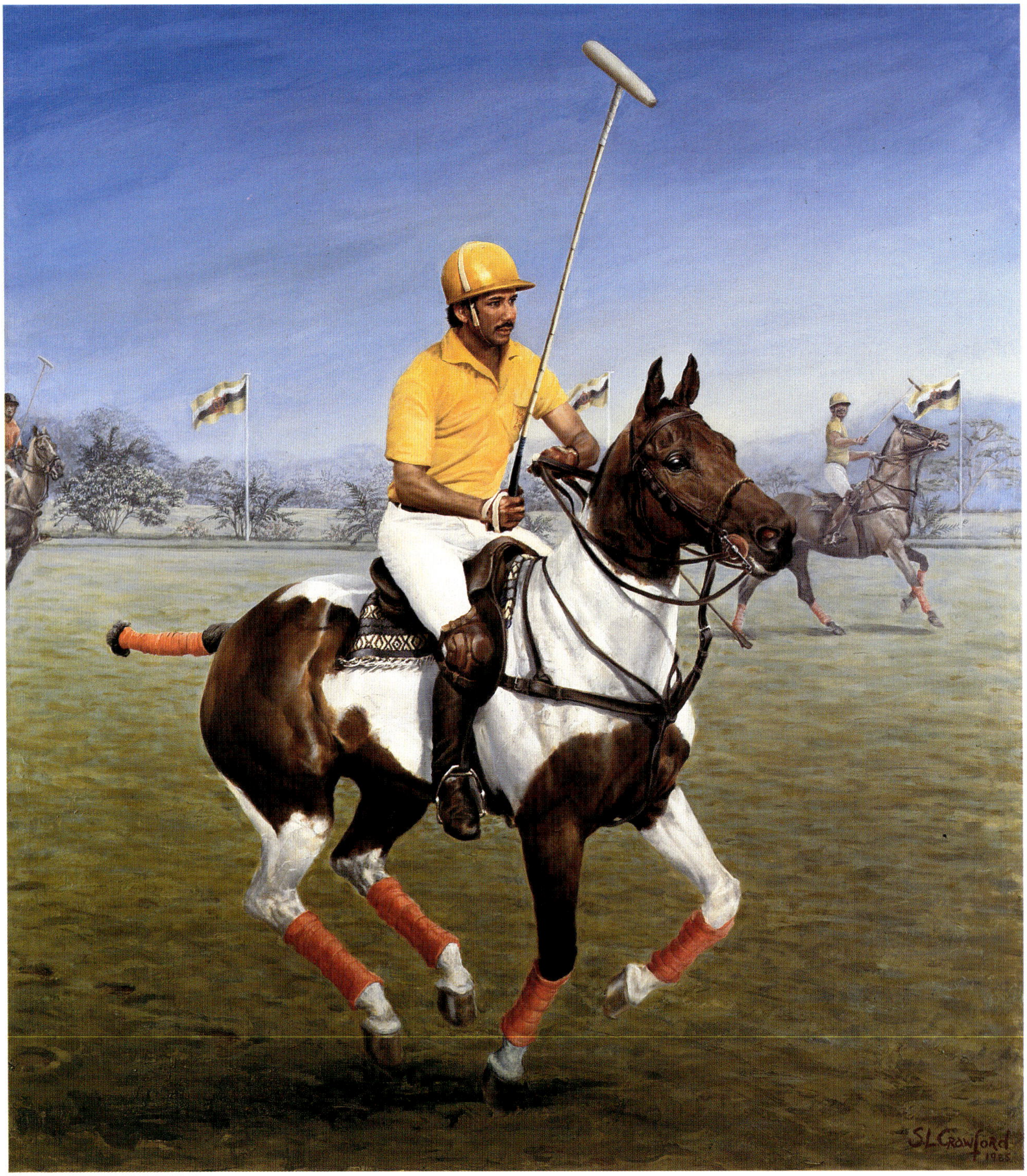

PLATE 20 Susan Crawford, *The Winning Goal: HM The Sultan of Brunei*, 1986.
Oil on canvas, 46 × 56 in (116.8 × 142.2 cm).

A leader of the prolific and innovative Newlyn Society of Artists, Samuel John Lamorna Birch, another noted flyfisher, painted between the wars some delightful angling studies, several of trout and salmon rivers devoid of assertive episode. His talent for using reflection mirrored in shimmering pools in Welsh and Scottish compositions in a free impressionist style brought a refreshing vitality to angling art of the period. For Walter Shaw Sparrow's classic *Angling in British Art* he painted the oil sketch *Fly Fishing in Lamorna, Cornwall* – a typically sparkling example. In an alleged self-portrait (exhibited at the Royal Academy in 1938) of Birch fishing in *Ella's Garden, Trewoofe, Lamorna*, the home of his friends the Napiers, both Cornish artists, sport admittedly plays a minor role with the scene dominated by the blues and greys of the limpid pool and its reflected tall trees. Such sensitive works tend to emphasise the mutual relationship between landscape composition and sport participation which form an inescapable facet of sporting art. An acceptable and convincing ratio lies wholly within the skill and vision of the artist.

As might be expected, the foxhunting specialists only occasionally diverted to the quieter pursuit of fishing but it should be remembered that one of Alfred Munnings' first two exhibits in the Royal Academy in 1899 had been that wintery evocation *Pike-Fishing in January* near Lavenham Mill. George Armour produced pleasing little angling scenes in gouache on linen and Lionel Edwards applied his landscape talent to some effect in studies of dry fly fishing on the Test. But it was his fellow sporting artist Frank Wallace, a dedicated angler, who used watercolours with outstanding fluency in many Scottish scenes such as *The Hon. Mrs Robin Grosvenor Fishing at the Fells Pool* in 1925.

Shortly before his death in 1974 John Kenney forsook the hunting Shires to paint some sparkling angling compositions as in *May Morning near Pangbourne* with its pollarded willows and adroitly posed fisherman, to suggest that he might have become one of our finest contemporary exponents of this more leisured pastime (97).

All artists in their angling pictures seem to acquire an innate spontaneity that distils the quiet engrossing delights of the moment. Few works are specifically commissioned and perhaps painting purely for pleasure and not for profit brings its own bonus, especially within a lovely environment. In the 1970s a fine series of paintings by Tim Havers of four famous fishing

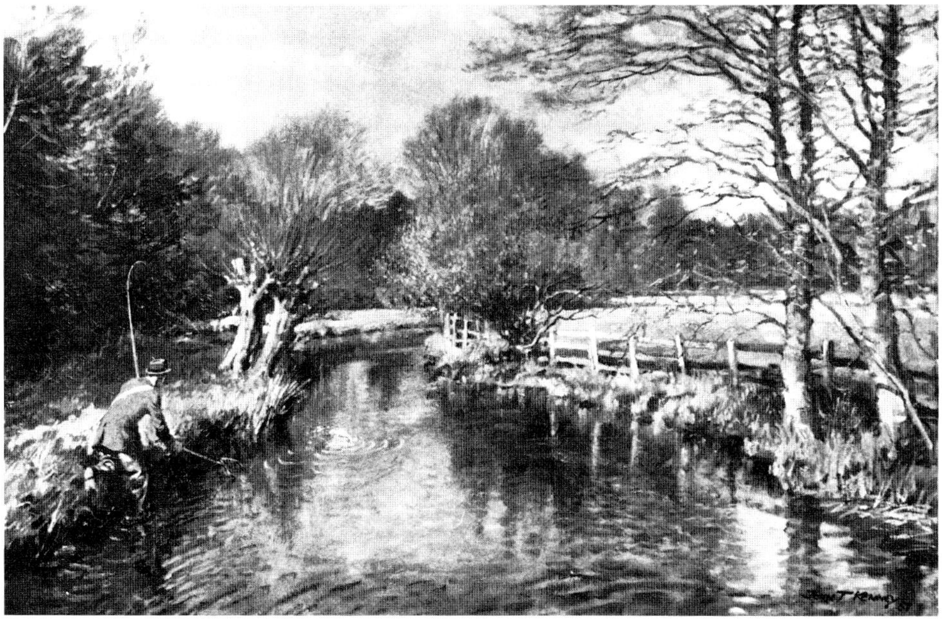

97 John Theodore Eardley Kenney, *May Morning near Pangbourne*, 1967. Oil on canvas, 25 × 30 in (63.5 × 76.2 cm).

rivers – the Test, Itchen, Kennet and Dove were published as prints and this artist, also a prolific illustrator, produced hand-coloured etchings of rainbow trout and salmon which conform both to the technical accuracy demanded by the critical fisherman and to decorative pictorial design.

William Garfit, a contemporary artist of talent born in 1944, who studied at the Cambridge School of Art and also at the Royal Academy Schools, is himself a keen angler and conservationist. In four exhibitions at the Tryon and Moorland Gallery his scintillating oils and watercolours of pools and rivers, which range from the chalk streams of the south to the Scottish rivers in spate, almost exclude the human element.

Modern pictorial records of angling, also shooting and other rural interests, have been enriched by the observant and individual approach of Rodger McPhail (*Plate 23*). Born in Lancashire in 1953 and trained for three years at the Liverpool School of Art he must, however, be considered as much the naturalist as the sporting artist for his delicate studies of foxes, stoats and badgers, heron, blue tits and duck fulfil specialist demands whilst possessing a beauty and integrity that delights the true country lover. His draughtsmanship of animals and their habitat is brilliant, his colour sense perceptive and subtle; in addition his strong feeling for landscapes and obvious personal enjoyment in an organised shoot, in angling and coursing produce lively work that is keenly observed and full of vitality.

Painting mostly in watercolours he has travelled widely, fulfilling commissions on the Continent, in the United States and in Africa. The Tryon Gallery has put on three major exhibitions of his work and he is much in demand as an illustrator. His own book *Open Season: An Artist's Sporting Year*, published in 1986, captures all facets of his considerable talent, and especially memorable is the reproduction on the dust jacket of the ghillie and laden garron after a successful stalk descending the steep lonely glen.

Amongst the British naturalist artists of this century, and prolific illustrators, Charles Frederick Tunnicliffe, RA, stands alone. His ornithological studies are exquisite and even his measured drawings of birds give postmortem subjects a kind of vitality of their own. His records in oil paintings, etchings and engravings of rural life are executed with superb observation, dignity and power, but Tunnicliffe's talent cannot be contained within the confines of the school of British sporting art, though his studies of heavy horses received the acclaim of Munnings who hailed him as an 'English genius'. Certainly he painted a few isolated pictures of racehorses on the beach, of ponies amongst the gorse of the Welsh hills, and of a scene in the farrier's shop, but the nearest he came to it, perhaps, were in his wood engravings illustrating Henry Williamson's *Tarka the Otter* where hounds are depicted with tragic intensity. During his long life (1901–1974) his output was prodigious and, though his role was that of the dynamic naturalist artist and observer of country life, his influence, indirectly, on the sporting scene will endure long after the end of this century.

As a sport, coursing has existed from time immemorial; carvings on Egyptian tombs dated BC 1400 show dogs of greyhound type, the Roman occupiers of Great Britain were accompanied by their long-dogs. The strict Forest Laws instigated by the Norman Kings ensured that the exercise of coursing was reserved for royalty and the aristocracy, but that devotee of field sports, Queen Elizabeth I, broadened these rulings so that both greyhounds and the quarry shared protection under the law and allowed a more plebeian public to participate.

In 1775 the first coursing club was formed at Swaffham and the popularity of the sport reached a peak in the nineteenth century under a central control and the first Waterloo Cup event was organised in 1836. But even within the prevailing heyday of sporting artists relatively few pictures were commissioned. Richard Ansdell's huge kaleidoscope of *The Waterloo Cup Coursing Meeting* dated 1840 was something of an exception and other more spontaneous compositions of unnamed greyhounds coursing in an anonymous landscape appeared but were not frequent.

Today, in the latter part of this century with this traditional sport threatened by abolition (it already has had to survive a projected Hare Coursing Bill in 1975), its records must be valued as future documentaries. Though the actual number of organised coursing clubs has diminished in the past fifty years, active support has certainly not lessened but since the Victorian era few pictures exist of this sport which combine the thrill of speed with the beauty of form. Instantaneous photography has become ever more frequently an accepted alternative.

Only Michael Lyne [and John Skeaping – see Chapters 16 and 17] has dedicated time and talent in any depth to depicting the excitement and technicalities of the sport today in all its phases. In his many London exhibitions the world of coursing has regularly played its part in such paintings as *A Cotswold Coursing Meeting* and in such rich character studies as *The Slipper*, (*Plate 23*). He excels both in his sketches depicting the lightning speed of greyhounds and also in more static portrayals of the 1971 Waterloo Cup winner, *So Clever*. He was himself a breeder of Salukis and a Steward of the National Sporting Club. He is one of the few contemporary artists with practical understanding of the sport and he was responsible for a set of coursing studies for the British Field Sports Society. In 1974, impelled perhaps by the genes of his sculptor ancestor, he modelled three small bronzes of greyhounds and a hare, each a separate entity. Speed is the theme and it is a striking foray into (for him) a contrasting medium. Other works in three dimensions have been carved models of his fine collection of waterfowl which is such a feature of his fourteenth century home in Gloucestershire.

Coursing greyhounds were to provide a constant subject for the increasing number of animal

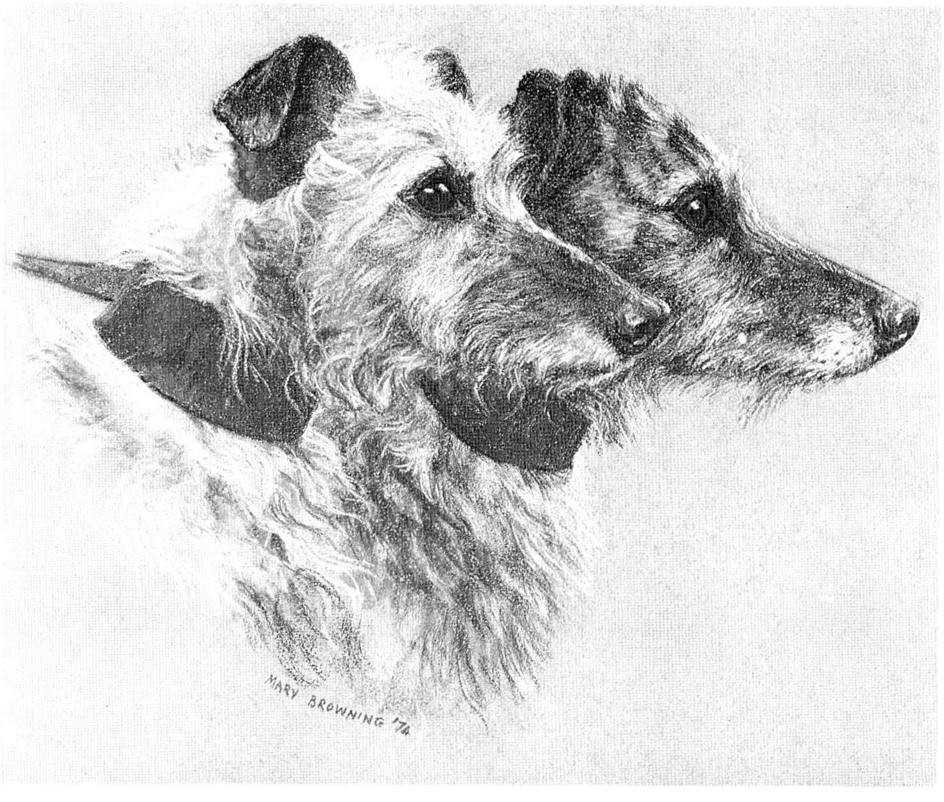

98 Mary Browning, *A Brace of Lurchers*, 1975. Pastel, 18 × 22 in (45.7 × 55.9 cm).

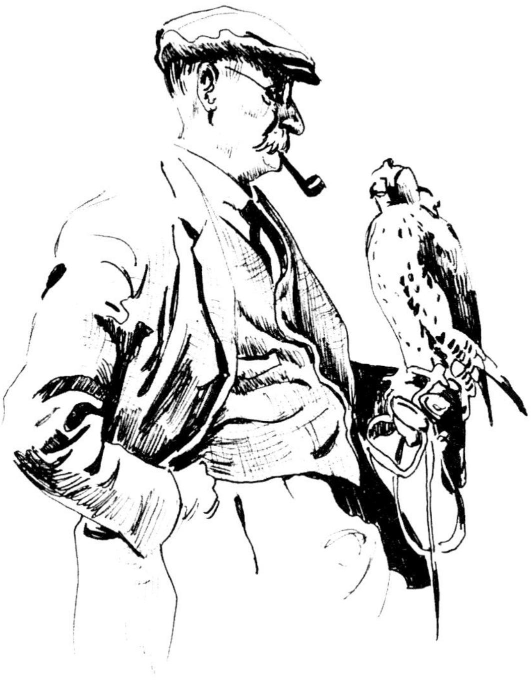

99 Peter Upton, *George Lodge with a miniature Peregrine Falcon.* Pencil drawing, 1988, from an old photograph.

sculptors that began to appear in the 1960s. In the detailed and finely produced work *Coursing: The Pursuit of Game by Gazehounds*, published in 1975 by the Standfast Press, Michael Lyne was also responsible for many of the illustrations. Here also Mary Browning's skilled portrayals of Afghan Hounds, borzois, deerhounds and whippets differentiate between the breeds with subtle contrasts of these coursing hounds. Also in the book Leslie Benenson, better known for her paintings of the Arabian horse, has contributed some fine woodcuts of the greyhound in action and repose.

Earlier in the century Arthur Wardle, a master artist of the sporting dog, received commissions for portraits of winners of the Waterloo Cup before the Second World War; particularly effective are the portrayals of Dee Rock who won the event in three consecutive years 1933–35 and of his son Dee Flint, victor in 1940. Leesa Sandys-Lumsdaine, a breeder herself of greyhounds, whippets and lurchers gave us some deft studies of their grace and mood and Susan Crawford's oil painting of a whippet quietly emphasises the alert, lithe fascination of this smaller breed. It should not be forgotten also that the versatile talent of Raoul Millais occasionally explored the coursing scene and, inevitably, almost every sporting sculptor of the day used the greyhound as a favourite subject.

Quite outstanding in pastel are the heads of *A Brace of Lurchers* by Mary Browning, a beautifully executed and keenly observed study of canine character (*98*) and equally effective in the same medium the two greyhounds *Fortina's Palace* and *Grim Reality*. Encouraged by Michael Lyne, the sensitive talent of this woman artist who lives near Banbury has received little acclaim but a print after her study of working Suffolk Punches illustrates her expert draughtsmanship and deserves wider publicity.

In the Middle Ages and earlier the popularity in Europe of falconry as a leading field sport can hardly be exaggerated. It was not merely an exciting pastime but for centuries an important means of providing the household with fresh meat. Basically the sport is the pursuit of wild quarry in natural surroundings by trained hawks of different species; and in the seventeenth century, Barlow and Hollar depicted with clarity the technicalities of the pastime; later Jan Wyck and John Wootton painted decorative compositions of mounted hawking parties with lords and ladies in splendid array. By Georgian times hunting had become the major country activity, nevertheless the notorious Colonel Thomas Thornton still made hawking one of his major enthusiasms with organised forays in the north, also down at Newmarket and on Salisbury Plain. A brilliant relaxed portrait by Philip Reinagle inevitably included the Colonel's favourite hawk and greyhound.

The works of naturalist artists have produced some splendid pictures of birds and animals but the genre differs from the context of sporting art. Exceptions exist, especially in the works of such observant exponents as George Lodge, whose portrayals of falcons at rest and in action have an innate sporting motif as seen in his gouaches of *The Hooded Greenfoot* and *A Peregrine Tiercel*. His studies of the art of falconry serve as a reminder that hawking at the turn of the century still existed under the aegis of the Old Hawking Club and many private establishments. His picture *Thomas Mann's Hawking Party in Cambridgeshire* dated 1889 is a typical example of contemporary sport with the host wearing the green coat of the Old Hawking Club and the artist (himself a keen falconer) seated on the ground on the left. In George Lodge's career as an ornithological artist such scenic compositions are rare. Contemporary with this, Spy was including Thomas Mann, that specialist of hawking in his *Vanity Fair* series of caricatures of sporting personalities.

Historians of falconry in this century will find their most valuable information in the photograph albums of the country houses of the sporting gentry (*99*). Few artists have attempted to compete with the camera except, more recently, the most prolific and successful twin brothers, Roger and Peter Upton, both falconers in their own right and artists of talent, though Peter has found his dominant inspiration in fine studies of the Arabian horse. Roger is author of *A Bird in Hand*, published in 1980, an informative work on celebrated falconers of the past and also of many of their most famous hawks, and in 1987 of *Oh, For A Falconer's Voice: Memories of the Old Hawking Club*.

In our era, due to pesticides and mechanisation the number of birds of prey has steadily declined. A charitable Hawk Trust has been founded and a few centres of instruction exist, thus ensuring that the ancient sport of hawking still persists with its traditional techniques. At the Game Fair, modified demonstrations of falconry attract the attention of a wide public but few sporting artists today seem to have the volition or expert knowledge to try their hands at contemporary pictures of this sport actually taking place.

At the end of the century it must be accepted that, pictorially, in the world of field sports, the camera has achieved considerable prestige. The photograper's established expertise and artistry in the use of colour and light has become equally appreciated by both sportsmen and publishers of topical books; in many cases commissioned paintings have been superseded.

NOTES

1 Lionel Edwards, RI, *Reminiscences of a Sporting Artist*, p. 162.

2 Walter Shaw Sparrow, *Angling in British Art*, John Lane, The Bodley Head, 1923, p. 25.

3 Ernest E. Briggs, RI, *Angling and Art in Scotland*, Preface.

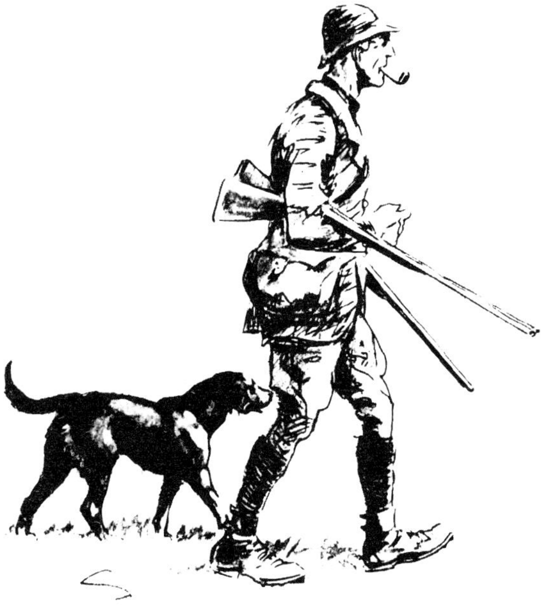

100 Snaffles – Charlie Johnson Payne, *Tom Cobb, who was walking behind the other loaders.*

16

British Sporting Sculpture in the Twentieth Century

The French finesse and subtlety of the bronzes of Les Animaliers at the end of the nineteenth century are difficult to equate with the simpler hunting, shooting and fishing traditions of British sporting art; nevertheless our sculptors in the late Victorian era reflected something of this romantic Gallic style whilst substituting a more robust and sturdy approach.

However, in this country, the actual sporting scene during this period had found few exponents in sculpture. Commissions for monuments, many of them equestrian portrayals, had certainly been forthcoming but this lack of sporting context was to remain more or less unchanged until after the First World War.

John Willis Good, who died in 1874, was one of the few Victorian sculptors who produced fine racing and hunting subjects. But it was Adrian Jones, though born as early as 1845, who must be recognised as the major talent of equestrian sculpture to bridge the centuries both in the ceremonial and sporting sphere. As late as 1924 (when he was in his seventy-ninth year) his magnificent Cavalry Memorial in Hyde Park was unveiled.

Born in Ludlow and educated at the local Grammar School he was dedicated to rural sports and drawing. He qualified in 1866 at the Royal Veterinary College and was gazetted to the Royal Horse Artillery. During service in India, Ireland and South Africa (in the Boer War) official duties always shared priority with polo, racing and hunting. He started painting portraits of favourite horses for brother officers but though he continued working in oils most of his life, the results raise little enthusiasm. He found his ultimate *métier* when he frequented the London studio of C.B. Birch, ARA, the well known sculptor. With a natural flair for form plus his professional understanding of equine anatomy Adrian Jones' first sculpture, a model of his own hunter, *One of the Right Sort*, was accepted in 1884 by the Royal Academy. This was followed by the premier prize the same year in the Goldsmiths' Company competition for the best group model – his plaster cast of *Gone Away!* – a huntsman and two hounds. However the judge, H.H. Armstead, RA, had reported it was not a question of selecting the most excellent but the least objectionable entry![1]

Commissions for models of hunters, racehorses, polo ponies and such champion foxhounds as *Pytchley Forager* from leading owners and trainers came flooding in. Most prestigious was a request from the Jockey Club for a larger than life bronze of Persimmon as a stallion to be presented in 1909 to King Edward VII for the royal stud at Sandringham, where it stands today. Earlier he had made a model for the King of the horse as a three-year-old and also of Diamond Jubilee and Ambush II. Once his career as a sculptor was established he resigned his army commission.

In addition he later produced many important official monuments including the Royal Marine Memorial in the Mall and the Australian War Memorial in the City of Adelaide. But this ultimate success had to be achieved after surviving denigration by the leading artists of the day, who questioned the ability of an army captain, qualified merely as a veterinary surgeon with no formal art training, to model any major sculpture of merit. Adrian Jones' reply was to take as his subject Duncan's horses in Macbeth 'beauteous and swift the minions of their race turn'd wild in nature'[2] which went mad in their stables the night of the King's murder. The three frenzied horses, modelled almost lifesize, were exhibited in the Royal Academy in 1892 and created a sensation, followed by inferences that the work was by other unnamed sculptors working incognito. Legal admonitions brought a retraction, clearing Jones' reputation completely. In 1986 the original plaster cast of the famous Duncan's Horses which had been bequeathed to the Royal Veterinary College became, with time and weather, in danger of acute deterioration; but by public and private subscription they were cast in bronze and installed permanently on the premises of the Royal Veterinary College's referral hospital at Hawkshead.

The major masterpiece of Adrian Jones' career is, of course, the *Quadriga of Peace*, the forty ton bronze on the Wellington Arch at Hyde Park Corner, completed in 1912, its motif realised in a classic composition of equine beauty and power.

In the actual sphere of sporting art the sculptor will be remembered for such pleasing models as the conspicuous racehorse, The Tetrarch and of the Earl of Lonsdale on his favourite hunter, Patsy, with the Cottesmore hounds. In 1899 the trophy for the Tally Ho Cup at Cork Park had been *The Silver Huntsman*, a lively and sensitive model of Mr W.F. Oakeley, Master of the Atherstone from 1871–1891 on Icicle with hounds Trimmer, Regulus and Rodney (*101*). Later this was recast in bronze.

This same appreciation of the animal subject in sculpture also appears at the turn of the century in studies by the popular sporting painter of the day, Alfred Haigh, who sometimes alternated large hunting compositions in oils with models of horses, foxhounds and greyhounds and, on one occasion, a gamecock. But his real triumph of characterisation is illustrated in an eleven inch bronze of Mr Jorrocks on Arterxerxes, based obviously on the incomparable John Leech illustration for *Handley Cross*.

Of outstanding ability as a sculptor was John Henry Monsell Furse who lived until the mid-twentieth century and was brother of Charles Furse, the artist. Owing to ill health, injury and personal tragedy he virtually completed all his work before 1910.

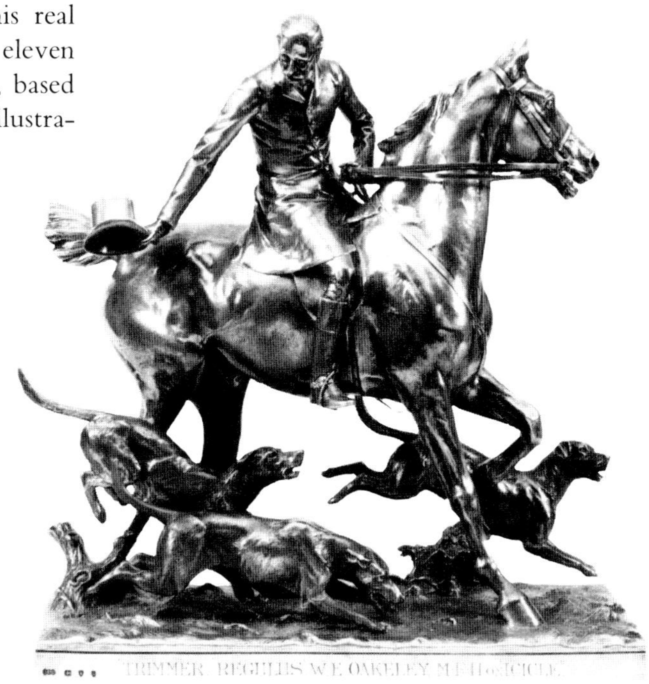

101 Adrian Jones, *The Silver Huntsman*, *c* 1899. Bronze, h. 21½ in (54.6 cm), l. 20 in (50.8 cm).

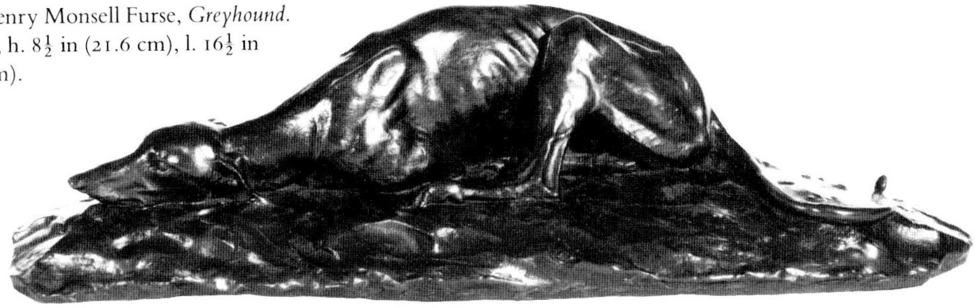

102 John Henry Monsell Furse, *Greyhound*. Bronze, h. 8½ in (21.6 cm), l. 16½ in (41.9 cm).

Exhibiting at the Royal Academy and many major city art galleries between 1892–1907, critics of the day praised his keenly observed presentation of form and action. The compelling quality of his work is illustrated in such bronzes as *Shire Horses at Play* to contrast with the sleek symmetry of a recumbent greyhound (*102*).

In the world of art it is undeniable that many painters and sculptors of outstanding gifts fail to achieve even minor fame. Publicity cannot instil talent but recognition and appreciation often provide the spur for inspiration. The name of Cecil Brown, born in 1868, rarely aroused much comment in his own time and is virtually unknown today, a curious fact as any work by this sculptor seldom fails to impress by its definition and discernment.

Born in 1868 at Ayr he was educated at Harrow and Exeter College, Oxford, and studied art in London and Paris. He was appointed art master at Charterhouse and later, in 1920, at Bedford School, a post he held for the rest of his life and which probably accounted for his lack of public acclaim, though he worked successfully in oils before concentrating on sculpture with horses as his dominant subject. He was himself an expert on matters equestrian, wrote several articles for periodicals and also the book *The Horse in Art and Nature*. Though over military age at the outbreak of the First World War he served with the Middlesex Yeomanry in Egypt and Palestine, which resulted in his splendid monument to the Camel Corps on the Victoria Embankment.

Brown exhibited at the Royal Academy and the Paris Salon and was elected in 1909 to the Royal Society of British Sculptors. His approach to the horse varied from studies of a hackney, reminiscent of Antoine-Louis Barye, to a detailed pair of draught horses with a farmhand, one of his finest works, and purchased in 1987 by the British Sporting Art Trust for its permanent collection, a gesture, which may, at last, open eyes to an important talent (*103*).

There was certainly a dearth of sculptors using the sporting idiom in the first part of the new century, in marked contrast to the numerous painters of the day who were all putting new life into the pictorial scene. However between the two world wars the outstanding calibre of John Skeaping was to bring a liberating element to animal sculpture. His important influence on sporting painting in this century has already been assessed but his ultimate reputation will rest as a sculptor of the animal kingdom.

After his early training at Goldsmiths' College and the London County Council Central School of Arts and Crafts, Skeaping entered the Royal Academy Schools. Here he won the Gold Medal, the Travelling Scholarship and finally, in 1924, the Prix de Rome with his relief of *Diana and Endymion* – a classical theme which gave little indication of his future career in animal subjects. In Italy he also studied the techniques of direct carving in stone – the character and quality of materials were always to influence strongly his reactions to design and form.

In 1930 he held an exhibition at Tooth's Gallery in London with his wife, the sculptor Barbara

Hepworth, where his model of a pony in alabaster brought praise from the critics. Four years later in the same gallery a lifesize figure of a horse carved in wood caused something of a sensation, especially amongst the sporting fraternity, one *aficionado* suggesting it ought to be bought for Tattersalls! It was, however, his only exhibit that remained unsold. This carving might be considered the forerunner of his later large portrayals of leading racehorses of his day. In his autobiography, *Drawn from Life*, John Skeaping wrote, not with arrogance but with sheer simplicity; 'I can model a horse and portray its movement better than anyone else,'[3] a fact admirably illustrated in his memorable bronzes, some lifesize, of such Classic winners as Hyperion, Mill Reef and Chamossaire, of the indomitable Brigadier Gerard and such American champions as Secretariat and Fort Marcy.

The statue of Hyperion was commissioned in the early 1960s by Lord Derby after the horse's death at the age of thirty. Skeaping, working from the skeleton and photographs, aided by interviews with Hyperion's stud groom, stable lad and his jockey, Tommy Weston, achieved a striking likeness of this little wonder horse. Nevertheless, exhibited in the Royal Academy the lifesize model appeared static and, understandably, out of place, but set up in its final home at Lord Derby's stud at Newmarket, by Skeaping's uncanny alchemy, it achieved a subtle animation, with passing mares allegedly giving it a suggestive whinny!

Another posthumous commission was Mr Stanhope Joel's Chamossaire, completed in only nine months from photographs and recorded statistics. Also lifesize, this bronze of commanding presence, sited at the Snailwell Stud at Newmarket, is a brilliant portrayal with the horse striding forward, head held high, neighing defiance to the world.

Equally appealing are the sculptures of the arch rivals Mill Reef and Brigadier Gerard, both described by Skeaping as magnificent horses. He remembered Mill Reef as 'a charming character and full of grace . . . walked like a ballet dancer!'[4] Modelled half lifesize, the sculptor haunted Ian Balding's training premises, taking measurements and hundreds of photographs and his portrayal subtly suggests the underlying stamina and power that led Mill Reef to become one of the legendary horses of the century. First exhibited at Ackermann's gallery in London, the bronze now stands at Mr Paul Mellon's Rokeby Stables in Virginia (*1, page 8*) with replicas for his trainer Ian Balding at Kingsclere and at the National Stud, Newmarket.

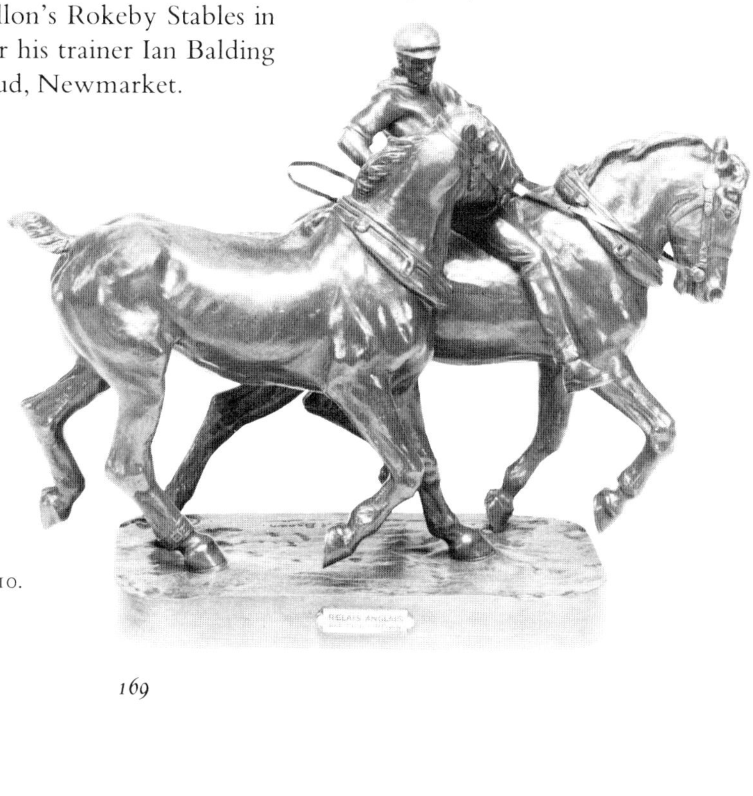

103 Cecil Brown, RA, *Draught Horses*, *c* 1910. Bronze, h. 15 in (38.1 cm), l. 14 in (35.5 cm).

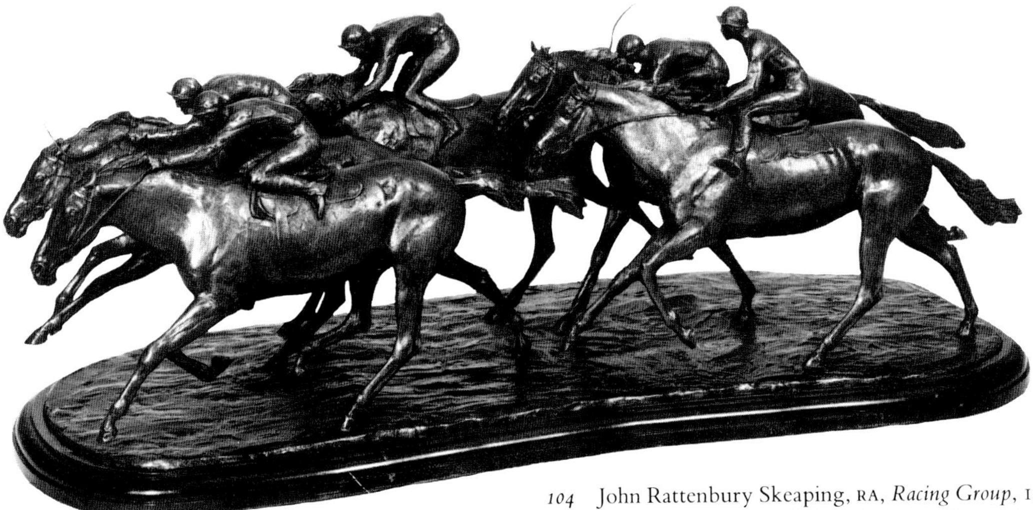

104 John Rattenbury Skeaping, RA, *Racing Group*, 1977. Bronze (artist's proof), h. 13 in (33 cm), l. 34 in (86 cm).

Models of Brigadier Gerard, lifesize and splendid, the lovely American 1972 Champion three-year-old, Key to the Mint and the three-quarter lifesize bronze of the great Secretariat at full gallop established the truth of Skeaping's assertion – 'I have been the only professional sculptor in this field. This is no boast, it is the simple and regrettable fact. But I am hoping that it will not always be so.'[5]

In all Skeaping's own life artistic inspiration had been allied to practical experience in many spheres. He could ride and drive horses, plough with them, race-ride and shoe them. The Zoo provided other animal subjects and a spell 'away from it all' in Mexico taught him age-old techniques in pottery. Visits to quarries and stone masons started him on the road to direct carving in granite. He learnt to work in marble, to forge his own tools; while other enthusiasms included Celtic carvings, fishing, writing and the bull fiestas of the Camargue.

But a price was demanded for this excess of versatility to be summed up in Skeaping's own words, 'I chose my way of life which has given me great pleasure, but I have paid dearly for it in that I have not achieved my potential as a sculptor.'[6] Nevertheless his attitude to art never lacked total integrity. In the early 1930s as the avant-garde trend for the abstract became ever more dominant, with initiative and courage he broke away from the modern movement in sculpture. Twenty years later in 1953 when Skeaping succeeded Frank Dobson as Professor of Sculpture at the Royal College of Art, he still encouraged the basic truth of a simplified realism. He became a full Academician in 1959.

His small models of birds, deer, dogs and cats possess a creative observation rare in their own time and in his equine bronzes, whatever the diversity of type and mood, mobility is the keynote. Vitality pervades even a static pose and in this quality lies the visual satisfaction of his work. Movement inevitably produces alteration in the appearance of form and structure – sometimes it elongates and distorts – but in all Skeaping's sculpture a balanced rhythm remains. Pace and tension are never lacking in his racing Thoroughbreds, over fences and on the flat. His bronze action trophy for the Ackermann-Skeaping Hurdle Race at Sandown and the brilliant group of five racehorses in a tight finish typify this magic (*104*).

A year before his death in 1980 an exhibition of his bronzes was held in Ackermann's Galleries when his true genius was apparent in the contrasting impact made by the diversity of subjects;

from the dynamic *Work Horse* and the lightning manoeuvres of *Polo Group*, both however eclipsed by the superb model of two racing greyhounds (*105*). In John Skeaping the twentieth century had found a great master of animal sculpture.

The recognition and exhibitions of his work were in no small way responsible for the extraordinary resurgence of sporting sculpture during the decades following the mid-century. Suddenly animal models by aspiring sculptors, both male and female, began to appear in ever increasing numbers. The subjects were predominantly equestrian and though skill in execution might be lacking, inherent talent, plus a conscious endeavour to apply something of Skeaping's mobile style, was nearly always apparent. But though this brought a liberating animation it was often unallied to any understanding in depth of the basic bone structure and the muscles and sinews that underlie animal form. However, amongst the numerous animal sculptors of the day many merit acclaim for a serious and new approach to their subject. Several sporting painters with varying success also accepted the challenge of working in three dimensions including, earlier of course, Munnings with his splendid statue of Brown Jack but also Michael Lyne with his coursing greyhounds, John King with bronzes such as *Well Ridden* for the Chatsworth Horse Trials Trophy and Susan Ponsonby with the five phases of the Galloping Horse.

A decisive feature of the epoch was the prestige status given to sporting sculpture by awards for major equestrian events of specially commissioned models in bronze or even silver as commemorative trophies instead of the traditional silver plate cups of mundane design.

First to become popular in this sphere with eventually forty-nine examples to her credit, was Jean Walwyn and the most notable was *The Winner*, her lifelike bronze for the National Hunt Champion Trophy of a tired 'chaser and a jockey after a race. She modelled a formal horse's head in unpolished gold for the prestigious John Player Show Jumping event and, for the Schweppes Gold Trophy, a model of a hurdler at the winning post.

Herself the daughter of Colonel 'Taffy' Walwyn, President for many years of the British Show Jumping Association, and also a cousin of Fulke Walwyn, the trainer, her career started as a professional physiotherapist, practising in her native Cotswold country treating casualties from the hunting field. As an alternative diversion she found herself modelling their horses and dogs (baking the results in the kitchen oven). Practical expertise was acquired at informal classes under Doris Lindner and her first major success was winning the Topham Trophy Art competition in 1959 with a plaster cast of a horse with jockey adjusting his leathers in the paddock (*106*). Many commissions followed, including in 1966 the exciting assignment from the United Services Club to commemorate its 150th anniversary with a statuette of HM The Queen on the chestnut gelding, Imperial, and the Duke of Edinburgh at the Trooping the Colour ceremony. As long ago as 1962 her model of *A Lady's Hack*, elegant and refined, received a Medaille de Bronze in the Paris Salon.

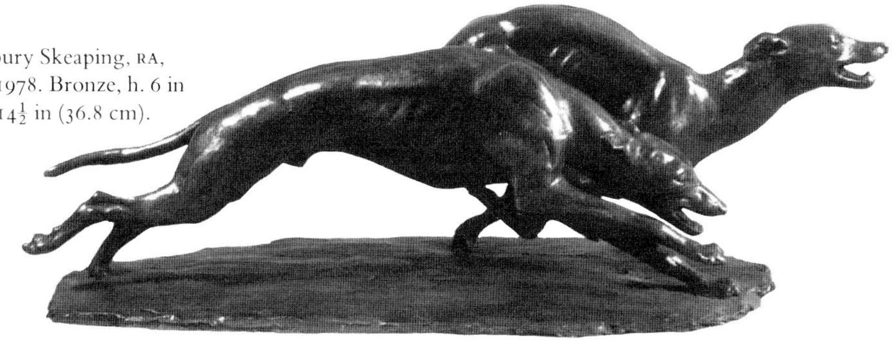

105 John Rattenbury Skeaping, RA, *Greyhounds*, 1978. Bronze, h. 6 in (15.2 cm), l. 14½ in (36.8 cm).

Much of her most pleasing work has been presentation pieces for sporting VIPs on retirement and for trophies for point-to-points, such as the bronze of HRH The Prince of Wales on Allibar for the Amateur Riders' Steeplechase at Ludlow. Her commissioned portraits of horses in the UK and abroad with, and without, jockeys, number over a hundred, the most recent being Dawn Run and Reference Point. Her plaster cast of the 1961 Derby winner, St Paddy, specially modelled for Watneys was to be seen for many years in the Tattersall Tavern in Knightsbridge. Though Jean Walwyn's animals are strictly representational they are rarely static, a certain mobility being cleverly achieved by the tilt of the head and the drift of a tail. Her own professional training in anatomy and lifelong experience as a horsewoman stamp her work with quiet conviction.

In 1960 Douglas Bunn's initiative in establishing the splendid All England Jumping Course at Hickstead brought a new and stimulating element into this popular sport. The British Show Jumping Derby drew the holiday crowds to Sussex and Irish-born Emma MacDermott modelled, in 1979, the perpetual trophy for this event after it had been won three times by the Irishman, Eddie Macken, on the superlative Boomerang. Executed in bronze it shows this horse and rider negotiating the daunting Derby Bank with a clever suggestion of intelligent care allied to mutual courage and confidence.

Coming from a sporting background, racing, polo and hunting had always played a large part in Emma MacDermott's life before she trained for three years at the St Martin's School of Art in London. Her work has been exhibited in the United States and on the Continent and commissions have included the Airlie Coolmore Trophy for the Irish 2000 Guineas and the Pacemaker International Trophy. Some of her most effective models have been coursing greyhounds and steeplechasers in action.

A spate of trophies for important equestrian events were demanded at this time from contemporary sculptors. Edwina Emery, a member of the Royal Society of British Sculptors, was responsible in 1984 for the Champion of Champions Trophy at the Horse of the Year Show, a commission that was to signify 'the pursuit of excellence in horsemanship' but applicable to any type of horse. The motif she selected was Pegasus, the winged horse of mythology.

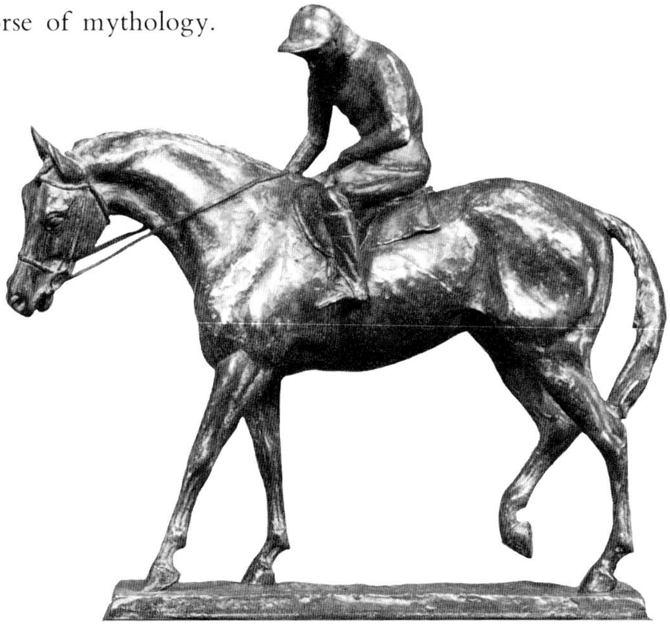

106 Jean Walwyn, *The Topham Trophy*, 1958. Bronze, h. 12 in (30.4 cm), l. 14 in (35.5 cm).

Almost a dozen special trophies have been amongst her most important assignments, including, in 1986, a model of Lester Piggott, *The Final Frame*, for Garrards the Crown Jewellers.

Sculpture was not taken up by Caroline Wallace professionally until she was thirty and married with two children. Drawing and painting in watercolours had been a hobby but her life had been dedicated to sporting interests which were to provide her with a useful visual background. In Alan Oliver's eventing yard she became closely involved with the competitive horse world, looking after Princess Anne's horses, which later led to her executing a bronze of the Princess in full *de rigueur* dressage kit on Goodwill, to be sold in aid of the Save Children Fund Operation, Daka. Her first commissioned trophy was for the Police Horse of the Year at the Show in its Harringey days; amongst the many that quickly followed were bronzes for the Locko Park and Gatcombe Horse Trials and models of such eventing champions as Lucinda Green on Regal Realm and Virginia Leng on Priceless. She has also established a close liaison with such international jewellers and equestrian luxury stores as Aspreys, Tiffanys and Swaine Adeney who commission hunting and racing models. Her natural talent and intimate understanding of the sporting scene brought success almost too swiftly for Caroline Wallace. Horses are obviously her *métier* but their riders lack the same vitality and conviction.

Another young woman without any formal art training also to rocket to almost instant recognition in the world of sporting sculpture was Annette Yarrow. Being champion amateur jockey in Madras in her youth for three years in succession and riding there constantly an Arab stallion and Part-breds may have facilitated her skill in depicting the horse in action. Birds of prey are also amongst her subjects, which led later to her splendid lifesize golden eagle on a globe of the world at the Army Air Corps Memorial at Middle Wallop.

Among major commissions have been two models of Red Rum half lifesize, one for his home town of Southport and the other unveiled at Ayr Racecourse in 1975 to commemorate his victory there in the Scottish Grand National. But her most spectacular achievement, somewhat outside the context of British sporting art, was accomplished in 1983, *Bedouin Heritage*, a lifesize native horseman brandishing his rifle on a rearing desert mare executed for HM King Hussein of Jordan, to stand outside the Parliament Buildings in Amman as a memorial to the 1916 Arab Revolt. In her own country Annette Yarrow's studies of the Arabian horse with their unique conformation and action have brought her special acclaim.

Equally effective with the Arabian as her major subject is Pamela du Boulay, a woman sculptor, also self taught but she admits to spending two years carefully studying Stubbs' classic *The Anatomy of the Horse* and then more experimenting in various media before she allowed her work to be cast in bronze. She also completed a mammoth commission for the Near East with a one and a half lifesize Arab stallion for a public square in Baghdad.

The sculptor's own Arabian mare, Shammah, who originally came from the Royal Stud in Jordan, often appears in her somewhat stylised models of the breed, the typical small head and flaunting tail exploited with artistic license to illustrate the elegance, refinement and 'dryness' that epitomise the desert-bred Arabian (*107*); sometimes initially she exaggerated the fineness of bone to the point of excess. A formalised study of the Godolphin Arabian (one of the famous original progenitors of the Thoroughbred) worked in an unusual medium of vinyl composition and then painted, was exhibited in the Moorland Gallery in 1975 and appeared with decorative effect. Pamela du Boulay's talent is at its best in expressing the generous full bodied quality of Arabian mares and in her dramatic studies of greyhounds and salukis, the hunting dogs of the desert.

Virtually unknown except by the *cognoscenti*, the Arabian horse owes a most perceptive

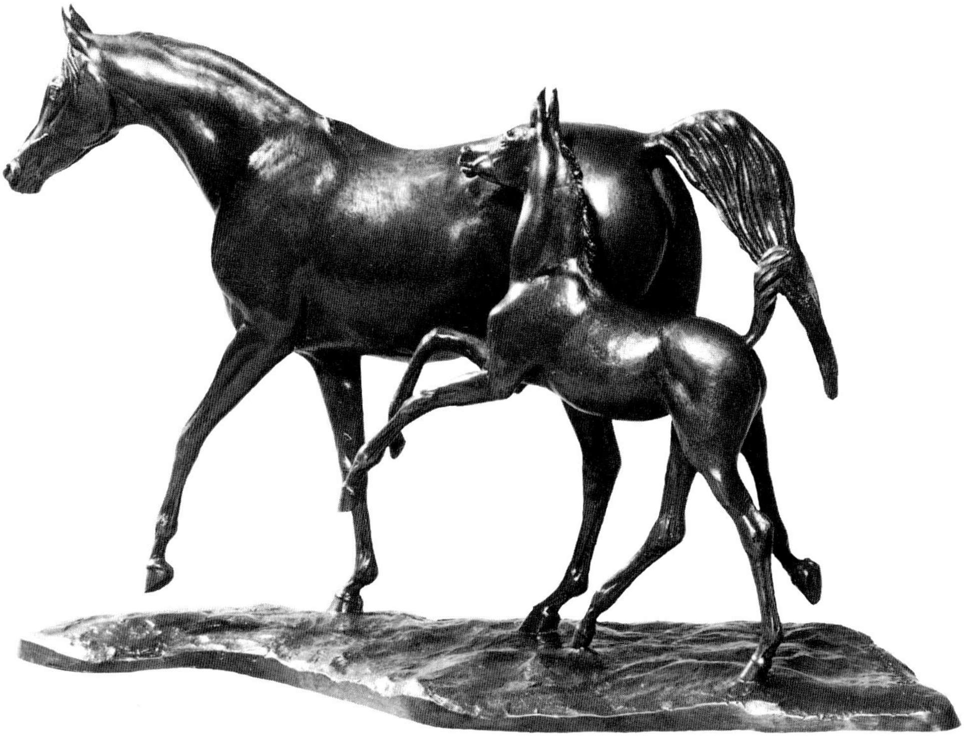

107 Pamela du Boulay, *Arabian Mare with Foal*, 1973. Bronze, h. $7\frac{1}{2}$ in (19 cm), l. 11 in (27.9 cm).

108 Geoffrey Snell, *After the Game. The Charles Heidsieck Trophy for the Warwickshire Cup*, 1975. Bronze.

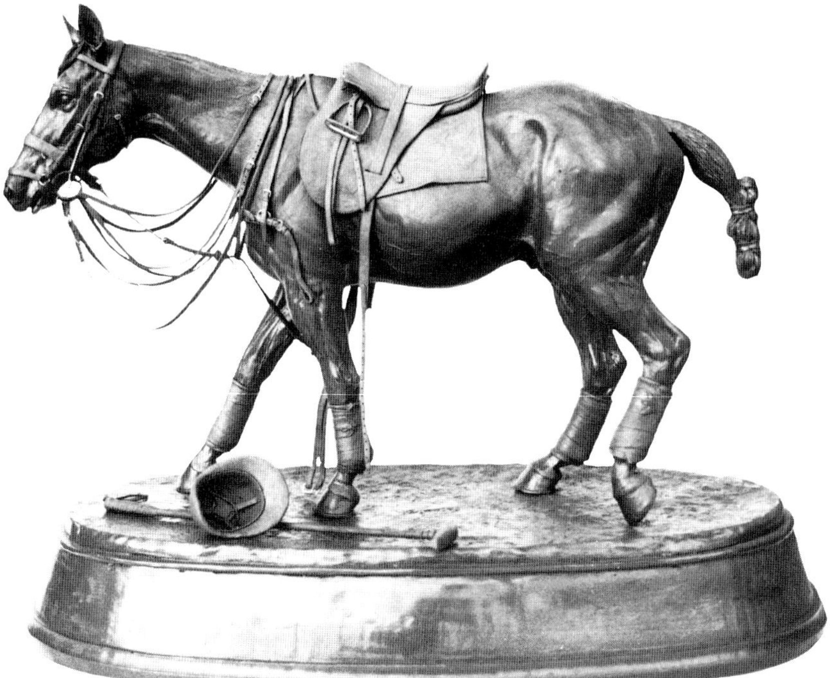

realisation in bronze and in watercolours to Marjorie Stevens, who lived in Devon after the Second World War and, sadly, dedicated her life to breeding Arabians and not to art. Her bronzes of a stylised head of Skowronek and of a lively Nassik possess unusual discernment of the breed.

Another woman sculptor missing publicity has been Priscilla Hann, trained at the Wolverhampton College of Art and the Tyler School of Art in Philadelphia where she won the Sculpture Prize. Successful in her models of greyhounds and lurchers, she hit the press headlines in 1988 with her bronze of Aldaniti and Bob Champion on their charity ride from Buckingham Palace to Aintree, and later that year she won the British Sporting Art Trust's award for sculpture at the annual Society of Equestrian Artists' Exhibition for her equestrian study *Winner's Enclosure*.

In 1976 the world of polo received a welcome fillip when Charles Heidseick Champagne commissioned a trophy for the Warwickshire Cup, the high goal polo tournament, at Cirencester Park. Geoffrey Snell, a talented but little known Buckinghamshire sculptor, was given the assignment. The quality of previous works in bronzes of *A Saddle Horse Racking* and a *A Pair of Setters Flushing a Grouse* had illustrated his keen observation of animal form. Using as model the pony Brigorita, (the property of the famous England Player, Paul Withers) at the end of a match resulted in a little masterpiece, *After the Game*. Though somewhat inhibited by the tack and trappings necessitated by top class polo, utter exhaustion is depicted in the relaxed pose; there is a hint of injury to the near hind leg and a subtle suggestion of tired satisfaction in the head which makes this trophy a wonderful acquisition (*108*).

In complete contrast but also one of the most outstanding awards in equestrian events, and one of the most valuable outside the racing sphere since the Second World War, is the John Pinches Trophy, first presented in 1979 to the winner of the International Dressage Championship at Goodwood, modelled in silver by the woman sculptor Lorne McKean (*109*). It shows a dressage rider executing a canter pirouette and skilfully combines representational composition with some artistic licence. Though silver is a notoriously difficult medium a dulled patina has been produced subduing the hard brilliance of the metal.

From her first one man exhibition in 1970 at the Sladmore Gallery, when already a member of the Royal Society of British Sculptors,[7] it was obvious that Lorne McKean was destined to become an important name in contemporary sculpture, for she has enriched a natural talent by years of serious application and academic training. As a child her ambition was to become a sculptor, and at the age of eleven her model-

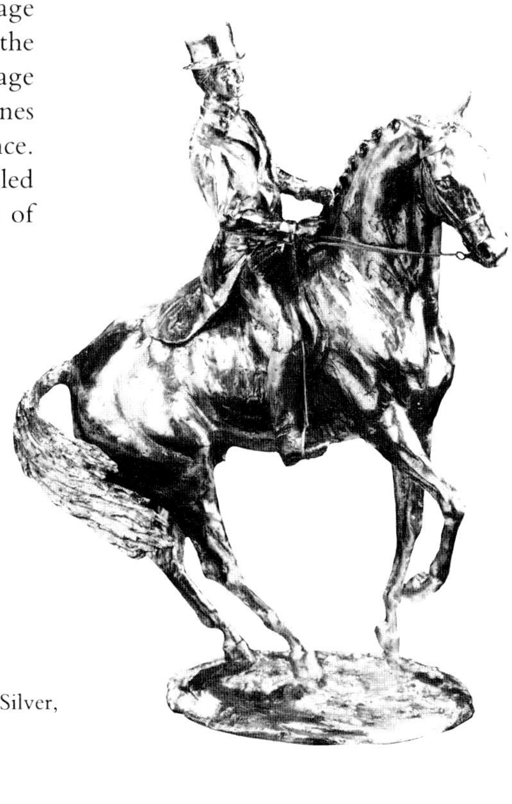

109 Lorne McKean, *John Pinches International Dressage Trophy*, 1974. Silver, h. 14 in (35.5 cm).

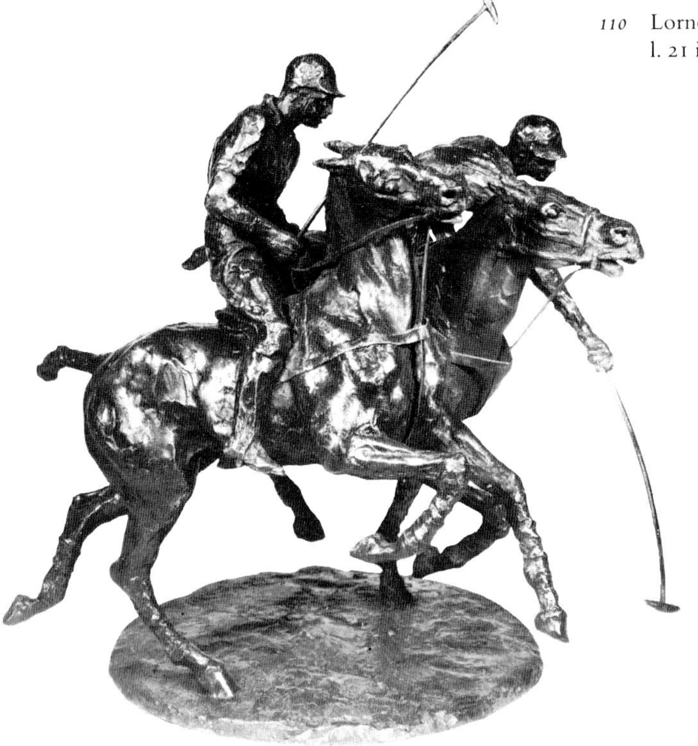

110 Lorne McKean, *Riding Off*. Bronze, h. 10 in (25.4 cm), l. 21 in (53.3 cm).

ling attracted the attention of Prince Serge Yourievitch, a friend of Rodin. He guided her work at his studio with encouragement spiced by criticism, until she attended the Guildford School of Art and, later, the Royal Academy Schools where she won the Leverhulme and the Feodora Gleichen Scholarships and the Silver Medal for Sculpture. She then came under the influence of Annigoni in Florence where she studied drawing; thus Lorne McKean has been well equipped for her vocation.

Though successful in portraits of the famous, and especially in studies of children, animals have proved her most constant inspiration. Of all the equestrian sports polo, perhaps, provides any artist with insoluble difficulties. The moment of truth is indeed brief and the poses almost inevitably appear, at the best, exaggerated and, at the worst, impossible. However Lorne McKean's polo models never lack impetus and suggest with skill the rigours and excitements of the game as in *Riding Off*, (*110*). A great triumph was the commission from Queen Elizabeth for a model of the Duke of Edinburgh on his polo pony, Portano, as Her Majesty's personal gift to the Duke on the occasion of their Silver Wedding Anniversary. Equally successful are her bronzes of a Lipizzaner of the Spanish School executing the piaffe and, in the famous Welsh cob Llanarth Braint, all the toughness of his breed is portrayed in spectacular action with flying mane and feather. Her canine portraits, happily devoid of any hint of sentimentality, possess a curious dignity and charm, whether boxer, basset hound, sheltie or greyhound. But more recently unusual commissions from the business world have included an eight foot osprey in bronze for Greenwich, USA, and a composition of herons for the Thames Water Board at Reading and, most stimulating of all, a nine foot bronze of flying herons for a private lake.

This sculptor has not only fulfilled her early potential but with her work in demand all over the world she can now select her subjects and experiment with new techiques for she and her sculptor husband, Edwin Russell have established an atelier in Surrey with four working apprentices and two assistants.

By the late 1970s there was a wealth of young sculptors drawn to animal life: Jonathan Knight, Gill Parker, Gill Wiles, Amy Oxenbould, Simon Erland, David Wynne and several others all shone in this sphere, with Jill Tweed, a pupil of the Slade, tackling the lifesize and on occasion using boxing as a subject. Althea Wynne also found success in studies of birds – her *Leda and the Swan* is delightful in addition to a lifesize mounted *Warrior*. Ann Baxter skilfully uses wood as her medium, allying form to the natural colour and grain. There are no limits to Angela Conner's versatility – distinguished portraits of the famous as well as Classic

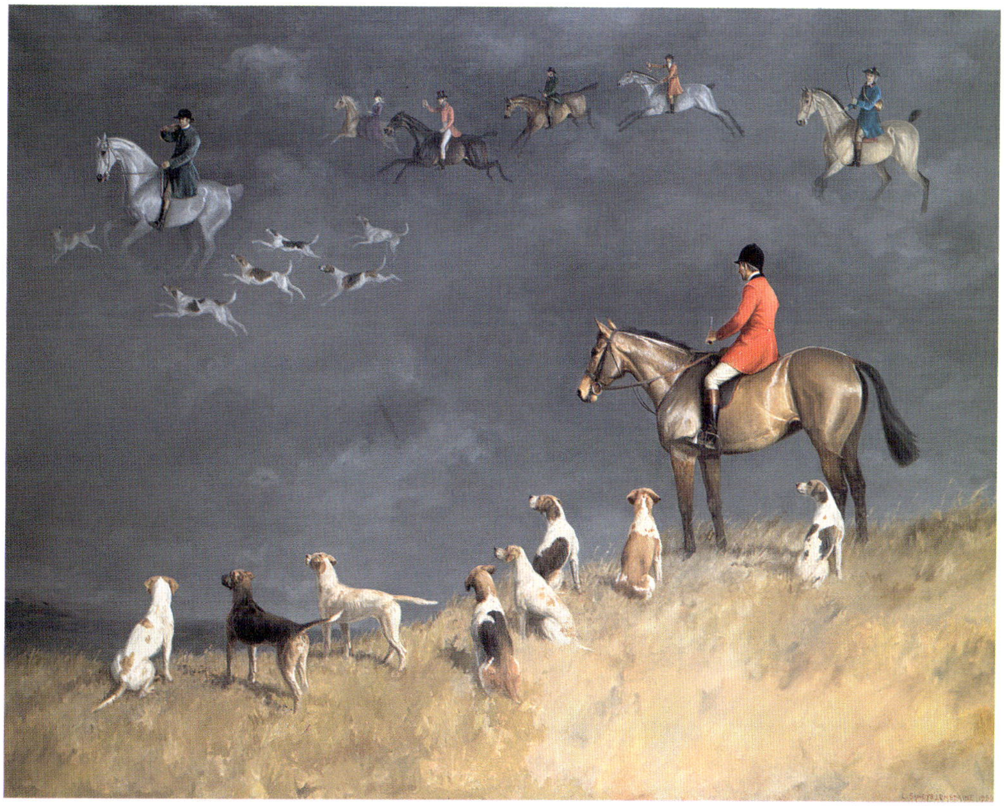

PLATE 21 (*above*) Leesa Sandys-Lumsdaine, *Echoes from the Past*, 1984. Oil on canvas, $49\frac{1}{2} \times 39\frac{1}{2}$ in (125.7×100.3 cm). (*below*) Susan Crawford, *Sun Princess, Winner of The Oaks and St Leger 1983*. Oil on canvas, 36×28 in (91.4×71.1 cm).

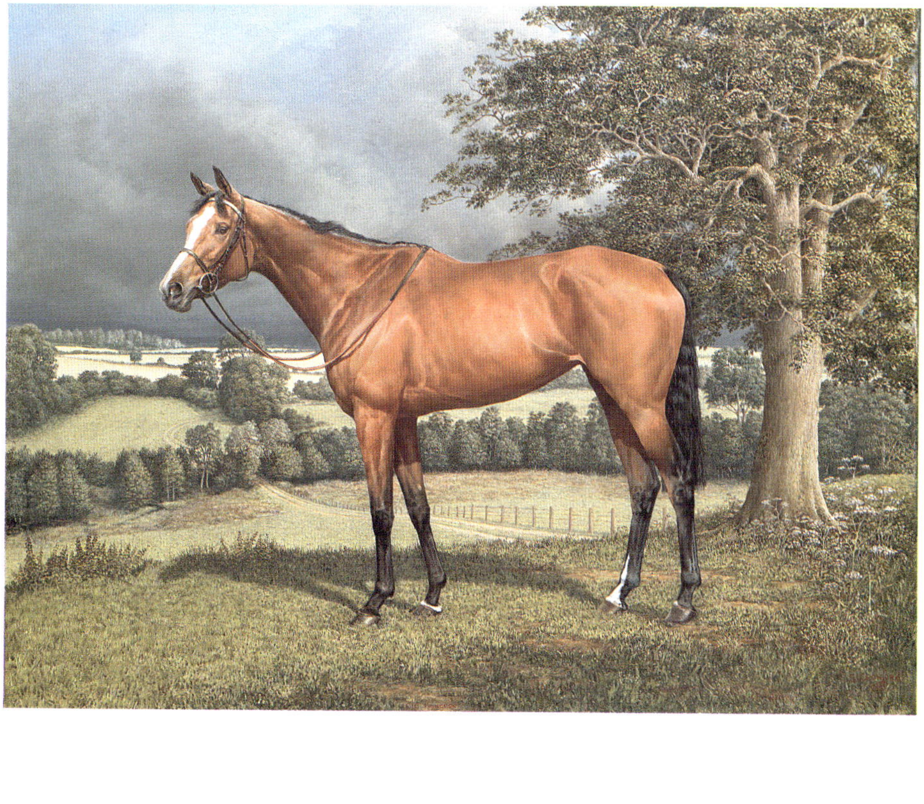

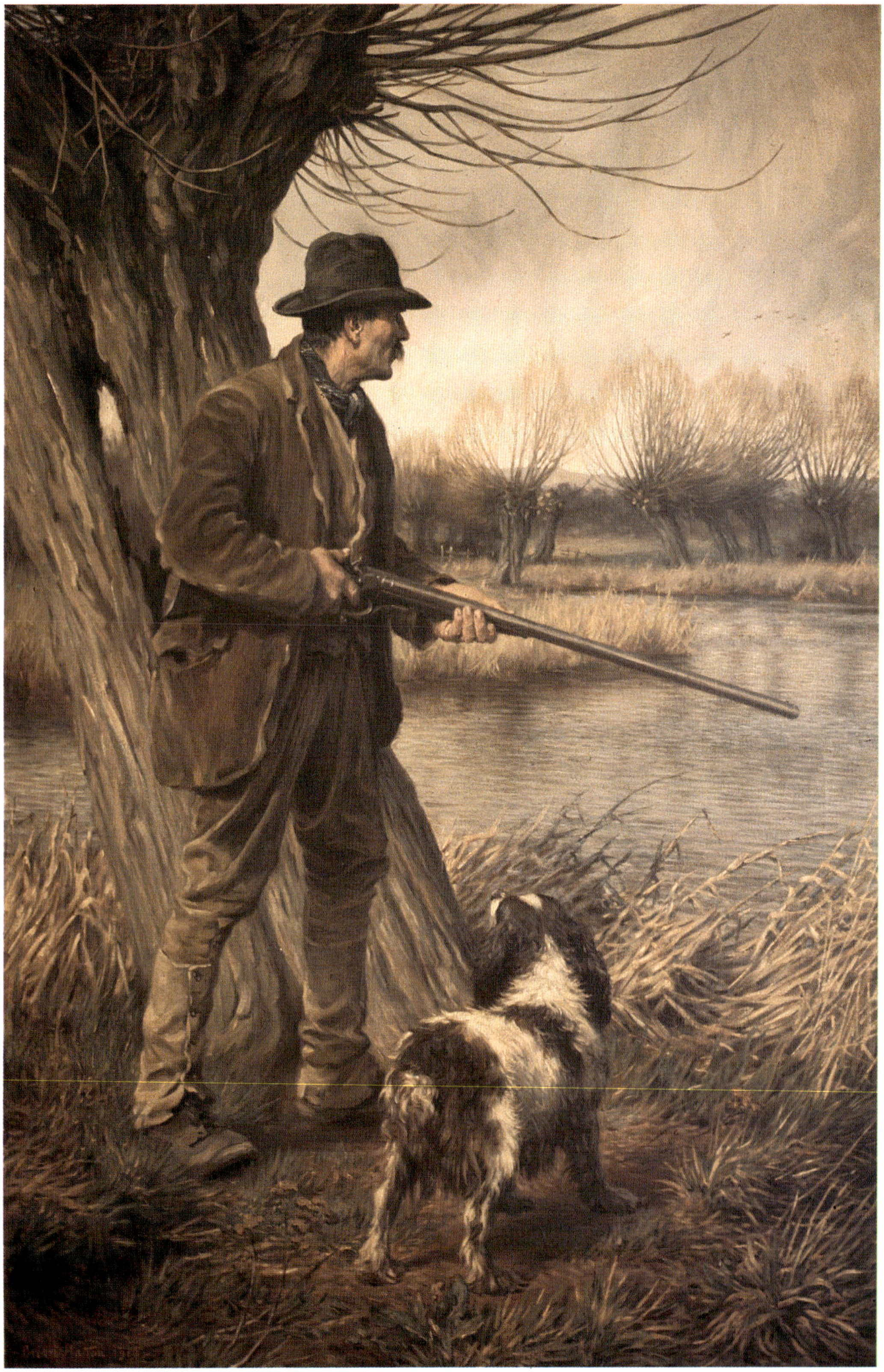

PLATE 22 Brian Hatton, *Man Duck-Shooting with Dog on Lugg*, 1910. Oil on canvas, $53 \times 35\frac{1}{2}$ in (134.6×90.1 cm).

winners. Her bronze of Park Top is the Duke of Devonshire's TBA Breeder's Award and her model of *Vaguely Noble* received the British Sporting Art Trust's award at the 1985 Society of Equestrian Artists' Exhibition. Her work can be seen in major public and private collections on both sides of the Atlantic.

Two other important women sculptors to make their mark in the 1970s have been Sally Arnup and Tessa Pullan, pupils of John Skeaping. Predictably, strong creative talent harnessed to expert instruction produced results of quality and some innovation. Sally Arnup, trained at the Royal Academy Schools, always works directly from live animals, whether frogs, Chinese geese, calves or horses. Her penetrating observation is expressed in the mobility and sensuous form of her models. Her work holds wide appeal with over thirty exhibitions as far afield as Norway, Italy and New Jersey, and in 1984 she was appointed a Fellow of the Royal Society of British Sculptors.

In the sporting sphere commissions have included several dogs, many lifesize; especially successful have been Labradors and a seated bloodhound (*111*). As visually satisfying are her studies of whippets and greyhounds, but it is a bronze of an otter with trout that illustrates Sally Arnup's talent for engaging the emotions without sentimentality.

Born in 1953, Tessa Pullan's success has been achieved after three years' apprenticeship from the age of eighteen with Skeaping in France, then a three years' diploma course at the City and Guilds of the London Art School and finally post graduate studies 1977–1980 at the Royal Academy, where her work has been regularly exhibited in the Diploma Gallery and at the Summer Exhibition. In the words of Paul Mellon, 'Her subjects are sought in attitudes so natural and instantaneous that live animals spring to one's mind in a sudden illumination, a flash of sunlight.'[8]

Amongst many commissions have been a bronze of a mare and foal which won her, with Ann Baxter, the sculpture prize awarded by the British Sporting Art Trust at the seventh Exhibition of the Society of Equestrian Artists; also a portrayal of the ill-fated Derby winner Troy for Willie Carson, completely Skeaping in its vibrant fluent style. But in 1980 she produced by direct carving, lifesize and with stark effect, a pair of recumbent greyhounds in Portland stone. Even more original, also lifesize and causing something of a sensation at the 1982 Royal Academy Summer exhibition was *Dobbin*, an equestrian construction in wood created with skilful technique (*112*). Other studies of foals in the same medium make impact by their curious but acceptable angularity to suggest that Tessa Pullan's future work will not be sterotyped.

John Skeaping's aspirations that contemporary animal sculptors might once again attempt half or lifesize models began to be realised as architects and racecourse committees began siting animal sculptures in various media to enliven shopping precincts and grandstand locations. Included in these were Judith

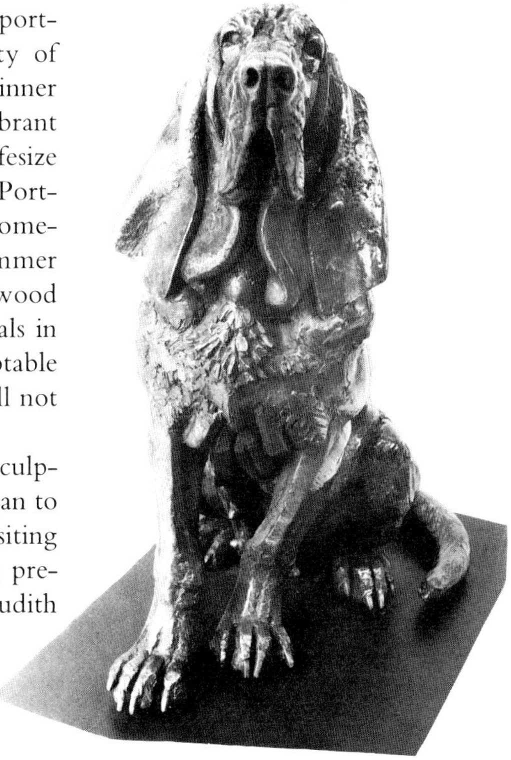

111 Sally Arnup, *Seated Bloodhound*, 1975. Bronze, h. 22 in (55.9 cm), l. 18 in (45.7 cm).

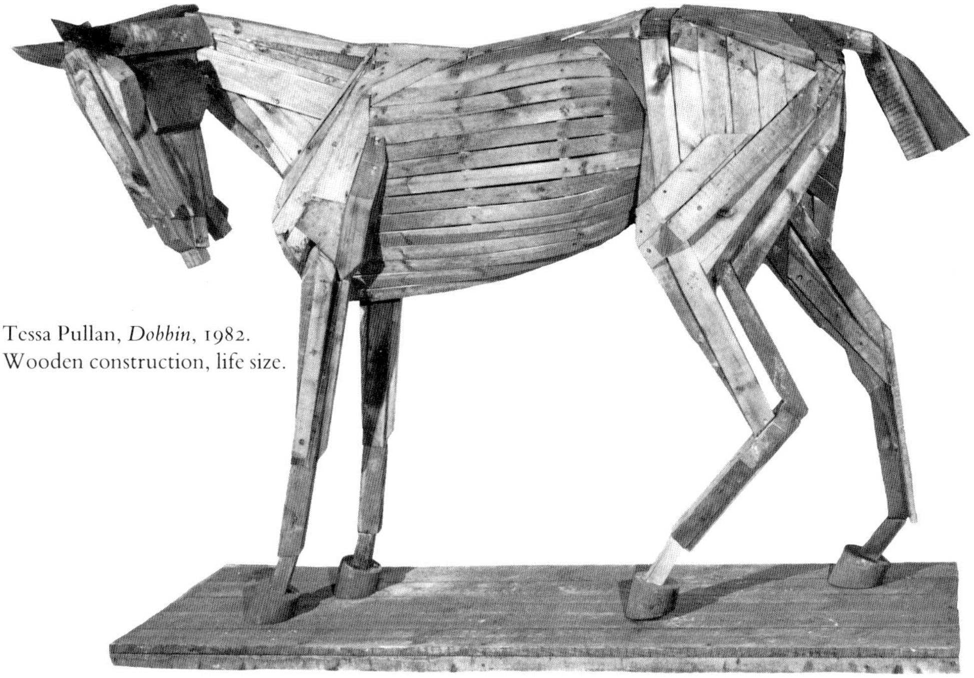

112 Tessa Pullan, *Dobbin*, 1982.
Wooden construction, life size.

Bluck's sturdy and popular model for the Ealing Broadway Centre and, in this same mood, a 9 ft bronze of a dray horse by the Sussex-born sculptor, Shirley Pace, is to take a commanding position in 1989 in Queen Elizabeth Street, Bermondsey.

More important in the sporting context is Jonathan Knight's half lifesize model at Cheltenham of Dawn Run, the first horse to have won both the Gold Cup and Champion Hurdle there, where this good likeness of the miracle mare shares artistic honours with a splendid bronze of the legendary Arkle, also half-lifesize modelled by Doris Lindner.

It must be regretted that the greater part of the career of this talented woman sculptor was devoted to modelling equestrian celebrities in porcelain. Trained at the St Martin's School of Art, at Calderon's and at the British Academy in Rome, Doris Lïndner's Art Deco and abstract work was exhibited at Heals in the 1920s where its quality was immediately recognised by a Director of the Royal Worcester Porcelain Company. She was to work for the firm for almost the next fifty years, first modelling small animals, then hunting groups and in 1948 HRH Princess Elizabeth riding Tommy was issued as her first equestrian limited edition to establish her reputation. Many renowned riders and horses became her subjects – Harry Llewellyn on Foxhunter, HRH The Duke of Edinburgh on a polo pony, then Hyperion and Nijinsky, but it must be admitted her humans were never as visually satisfying as her horses. Nevertheless such finely observed and beautifully executed breed models as an Arabian stallion, American Saddlebred and Welsh Mountain Pony must be considered ceramic masterpieces. In the 1960s her limited editions attracted an admiring public and augmented in price to heirloom proportions.

But it was in her few bronze and stone models that Doris Lindner's true calibre as a sculptor is revealed and in Arkle she has captured with inimitable flair the horse's high head carriage, air of confidence and impression of greatness. Photographs rarely reproduce the full scope of an outdoor statue but Michael Lyne's painting of Doris Lindner's bronze against the panorama of the Cleeve Hills at Cheltenham reveals something of the quality of the work.[9]

In 1987 John Osborne completed, in an edition of three, a half lifesize bronze of the black Metropolitan Police horse, Burmese, ridden by HM The Queen for eighteen years at the Trooping the Colour Ceremony, an assignment complicated for the sculptor by the intricacies of the full ceremonial tack of the Grenadier Guards. One model was sold for £40,000 in aid of the St John's Ambulance Centenary Appeal, destined for a big department store in Tokyo.

With no conventional training but only itinerant experience found in Tangier, woodcarving in Spain and work in an iron foundry in Paris, John Osborne established his own foundry in Sussex whilst improving his own considerable gifts as a sculptor. His models of Arabian stallions and Grand National 'chasers, racing greyhounds and flying birds illustrate his ability to depict animals in action in many forms.

To become one of the most important names in the 1970s was Philip Blacker, whose formal art background had also been negligible. However for thirteen years he had been a top professional jockey over the sticks and he concedes that, in an age when a total lack of facilities for serious anatomical studies prevailed, his mastery of skeletal truth had been obtained by riding out every morning for fifteen years. When his bronzes were exhibited in 1978 at the Tryon and Moorland Galleries in London it was obvious that an important new talent had arrived where a keen understanding of the rigours of the sporting scene were allied to strong inherent ability and appreciation of animal movement. His one man exhibition in 1983 showed growing skill in finesse and presentation as in *Stewards' Enquiry* with three 'chasers in a tight finish, and in his poise and angle of horse and rider in *Jumping the Canal Turn*. In both he motivated the imagination of the beholder to appreciate the magic and miseries of being in the saddle which are incomprehensible to the pedestrian with two feet on the ground.

Amongst many commissions for trophies perhaps the most striking is the Seagram Grand National Steeplechase Trophy which, with considerable invention, shows three phases of a horse landing over Becher's Brook to illustrate Philip Blacker's mastery of his subject. But in contrast a study *Tired Greyhound*, with sheer exhaustion subtly understated, suggests there

113 Philip Blacker, *Red Rum*, 1988. Bronze, life size.

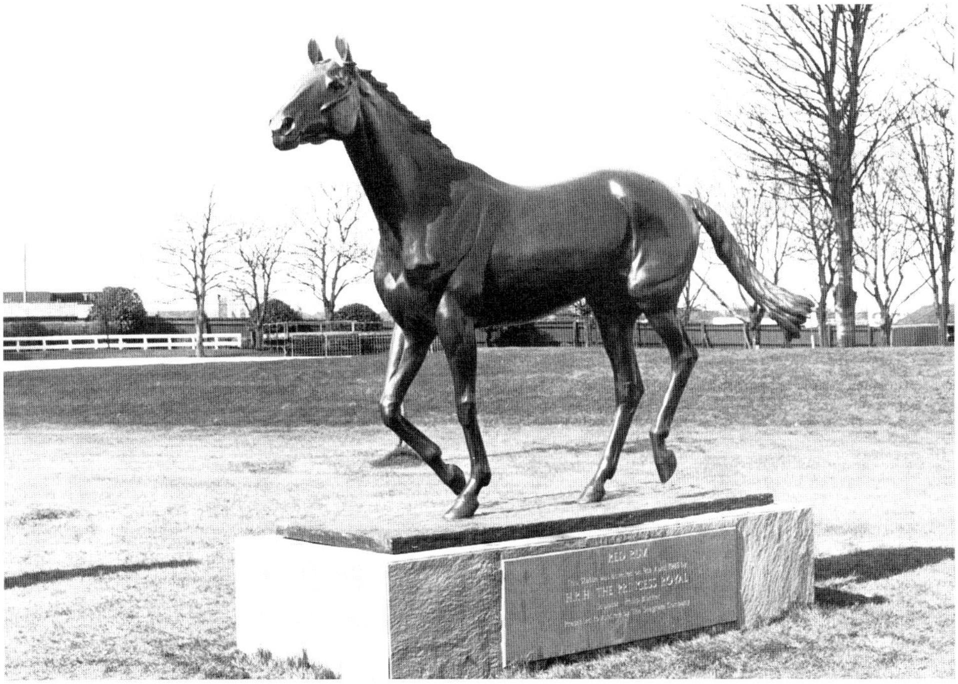

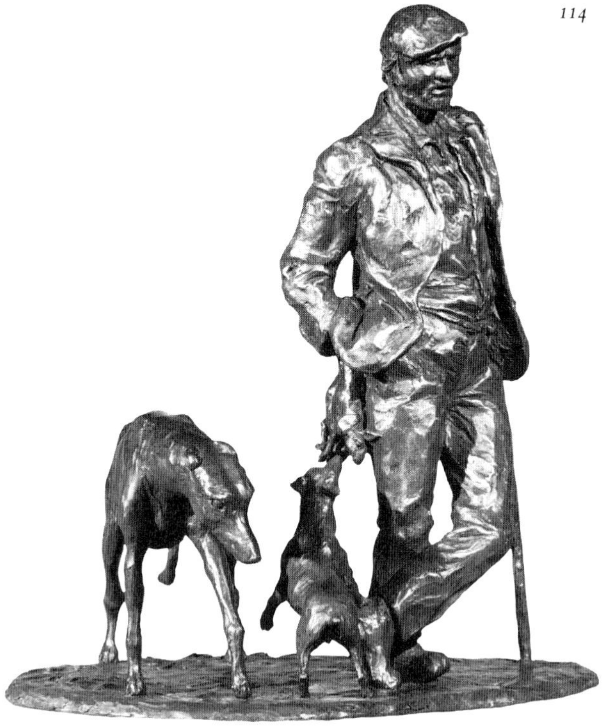

114 Philip Blacker, *Study from Appleby Horse Fair*, 1987. Bronze, h. 14 in (35.5 cm), l. 24 in (60.9 cm).

are unexploited facets to the sculptor's talent. He has portrayed such leading horses as Cormorant Wood, Blakeney and Morston and, for Sheikh Mohammed Maktoum, the famous Pebbles.

Proving finally that sculptors of today are undaunted by the challenge of the lifesize horse, Philip Blacker's statue of Red Rum was unveiled by the Princess Royal at Aintree on 9 April 1988 (*113*). It was commissioned by Seagram UK Ltd to commemorate the 150th anniversary of the race. No other horse in equine history has been exposed to the creative efforts of painters, sculptors and, of course, photographers in such excess as Red Rum, the triple winner of the race. A top personality on television and in the press 'Rummie' became the idol of thousands, horsemen and housewives alike. It was not an easy assignment for any sculptor. After several weeks visiting the horse at Southport, getting to know him, watching him being ridden on the sands, Philip Blacker decided on a romantic pose, the horse, characteristically on his toes, moving slightly sideways with the wind swirling into exciting movement the mane and tail. This bronze of Red Rum captures not only the physical likeness, the intelligent head, the magnificent front, strong quarters and even the slight dish of the off fore, but also something of the indomitable spirit of the horse – the greatest of all Grand National winners.

In his 1988 exhibition at the Tryon Gallery, Philip Blacker further displayed his interesting potential with rural studies from Appleby Horse Fair (*114*) to contrast with the cubist connotations of a galloping Thoroughbred, *Racehorse from Another Angle*.

Animal and sporting sculpture in the latter part of the twentieth century owes much of its growing prestige to the initiative of the Sladmore Gallery in Bruton Place, London. Established in 1967 by the Horswell family it quickly achieved an international reputation. Its early exhibitions were devoted in the greater part to the French Animaliers School, shared with some bronzes by British Victorians. However, with admirable expedition, works by young and unknown contemporary sculptors were soon regularly exhibited, sometimes sharing the honours with such superlative masters as American-born Herbert Haseltine and the Italian genius, Rembrandt Bugatti. Such talented newcomers as Lorne McKean, Gill Wiles, Gill Parker and others were given their chance to make a London debut.

An encouraging feature in this same period has been some stimulating designs being incorporated into modern functional buildings. Some of these have used a sporting motif and most interesting in this area has been the innovative work of Walter Ritchie. He first studied at the Coventry School of Art and his early works were modelled and cast, but direct carving quickly became a major interest. He gained experience at the Horton Quarries in North

Oxfordshire and later Eric Gill was his master. Walter Ritchie initiated an effective form of brick sculpture, designing for the offices and amenity buildings of George Armitage and Son Ltd, Brickworks, at Hurley near Wakefield a series of *Sport in the Ridings* in Robin Hood red, antique brown and pale cream Ebor bricks. In the shooting composition of sportsman and sportswoman with loader and labrador a traditional scene acquires contemporary activation in a new medium (*115*).

In particular, Wates Building Group have allied sculpture to their post war constructional planning. Their commissions from such leading sculptors as Sydney Harpley, Jonathan Kenworthy, Michael Rizzello and David Wynne have frequently involved an animal subject. Outside Norwich Union House in Croydon the immortal John Jorrocks on Arterxerxes rides again in his own home town in striking action in a nine foot bronze modelled by John W. Mills, ARCA, FRBS. This sculptor, born in 1933, studied at Hammersmith and the Royal College of Art. Examples of his work are in collections in many European countries and in the United States and Canada. But the Jorrocks sculpture contrasts in concept with John Mills' *A Ride of Horses* exhibited at the Alwin Gallery in London in 1986, non-representational in approach, nevertheless relevant to the contemporary age and much enhanced by the ancient Florentine technique of a tawny patina.

At the end of the century sculpture outside the defined sporting context cannot be ignored, certainly not the work of Dame Elisabeth Frink who has forged a tenuous link between academic and 'modern' art in her animal bronzes. She has made a transition that is comprehensible and acceptable to the general public, if not wholeheartedly admired by the hunting fraternity. In 1974, at the Artists Gold Exhibition at the Goldsmiths Hall, her *Rolling-over Horse* in eighteen carat gold measuring only 13 cm in height gave indication in miniature of the distinctive qualities that brought her public commissions from all over the world. These have included in the equestrian field the timeless *Horse and Rider* at the corner of Piccadilly and Dover Street, commissioned by Trafalgar Property Development, and the lifesize bronze in 1980 for Goodwood Racecourse (*116*). With a strange serenity that appeals to the mind as well as to the eye, these horses suggest the spirit and energy that comes from within. Frink drawings were used as the catalogue cover motif for the 1980 International Show Jumping Championships at Olympia. Her Expressionist birds, dogs and horses demand time and thought for assimilation but enrich the animal sculpture of this age. Elected an RA in 1977, a Dame of the British Empire in 1982 with honorary doctorates from various universities, a Trustee of the British Museum and a member of the Royal Society and the Fine Arts Commission, Elisabeth Frink also finds time for enjoying her own horses at her home in Dorset.

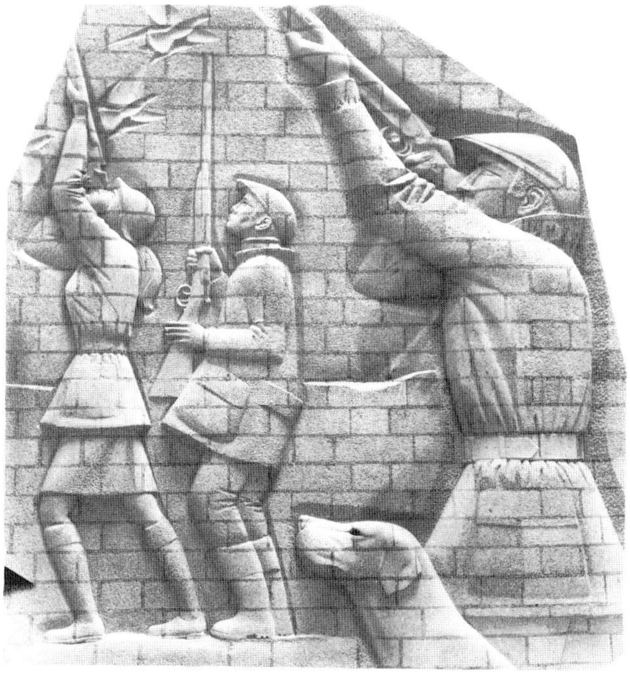

115 Walter Ritchie, *Sport in the Ridings* (detail), 1977. Robin Hood red, antique bronze, pale cream Ebor bricks, h. 132 in (335.2 cm), l. 168 in (426.7 cm).

As the century nears its end, there appears to be a watershed developing in sporting and animal sculpture. On the one hand the strictly representational is executed with a certain skill and observation by several young exponents to vie with animated form, basically and predominantly equine in character but enigmatic and expressionist in style and not directly relevant to sporting art. Puzzling equestrian works in this sphere by Sean Crampton and Robert Clatworthy, RA, cannot be ignored and perhaps we should begin to learn to take a wider perspective in assessing their implications. Sean Crampton was born in 1918, trained at the Birmingham School of Art, and after distinguished war service won a national competition in 1951 for the Royal Armoured Corps Memorial. Working on private commissions of heroic proportions, (including a spectacular Third Horseman of the Apocalypse), he began to abandon three dimensional modelling for abstract studies in iron, nails and bronze strips which have included equine form but also, more effectively, a heron for cascading water. He was President of the Royal Society of British Sculptors from 1966–1971.

Robert Clatworthy initially studied at the West of England College of Art in Bristol and later at Chelsea School of Art and the Slade. In his very personal interpretation of animal life he has declared an intention to express the way a living animal feels in movement rather than how it appears to human observation. Elected an RA in 1973 his works now form part of the permanent collections of the Tate Gallery, the Victoria & Albert Museum and the Arts Council. A recent commission of a 25 ft bronze of a menacing horse and rider can be seen in the business precincts of Finsbury Avenue, London, EC.

Though these innovations remain outside the concept of sporting art *per se*, and the way ahead for animal sculpture is by no means easy to interpret, nevertheless these approaches will, conceivably, play some unpredictable part in the sporting art of the next century.

NOTES

1 Letter to the Committee for Technical Education, Goldsmiths Company, from H.H. Armstead, RA, 2 December 1884.

2 William Shakespeare, *Macbeth*, Act 2, Scene 4, 15.

3 John Skeaping, *Drawn from Life*, p. 231.

4 ibid, p. 243.

5 ibid, p. 245.

6 ibid, p. 231.

7 Lorne McKean became a Fellow of the Royal Society of British Sculptors in 1972.

8 Foreword in Tessa Pullan's personal folder.

9 In 1989 a half life size bronze of the great Golden Miller, by the Wiltshire sculptor, Judy Boyt, will be erected at Cheltenham overlooking the scene of his five successive Gold Cup triumphs (1932–36).

116 Elisabeth Frink, DBE, RA, *Horse*, 1980. Bronze.

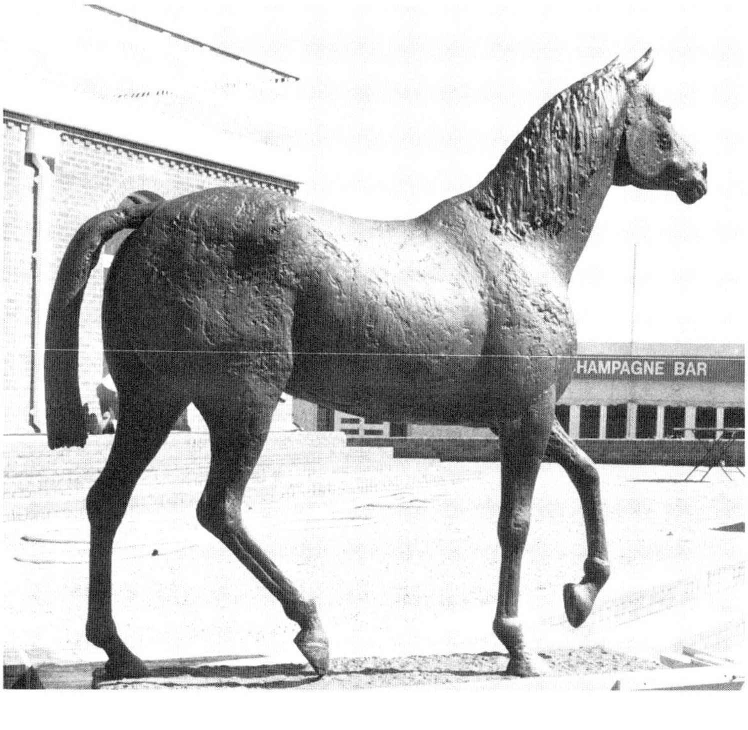

17

Cricket and Other Diversions

The Shorter Oxford English Dictionary attributes to the noun 'sport' a variety of meanings. In the fifteenth century the definition given is 'pleasant pastime, amusement, diversion.' Two hundred years later it has developed into 'pastime afforded by the endeavour to take or kill wild animals, game or fish' and here is reflected the growing national partiality for hunting, shooting and fishing. Another couple of centuries elapse and 'sport', probably to counteract the drab materialism of the industrial revolution, has expanded to include 'participation in games or exercises, especially those pursued in the open air.'

Thus the significance of the term has few limitations but, in the actual context of British sporting art, activities involving animals in outdoor situations have remained for three centuries its most constant interpretation. Even such particular 'amusements' as bull baiting, cock-fighting, wild fowling and ferretting in their day had been given pictorial recognition and, in addition, such pedestrian diversions as archery, fencing, pugilism, cricket and other ball games had also produced some intriguing pictures. But the fact remains that the horse continued as the paramount motif and hunting and racing reigned perpetually supreme as the commissioned subjects.

In this present survey of twentieth century sporting art the same equestrian imbalance persists and its most successful artists have rarely ventured far from the sphere of field sports. This is paradoxical for since Hitler's war a world of leisure and social security has prevailed with soaring popularity of pastimes outside these limited boundaries. Never have cricket, football (both soccer and rugger), golf and tennis reached a wider circle but with an observing rather than participating public – the comfort of the armchair in front of the television set is substituted for the great outdoors. In addition in recent years even basket ball, volley ball, bowls and snooker have all become headline news in the popular press after excessive exposure on 'The Box'. As a result one might have expected that sporting art would have established a new specialist genre of its own with 'the pursuit of the ball' as its focus.

The ramifications of contemporary recreations are boundless – athletics, ballooning, canoeing, skiing, hang-gliding, wrestling all play their part; and even in an abbreviated list in *The Guinness Book of Sports Facts* over fifty popular activities are mentioned.[1] But inevitably in this century the role of the sporting painter has been effectively diminished by the phenomenal development of action and colour photography. Today the camera is used with a creative skill never envisaged by that pioneer, Eadweard Muybridge, and the sporting artist, however talented and variable, must now always vie for supremacy with the photographer and his telephoto lens.

However, in 1977 an exhibition 'Play the Game' put on by Frost & Reed in their Bristol Galleries illustrated the fact that certain artists were accepting the challenge in ball games with successful innovation. Of course, a book of some length and detail on the art of these peripheral aspects of the British sporting scene demanded publication and one has recently appeared.[2] In this present general survey of the twentieth century only a few of these subjects can be very superficially observed and sparsely illustrated.

Many national recreations outside the sphere of field sports have always received contemporary pictorial recognition but 'the noble art' of cricket has, from medieval times, remained a constant subject amongst our 'pleasant pastimes'. Even traditional animal and sporting artists such as R.B. Davies, Edwin Landseer, George Morland and James Pollard had all painted, on occasion, pictures involving cricket (though admittedly with an indirect emphasis). But more important masters which include Gainsborough, Turner, Zoffany and Joseph Wright of Derby have also added their lustre to the cricket theme. Such classics of the past as Rowlandson's bawdy female *Cricket Match Extraordinary*, Peter de Wint's lovely watercolour *The Cricketers* and Thomas Henwood's sturdy portrayal of *The Scorer* effectively epitomise a pastime that ranks as a national institution. Artists of variable talent were to continue this convention in the twentieth century but to a far lesser degree, as other games assumed major public popularity and action photography acquired ever increasing expertise.

The game of cricket was first enjoyed by the landed gentry but was later played by all levels of society, especially in the North of England, from squire to villager, though for formal occasions the category of 'Gentlemen and Players' was to be observed until 1962. Contemporary rural matches in lovely surroundings never lost their artistic appeal and had attracted such Victorian landscape painters as Sir David Murray, John Ritchie and John Robertson Reid and included minor names, such as the Sussex watercolourist James Matthews with a delightful little scene *The Boundary Bench*, dated 1901, to serve as a reminder of long summer afternoons watching local worthies seeking glory with bat and ball (*117*).

But the end of this era has seen a rise of professionalism in the game with teams capable of large scores and expert bowling. Such impressive and picturesque players as the Indian, K.S. Ranjitsinhji, C.B. Fry and Pelham Warner gave prestige to the new century, followed by G.B. Jessop, J.T. Tyldesley and Jack Hobbs, all to be enshrined for posterity, with leading personalities of other sports, in observant caricatures in *Vanity Fair* by 'Spy' (Sir Leslie Ward, a great-grandson of James Ward, RA, that master of sporting and romantic art in the late eighteenth century). The cricket hero had already been lionised in 1898 in William Nicholson's woodcuts in *An Almanac of Twelve Sports* where the month of June is represented by cricket in a period evocation of stalwart Alfred Mynn, the great Kent and England all-rounder. The legendary William Gilbert Grace dominated the game for over forty years and, of course, had inspired numerous notable portraits including young Max Beerbohm's caricature celebrating WG's feat of completing 1000 runs in the month of May 1905, to receive from the cricket obsessed editor of the *Daily Telegraph* a cheque for £10,000. In 1908 Henry Tuke, the portrait and genre artist, portrayed in watercolours the great man, now aged sixty, posed in Ranjitsinhji's turban, relaxing after a match played at the Indian's home in Sussex.

Pictures of celebrated cricketers and of public school matches were a popular feature of the Edwardian era but scenes of country house and village matches typify the real enchantment of this English game. In this category Frank Batson's *Playing Out Time in an Awkward Light*, exhibited in the Royal Academy in 1901 with its stiff white flanneled figures set in deepening shadows against leafy trees, seems to epitomise the tranquillity of life before the First World War.

That Post-Impressionist and Anglophile, Camille Pissarro, had, during his visits to England

117 James Matthews, *The Boundary Bench*, 1901. Watercolour, 6 × 7¼ in (15.2 × 18.4 cm).

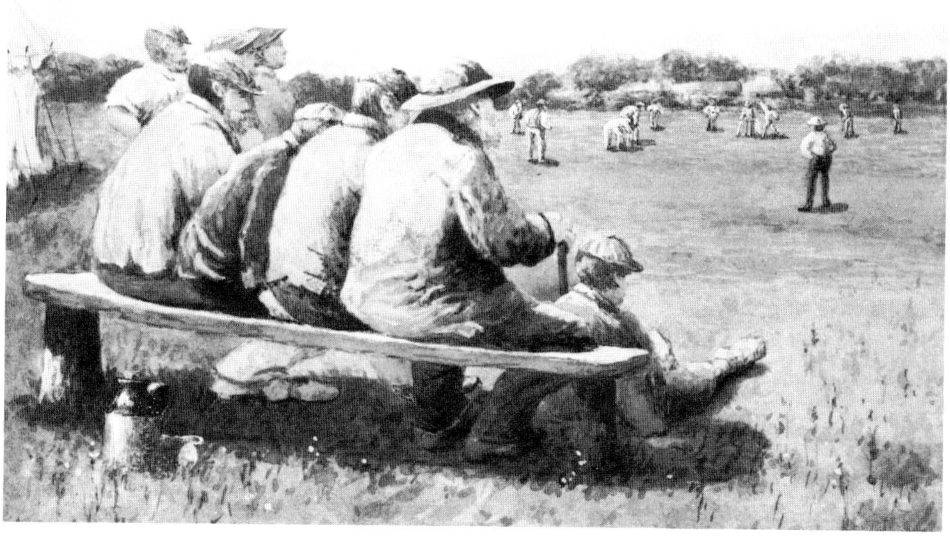

in the 1890s, made several studies of cricket matches and their subtle nuances of light and shade were to be reflected in many future compositions of the game. In his cricket classic Albert Chevallier Tayler, a genre artist and gifted member of the Newlyn School, accurately depicts the Kent County 1906 Champions playing Lancashire but evening shadows provide a touch of magic and mystery (*Plate 24*). Eighty years later the distinguished watercolourist John Ward was to record a similar occasion with all the verve and gaiety typical of Canterbury Cricket Week. Chevallier Tayler's more formal contributions to the game appear in *The Empire's Cricketers*, where forty-eight of his drawings appeared in 1905 in a twelve part series produced as lithographs (and later in a bound edition) in conjunction with George W. Beldam, the Middlesex batsman and a brilliant pioneer of action photography in sport. Published by the Fine Art Society they made an important factual record of fifty years with bat and ball, though their merit artistically is disappointing. Spencer Gore, one of the founders of the Campden Town Group also reflects this Gallic influence in his painting *The Cricket Match*, painted in 1929 in soft tones and the figures indistinct in detail; nevertheless the scene remains unequivocally English.

Between the two World Wars few sporting artists used cricket as a subject though the game ranked high in the country's recreational priorities. In the 1920s and '30s its popularity along with other sports was endorsed by such tobacco companies as Players and Wills who used cigarette cards as advertising material; they included many sets featuring cricketers which are today much esteemed by 'cartophilists', especially characterisations by 'Rip' of such stars as Jack Hobbs, Phil Mead, Patsy Hendren, etc.

London Transport also emphasized cricket's public appeal in its poster by Anna Zinkeisen for the Oval Test Match in August 1930 in a cheerful design of an Australian kangaroo and British lion in the role of wicket keepers. This was matched the same year by her decorative tennis girl publicising the Wimbledon Championships.

One of the few action pictures of merit of the day came from the brush of Algernon Newton,

RA, (a grandson of the founder of the famous firm of Winsor and Newton, the art colourists). In 1929 to celebrate the Jubilee of the firm, Messrs Cadbury Limited, the painting *A Cricket Match at Bournville* was commissioned by a director, William Cadbury; with its urban background of tall buildings and dark shadows sweeping across the ground the small white players stand out with crystal clarity.

After the Second World War county games continued in their traditional fashion but aroused little pictorial interest. Charles Cundall, that faithful recorder of our sporting English occasions, painted in 1953 play in progress in *A Hastings Cricket Festival*; nevertheless the leisurely world of cricket was on the brink of metamorphosis.

Influential business sponsorship was to arrive stimulating high powered one-day contests, the first inter-County competition being initiated by Gillettes in 1963. With speedy runmaking the vital issue, public support for these games brought packed grounds. Obviously the speed and clarity of the modern camera captured magnificently the exciting incidents of this new era and only a few artists made any significant attempt to project these innovations.

It was perhaps an indicative nostalgia that inspired Lawrence Toynbee's important work dated 1974 of *Cricket at Hovingham Hall*, the home of Colonel Sir William Worsley, one of the great Yorkshire supporters of the game, where the picture evokes the charm and pleasures of the disappearing country house match. Also in this same category comes David Inshaw's tranquil composition of 1974 of *The Cricket Game* played against a silhouette of leafy trees and rolling downland – another memorable picture of vanishing England.

But Lawrence Toynbee also possessed the talent and eye to depict contemporary sport in the modern vein. Born in 1922, son of a historian Arnold Toynbee and grandson of the classic scholar Gilbert Murray, he was trained at the Ruskin School of Art to become a skilled draughtsman which, allied to his personal dedication to ball games, enabled him to bring a transforming spontaneity to athletic movement. This was particularly effective in illustrating sparkling shots in cricket such as *Hit to Leg* by a West Indian batsman and *Cover Slash*; though players are

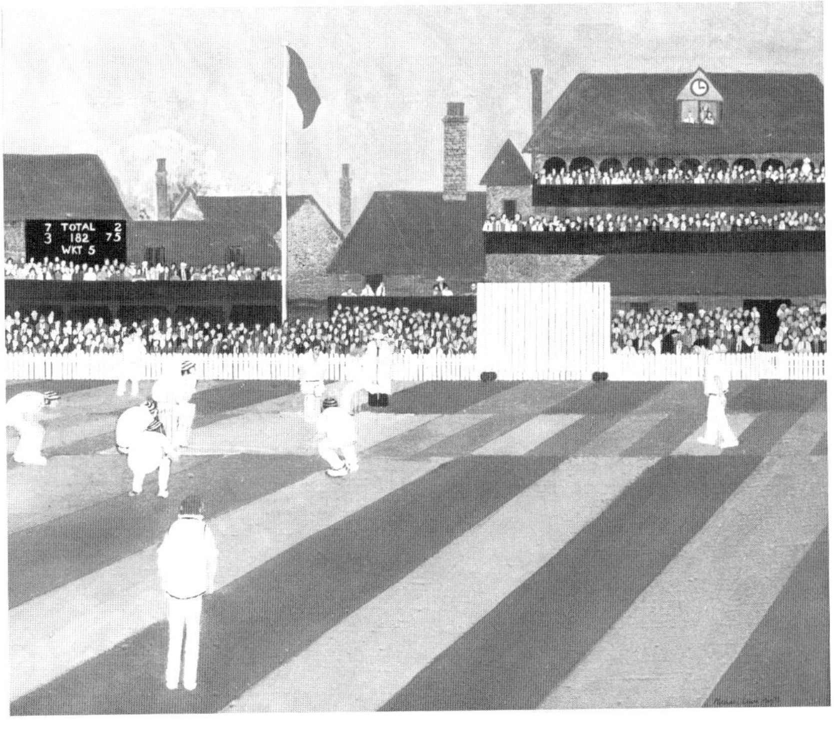

118 Michael Lewis, *Cricket Match*, 1978. Oil on canvas, 20 × 22 in (50.8 × 55.8 cm).

unidentifiable and blurred in action, stance and stroke are always correct and vigorous. Equally pleasing, using dim colour tones, are his pictures of rugby football, soccer, tennis and squash and other diversions. Toynbee must be considered one of the very few artists of his day able to use minor sporting subjects to enhance an important artistic career, and in contemporary style also can be included Michael Lewis's *Cricket Match*, (*118*).

Ruskin Spear, a distinguished portraitist and Royal Academician, rather as an afterthought in his career discovered cricket as an artistic stimulus. His portrait of 'Fiery Fred' Truman in 1963 succeeds in suggesting the menacing aggression of the player with the innate charm of the man; and many years later his masterly action study of *Bowler and Batsman*, exhibited at the Royal Academy in 1985, expresses vividly the speed and tension of the modern game. By contrast, portraits in the late 1970s by Roger Marsh, though achieving good likenesses as typified in the rubicund features of the Gloucestershire player M.J. Procter, in their muted colouring and static pose lack any comparable distinction. Often the artist reverts to the stars of yesteryear such as K.S. Ranjitsinjhi, W.G. Grace and Jack Hobbs for his models.

The pictures by Gerry Wright also reflect retrospective occasions and have been referred to as flowery Edwardiana with their stiffly posed teams in rainbow blazers. Colourful horticulture perennially blossoms in his backgrounds explained, perhaps, by the fact that the artist was, allegedly, once a market gardener as well as a member of the Kent County staff. Painted in primary colours these portrait compositions have a Rousseau stylised naïvety.

Amongst the few artists competing with the camera in various sports must be noted Phillip Gardner with his pulsating impressions of players in action, though his professional career in art started late in life, after thirty years spent as a copywriter and creative director of an advertising agency. But his first exhibition in 1971 brought immediate success and his striking watercolours of individual human action make impact with deceptive simplicity.

In a different category is Rhodesian-born Rosemary Taylor, a woman artist with an idiomatic approach to the contemporary sporting scene in vast oil paintings of free assertive brushwork. Her backgrounds verge on the abstract but her cricket players, often unidentified by name, are recognisable in an instantaneous exaggeration of style and stroke, as in her study of *Walker, Grieg and umpire Dickie Bird*. Animation may be taken to excess but it sparkles, nevertheless, with a bizarre revelation of pace and power. William Bowyer, a newly elected Royal Academician in 1982, with something of this same vitality, enlivened the Summer Exhibition of that year by a brilliant action study of Clive Lloyd the Guyanian cricketer. A keen player himself, Bowyer aims to produce an annual picture of the game. In 1987 to commemorate Lord's Centenary Year he presented a study of the ground with cricket in progress.

Enthusiasm for the game in this century has certainly not diminished. The summers are still enlivened not only by the sponsored tournament but also traditional matches continue on the village greens. At the National Portrait Gallery both W.G. Grace (by an unknown artist) and Ian Botham by John Bellany – an undistinguished portrayal – have their place. Though the pictorial approach to the actual game has changed and increasing emphasis is given to action and transitory incident nevertheless, during the past hundred years, cricket has certainly provided the major contribution to the pictures of England's pastimes and diversions.

In contrast the game of football seems to have activated artists less frequently, possibly because originally its players had been mostly lads of the lower classes, but by the 1840s it had been introduced into the public schools and in this century soccer and rugger have become the nation's most popular ball games; nevertheless artistic recognition has been comparatively limited. By 1912 Spy's caricature in *Vanity Fair* shows the distinguished Lord Kinnaird, with

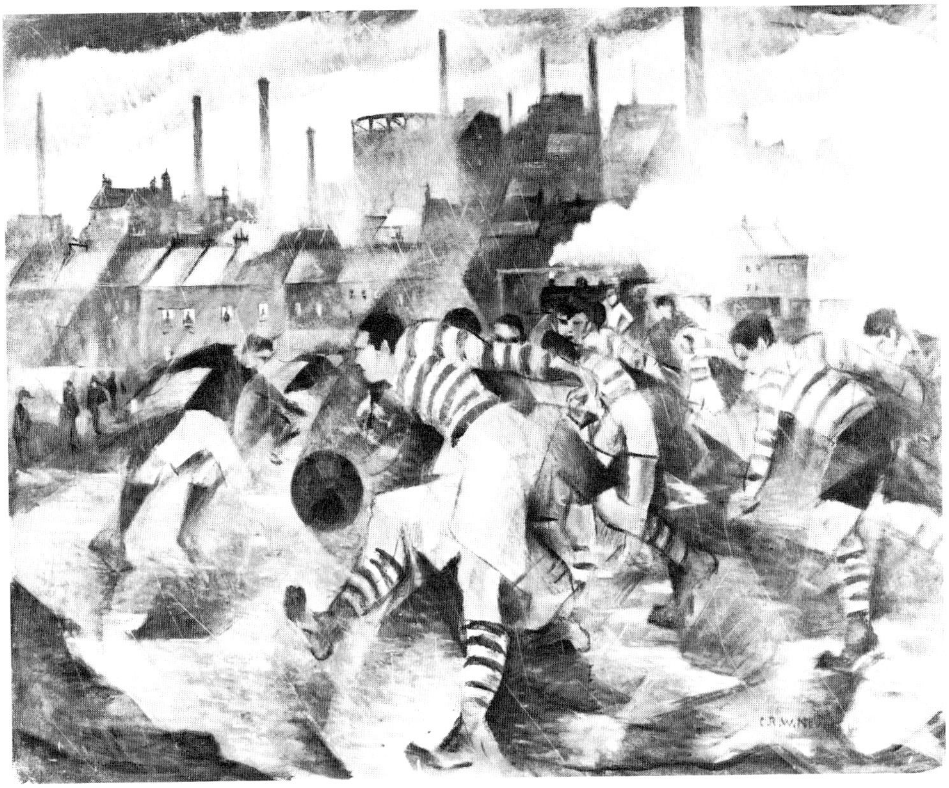

119 Christopher Richard Wynne Nevinson, *Any Winter Afternoon in England*, 1930. Oil on canvas, $18\frac{1}{4} \times 30$ in (46.3 × 76.2 cm).

the simple title *Soccer*, all ready for play in long white flannels and brown boots. Frank Stratton, a landscape painter working in the 1920s, uses a melée of players in *The Football Game*, clad in modern conventional shorts and shirts and capturing the rigours and tensions of some indeterminate occasion. Charles Cundall found a constant subject in soccer matches with lively Cup Tie scenes, especially of Chelsea in play as in his 1937 Royal Academy exhibit of *Chelsea v Arsenal at Stamford Bridge*.

The century's major contribution to football art was the competition with prize awards of £3,000 put on in 1953 by the Football Association in celebration of its ninetieth anniversary. From 1700 items submitted and judged by Professor Coldstream, Sir Philip Hardy, Mr Philip James and Sir John Rothenstein 150 paintings, engravings and sculptures were selected for exhibition at Park Lane House, followed by a tour sponsored by the Arts Council to thirteen provincial towns. Contrasts of style, media and presentation made up a stimulating collection to illustrate the exciting possibilities of football as a major subject in contemporary sporting art. Especially lively were H. Andrew Freeth's incursion into *Watford F.C. Dressing Room*, and C. Chamberlain's huge oil painting ($94\frac{1}{2} \times 46\frac{1}{2}$ in) *Chelsea Plays the Arsenal* was presented to the Football Association by the Football League.

In *Going to the Match*, L.S.Lowry's lifelong devotion to the game is reflected in his own inimitable style, a quality that also comes over in S.R. Badmin's little watercolour *Here They Come – The Valley* with players streaming on to the pitch against a jigsaw of crowded stands. And, against a background of tall smoking chimneys, C.R.W. Nevinson in *Any Winter Afternoon in England* typifies artisan escape from the dark satanic mills of industry (*119*). In quieter mood Lawrence Toynbee's *Mid-Week Practice at Stamford Bridge* contrasts with tough studies of his rugger scenes at Twickenham.

Joyce Bidder, a woman sculptor of underestimated talent working from the early 1930s, made a fine contribution to rugby football with her model *Tackled* exhibited in plaster in the Royal Academy in 1931 and finally cast in bronze in 1987 (*120*). Here is illustrated the powerful aggression of the human male at play, a theme developed in impressionist watercolours with stark economy of line by Philip Gardner in *Charging All Blacks* which suggests the rampant menace of the game (*121*). Although an invigorating kaleidoscope of paintings certainly does exist of both rugger and soccer, photography has become their most popular illustrator.

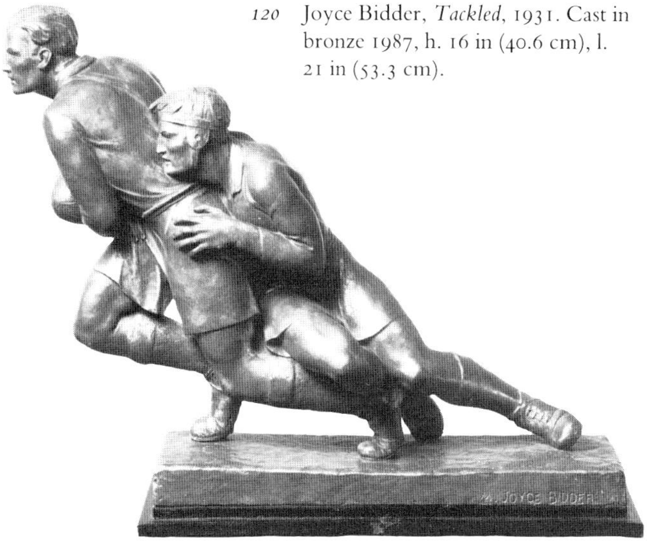

120 Joyce Bidder, *Tackled*, 1931. Cast in bronze 1987, h. 16 in (40.6 cm), l. 21 in (53.3 cm).

Modern tennis (originally Lawn Tennis) derives from the historic game of Real Tennis mentioned in six of Shakespeare's plays and played with enthusiasm by Henry VIII at Hampton Court. It must be reckoned as a relative newcomer amongst our popular sports and pastimes; the first Club was not formed until 1872 at Leamington Spa and five years later the All England Lawn Tennis Championships were established at Wimbledon, today a venue of world fame where its Museum includes a selection of paintings and drawings.

At the turn of the century as an exercise enjoyed socially by both sexes against the pleasant background of English gardens several artists found the subject appealing; not least of its charms were the graceful neat waisted dresses of the ladies worn with alluring boater hats. As early

121 Philip Gardner, *Charging All Blacks*, 1979. Watercolour, $12\frac{1}{4} \times 15\frac{3}{4}$ in (31.1 × 40 cm).

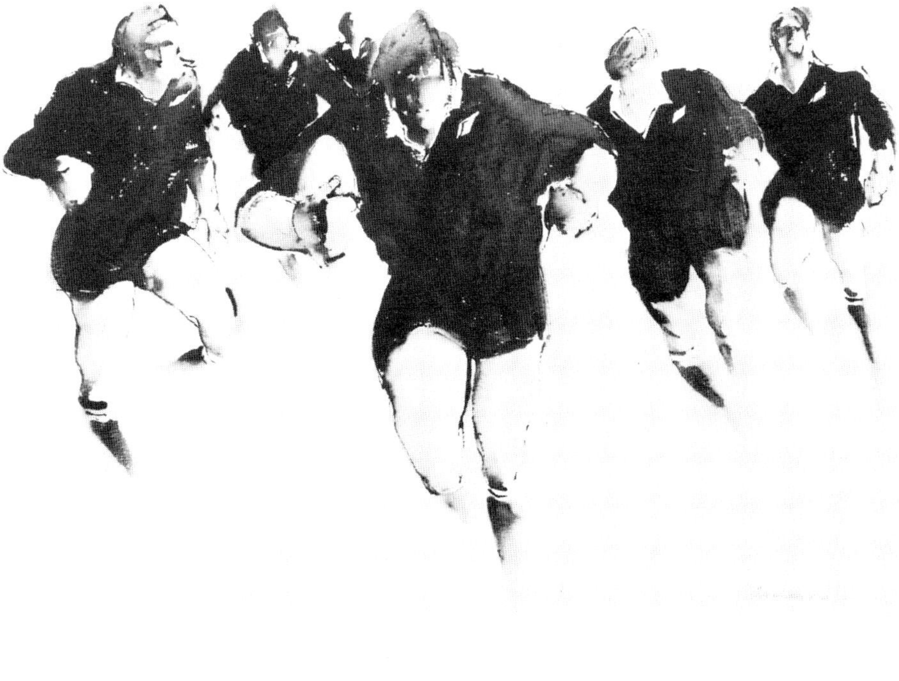

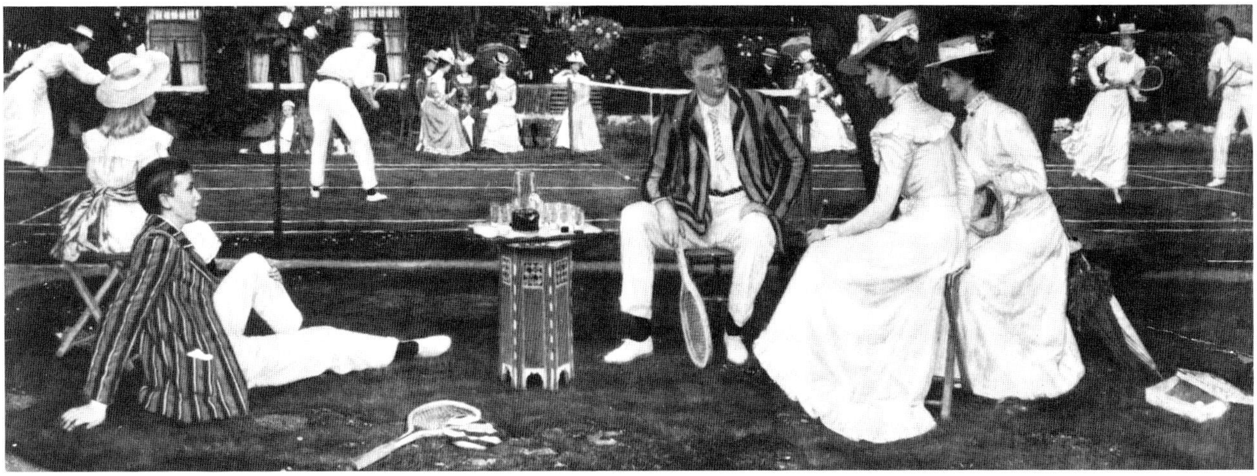

122 Charles March Gere, *The Tennis Party*, 1900. Oil on canvas, 38 × 107 in (96.5 × 271.2 cm).

123 Eric Ravilious, *Tennis* (detail), *c* 1930. Tempera on plywood panels, three panels each $32\frac{1}{4} \times 19\frac{1}{2}$ in (81.9 × 49.5 cm).

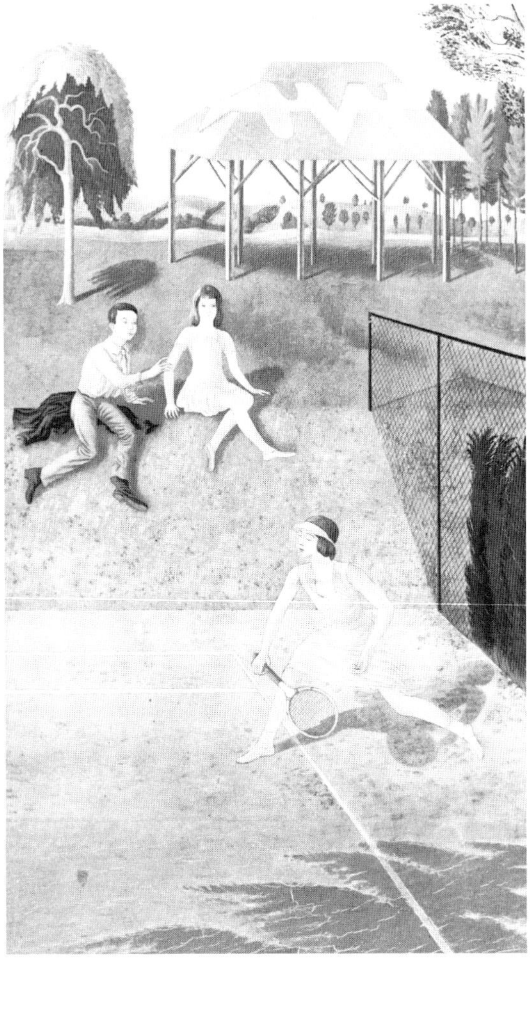

as 1896 Sir John Lavery's minor masterpiece *The Tennis Party* was exhibited at the Royal Academy. Painted in watercolours, this decorous but animated mixed doubles was received with public admiration but denigrated by certain critics for its impressionism which to the conventional Victorian eye still appeared merely capricious and imprecise. But its mood was to influence tennis compositions of the future and in particular Charles March Gere's decorative picture of the same title dated 1900 (*122*). This portrait painter and illustrator, trained at the Birmingham School of Art, where he was for many years a teacher, also subtly suggests the more serious diversion is well-bred flirtation rather than the rigours of the game. This happy social inference even three decades later is still delightfully emphasized in Eric Ravilious' lively triptych of the game executed on wooden panels (*123*).

But in the interval the approach had actually changed dramatically, as recorded in Marjory Violet Watherston's *Wimbledon*, 1923, a scene from the Centre Court Stand with the 1923 Ladies Singles Final being fought out between the invincible but temperamental Suzanne Lenglen and Kitty McKane (*124*). The composition is perhaps overdominated by a standing spectator, of obviously some importance – but who is he?

Fifty years later a contrasting Centre Court painting by Michael Lewis, the Devon humorous artist, records in bright naïve style the final awards being presented against serried ranks of officials, ballboys and grinning spectators. A still life approach to the game can be found in a modern print based on Mike Potter's *Balls Please* – a geometrical work of green grass, white lines, taut net and three unsullied balls.

By the 1970s Rosemary Taylor's huge dramatic studies of such international players as Jimmy Connors, Bjorn Borg and Virginia Wade (*132, page 206*) brought a new dimension in every sense to pictorial tennis. With canvases measuring 60 × 84 in the artist's flair for instantaneous action competes with the sharp efficiency of the camera and could perhaps be exploited more effectively in compositions of less grandiose proportions. Tennis at home and abroad absorbs many hours of television and, now played both indoors and outside, it is surely only a matter of time before contemporary artists discover exciting new facets to use pictorially; the potentials are considerable.

In contrast Real Tennis in the twentieth century has remained the esoteric diversion for the few, though since the 1970s it has certainly enjoyed a revival with a strong feminine participation. Minor artists of royal circles in the seventeenth century have left interesting records of the game but today pictorial impact is negligible. An exception can be found in the oil painting *The Dinner Match at Leamington* by Anthony Hobson, an artist himself dedicated to the game and who has also painted portraits of its great professionals, Jim Dear, a former World Champion, and Harry Johns, head professional at Lords. The picture was completed in 1982. It faithfully represents the court at Leamington and though by necessity the composition is stiff in design, there is some indication in the players' stance of the intellectual challenge of the game which has been described as an amalgam of squash and chess (*125*).

According to folklore the game of golf was originated by Scottish shepherds using their crooks to knock pebbles into rabbit holes. More credibly its roots seem to spring from the Low Countries which have considerable early pictorial records of the game. In Great Britain there are only three known paintings of golf before 1868; nevertheless by the mid-fifteenth century its popularity had jeopardised the more important martial pastime of archery. It had been played at the court of Henry VIII and by the Stuart Kings and had become known as the Royal and Ancient Game of Golf.

Its prestige accelerated at the end of the Victorian era, and many clubs had been formed, several on the outskirts of London. Artists of talent in other spheres turned to golf with its

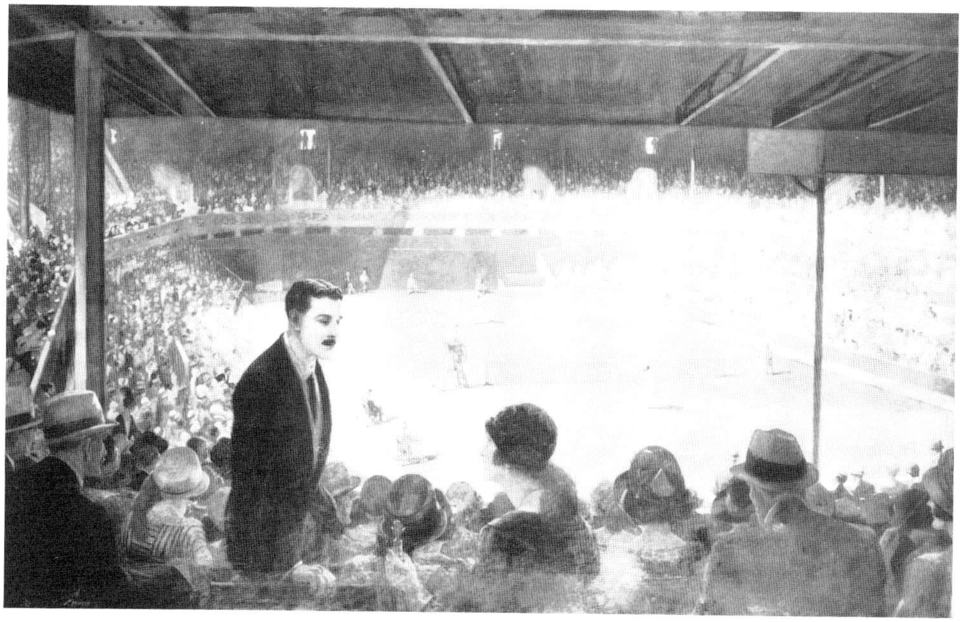

124 Marjory Violet Watherston, *Wimbledon* *1923*. Oil on canvas, 50 × 78 in (127 × 198.1 cm).

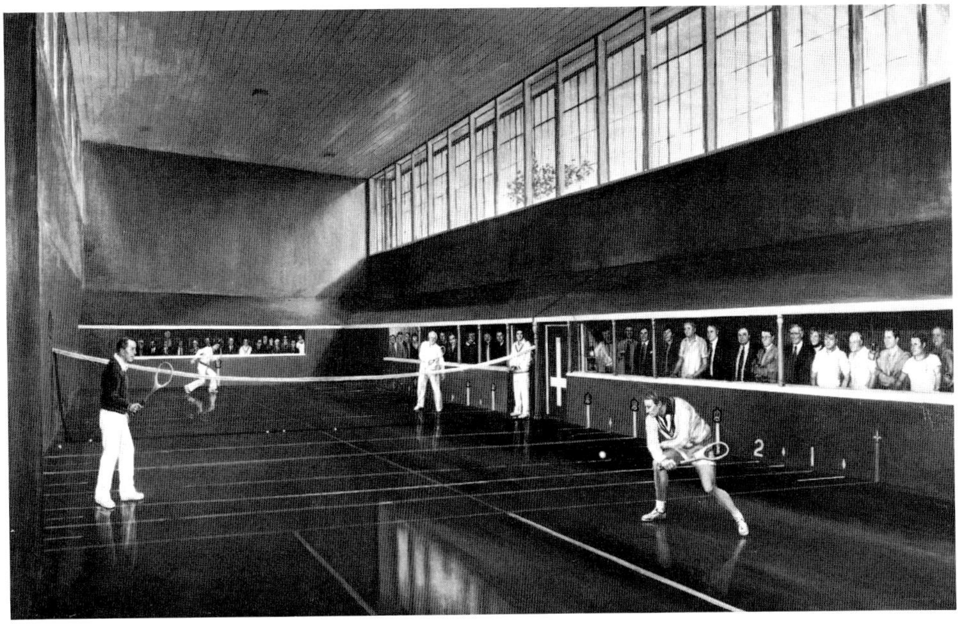

125 Anthony Hobson, *The Dinner Match at Leamington*. Oil on canvas, 60 × 96 in (152 × 243.8 cm).

appealing landscape as a subject. Sir John Lavery's splendid oil painting in the Tate Gallery of *The North Berwick Golf Course from the Ladies Tee*, dated 1918, and a complementary study of Nancy, Lady Astor, driving a long ball at the same venue come into this category. Many country clubs possess pictures of local golfing occasions, mostly of small merit but sometimes a little gem in watercolours will give unexpected pleasure.

At the beginning of this century Charles Edmund Brock, a book illustrator and portrait painter, was producing some attractive golfing studies, including a series of sepia prints of players in action on the links after Frank Paton's earlier works, and these in the sporting euphoria of the 1980s were fetching high prices in the auction rooms. Drawings by Charles Ambrose were a feature of *Country Life* in 1909/10 and these portrayed such star figures of the day as Ted Ray and James Braid (*126*). Here it was noticeable that though knickerbockers were sometimes worn by the younger fraternity, a baggy suit and cap were more often accepted costume. It was not until Sir William Orpen's fine portrait in 1929 of the Prince of Wales (later the Duke of Windsor) as Captain of the Royal West Norfolk Golf Club that exaggerated plus fours became *de rigueur*; worn with a bright Fair Isle sweater, holding a driver, the heir to the throne fills admirably the role of Prince Charming.

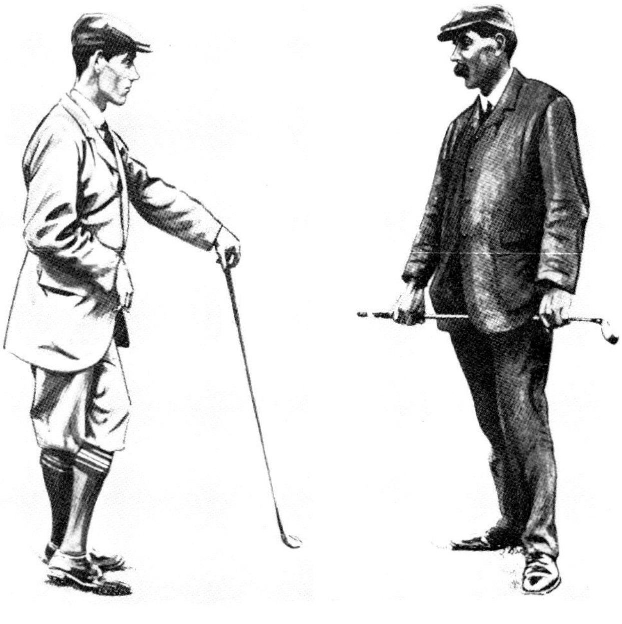

126 Charles Ambrose, *Ted Ray in 1911* and *James Braid in 1910*. Drawings from *Country Life*.

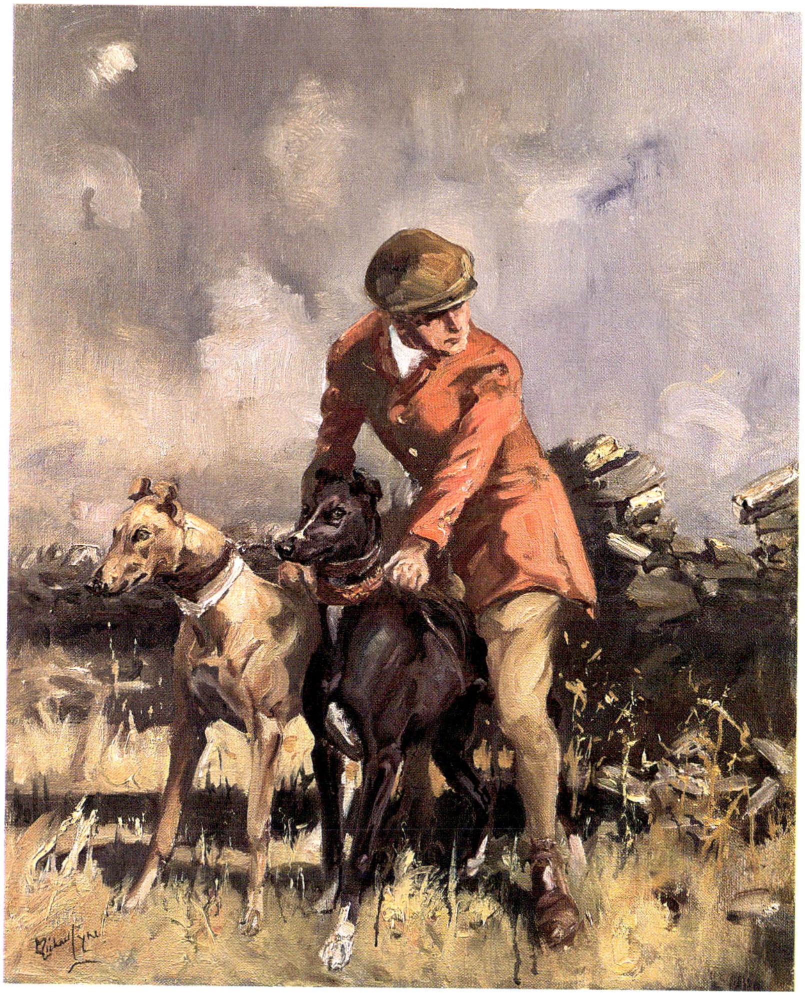

PLATE 23 (*left*) Michael Lyne, *The Slipper*, 1969. Oil on canvas, 24 × 30 in (60.9 × 76.2 cm).

(*below*) Rodger McPhail, *Roe Deer* (detail), 1984. Watercolour, $12\frac{1}{4}$ × 18 in (31.1 × 45.7 cm).

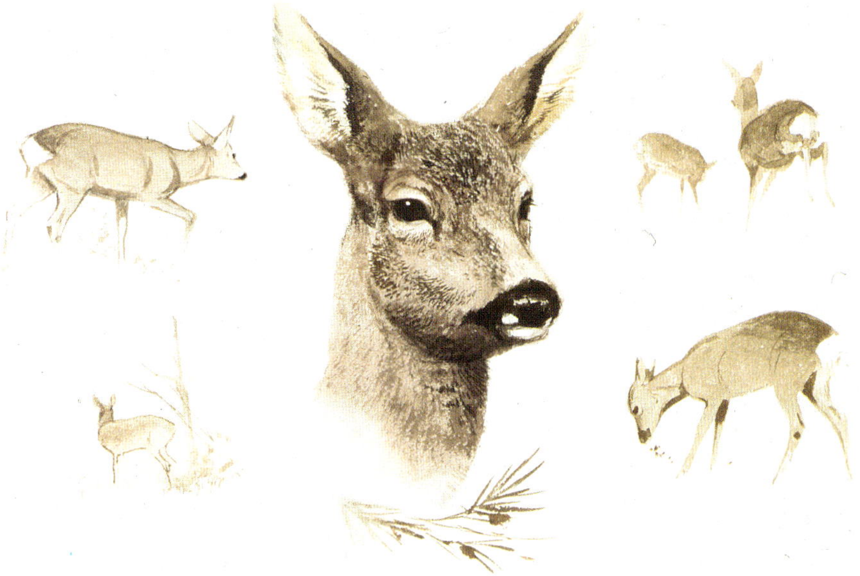

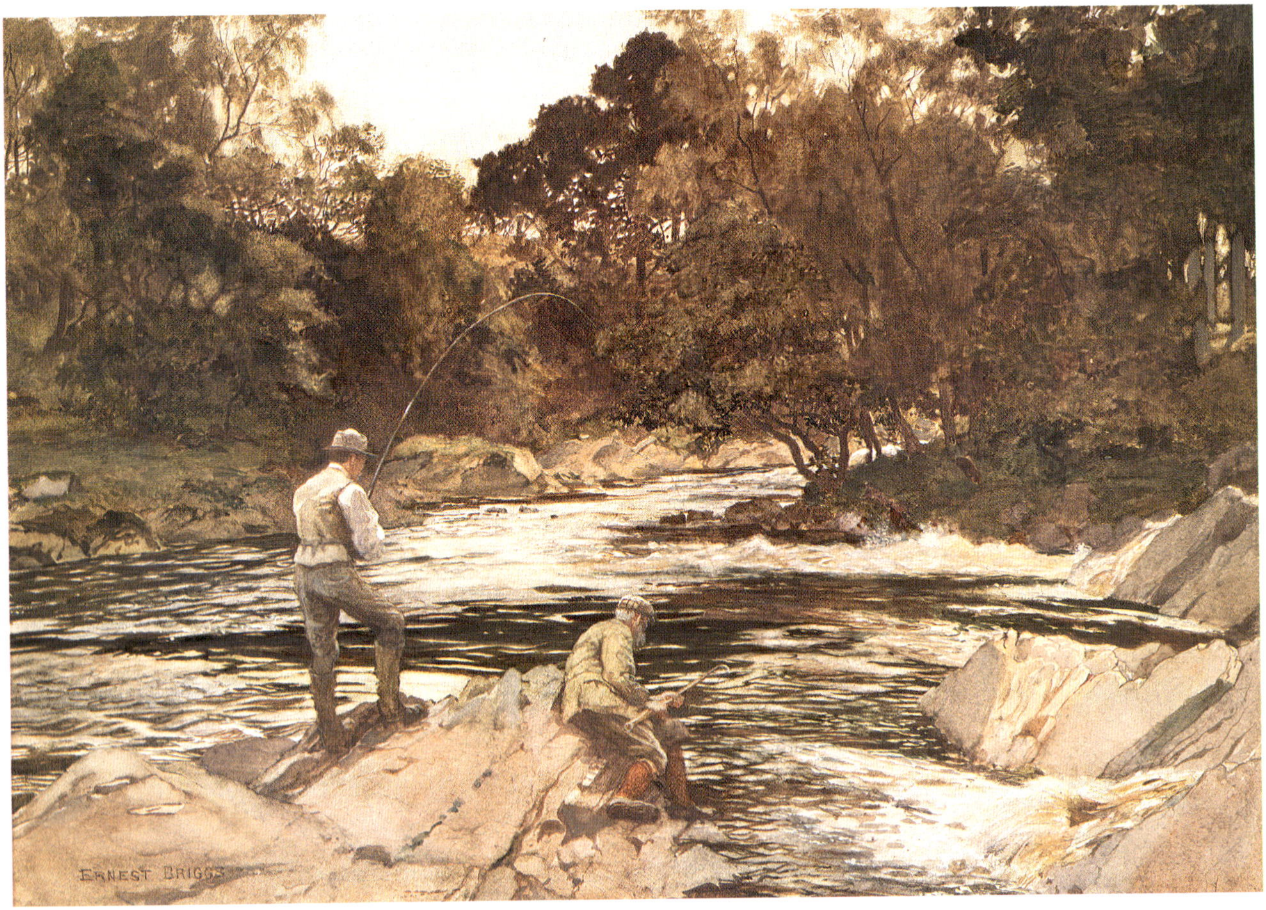

PLATE 24 (*above*) Ernest Edward Briggs, *Hooked! Salmon Fishing on the Innerwick Waters of the Lyon*, 1908. Watercolour, $12\frac{1}{2} \times 17\frac{1}{2}$ in (31.7×44.4 cm). (*below*) Albert Chevallier Tayler, *Kent v Lancashire – Canterbury*, 1906. Oil on canvas, 90×42 in (228.6×106.6 cm).

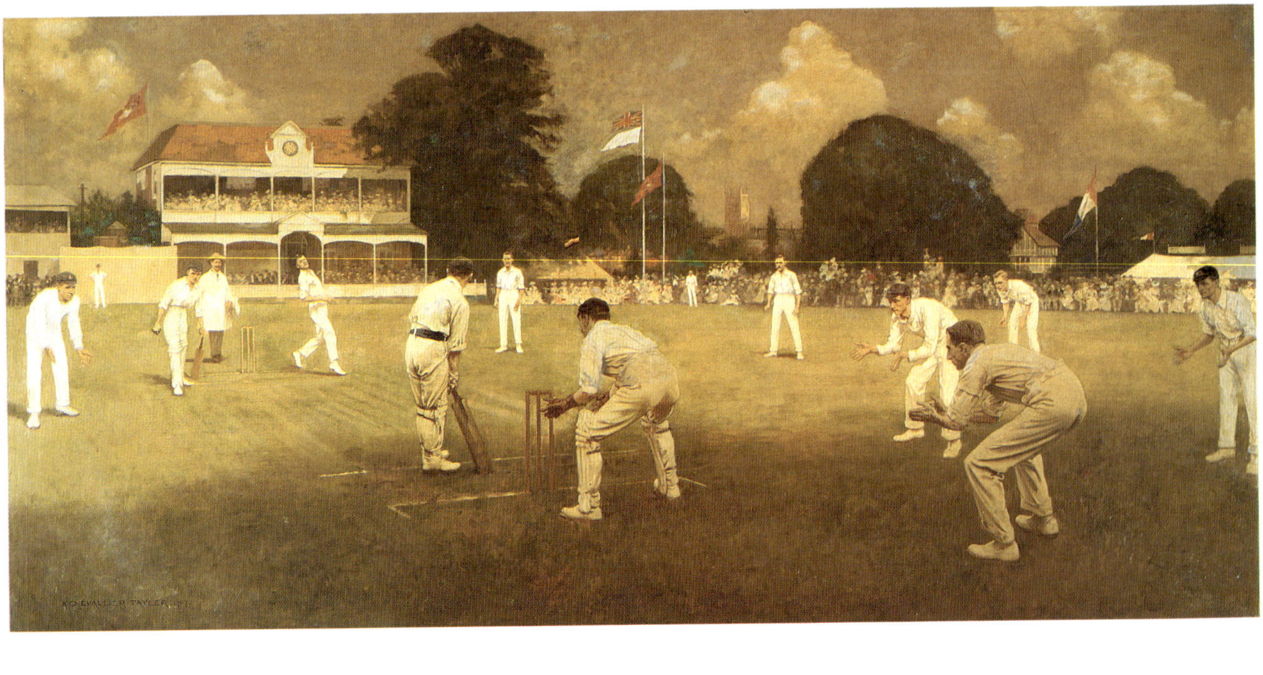

Many of the popular illustrators found rewards in using golf as a subject including that imaginative mystic Arthur Rackham and more understandably, in humorous vein, G.D. Armour, and Cecil Aldin with his set of prints of British Courses. Of course 'Spy' portrayed leading players in *Vanity Fair* and such fellow contemporaries as John Hassall, E.H. Shephard, Harry Furniss, Harry Rountree and Frank Reynolds were all regularly supplying drawings to *Punch*, for golf had developed into the people's game with a general appeal and many municipal courses were maintained. Much esteemed were Reynolds occasional watercolours in addition to his black and white drawings and Rountree illustrated Bernard Darwin's book on *British Golf Courses* with a series of watercolours. Such paintings as *Westward Ho* by Stephen Laws, with its view of the Club House and *Golf at East Brighton*, *c* 1940, by the Sussex landscape and sporting artist, Conrad Leigh, with a glimpse of St Dunstan's Castle, typify pleasing golfing scenes of the mid-century. More important, as factual record, is the painting of Severiano Ballesteros playing his tee shot at the 18th hole at Walton Heath in the 1987 European Open Championship (*127*). The artist, Julian Barrow, a specialist in stately home subjects, has found a new metier in his atmospheric pictures of golfing occasions.

Allegedly badminton is said to have developed during the last century from an informal diversion with battledore and shuttlecock to mitigate the *longeurs* of a rainy afternoon at Badminton, the Duke of Beaufort's stately home, but in actual fact India was its original cradle. But wherever its background, many visitors to the Tate Gallery will have been beguiled by David Inshaw's evocative picture *The Badminton Game*, dated 1972/73 (*128*). Originally called *Remembering Mine the Loss is, Not the Blame* from a poem by Thomas Hardy, it was painted shortly after the twenty-six-year-old artist moved to Devizes in 1971 when he fell in love, not only with the Downs and the Vale, but also with the girls playing badminton. The strong sunlight reflects this devotion and invests the picture with something of the same timeless quality of David Inshaw's lovely cricket composition.

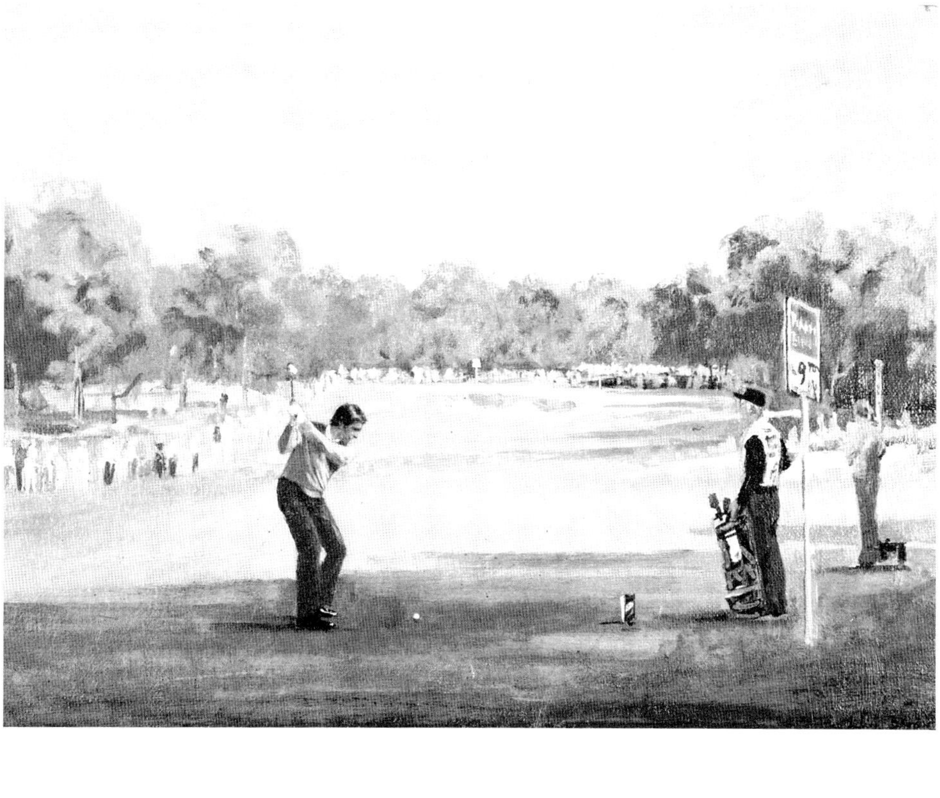

127 Julian Barrow, *The European Open Championship 1987. Seve Ballesteros playing his tee shot at the 9th hole. Old Course. Walton Heath*. Oil on canvas, 20 × 30 in (50.8 × 76.2 cm).

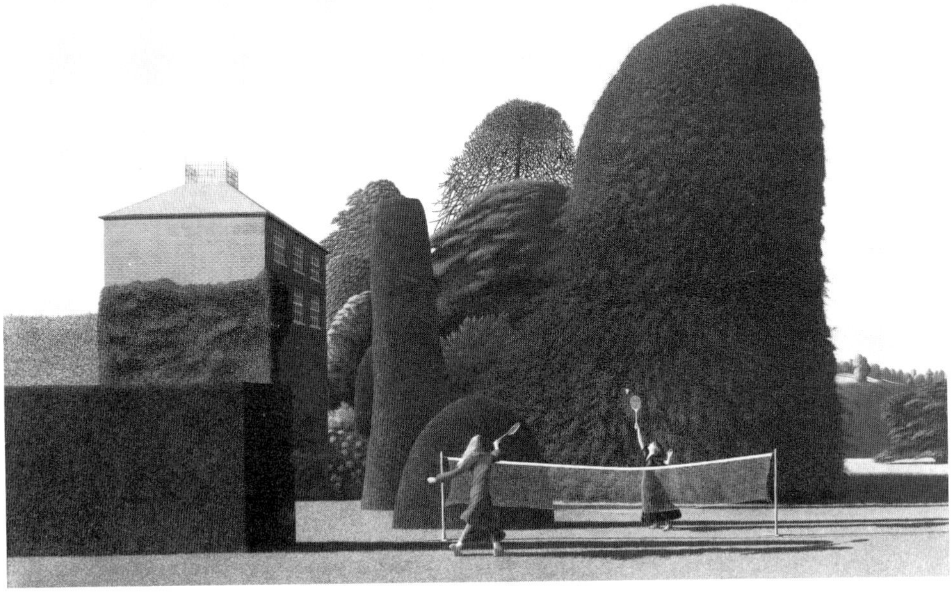

128 David Inshaw, *The Badminton Game*, 1972–3. Oil on cotton canvas, 60 × 72½ in (152.4 × 184.1 cm).

Ball games of every category have initiated many pictures of play in progress and styles and mood certainly vary from the sublime to the slightly ridiculous. Croquet was depicted by Manet with a romantic impressionism to be followed by many tranquil Edwardian studies but forty years later John Northcote Nash, RA, records its finer points with caustic caricature.

Bowls, today soaring to top popularity with regular television coverage also possesses an ancient lineage; Charles II, after his Restoration, in 1663 ordered a new bowling green at Windsor Castle. Recently the game has merited a picture by Henry Cotteril Deykin (the competent and prolific portrayer of all ball games) with concentrated play at the Saffrons Ground in Eastbourne against the red Town Hall and its clock as background. Billiards possesses pictorial records going back to the seventeenth century and in our own day Ruskin Spear celebrates the modern euphoric craze for snooker in a clever oil painting which merges tension with a comic expertise.

But outside the orbit of ball games other activities, pleasant pastimes, amusements and diversions have inspired the contemporary artist in many different directions. Rowing offers most pictures of important talent and the sport deserves its own serious artistic appraisal. In the nineteenth century the rewards could be considerable, for Henley Royal Regatta was inaugurated in 1839 for amateur oarsmen and this event alone, now one of the major social, as well as sporting, occasions of the year, has produced innumerable compositions. In our own day artists such as Charles Bone, Jeremy C.G. King and of course Charles Cundall have brought the colourful scene alive in varied style and all using sunlight, river reflections and animated figures as also observed with such clarity by Sir John Lavery in his *Maidenhead Regatta*. John Jonas, who specialises in the 1980s in depicting the spectator view of sport at the more fashionable meetings has also evoked the sunlit Thames-side scene of pretty girls, handsome young men and a glimpse of toiling oarsmen. In a different aquatic context yachting holds a paramount position ever since King Edward VII was fired with enthusiasm for *Britannia* and the Cowes festivities. In the first edition of the periodical the *Yachting Monthly*, (now over eighty years old), the King was featured as 'The Yachtsman of the Month.' The royal context was probably responsible for the extravagant sum of £23,100 paid in January 1988 for a sparkling picture by Charles E. Turner after an estimated price of £2000–£3000. With the title *Before the Start*, it shows *Britannia* with *Shamrock V*, *Astra* and other famous contenders at Cowes in the 1930s with the royal yacht *Victoria and Albert* in the distance – a record price for a delightful painting which presages soaring values for similar scenes (*129*).

It is curious that the establishment of greyhound racing at the White City and the Belle Vue Stadium at Manchester in the 1920s has produced so few contemporary pictures for it triggered off a wave of enthusiasm for the sport. Though teeming in atmosphere and colour with excited crowds and competing greyhounds in sweeping floodlights, the scene has been largely neglected by artists of proven talent. Certainly between the Wars Gilbert Holiday used this subject effectively on one occasion; John Skeaping, even with his close personal involvement with the sport, only rarely painted the actual stadium environment, though these few studies in gouache and oils brilliantly capture the split second speed and tension. More recently Vic Grainger, born in 1931 in Mansfield, Nottinghamshire, and a student of commercial art, early in his career became steeped in the local world of whippet and greyhound racing. Today sporting commissions have taken over and his stadium studies also cleverly suggest the thrill of a race in progress (*130*).

Early in the century Jack Yeats brought to life the boxing world of East End London in arresting black and white drawings and Anna Zinkeisen painted a vivid boxing scene at the National Sporting Club. Nearer our own day Philip Gardner has also found aggressive males in the ring an exciting motivation for swift impressions of sport in action.

Many other activities could be mentioned, some only recorded in isolated pictures, but it is notable how certain artists of the traditional sporting equestrian school have veered on occasion to a completely divergent subject such as Cecil Aldin in skating and Charles Simpson, memorable for those galloping scenes of the Shires, with a clever fencing study ably executed in grisaille.

129 Charles E. Turner, *Before the Start – Cowes*. Watercolour heightened by bodycolour, 16½ × 29 in (41.9 × 73.7 cm).

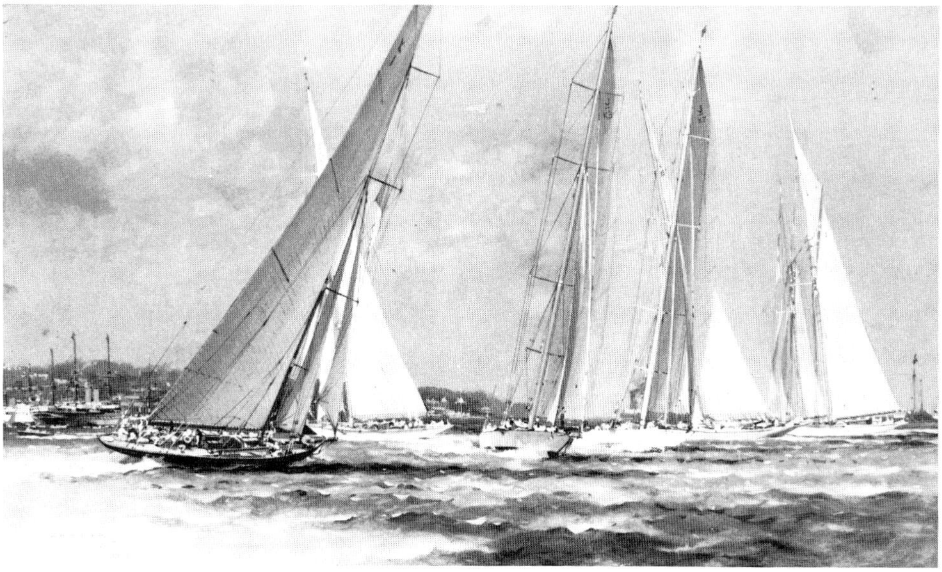

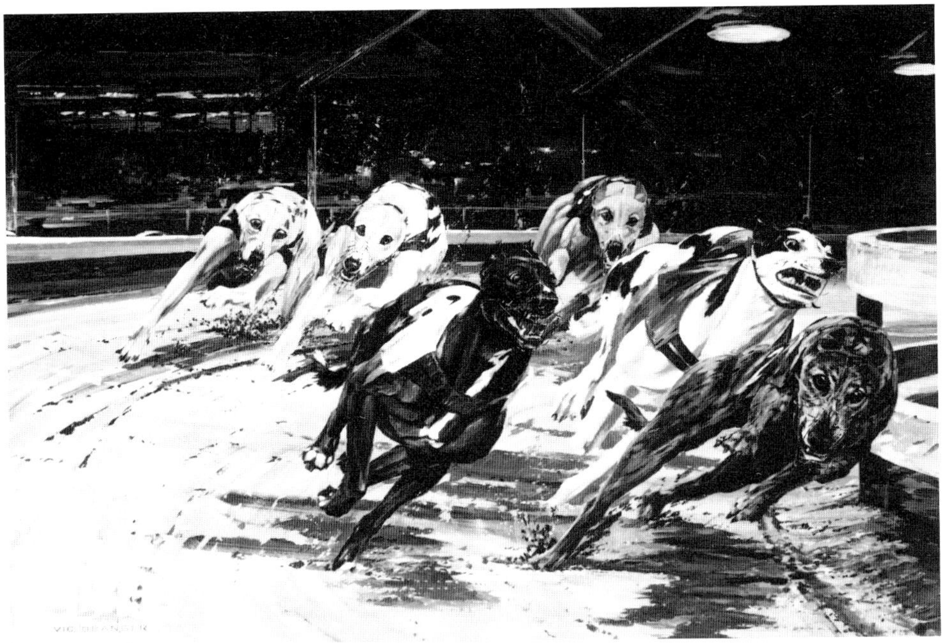

130 Vic Grainger, *At the Last*, 1988. Acrylic, 20 × 30 in (50.8 × 76.2 cm).

Sporting art has been termed a narcotic against mechanisation but one of the most exciting and hazardous sports of this century has been concerned with the motor car, whether in active track racing at Brooklands, the Grand Prix Endurance Test at Le Mans for touring cars inaugurated in 1923 and lasting 24 hours or in such contests as the Monte Carlo Rally and local hill climbs. This new vision of speed offered abundant pictorial material for the twentieth century artist and many found the challenge irresistible. Frank Wootton, Terence Cuneo and the big game specialist David Shepherd painted scenes alive with split-second cornering, glistening tarmac and hot oil. But the real master of the romance and drama of motor sport in the 1930s was the incomparable Gordon Crosby. His technical knowledge acquired in the Daimler drawing offices, allied to burning enthusiasm made his studies of Bentleys, Bugattis and Maseratis vying for the lead in some international contest as colourful and as pictorially exciting as any equine drama at Becher's Brook. By brilliant use of colour and contrasting light and shadow he invested cars and their drivers with an heroic glamour. An exhibition of his work was put on at the National Book League in 1978.

It is obvious much information awaits collation on many more activities of the twentieth century but in the meantime the modern sporting artist need find no lack of stimulating subjects outside the conventional confines of the horse world.

As recently as Boxing Day 1987 Simon Barnes, Sports Correspondent of *The Times*, was lamenting the deplorable design, material and craftsmanship of trophies presented for such contemporary sports and pastimes as badminton, cycling, snooker and even football and tennis. Skill and beauty had all played their part, he maintained, in the attainment of victory, and these qualities should surely be reflected in their trophies. What an opportunity here for the talent and initiative of artists and sculptors of the twenty-first century!

NOTES

1 *The Guinness Book of Sporting Facts*, Guinness Superlatives Ltd, 1984.

2 Mary Ann Wingfield, *Ball Games*, Antique Collectors Club, 1988.

18

The Century in Retrospect

As Dogberry so succinctly declared in *Much Ado About Nothing* 'comparisons are odorous' so perhaps it is inappropriate to relate the school of British sporting art in our own time to the preceding centuries. From 1700–1900 there had been a certain calm continuity in the way of life; admittedly the Enclosure Acts, the Repeal of the Corn Laws and the Industrial Revolution had been major influences which sporting pictures had in various ways reflected. But with the twentieth century a totally new mechanised world emerged, followed by two major wars, nuclear fission and the arrival of man on the moon. Life was never going to be the same again for either the rural or the urban population of this country.

Understandably, contemporary art had reacted in a gamut of excess ranging from Cubism to Abstract Impressionism. In contrast the sporting school remained almost impervious to the impact of these startling new horizons. Its stylistic innovations during the century have been comparatively restrained and it must be admitted that even today when the countryside has become the accepted playground of the town dweller, sporting art still tends to remain constant to its past traditions, with its hunting scenes and equestrian portraits echoing the style and approach of commissions in vogue before the two World Wars. Certainly an infiltration of effective impressionism has gradually stimulated mood and movement and since the 1970s has assumed increasing dominance in the racing scene and in studies outside field sports. But Edwards, Munnings and Skeaping have each, in their individual style, predominantly stamped this century with their recognisable hallmarks.

The school of British sporting art is a genre in which masterpieces rarely appear, possibly because its artists, not infrequently, must submit to the dictates of their patrons – horse owners in particular wear determined rose-coloured spectacles – and, as Walter Shaw Sparrow so neatly expressed their predicament, 'Those who live to please must please to live'. Yet in spite of this Cinderella role many pictorial gems have appeared in this century as in the past.

Though the popularity of hunting, racing and all field sports was growing apace, exhibitions of sporting art in actual public galleries were rare – such indigenous subjects lacked cultural appeal. Of course, London art dealers regularly put on sporting collections and the capital was rich in such long established firms as Arthur Ackermann & Son, Frost & Reed, Fores and others who for more than a hundred years had been the shop windows of sporting art.

But it was left to charitable causes to trigger off some public initiative. And in 1928, in aid of hunt servants and jockeys fallen on hard times, an exhibition, 'Sport in the Midlands', found an appropriate venue in the Leicestershire Museum and Art Gallery. Though somewhat hampered by the geographical limitations of the title, it included four Stubbs, and, of course, generous representation of the local masters, Marshall and Ferneley. Also finding a place was

Munnings' fine portrait of the Prince of Wales on Forest Witch. His Royal Highness was hunting regularly in Leicestershire at that time.

Three years later in 1931 a loan collection of over 100 sporting paintings was put on, under the aegis of the Viscount and Viscountess Allandale, to boost the funds of the London Foot Hospital. Works by most of the important sporting artists of the eighteenth and nineteenth centuries, including half a dozen Stubbs, were among the treasures emerging from stately homes. Some modern exponents, such as Lionel Edwards, Charles Simpson and Alfred Munnings also shared the welcome publicity.

In 1937 the magazine *Country Life* sponsored an exhibition in aid of the National Trust, depicting facets of 'British Country Life Through the Centuries'. Amongst over 800 items, and sharing space with such artefacts as eighteenth century badger tongs and pillion saddles, the exhibits of sporting paintings included works by John Wootton, James Ward and Thomas Rowlandson with George Stubbs' *Racehorses Training at Goodwood* to provide the *pièce de résistance*. Again the contemporaries were not ignored with Michael Lyne, John Skeaping and A.J. Munnings taking their place.

Most remarkably, in 1943, with the Second World War reaching its most desperate stage, to its eternal credit the County Borough of Preston opened the doors of its Harris Museum and Art Gallery, under its Art Director S.H. Pavière, to an admirable loan selection of British Sporting Paintings. Amongst nearly 150 exhibits (no mean feat of assembly with transport heavily restricted) especially notable were eleven works by Henry Chalon. His Majesty King George VI had generously sent from Windsor, to face the hazards of travel and enemy action, a George Stubbs' masterpiece *The Prince of Wales' Two Chestnut Saddle Horses with Anderson the Groom*.

Significantly, and not unusual on these occasions, the writer of the foreword of the catalogue was Major Guy Paget, the instigator and organiser of most of these private exhibitions. This indefatigible foxhunter of the Shires also carried a burning enthusiasm for the school of British sporting art. He was amongst the first to realise that the increasing purchases of these pictures between the wars by such appreciative Americans hunting in Leicestershire as Ambrose Clark, Victor Emmanual and later Paul Mellon, and in the racing sphere such international sportsmen as Sir Abe Bailey and Mr 'Solly' Joel, would eventually lead to the general exodus overseas of our finest works. His was a repetitive voice calling loud and long in the wilderness for a National Gallery of British Sporting Art. As early as 1922 Walter Shaw Sparrow had written 'The old British pictures belong to the nation's history'[1] Alfred Munnings echoed this *cri du coeur*, and even more vociferously from 1925 onwards the annual plea for the same cause by A.C.R. Carter, editor of *The Year's Art Annual*, makes salutory reading. He cautioned 'there seems to be no end to the resources of America,' and 'note should be taken of their growing cult of acquiring sporting, hunting and racing pictures of Old England,' and continued in 1932 'we still wait that yearned for necessity a National Gallery of Sporting Pictures'.[2]

Admittedly in 1934 part of the private collection of Mr H.W. Arthurton and Mrs Carstairs had been briefly exhibited in a small sporting room at the Tate Gallery but within two years it was transferred to the Whitechapel Art Gallery. Nevertheless, David Fincham, the art historian, in *Apollo*, hailed these pictures as 'of such historical interest . . . that their artistic merits can speak for themselves'.

But great opportunities were lost: Sir Abe Bailey could find no British gallery to give a home to his fine collection so it was bequeathed to his native National Gallery at Cape Town; Mr Walter Stonor's eighty-five sporting paintings were accepted by the Walker Art Gallery at Liverpool but then relegated to the store below stairs for almost fifty years. At the end of the 1930s it had seemed possible that Lord Duveen might contemplate the funding of a national scheme in spite of his own total disinterest in sport of any kind; but any generous gesture was inhibited by his belief that Sir Philip Sassoon intended to finance a sporting national gallery. The onset of the Second World War, of course, terminated all such ideas.

Nevertheless a year before peace was declared Major Guy Paget in April 1944 contributed three long articles to *The Field* on 'Planning a National Sporting Gallery'. Never in the blackest days of imminent invasion did he lose his enthusiasm for the cause of British sporting art. As already briefly recorded it was Walter Hutchinson, the publisher, who gave the dream a transient reality in 1949 when he opened the National Gallery of British Sports and Pastimes at Derby House. It was a polyglot collection of 618 paintings (with over another 2000 in reserve) and though badly hung, ineffectively lit and with some doubtful attributions, it must be hailed as a courageous achievement of great potential. But organised with basic financial weaknesses, the untimely death of Walter Hutchinson forced the swift dispersal of the collection in 1951–52 by Christie's at three auction sales for derisory sums. Today it seems hardly credible that John Wootton's *Flying Childers* was sold for fifteen guineas. Pictures by Seymour, Sawrey Gilpin, Herring and Marshall went for a few hundreds. Similarly, this sale had been preceded by the dispersal of the Arthurton collection in 1949 in which only the Agasse picture of *Lord Rivers Stud Farm at Stratfield Saye* reached four figures (1800 guineas) and very few even hundreds. Thus was the nucleus of a magnificent national collection of sporting art irredeemably scattered for the lack of any national initiative and appreciation.

However, a tiny flicker of public interest had been aroused. In 1951 the Walker Art Gallery put on an exhibition of works by Stubbs and this was followed in 1957 by a fine display of the artist's pictures in the Whitechapel Art Gallery, the first important Stubbs' exhibition in London for over seventy years. This had been initiated and selected in greater part by Mr Basil Taylor, the art historian, whose scholarly articles and a monograph published in 1971 of Stubbs were to precede his definitive work on the artist, sadly never accomplished owing to his tragic death in 1975. The impact, however, of these two exhibitions outside the converted cognoscenti was small. Paradoxically it was left to the quiet enthusiasm of an American, Mr Paul Mellon, who once described himself as 'a galloping anglophile', to awaken the British public to the merits of the school of British Sporting art in a winter exhibition in the Royal Academy 1964–65 of 'Painting in England 1700–1850 from the Collection of Mr and Mrs Paul Mellon.' In his youth at Cambridge University where he read history, Paul Mellon had also acquired his lifelong dedication to the culture of this country and his love of English foxhunting.

Over the years he had steadily, with discrimination and genuine appreciation, under the guidance of Mr Basil Taylor assembled his collection of pictures, drawings and engravings. In 1962 he had generously established in London the Paul Mellon Centre for Studies in British Art. The *Daily Telegraph* hailed the Royal Academy exhibition of 304 paintings in headlines of 'delight and dismay' for here, to our eternal shame, was a national collection this country had never made. One gallery alone was devoted to fifteen works by Stubbs, but fine paintings by Seymour, Wootton, Marshall and Ward all bore splendid evidence of the rich talent and variety of the British sporting school, and minor works of great appeal by such lesser names as Pollard, Webb and Gooch only served to emphasise our lost heritage. In 1977 Paul Mellon built the Yale Center for British Art for his English collection, a magnificent gift for his old American university – but a nucleus of sporting pictures is still retained at the Mellon home in Virginia for personal enjoyment.

Though this exhibition in the Royal Academy had brought an attendance of only 47,195, the lowest since the war, it was to prove a catalyst. Two years later at the Queen's Gallery at Buckingham Palace a collection of 'Animal Painting from Van Dyke to Nolan' was put on with many fine examples of sporting pictures from the Royal private apartments. Several works by Sawrey Gilpin, originally commissioned by the Duke of Cumberland, and J.F. Herring's *Tajar and Hamar* that had not been seen in London for a long time were on display. In addition never had George IV's extravagant, and often unpaid patronage of George Stubbs seemed more justified with the appearance of such gems as *Laetitia, Lady Lade riding in the Park* and *The Prince of Wales' Phaeton*.

In 1967, the bi-centenary of the birth of Ben Marshall had been commemorated (a year too early it was later discovered) and the 150th anniversary of the birth of John Leech by a joint exhibition at the Leicester Museum and Art Gallery with two first class collections of the sporting scene under the guidance of Lionel Lambourne. Impetus slowly continued and in 1974 the Arts Council of Great Britain was responsible for an exhibition of 'British Sporting Paintings 1650–1850' at the Hayward Gallery which later, in modified form, travelled to the Leicester Museum and Art Gallery and then to the Walker Art Gallery in Liverpool. This was a major triumph, for Sir Oliver Millar in his scholarly introduction to the catalogue admitted that 'sporting painting cannot continue to be treated as if much of it did not exist. And it does not become the art historian to suggest that the study of sporting art in England leads him to fields in which he is not required to trespass.'

Even in the forbidding concrete environs of the Hayward Gallery the impact of these 304 pictures was impressive. Numerous loans for the exhibition from stately homes, country houses and more humble sources dispelled the smear of overall artistic mediocrity with which the art purists had denigrated the sporting genre for more than half a century. Here was stimulating evidence that many of these pictures, in addition to being pleasing records of social history and vanished rural scenes, were pleasing works of art in their own right.

It was gratifying to see that so many still remained in this country – but for how long? Admittedly the sale overseas of the James Seymour painting *A Kill at Ashdown Park* had, in 1969, been held up by the Reviewing Committee of the Export of Works of Art and had been acquired by the Tate Gallery for the record sum of £63,000 with the help of various organisations and unexpectedly generous subscriptions from the public. But there was no cessation to the number of pictures being sold abroad. Mr Mellon's acquisitions quietly continued and now, in the late 1960s, he was joined by an impatient American rival in the person of Mr Jack R. Dick, a wealthy cattle contractor, who decided to amass a comparable collection with no loss of time, and money no object. A flood of our finest works crossed the Atlantic. But within a few years the collection had to be dispersed on behalf of the United States Government for tax debts. The 466 pictures were brought back to London to be sold by Sotheby's in four separate sales between October 1973 and April 1976. However considerable legal controversy preceded the first auction regarding alleged forged invoices and an Extraordinary Meeting of the Society of London Art Dealers was held before the matter was cleared up and authenticity of ownership unequivocally established.

Knowledgeable dealers had guided the Dick purchases so it was a fine galaxy of sporting art released on the market. The suggestion of scandal and chicanery had aroused world interest and it was no surprise when the paintings realised record prices. Jack Dick himself died at the age of forty-six before the second auction.

These events brought no hint of a national collection. However, when an appeal had been made at the end of 1971 to save Titian's masterpiece *Death of Actaeon* for the National Gallery, letters had appeared in the press suggesting that money might be better spent on safeguarding works by our own native artists.[3]

But the idea of a British collection of sporting art had never been totally in abeyance in the minds of both Mr Peter Johnson, Director of the Lowndes Lodge Art Gallery, and the author of this book. A search over the years for suitable premises, finance and pictures had been continuous but inauspicious – 'never the time and the place and the loved one altogether' – and time was certainly running out. Many of the organisations and individuals approached considered that the door was being locked long after the horses had departed. Nevertheless under the aegis of Peter Johnson and Stella A. Walker in 1974 a small committee was formed of which Mr Anthony Barbour, a collector of sporting art, Mr A.L. Gates, Director of Ackermann & Son, Mr John Wood, author of *A Dictionary of British Animal Painters* and Dr R.B. Fountain, a writer on the subject and lifelong devotee, were members. (It was through Robert Fountain's initiative and dedicated work as the second Executive Chairman of the British Sporting Art Trust that so many future plans came to fruition.) They were joined later by Mr N.C. Selway, a writer and specialist on the works of James Pollard, and the Marquess of Dufferin and Ava who had been responsible for much of the organisation of the exhibition at the Hayward Gallery.

In its Annual Report of 1966 the Tate Gallery had stated that 'it was particularly regrettable for instance that so characteristic a feature as the English School of Sporting Art should remain comparatively unrepresented at the centre. It becomes yearly more apparent that unless we can improve our showing within this field scholars will have to go in future as far as the USA where the Mellon Collection will provide what Britain is failing to do.' This was the guideline for the newly formed committee to make an approach to the Tate Gallery. Its Director, Sir Norman Reid, eventually announced that his Trustees had agreed that when current building operations were completed, accommodation would be made available for a collection of British sporting art in the Tate Gallery. Dr Martin Butlin, Keeper of the British Collection and Mrs Judy Egerton, art historian and specialist on George Stubbs, joined the Committee to represent the Gallery.

In 1977 the British Sporting Art Trust was then formed with the Committee members as its original Trustees. Charity status was approved and an advisory Honorary Council appointed amongst whom were the Duke of Beaufort, The Earl Fitzwilliam, Major Sir Reginald and Lady Macdonald-Buchanan, Mr Dorian Williams, the Marquess of Townshend and Mr Paul Mellon. The final seal of approval was the gracious patronage of Queen Elizabeth the Queen Mother. The liaison with the Tate was to work well with the Gallery having first call on any works offered to the Trust.

Once launched, gifts and loans of some good pictures became available. Lady Price presented the Trust with two paintings of sporting dogs by George Stubbs. Works by Ferneley, Herring, Pollard and Landseer were forthcoming but without the support of Mr Paul Mellon progress would have been minimal. An approach was made to him (somewhat tentatively it must be admitted) for the loan of perhaps a couple of pictures from his collection. His generous response brought amazed delight – fifteen could be expected with a view perhaps to eventual bequest! After twelve months this proposition was revised and became the outright gift of thirty sporting paintings to the Tate Gallery through the British Sporting Art Trust. In his letter to Sir Norman Reid, Mr Mellon wrote 'by making this gift I have been encouraged by the fine efforts of the British Sporting Art Trust to assemble at the Tate a good and representative collection of British sporting art.' It was a splendid nucleus for a national collection with works by Agasse, Alken, Herring, Stubbs, Ward and other major artists of the British sporting school.

Within two years, under the will of Mrs Ambrose Clark, widow of that enthusiastic American foxhunter in Leicestershire between the Wars, the Trust received seventeen paintings from his collection, which were then given to the Tate. Fine examples by Ferneley, Marshall, Cooper and Pollard established with other individual gifts and loans to the Trust, a collection of pictures that can be considered admirably representative of the school of British sporting art. Adequate gratitude to our American benefactors is hard to express for, in addition, their support continues in the formation of the Friends of British Sporting Art in the United States.

But the Trust stood on its own feet. Provincial interests were encouraged when Mr Richard Green, the Director of the York City Art Gallery, joined the Executive Committee and this northern venue became available for activities sponsored by the Trust. Various exhibitions were organised from 1977 onwards, first at the King's Lynn Festival, then through the generosity of the Earl of Halifax his important collection of racing pictures, seldom seen in public, were loaned for almost two years for exhibition at the Tate and York City Art Galleries. In addition it received on indefinite loan, and finally purchased, the British Council's collection of over 100 sporting prints, unseen for fifteen years. These were displayed in a dozen galleries in various parts of the country as far apart as Doncaster and Exeter.

Through the generous sponsorship of Mr Edmund Vestey it had been possible in 1985 to open a gallery of British sporting art at the National Horseracing Museum at Newmarket to complement the permanent collection at the Tate and periodic displays at the York City Art Gallery. Recognition had also been given by the Trust to twentieth century sporting art in three London exhibitions of works by Snaffles, by artists working from 1900–1950 and by a Lionel Edwards collection, which was also shown at the Leicester Museum and Art Gallery and seen by over 12,000 members of the public. A library has been established at the York City Art Gallery, a slide collection has been formed, twenty essays on sporting artists printed, lectures given and visits to public and private collections of pictures at home and abroad arranged. Two works of paramount importance to art historians have been compiled by Trust members and published – *A Bibliography of British Sporting Artists* by Norah M. Titley (sponsored by Sotheby's) and *An Inventory of British Sporting Art in United Kingdom Public Collections* by Gerald L. Pendred.

Obviously the work of the Trust is long term but already it has significantly enhanced the prestige and recognition of British sporting art in this country. It is, inevitably, a specialised interest, its finances are largely dependent on benefactors and sponsors in which up to date it has been uniquely blessed. A satisfying feature has been the generous support of the leading firms dealing in sporting art and by the big auction houses. But it cannot be envisaged that the Trust's assets will ever permit major purchases at current soaring prices. It has been possible to acquire a few paintings by minor artists, and some bronzes, but whatever the future holds for the British Sporting Art Trust it should not be forgotten that its formation was responsible for over fifty fine sporting works finding their permanent home in the Tate Gallery.

Looking back it is evident that a lively interest in the British sporting school has at last been aroused and at an influential level. Though the Royal Academy had failed to commemorate in any way in 1978 the centenary of the birth of its Past President, Sir Alfred Munnings, amends were made a year later with its Derby Day 200 Exhibition for the bicentenary anniversary of the first running of the race. AJ would certainly have rejoiced at this stimulating collection of pictures and memorabilia, selected and catalogued with imaginative flair by Patricia Connor and Lionel Lambourne. Posters, photographs and films and even a gypsy caravan in the hallowed quadrangle of Burlington House, all added to the impact of this splendid sporting occasion. Another encouraging straw in the wind was an exhibition of works by John Wootton 'Landscape and Sporting Art in Early Georgian England' initiated in July 1984 by the Greater London Council in the fine setting of Kenwood.

But greater glory lay ahead at the Tate Gallery where in October of that year George Stubbs was honoured with an exhibition at last worthy of the genius of the artist. The brainchild of Judy Egerton, Assistant Keeper of the British Collection at the Tate Gallery and erudite compiler of the Catalogues of 'The Paul Mellon Collection of British Sporting and Animal Paintings', this exhibition with nearly 200 items was an unforgettable experience and was certainly one of the great occasions for British sporting art in the twentieth century.

Though articles on current exhibitions and sporting artists, past and present, received regular coverage in such periodicals as *Country Life, The Field, Art, The British Racehorse, Horse & Hound* and even an occasional feature in such art glossies as *Apollo* and the *Burlington Magazine*, the national press rarely vouchsafed a serious review of current sporting art exhibitions (Stubbs at the Tate, was of course, an exception). Collections of important eighteenth and nineteenth century sporting pictures were exhibited twice a year by such established London firms as Ackermann & Son, the Richard Green Gallery, Frost & Reed and Pawsey & Payne but left the art critics silent. New names were launched by the Tryon and Moorland Gallery and the Malcolm Innes Gallery but merited not a word. Sporting art had still to emerge from its Cinderella image.

However, money speaks louder than prejudice and nothing in the sale rooms has been more remarkable in this century than the soaring price of sporting pictures. In the 1960s the American purchasers, followed by the investments in this sphere of the British Rail Pension Fund, had launched a price spiral of all the major eighteenth and nineteenth century sporting artists. Though there had been a general art market recession between 1980–1984 the price surge had continued for sporting works, to reach six figures for paintings by Stubbs, Wootton, Marshall and Munnings.

By July 1986 the Herring/Pollard painting of *The Doncaster Gold Cup 1838*, had sold at Christie's for £777,600. Three years later, in June 1987, national newspapers certainly headlined the sale in New York of Stubbs' *Baron de Robeck* riding a Bay Hunter for a world record price of $2,420,000 – nearly a million and a half pounds for a Stubbs! One of our oldest and most respected London art dealers remembered in his youth paying £35 for the artist's portrait of the racehorse Tristram Shandy, sold on this same American occasion for £655,523. *Autres temps autres moeurs* – indeed! The British sporting art Cinderella had at last acquired her crystal slippers!

As the value of these works of the eighteenth and nineteenth century show no signs of lessening, the less wealthy collectors have turned to artists working at the end of the Victorian era. Pictures by Heywood Hardy, Thomas Blinks and Godfrey Giles are now approaching the five figure bracket. Munnings' racing painting *At the Starting Post: Study No. 4*, a subject never considered amongst his major masterpieces, in 1987 sold in New York for £703,488. But it is safe to prophesy where Munnings is concerned the sky will be the limit; in the last fifteen years his prices have risen by 540 per cent in the Art Index. Works by Lionel Edwards, available for a few hundreds at the time of his death in 1966, as the century nears its end, are eagerly bought for many thousands. Equally, Gilbert Holiday's values have already taken a steep jump upwards. In November 1988, to general amazement, a life-size bronze of a mare and foal by Adrian Jones was sold by Sotheby's to a private buyer for £286,000. Does this presage a revival in monumental animal sculpture? It is safe to say that British sporting art will never be undervalued again; however, it is probably true, that in this late twentieth century euphoria, its merits in many cases may be over estimated. Popular appeal and investment prospects have played their part but quality must be the ultimate and lasting criterion.

Today, as in the past, it is still the horse that sustains the leading role in the sporting school and the formation in 1978 of the Society of Equestrian Artists by Air Vice-Marshal Norman Hoad, CVO, CB, AFC, with Terence Cuneo as President, by its annual London exhibition, has provided a welcome new forum.

In the 1980s a multitude of new names of sporting artists and sculptors has appeared in London and Provincial galleries. Talent fluctuates and a certain monotony tends to pervade style and interpretation, nevertheless a new approach and innovation have certainly made a tentative appearance to contrast with former traditions. A feature of the decade, however, has been a decline of hunting as a subject with a swing to the racing scene where speed and lively action have been the keynote based, perhaps too obviously, on the current expertise of colour photography.

In retrospect it must be appreciated that the twentieth century has enjoyed a wealth of talent which has been used with vision and versatility to enhance the rich heritage of British sporting art.

NOTES

1 Walter Shaw Sparrow, *British Sporting Artists*, p. 62.

2 *The Year's Art Annual*, 1925–1932.

3 Appendix Two, p. 209.

131 John Gilroy, *Derby Day 1968*. Oil on canvas.

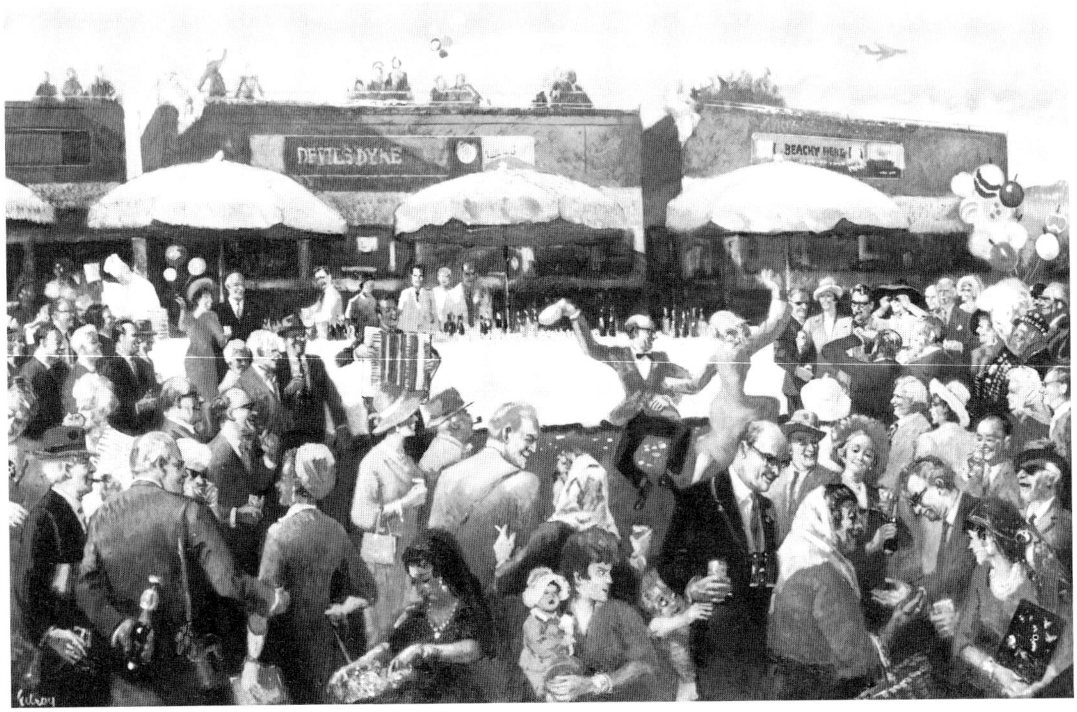

19

The Way Ahead

For over 300 years British sporting art has reflected our traditional country way of life and its recreations. But times are rapidly changing and in the twenty-first century sporting artists face a challenge as radical as the elucidation of animal action presented by Muybridge a hundred years ago.

Even if future government legislation fails to ban blood sports completely, many rural areas are now extensively occupied by town-bred commuters who, often ill informed, fail to understand that hunting, shooting, stalking and fishing form an integral ingredient for the conservation of the countryside which they wish to enjoy.

The granting of general access to commonlands, moors and mountains now widely demanded will inevitably ensure votes for any political party but, in this over-populated island, such a hikers' paradise will drastically diminish animal wild life and the undisturbed terrain neccessary for its existence. With country sports under threat of extinction (except perhaps fishing which with almost four million regular anglers might escape an official ban) sporting artists of the twenty-first century will inevitably find their traditional subjects and the landscape settings considerably curtailed.

Racing would appear to be the only activity that will still offer, as in the past, familiar opportunities. The Derby and the Grand National continues to make headline news. Owners will, as ever, demand portraits of their successful bloodstock and the important races in spite of the skills of the modern photographer. In 1958 all the Classic races were sponsored; perhaps in future these generous donors will, in addition, commission paintings of these occasions for their boardrooms.

But artists will have to consider more seriously the horse in alternative activities – in drag hunting, in the show arena, in long distance competitions, in trekking and gymkhana events. Arab horse racing offers an exciting and unexploited subject and facets of dressage, like polo, hold considerable diversion. It is inconceivable that the horse will not retain its status as a leading inspiration in any new approach to the sporting scene.

However, it is often ignored that such masters of the past as Ward, Marshall, Alken, Ferneley and others painted pictures outside the actual sphere of field sports from archery to bull-baiting, pugilism to cock-fighting. In our own more humane era it would seem that such alternative subjects as competitive ball games, athletics, water and winter sports, not forgetting the periodical impact of the Olympic Games could assume important pictorial prestige. Fifty years hence the present rather limited concept of sporting art may be considerably widened.

The recent influences of Edwards, Munnings and Skeaping will not disappear but young artists, faced with a changing world, will introduce innovations, probably controversial, which will have to be absorbed. But an awareness of the past must not be lost and, therefore, for future generations, the pictures and sculptures of the sporting school of the twentieth century will rank of paramount importance as records of British sporting art before an eventual transformation. The way ahead is certainly unpredictable!

132 Rosemary Taylor, *Virginia Wade*, *c* 1976. Oil on canvas, 62 × 86 in (157.4 × 218.4 cm).

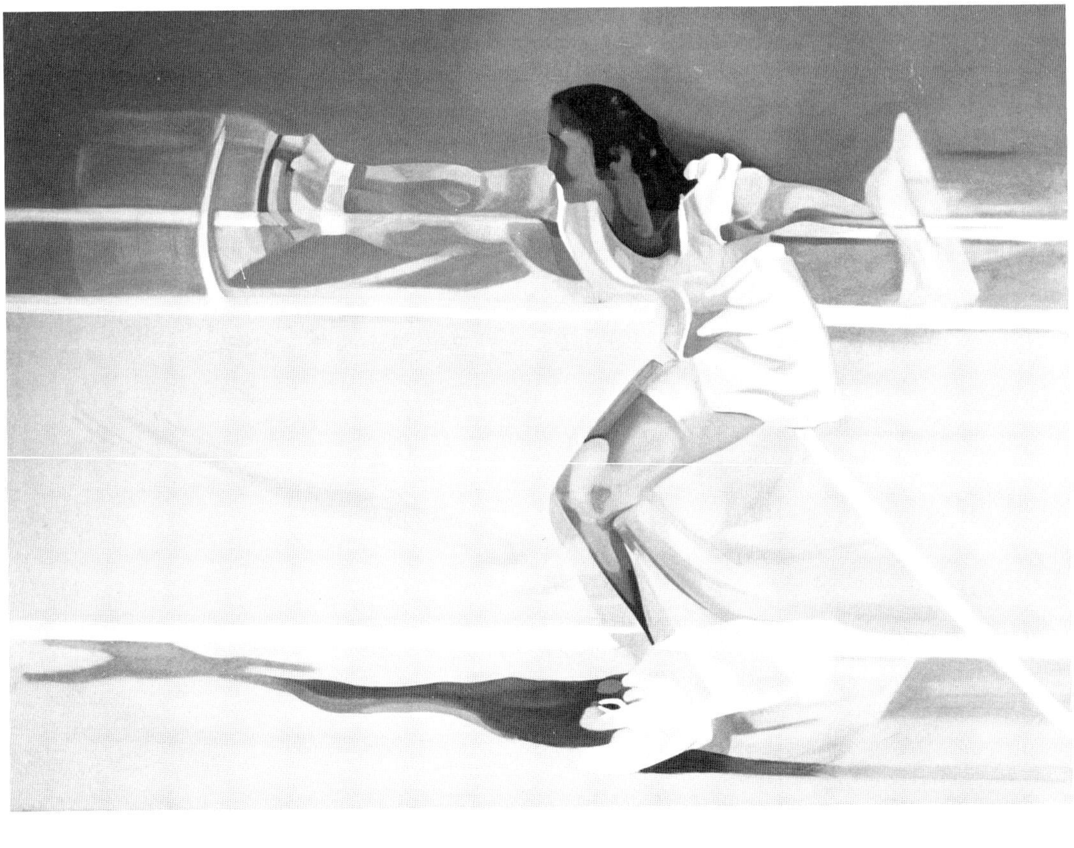

APPENDIX ONE

Sir Alfred Munnings' Presidential Speech

28 April 1949

Your Royal Highness, my lords and gentlemen, I am getting somewhat distressed. Through some extraordinary arrangement, these toasts have all been put on the President. There are men in this Academy who could easily have proposed the toasts of the Guests or the toast of The Ministers, but here am I, giving toast after toast; as they say in hunting – I've been up in the air all the time. I have never been on my seat but for a few minutes, and am feeling like a most awful interrupter. I know what it is – and have known what it is – to sit at these tables when there has been much more company – carousing and drinking – little thinking of the poor President at his table . . . regardless of all what he has to go through and to *get away with*, to put it in a common term of speech . . . .

Here am I, responding for The Academy. If I glance at my notes you must excuse me. Now, the Archbishop of Canterbury has spoken well – I should say in a very accomplished way – about this body of men. But what of the body? Are they worthy of this building in which they are housed? Are we all doing the great work which we should do? Well . . . my Lords and Gentlemen; it is not for me to stand here on my feet tonight and find one fault with the Royal Academy. Sitting here with members on either side of you . . . and you will have found out what intelligent men artists are.

But I find myself a President of a body of men who are what I call shilly-shallying. They feel that there is something in this so called modern art. You will say, I am getting right away into the subject. Well, I myself would rather have – excuse me, my Lord Archbishop – a damned bad failure, a bad, muddy old picture where somebody has tried to do something, to set down what they have seen, than all this affected juggling, this following of what – shall we call it of the School of Paris? (I trust the French Ambassador is not here tonight.)

Not so long ago I spoke in this room to the students, and in my poor discourse I said to these boys and girls: they are not boys and girls – more than half of them are grown up, and they are receiving all sorts of gratuities from the Government – for what? To learn Art and to become what? Not artists . . . I said to those students, 'If you paint a tree – for God's sake try and make it look like a tree, and if you paint a sky, try and make it look like a sky . . .' Only these last two days I have been motoring from Dedham to Newmarket and back . . . On Sunday I motored through Suffolk, and was looking at skies all the time . . . and on Monday, what skies there were! . . . And still, in spite of all those men who have painted skies in the past, we should be painting skies still *better*. But there has been a foolish interruption to all efforts in Art, helped by foolish men writing on the Press, encouraging all this damned nonsense, putting all these younger men out of their stride . . . I am right – I have the Lord Mayor on my side and *all* the Aldermen and *all* the City Companies. There is a Master of a City Company here tonight, the Master of the Mercers' Company – Lord Selborne – and I am sure he is with me; and on my left I have the famous newly-elected extraordinary member of the Academy – Winston Churchill. He, too, is with me because . . . And I know he is behind me because once he said to me, 'Alfred, if you met Picasso coming down the street, would you join with me in kicking his something, something, something . . .' (*Laughter*). I said, 'Yes sir, I would!' (*More laughter*).

Now we have all sorts of highbrows here tonight, experts who think they know more about Art than the men who paint the pictures, even the poor devils who have sat out in the open and tried to paint a landscape and failed. They are – if I may use a common expression – so fed-up to the teeth in pictures, they move among pictures, they see so many pictures, as I have seen this afternoon – that their judgment becomes blunt, yes, blunt! . . . . That reminds me of Anthony Blunt . . . Anthony Blunt, is he here tonight? He once stood with me in this very room during an evening party when the King's pictures were here. There was a full-length Reynolds hanging on the end wall, a fine picture – and he was telling some people that Reynolds was not as good as Picasso. What an extraordinary thing for a man to say! . . . Perhaps I should not mention names, but I do not care, since I am resigning at the end of this year . . . I do not wish to go on with an Academy that says – their profound mind working and thinking – 'Well, there *must* be something in this modern art; these writers are getting busy, we must give the jugglers a show' – and so, if you go into Number Eleven, you will see faint zephyr breezes – very faint zephyr breezes . . . I should call them violent blows of nothing. Here we are in this Academy, and you, gentlemen, were assembled to take sherry in the Octagon Room, where there was a woman carved out of wood, and God help us if all the race of women looked like that! (*Prolonged laughter.*) Sculptors today are sinking away into a fashion of bloated, heavy-weight monstrous nudes. You saw the things exhibited in Battersea Park. They were put there by the London County Council. We are spending millions every year on art education, and still we exhibit all these foolish drolleries to the public. I have stood in the Park; I have been with the people who were there, and asked them questions, and they were disgusted and angered, as were those whom I met looking at the Madonna and Child in a church in Northampton. I happened to be up there at a Horse Show, and not being a very great rider, was one of the judges of hunters, the others being the head of the Mounted Police, Colonel de Chair, and Lord Allerton. On the preceding day, after our arrival, I said to my wife, 'Before we get any further – before we go to the hotel, let us hunt these churches – let us seek out this masterpiece which *The Times* eulogised during the war, with a photograph shown on the back page.' After visiting other churches, we found the church at last, and I said to my wife, 'You wait in the car, I will come back and tell you if it is there.' I came back and said, 'Come along,' . . . and we walked up the aisle, and there was this 'graven image' . . . Well, Canon Hussey, or whoever it was, wished for this thing, and other gentlemen may have suggested it but I would like to ask everybody here if they could – if they have a day or weekend to spare – to travel up to Northampton and see the statue of the Madonna and Child in this church. I am speaking plainly. My horses may be all wrong – we may all be wrong – but I'm damned sure that isn't right.

I am not going on too long, for a great man is speaking after me – but I would like to say that I took a car this afternoon and went to the Tate Gallery and the National Gallery. I went to that room in the Tate – I would ask you all to go and see it – the second room on the right with white walls, which is nothing but wall with a few pictures spotted around, and there you will see a picture by Matisse, *Le Forêt*. (*Interruptions from members 'Beautiful work . . .'*) I hope you hear the other members interrupting me at the end of the room. As I am President and have the right of the Chair, allow me to speak. I shall not be here next year, thank God!

In the *Telegraph* I was reported as having said in an address to Academy students –'. . . If you paint a tree, for God's sake let it look like a tree . . .' Well, a lady called Mary Borden wrote a long letter to that same paper, a column in length, ending up with saying how, if she sat in a wood cluttered up with trees, she would have welcomed this canvas – *Le Forêt* – if it had come crashing through the delicate green of the undergrowth to her feet – 'the very spirit of a tree!!' . . . I can say no more. Go and look at that spirit of a tree. But hear what Robert Louis Stevenson wrote of a forest in his story, *The Treasure of Franchard*. 'The sound of innumerable thousands of treetops, and innumerable millions on millions of green leaves was abroad in the air, and filled the ear with something between whispered speech and singing'!! . . . I think that expresses more than Mary Borden's letter did to the *Telegraph*. Gentlemen may I say one last word? In the National Gallery today, amongst those Munich pictures, there is one by Rubens of himself and his wife which brought back many early memories to me of when I used to go to Munich fifty years ago. What a picture! and I see that *The Times* art critic has dared to write that the technique and painting of the gold and silver on the wife's dress made the work of Renoir look like that of an amateur. A great thing for that critic to say, and I entirely agree with him.

Gentlemen, as President here, and resigning President, I thank you for drinking the health of the Royal Academy, as you have done, and I wish you all well.

APPENDIX TWO

ART WITH AN ENGLISH APPEAL

Sir – It would seem from your leader of Dec 31 that the chances of the £231,000 being raised by public appeal to save the Titian are slim. One cannot help but feel some relief if this is so.

To many people the idea of the National Gallery mortgaging their income for four years is ludicrous. They have already lost the chance of purchasing three paintings to fill gaps in the collection, and who can tell what further works will appear on the market during the period in question?

To be perfectly frank, the Titian is a picture of little popular appeal, and, although Mr Martin Davies states that over 10 million people have seen it since it went on view at the National Gallery, what he really means is that number of people have visited the collection. I would hazard a guess that few of the 10 million have been especially to see the Titian.

What would have been the public response, however, if instead of Lord Fitzwilliam's generous loan of Stubbs's 'Whistlejacket' to Kenwood the picture had been put up for sale? Maybe the trustees of the National Gallery and the Reviewing Committee for Works of Art would consider it of little national importance, but the man in the street would, I am sure, derive far more pleasure from this particular painting, and indeed support any appeal that was necessary.

Our firm, as specialists in English sporting pictures, have often deplored the lack of interest shown by the majority of the museum directors to this school of painting. Year by year fine paintings are exported which are of national importance.

This is a school unique to our country, and surely as such should be better represented in our national collections. The National Gallery shows one picture by Stubbs, which has been somewhat neglected. Is this really fair to one of our greatest artists or to our native school as a whole?

Daily Telegraph, 6 January 1972

A.L. GATES
Managing Director
Arthur Ackermann & Son Ltd
London W1

USE OF PUBLIC MONEY

Sir – I support your view that the loss of the Titian should not be regarded as a major disaster, and your point that resources should rather be directed to preserving for this country works especially relevant to our own history.

Certainly the 'Death of Actaeon' is a very fine and attractive example of Titian's late manner, and it would set the crown on the representation of this master's work in the National Gallery. But it is a picture of international rather than national importance. Our galleries are already rich in the finest European masterpieces, and one can understand the taxpayers' lack of sympathy with apparent desire of the spenders of public money to purchase everything exceptional that comes on to the market regardless of cost.

I think it was Sir Osbert Sitwell who, when asked if he considered the English were indifferent to art, answered: 'No. They are not indifferent to art; they hate it with an implacable loathing.' This may be an exaggeration, but it is probably true to say that the current interest in works of art is inspired more by commercial than aesthetic considerations.

But had we not better stop regretting what we cannot afford, and concentrate instead on works by our native artists, which can still be bought at realistic prices, and which are a record of life in the towns and countryside of England?

Daily Telegraph, 6 January 1972

I.R.D. BYFIELD
London W1

BRITAIN'S SPORTING ART DESERVES A GALLERY

Sir – It was with great pleasure that I read Mr A.L. Gates' letter concerning sporting art (Jan 6), and his comments were not only relevant but also extremely important. I would like to take this point a stage further and suggest that Somerset House be used for a really first-class sporting gallery.

The question of retaining national art treasures is obviously of great importance to this nation, but surely of even more consequence is the collecting of sporting paintings which are a form of art unique to this country. We should be justly proud of this heritage, and the opportunity must be taken to collect these paintings for a suitable gallery as was originally envisaged by the Hutchison collection.

There are a considerable number of people who are anxious that this field of art should be duly acknowledged in the same way as, for instance, seascapes are shown at the Greenwich Museum or portraits at the National Portrait Gallery.

Daily Telegraph, 8 January 1972

PETER JOHNSON
London SW1

SOMERSET HOUSE

Sir – The timely plea by Sir John Betjeman and others for the use of Somerset House, when vacated, as a gallery for exhibitions of English painting, especially of the eighteenth century, deserves serious and immediate consideration. If this idea is realized I would suggest most strongly that one room of these collections should be reserved for examples of British sporting art of both the eighteenth and nineteenth centuries. These pictures, in a manner that is unique, illustrate not merely the national addiction to field sports but, what is of vital interest, they record for posterity the English country way of life before the advent of motorways and pylons.

As a genre British sporting art has no equivalent in any other part of the world and it should be recognized as a national heritage of importance. Perhaps if some responsible plan for public exhibition of these paintings could be evolved the frequent disappearance overseas of so many of its finest examples might be halted.

The Times, 9 January 1973

(MRS) STELLA A. WALKER
Heathfield, Sussex

List of Illustrations

Illustration Acknowledgements

Grateful acknowledgement is made to the following individuals and galleries for permission to reproduce photographs of pictures, prints and sculpture:

By gracious permission of Her Majesty the Queen, *Pl. 16*; By gracious permission of His Royal Highness the Prince of Wales, *66*.
Arthur Ackermann & Son; *Pl. 3*, *Pl. 7*; *3, 11, 28, 43, 47, 63, 68, 79, 105*; Mrs D. Arkell, *27*; Sally Arnup, *111*.
The Duke of Beaufort, *Pl. 16*; *36*; Captain J. Bell-Irvine, *77*; Mrs D. Biegel, *Pl. 13*; *60, 61*; Philip Blacker, *114*; Pamela du Boulay, *107*; Bridgeman Art Library, *73*; Brighton Art Gallery, *19*; City of Bristol Museum & Art Gallery, *123*; British Sporting Art Trust, *34, 35, 37, 55, 92, 103*; Mrs R.M. Brooks, *Pl. 21*; Mary Browning and the Standfast Press, *98*; H.M. The Sultan Haji Hassanal Bolkiah Mu'izzaddin Waddaulah of Brunei, *Pl. 20*; Burlington Gallery Ltd, *117, 127*.
Donald Cameron of that Ilk, *95*; Cheltenham Art Gallery & Museums, *122*; Christie's Fine Arts, *Pl. 10*; *4*; Christopher Cole Fine Paintings, Beaconsfield, *Pl. 5*; P. Colmore, *49*; Country Life, *126*; Court Gallery, London, *Pl. 6*; *29, 54, 100*; Crane Kalman Gallery, London, *118*; Major J. Crawford, *Pl. 13*.
E.G.F. Davey, Esq., *Pl. 22*; David Ker Fine Arts, *83*; The Duke of Devonshire, *90*.
Estate of Lionel Edwards, *Pl. 9*; *34, 35, 37, 38, 55, 92*.
Fine Art Photographs Ltd, *Pl. 24*; Fine Art Society, *120*; Fores Ltd, *14*; Mrs W. Frank, *64*; Frost & Reed Ltd, London and Bristol, *Pl. 15*, *Pl. 18*, *Pl. 23*; *44, 62, 112, 132*; Sir Stephen Furness, Bart, *76*.
Garrick Club, *131*; Glasgow Museum & Art Gallery, *Pl. 4*; Trustees of the Goodwood Collection, *116*; Vic Grainger, *130*; Richard Green Gallery, *Pl. 1*, *Pl. 2*; *10, 12*; Sir Stephen Lycett Green, *Pl. 5*.
Hereford Museum & Art Gallery, *56*; Roy Heron, *8*; *Horse & Hound*, *Pl. 18*; *88*; Peter Howell, *Pl. 17* (and Kiki Ward Platt), *Pl. 17* (and Frank Stronach).
Illustrated London News Picture Gallery, *7*; Imperial War Museum, *53*; *58*.
Oscar & Peter Johnson Gallery, *5, 9, 22*.
Mrs M. Kenney, *Pl. 14*; *65, 97*; Mr & Mrs J. Kennedy, *16*; Kent County Cricket Club, *Pl. 24*; Estate of Dame Laura Knight, *Pl. 11*; *50, 51*.
Leamington Tennis Court Club, *125*; Sir Nicholas Lyell, MP, *Pl. 3*; *23, 57*; Michael Lyne, *Pl. 15*, *Pl. 18*, *Pl. 23*; *62*.
Roger McPhail, *Pl. 23*; Malcolm Innes Gallery, *Pl. 19*; *6*; City of Manchester Art Gallery, *119*; The Marlborough Book Shop & Sporting Gallery, *Pl. 12*; Anthony Mason, Esq., *26*; Collection of Mr & Mrs Paul Mellon, *104*; David Messum Gallery, *46*; Sally Mitchell, *94*; The Sir Alfred Munnings Art Museum, *Pl. 10*, *Pl. 12*; *39, 40, 41, 93*.
National Army Museum, London, *45*; National Gallery of Ireland, *24*; Peter P. Nicholls, Esq., *Pl. 7*.
Phillips Fine Art Auctioneers, *Pl. 11*; Christopher Pilkington, Esq., *117*; Priory Gallery, Cheltenham, *31*; Tessa Pullan, *112*; Pym's Gallery, London, *20*.
Joy Stanley Ricketts, *84*; Walter Ritchie, *115*; Royal Academy of Arts, *50, 112*.
Seagram UK Ltd, *113*; Madeleine Selfe, *69*; Mrs M. Skeaping, *78, 79*; Sladmore Gallery, *80, 101, 102, 108, 109, 110*; Sotheby's, *15, 30, 48, 96, 124, 129*; John Southern, Esq., MBE and the Thorburn Museum & Art Gallery, *Pl. 1*; Spink & Son Ltd, *Pl. 8*, *Pl. 13*; Brian Stewart, Esq., *51*.
Tate Gallery, *Pl. 4*, *Pl. 11*; *18, 21, 42, 44, 74, 128*; Tryon Gallery *13, 25, 32, 33, 38, 67, 75, 81, 82, 85, 86, 87, 121*.
Peter Upton, *99*.
By Courtesy of the Trustees of Victoria & Albert Museum, *59*; Virginia Museum of Fine Arts, *Pl. 19*.
Lord Howard de Walden, *91*; Jean Walwyn, *106*; Joan Wanklyn, *70*; Lord Weinstock, *Pl. 21*; Whitbread & Company plc, *89*.
Private Collections, *18, 25, 52, 60, 68, 70, 71, 72*.

In some cases it has been impossible to trace owners of photographs and copyright, and to these I offer my apologies.

SELECTED BIBLIOGRAPHY

Aldin, Cecil, *Ratcatcher to Scarlet*, Eyre & Spottiswoode Ltd, 1926.

Scarlet to M.F.H., Eyre & Spottiswoode Ltd, 1933.

Time I Was Dead, Eyre & Spottiswoode Ltd, 1934.

Anonymous, *British Hunts and Huntsmen*, 4 Volumes, Compiled in conjunction with *Sporting Life*, The Biographical Press 1908–1911.

Armour, George Denholm, *Humour in the Hunting Field* with comments by Crascredo, Country Life Ltd, London, 1928.

Bridle & Brush, Reminiscences of an Artist Sportsman, Eyre & Spottiswoode, London, Charles Scribner's Sons, New York, 1937.

Barrow, C. ('Sabretache'), *Monarchy and the Chase*, Eyre & Spottiswoode, 1948.

Baskett, John, *The Horse in Art*, Foreword by Paul Mellon, Weidenfeld & Nicolson, London, 1980.

Bevan, Robert Polhill, *Robert Bevan 1865–1925, A Memoir by his Son*, Studio Vista, London, 1965.

Biegel, Peter, *Peter Biegel's Racing Pictures*, Michael Joseph, 1983.

Board, John, *Horse and Pencil*, Christopher Johnson, London, 1950.

Booth, Stanley, *Alfred Munnings 1878–1959, An Appreciation of the Artist & a Selection of his Paintings*, Sotheby Parke Bernet Publications.

Briggs, Ernest E., RI, *Angling & Art in Scotland*, Longmans Green & Co., London, 1908.

Bury, Adrian, *Joseph Crawhall, the Man & the Artist*, Charles Skilton, 1958.

Carr, Raymond, *English Foxhunting*, Weidenfeld & Nicolson, London, 1976.

Case, Walter O., *Ninety Years of Horse & Hound*, Compiled by Walter O. Case, Foreword by Colonel Sir Michael Ansell, CBE, DSO, Country Life Books, 1977.

Cook, Theodore Andrew, MA, FSA, *A History of the English Turf*, 3 Vols, H. Virtue & Co Ltd, London, 1901.

Coombes, David, *Sport and the Countryside*, Phaidon, Oxford, 1978.

Crascredo, (Charles Simpson), *Country Sense and Common Sense*, Illustrated by Lionel Edwards, Country Life Ltd, London, 1928.

Cuneo, Terence, *The Mouse and his Master, The Life and Works of Terence Cuneo*, New Cavendish Books, London, 1977.

Davies, Celia, *Brian Hatton*, Terence Dalton Ltd, Lavenham, Suffolk, 1978.

Eden, Ronald, *Going to the Moors*, John Murray, London, 1979.

Edwards, Lionel, RI, *Sportsman's Sketchbook*, Putnam & Co.

Reminiscences of a Sporting Artist, With illustrations by the Author, Putnam & Co, 1947.

Thy Servant the Horse, Written and illustrated by Lionel Edwards, Country Life Ltd, 1952.

Scarlet & Corduroy, Eyre & Spottiswoode, London, 1941.

Edwards, Marjorie, *Figures in a Landscape – Lionel Edwards RI, RCA*, Regency Press (London & New York) Ltd, 1986.

Eliot, Elizabeth, *Portrait of a Sport, A History of Steeplechasing*, Longmans Green & Co, 1957.

Ellis, Colin D.B., *Leicestershire and the Quorn Hunt*, Edgar Backus, 1951.

Flower, Mark & Donald Crawford, *Charles Johnson Payne (Snaffles)*, being a Selection of his Hunting and Racing Prints, Millwood Press, Wellington, New Zealand, 1983.

Furse, Charles Wellington, RA, *Illustrated Memoirs of – with Critical Papers & Fragments*. A Catalogue of the pictures exhibited at the Club in 1906 and a chronological list of works, printed for the Burlington Fine Arts Club, 1908.

Goodman, Jean, *Edward Seago, The Other Side of the Canvas*, Collins, 1978.

Graham, Clive and Bill Curling, *The Grand National*, Barrie & Jenkins, 1972.

Grant-Renwick, Richard, ed. by, *Coursing, The Pursuit of Game with Gazehounds*, The Standfast Sporting Press, Saul, Glos, 1977.

Grigson, Geoffrey, *Horse and Rider*, Thames & Hudson, London, 1950.

Grimshaw, Anne, *The Horse – A Bibliography of British Books 1851–1976*, Library Association Publishing Ltd, 7 Ridgemount Street, London WC1E 7AE, 1982.

Heron, Roy, *Tom Firr of the Quorn*, Nimrod Book Services, 1984.

Cecil Aldin: The Story of a Sporting Artist, Webb & Bower, 1981.

Higginson, Henry A., *British and American Sporting Authors, Their writings and biographies*, Huchinson & Co, 1951.

Two Centuries of Foxhunting, Collins, London, 1946.

Horswell, Jane, *Bronze Sculpture of Les Animaliers*, Reference and Price Guide, Baron Publishing, Woodbridge, Suffolk, 1971.

Huntly, The Marquis of, *Milestones*, Hutchinson & Co.

Knight, Laura, DBE, RA, *Oil Paint & Grease Paint*, Ivor Nicholson & Watson Ltd, London, 1936.

The Magic of a Line, William Kimble, London, 1965.

Lambton, George, The Hon., *Men and Horses I Have Known*, Thornton Butterworth, 1924.

Learmonth, David Livingstone, *The Horse in Art*, The Studio Publications, London & New York, 1958.

Lindsay, Lionel, *A.J. Munnings RA, An Appreciation: Pictures of Horses and English Life*, Eyre & Spottiswoode, London, 1927?

Longrigg, Roger, *The History of Horseracing*, Macmillan, 1972.

Luard, Lowes D., *Horses & Movement – From Paintings & Drawings*, Cassell & Co Ltd, London, New York, Toronto & Melbourne, 1921. Republished by J.A. Allen & Co Ltd, London, 1988. Edited by Oliver Beckett, FRSA.

The Horse – Its Action and Anatomy by an Artist, Faber & Faber, 1935.

Lyne, Michael, *A Parson's Son, Sporting Artist*, J.A. Allen, London.

Horse, Hounds and Country, Eyre & Spottiswoode, 1938.

McPhail, Rodger, *Open Season – An Artist's Sporting Year*, Airlife Publishing & The Tryon Gallery Ltd, 1986.

Messum, David, *The Life & Works of Lucy Kemp-Welch*, Baron Publishing, Woodbridge, Suffolk, 1976.

Mitchell, Sally, *The Dictionary of British Equestrian Artists*, Antique Collectors Club, Woodbridge, Suffolk, 1985.
Mortimer, Roger, *The History of the Derby Stakes*, Cassell, London, 1962.
Munnings, Alfred J., KCVO, PPRA, *An Artist's Life*, Museum Press, 1950.
The Second Burst, Museum Press, 1951.
The Finish, Museum Press, 1952.
Muybridge, Eadweard, *The Horse in Action: An Electric Photographic Investigation of Consecutive Phases of Animal Progressive Movements.*
Nicolson, William, *An Almanac of Twelve Sports*, William Heinemann, London, 1897.
Paget, Guy D.L., F.R.Hist.S., Lionel Irvine MBE, MA OXON, *Leicestershire*, Robert Hale Ltd, 1950.
Paget, J. Otho, ('Q' of the Field), *Memories of the Shires*, Methuen & Co, 1920.
Paul Mellon Collection, *Books of the Horse and Horsemanship – Riding, Hunting, Breeding & Racing 1400–1941*, Catalogue compiled by John B. Podeschi, the Tate Gallery Publications Dept for the Yale Center for British Art, New Haven, Connecticut.
Pavière, Sydney H. *A Dictionary of British Sporting Painters*, F.R. Lewis Publishers Ltd, 1965.
Payne, Charles J. (Snaffles), *'I've Heard the Revelly'*, Sale & Holden Ltd, Aldershot, 1953.
A Half Century of Memories, Collins, London, 1949.
Pendred, Gerald L., *An Inventory of British Sporting Art in United Kingdom Public Collections*, (Compiled by), British Sporting Art Trust, Boydell & Brewer, 1987.
Portland, The Duke of, KG, CGVO, *Memoirs of Racing and Hunting*, Faber & Faber, 1935.
Pound, Reginald, *The Englishman: A Biography of Sir Alfred Munnings*, Heinemann, 1962.
Randall, John and Tony Morriss, *Horse Racing – The Records*, Guinness Superlatives Ltd, Enfield, Middx, 1985.
Rickman, Philip, *Sketches & Notebooks from a Bird Painter's Journal*, Eyre & Spottiswoode, London, 1949.
Ritchie, Walter, *Sculpture in Brick and Other Materials*, Cheyney & Sons Ltd, Banbury, Oxon, 1978.
Ruffer, Jonathan Garnier, *The Big Shot – Edwardian Shooting Parties*, Debrett's Peerage Ltd, 1978.
'Sabretache', (C.F. Barrow), *Monarchy and the Chase*, Eyre & Spottiswoode, 1948.
Simpson, Charles W., RI, *Leicestershire and its Hunts*, John Lane, the Bodley Head Ltd, 1926.
The Harboro' Country, John Lane, the Bodley Head Ltd, 1927.
Animal & Bird Painting – The Outlook & Technique of the Artist, B.T. Batsford, London, 1939.
Photography of the Figure in Colour & Monochrome, W.H. & G. Witherby Ltd, London, 1938.
Stewart, F.A., *Hunting Countries*, Collins, 1953.
Cross Country with Hounds, Collins, 1936.
Hark to Hounds, Collins, 1937.
Skeaping, John, *Drawn from Life: An Autobiography*, Collins, 1977.
Animal Drawing "How to do it" Series 10, The Studio Publications, 1949.
Smith-Seth, Michael, *Bred for the Purple – A History of Monarchy and the Turf*, Leslie Frewin, 1969.
Sparrow, Walter Shaw, *British Sporting Artists*, John Lane the Bodley Head Ltd, London, Charles Scribner's Sons, New York, 1922.
Angling in British Art, John Lane the Bodley Head Ltd, London, 1923.
A Book of Sporting Painters, John Lane the Bodley Head Ltd, London, Charles Scribner's Sons, New York, 1931.
Titley, Norah M., *Bibliography of British Sporting Art*, (compiled by), The British Sporting Art Trust, Sotheby's, 1986.
Tubbs, D.B., *Art and the Automibile*, Lutterworth Press, Guildford & London, 1978.
Upton, Roger, *A Bird in the Hand – Celebrated Falconers of the Past*, Debrett's Peerage Ltd, London, 1980.
Oh for a Falconer's Voice: Memories of the Old Hawking Club, Crowood Press, 1987.
Underhill, George F., *A Century of English Fox-Hunting*, R.A. Everet & Co, 1900.
Vandervell, Anthony & Charles Coles, *Game and the English Landscape*, Debrett's Peerage Ltd, 1980.
Vandervell, Anthony, *So this was Shooting*, Flying Sporting & Leisure Press, Buckingham, 1986.
Walker, Stella A., *Sporting Art in England: 1700–1900*, Studio Vista, 1972.
Wallace, Frank, *Happier Years*, Eyre & Spottiswoode, London, 1944.
Watson, J.N.P., *Lionel Edwards: Master of the Sporting Scene*, The Sportsman's Press, 1986.
Millais – Three Generations in Nature, Art and Sport, The Sportsman's Press, 1988.
Watson, J.N.P., Edited by, *Collecting Sporting Art*, The Sportsman's Press, 1988.
Welcome, John & Rupert Collens, *Snaffles: The Life & Work of Charles Johnson Payne 1884–1967*, Stanley Paul & Co Ltd, 1987.
Willett, Peter, *The Thoroughbred*, Weidenfield & Nicolson, 1970.
Wood, Lieut Colonel J.C., *A Dictionary of British Animal Painters*, F.R. Lewis Publishers, 1973.
Yeats, Jack B., *Drawings & Paintings*, James White, Secker & Warburg, London, 1971.

INDEX

Names set thus ADAM, EMIL are of artists, and figures in **bold** indicate the main references to their work.

ABBREVIATIONS

A	Associate
b	born
c	*circa*
F	Fellow
H	Honorary
NEAC	New English Art Club
op	working
P	President
RA	Royal Academy
RBC	Royal British Colonial Society of Artists
RBS	Royal Society of British Sculptors
RCA	Royal College of Arts
RE	Royal Society of Painter-Etchers & Engravers
RHA	Royal Hibernian Academy
RI	Royal Institute of Painters in Water-colours
ROI	Royal Institute of Oil Painters
RO	Royal Society of Portrait Painters
RSA	Royal Society of Animal Painters
RSW	Royal Scottish Society of Painters in Watercolours
RWS	Royal Society of Painters in Watercolours
SEA	Society of Equestrian Artists
SWA	Society of Women Artists